REA

**FRIENDS
OF ACPL**

American Sports History Series

edited by
David B. Biesel

A related title by the series editor:

Can You Name That Team? A Guide to Professional Baseball, Football, Soccer, Hockey, and Basketball Teams and Leagues by David B. Biesel, 1991.

Major Leagues

Thomas W. Brucato

American Sports History Series, No. 18

The Scarecrow Press, Inc.
Lanham, Maryland, and London
2001

SCARECROW PRESS, INC.

Published in the United States of America
by Scarecrow Press, Inc.
4720 Boston Way, Lanham, Maryland 20706
www.scarecrowpress.com

4 Pleydell Gardens, Folkestone
Kent CT20 2DN, England

British Library Cataloguing in Publication Information Available

Library of Congress Cataloging-in-Publication Data

Brucato, Thomas W.
    Major leagues / Thomas W. Brucato.
        p. cm. — (American sports history series ; no. 18)
    Includes bibliographical references.
    ISBN 0-8108-3908-3 (alk. paper)
    1. Athletic clubs—North America—History. 2. Athletic clubs—North
America—Names—History. 3. Sports—North America—History. I. Title.
II. Series.
GV581 .B78 2001
796.04'4'097—dc21   00-063744

⊖™ The paper used in this publication meets the minimum requirements of
American National Standard for Information Sciences—Permanence of
Paper for Printed Library Materials, ANSI/NISO Z39.48–1992.
Manufactured in the United States of America.

To Julie,

my princess forever

Contents

Acknowledgments

I owe thanks first and foremost to God. He has given me great and innumerable gifts, among them family, friends, and both the ability and the desire to write.

I would like to thank my wife and Executive Research Assistant, Julie Brucato, for her help in creating this work. I thank her for her active participation in the seemingly endless research stages, as well as for her undying patience during the creation of the book itself.

I owe a deep debt of gratitude to my parents: my mom for instilling in me a love of sports (especially baseball) and my dad for instilling a love of writing.

I also owe special thanks to my sister-in-law Mary Ann Kasselmann for the contacts she provided.

I owe thanks to my good friend Dermid Strain, who has been an invaluable international resource.

I would like to thank Molly McCarthy of Modern Office Methods for her assistance and ever-present generosity.

I am deeply grateful to David B. Biesel, editor of the American Sports History Series, for providing sound advice, critical assistance, and a wealth of information. Without his help this book would be far less than it is.

Finally, I would like to offer special thanks to the following individuals and organizations for their willingness to share information with me and for their generous responses to direct inquiries:

Jodie Adams, Springfield Lasers (World TeamTennis)

Albany Firebirds (Arena Football League)

Anaheim Bullfrogs (Roller Hockey International)

Arena Football League

Ashley of Major League Roller Hockey

Robert Bradley, Founder and President, Association for Professional Basketball Research

Herb Branham of the *Tampa Tribune* (Tampa, Florida)

A. J. Carr of the *News and Observer* (Raleigh, North Carolina)

Sydney Carrick, General Manager, Idaho Sneakers (World TeamTennis)

Dick Clark, Society for American Baseball Research

Doug Colby, Manager—Community Relations and Promotions, British Columbia Lions (Canadian Football League)

Brian Craggs, Saskatoon Heritage Society

Anne Cribbs, Cofounder, American Basketball League

Susan Daly, Director of Marketing, New Jersey Red Dogs (Arena Football League)

Jefferson Davis, Archivist and Research Specialist, Hockey Hall of Fame

J. C. Dawkins, Director of Media Relations, Milwaukee Mustangs (Arena Football League)

Anne Marie Dixon, Media Contact, New York Saints (National Lacrosse League)

Tracey Donnelly, Communications Coordinator, World TeamTennis

June Flegg, Local History Room, Saskatoon Public Library

Jeff Gorlechen, New York CityHawks (Arena Football League)

Jon Greene, Vice President/Communications and Team Administration, San Diego Flash (A-League)

Jon Gustafson, Vice President of Operations, San Jose Rhinos (Roller Hockey International)

Houston Hotshots (World Indoor Soccer League)

P. K. Johnson, Business Manager, Orlando Jackals (Roller Hockey International)

Billie Jean King, Founder and Commissioner of World TeamTennis

Stan Kleine of the *Charlotte Observer* (Charlotte, North Carolina)

Ilana S. Kloss, Executive Director, World TeamTennis

David A. Litterer, U.S. Soccer History Archives

Amy D. Love, *Real Sports* magazine

Bob Markey Sr. of Prestige Property Investments, Inc. (Wellington, Florida)

Bob Markey II of the *Town-Crier Newspaper* (Wellington/Royal Palm Beach, Florida)

Oliver Mason

Sandi Mauer, Editor, www.lancasterpa.net

Amy McClure, World TeamTennis

David McLane, Roller Hockey International, founder of the World Roller Hockey League

Andy McNamara, Director of Media Relations, Portland Pythons (World Indoor Soccer League)

Ruth Millar, Local History Room, Saskatoon Public Library

Monterrey La Raza (Continental Indoor Soccer League)

Tim Parfitt, Business Development Manager, Netcel Ltd. (St. Albans, Hertfordshire, England)

Pennsylvania Posse (Major League Roller Hockey)

Mark Pray, Director of Media Relations, Women's National Basketball Association

Portland Pride (Continental Indoor Soccer League)

François Puchin, Montreal Impact Football Club (National Professional Soccer League)

Rachel Puig

Laura Reid, Assistant Media Relations Director, Los Angeles Sparks (Women's National Basketball Association)

Tom Rieger, General Manager, Kansas City Explorers (World TeamTennis)

St. Louis Aces (World TeamTennis)

John Scardino, President, Colorado Inferno (Major League Roller Hockey)

Viktoria Sergeyeva

Phil Simon, Media Relations Manager, San Jose SaberCats (Arena Football League)

Peggy Smith, Georgia Department of Industry, Trade and Tourism

Jeff Thomas, General Manager, Michigan Blast (Major League Roller Hockey)

Jim Ulman, General Manager, Baltimore Thunder (National Lacrosse League)

Jason Votruba, Director of Hockey Operations, Columbus Hawks (Major League Roller Hockey)

Rabbi Gerald I. Weider, Congregation Beth Elohim, Brooklyn, New York

Viviana Werber, Buenos Aires, Argentina

Betsy Yelich, Allstate Arena (formerly Rosemont Horizon), Chicago, Illinois

Yitzchok Zirkind

Introduction

Sports have likely existed since shortly after the dawn of humanity, and team sports for nearly as long. It is not really important whether, as some speculate, they emerged as pure recreation or, as others contend, they came into being as an energy-expending alternative to war. (After all, it's remarkably easy to envision two football teams as opposing armies, each trying to hold its ground, each trying to encroach upon its enemy's territory.) What *is* important is the fact that competition, on a team level, is a truly ancient—and even somewhat natural—concept.

The ancient Greeks and Romans brought sports to an unprecedented level, realizing that spectators would come from the four corners of the earth (a literal belief at the time) to watch the best athletes perform. People thrilled at the competition, especially at the prospect of seeing who would emerge as the best of the best.

Today's world has gone to yet the *next* level. Sports abound in our time as never before, in both the individual and the team variety, and multitudes love to play, as well as watch. Team sports have become big business in many parts of the world, and spectators continue to come from the four corners of the earth (figuratively speaking, of course) to watch. Those organizations today that have become the best of the best we have crowned the *major leagues.*

This book features a listing of major league teams in ten sports: baseball, football, basketball, hockey, soccer, indoor soccer, arena football, tennis, roller hockey, and lacrosse. It is designed to allow the reader to track a franchise through its complete history, including its origin, any name changes, transfers from one city or location to another, the league or leagues in which it played, the years it played, and its ultimate fate. The book accomplishes this through four parts:

"Part 1: The Teams" provides an alphabetical listing by location (for example, "Winnipeg" in the name "Winnipeg Blue Bombers"). "Part 2: The Leagues" provides a listing by league, while "Part 3: Team Names" does so by name or nickname. "Part 4: Team Name Origins" features an account of the origin, meaning, or significance of the names of most of the teams contained in this book.

This book focuses on North American leagues only. European teams that have played in North American leagues are included. Featured are leagues which are considered by most historians to have been the best of the best. Baseball's National Association, which is sometimes questioned because of its instability, is included here, as it was the very first professional league of its kind in any sport. Many of baseball's Negro Leagues are also included, those of which are generally considered to have been of major league caliber and whose players would undoubtedly have excelled in the white major leagues had they not been unjustly excluded from doing so. Also included is the All-American Girls Professional Baseball League, which featured the best women's professional baseball ever seen. In more recent times, the women's American Basketball League and the Women's National Basketball Association have revived popular interest in women's professional sports, and these leagues are also featured here, as is Women's Major League Roller Hockey.

A caveat to the reader: A few franchise moves are open to interpretation. Sometimes it is difficult to ascertain whether a team actually changed locations or folded and was replaced by a new team in another location. In some situations, such determinations are doubly difficult because the league owned the franchises; did the league move the team, or did the league simply cancel the team and start a new one elsewhere? In a few cases, there may be more than one "right" answer. I have attempted to determine, to the best of my ability and as my research led me, which was which, and to arrive at the best answer based upon the information available. If any errors are present, I claim full responsibility.

Also, in the nineteenth and early twentieth centuries, team names (or nicknames) literally came and went at the whims of local sportswriters. In *The Baseball Research Journal Number 27,* in fact, baseball historian Marc Okkonen points out, "In most cases, accepted team nicknames were coined by an individual baseball writer and stuck only if other writers eventually adopted the name in their own write-ups."[1] He also says, "Unlike today, when nicknames are clearly and officially designated as part of the team identification, the practice of arbitrarily attaching the same importance to them in an era that did not always offer the same recognition to nicknames seems to be an exercise in futility."[2] These early labels, therefore, should in large part be viewed as far less official and formal than they are today.

A book such as this is always a work in progress. Teams are constantly relocating, changing names, or folding, and leagues are being born and dying with amazing frequency as well. The market for major league sports is an everchanging one, and as long as people continue to seek entertainment through such contests, there will always be those organizations that attempt to seek them out and satisfy them. As this text was being written, there was already at least one planned franchise move in the works and plans for expansion teams in several leagues. Alas, those will have to wait for future updates. In the meantime, the author is always keeping a close eye on new developments . . . and they are guaranteed to be many.

The Major Leagues

Major Leagues features a complete listing of every major league team in the following leagues (with abbreviations used in this book):

Baseball

National Association	1871–1875	NA
National League	1876–present	NL
American Association	1882–1891	AA
Union Association	1884	UA
Players League	1890	PL
American League	1901–present	AL
Federal League	1914–1915	FL
Negro National League (1st)	1920–1931	NNL1
Eastern Colored League	1923–1928	ECL
American Negro League	1929	ANL
Negro Southern League	1932	NSL
Negro National League (2nd)	1933–1948	NNL2
Negro American League	1937–1950	NAL
All-American Girls Professional Baseball League	1943–1954	AAGPBL

Football

American Professional Football Association*	1920–1921	APFA
National Football League*	1922–present	NFL
American Football League (1st)	1926	AFL1
American Football League (2nd)	1936–1937	AFL2
American Football League (3rd)	1940–1941	AFL3
All-America Football Conference	1946–1949	AAFC
Canadian Football Council†	1956–1957	CFC
Canadian Football League†	1958–present	CFL
American Football League (4th)	1960–1970	AFL4
World Football League	1974–1975	WFL
United States Football League	1983–1985	USFL

The American Professional Football Association became the National Football League in 1922.
†*The Canadian Football Council became the Canadian Football League in 1958.*

Basketball

American Basketball League (1st)	1925–1931	ABL1
American Basketball League (2nd)	1933–1953	ABL2
National Basketball League	1937–1949	NBL
Basketball Association of America*	1946–1949	BAA

National Basketball Association*	1949–present	NBA
American Basketball League (3rd)	1961–1962	ABL3
American Basketball Association	1967–1976	ABA
American Basketball League (women's)	1996–1998	ABLw
Women's National Basketball Association	1997–present	WNBA

The Basketball Association of America became the National Basketball Association in 1949 when it absorbed some teams from the rival National Basketball League.

Hockey

National Hockey Association	1909–1917	NHA
Pacific Coast Hockey Association	1912–1924	PCHA
National Hockey League	1917–present	NHL
Western Canada Hockey League*	1921–1925	WCHL
Western Hockey League*	1925–1926	WHL
World Hockey Association	1972–1979	WHA

The Western Canada Hockey League became the Western Hockey League following the 1924–25 season.

Soccer

American Soccer League (1st)*	1921–1929, 1931–1933	ASL1
Atlantic Coast League*	1929–1930	ACL
American Soccer League (2nd)	1933–1983	ASL2
United Soccer Association†	1967	USA
National Professional Soccer League (outdoor)†	1967	NPSLo
North American Soccer League (outdoor)†	1968–1984	NASLo
United Soccer League	1984–1985	USL
Western Alliance Challenge Series‡	1985	WACS
Western Soccer League‡	1986–1988	WSL
Western Soccer Alliance‡§	1989	WSA
American Soccer League (3rd)§	1988–1989	ASL3
American Professional Soccer League§	1990–1994	APSL
Major League Soccer	1996–present	MLS

The first American Soccer League merged with the second Eastern Professional Soccer League to form the Atlantic Coast League in 1929, then became the first American Soccer League again in 1931.
†*The United Soccer Association and the National Professional Soccer League merged to form the North American Soccer League in 1968.*
‡*The Western Alliance Challenge Series became the Western Soccer League in 1986 and the Western Soccer Alliance in 1989.*
§*The Western Soccer Alliance and the third American Soccer League merged to form the American Professional Soccer League in 1990.*

Indoor Soccer

Major Indoor Soccer League*	1978–1990	MISL
North American Soccer League (indoor)	1979–1982, 1983–1984	NASLi
American Indoor Soccer Association†	1984–1990	AISA
Major Soccer League*	1990–1992	MSL
National Professional Soccer League (indoor)†	1990–present	NPSLi
Continental Indoor Soccer League	1993–1997	CISL

| Premier Soccer Alliance‡ | 1998 | PSA |
| World Indoor Soccer League‡ | 1999–present | WISL |

The Major Indoor Soccer League became the Major Soccer League following the 1989–90 season.
†*The American Indoor Soccer Association became the National Professional Soccer League following the 1989–90 season.*
‡*The Premier Soccer Alliance became the World Indoor Soccer League in 1999.*

Arena Football

| Arena Football League | 1987–present | AFL |

Tennis

| World TeamTennis* | 1974–1978, 1992–present | WTT |
| TeamTennis* | 1981–1991 | TT |

World TeamTennis became TeamTennis in 1981 and World TeamTennis again in 1992.

Roller Hockey

World Roller Hockey League	1993	WRHL
Roller Hockey International	1993–1997, 1999	RHI
Major League Roller Hockey	1997–1998	MLRH
Women's Major League Roller Hockey	2000–present	W-MLRH

Lacrosse

Eagle Pro Box Lacrosse League*	1987–1988	EPBLL
Major Indoor Lacrosse League*	1989–1997	MILL
National Lacrosse League	1998–present	NLL

The Eagle Pro Box Lacrosse League became the Major Indoor Lacrosse League in 1989.

Part 1

The Teams

In this section, teams are listed alphabetically according to their location (or other) names. (A location name would be, for example, "Detroit" in the name "Detroit Tigers.") Most major league team names are attached to a city (such as Detroit), while others are identified by a state or province. Some are named for a county or even for a country. There has even been a team named for a street (the Racine Cardinals) and one named for a dog kennel (the Oorang Indians). Some teams in the early twentieth century were identified by the companies that sponsored them. In all cases, the teams are listed alphabetically according to these designations. The Oorang Indians, for example, can be found under "Oorang." A soccer team like J & P Coats, named for the company that sponsored it, cannot in name be compared to a team like the Chicago Cubs, which is easily found under "Chicago." For the sake of consistency, however, J & P Coats is located under "J & P" and, similarly, a team like Todd Shipyards under "Todd."

Some teams' names are reversed (such as Football Club Seattle). These teams can be found under their *locations*, so that Football Club Seattle is under "Seattle," Team Hawaii under "Hawaii," Team America under "America," the Spirits of St. Louis under "St. Louis," etc.

Abbreviated locations, such as St. Louis and St. Paul, are alphabetized as if they are not abbreviated (as Saint Louis, Saint Paul, etc.).

Some teams used no location name at all. These clubs can still be found alphabetically and simply appear in parentheses to indicate that the team's name was not its location. For example, a team simply called the Aztecs is listed under the heading "(Aztecs)." The parentheses do not affect the alphabetical order.

A team's complete franchise history can be found under the *latest* name that team used. For example, the history of the Chicago Zephyrs can be found under "Washington Wizards," as can the history of the second Baltimore Bullets, because these teams were all the same franchise. Under each name, the reader is directed to the appropriate listing.

These histories are listed in sequential order from top to bottom. The first line lists the team's origin, and by reading down the page, the club's developments and ultimate fate become clear. Parenthetical notations appear where a sequence may be interrupted by an event such as a team suspending operations for a season or playing independently for a time.

Sometimes multiple teams in a single location used the same name. If these teams played in the same sport, they are distinguished by a number in parentheses following each team's name. For example, there were two teams

called the Tacoma Stars, both of which played indoor soccer. The first is listed simply as "Tacoma Stars (1)," the second as "Tacoma Stars (2)."

If two or more teams used identical names in *different* sports, they are identified by a letter representing the sports that they played as follows:

AF	Arena Football
B	Baseball
Bk	Basketball
F	Football
H	Hockey
IS	Indoor Soccer
L	Lacrosse
RH	Roller Hockey
S	Soccer
T	Tennis

For example, there have been two teams called the Dallas Stars, one in hockey and the other in tennis. The hockey team is listed as "Dallas Stars (H)," the tennis team as "Dallas Stars (T)."

Sometimes combinations of the letters and numbers are used. For example, there have been three teams called the Brooklyn Dodgers, one in baseball and *two* in football. The baseball team is listed as "Brooklyn Dodgers (B)," the first football team as "Brooklyn Dodgers (F1)," and the second football team as "Brooklyn Dodgers (F2)."

The notation "(S/IS)" is used for the duplicate name of a team which played both soccer and indoor soccer.

Some teams, especially in the nineteenth and early twentieth centuries, used more than one name, mainly because of local sportswriters. Whether or not many of these were "official" names is certainly doubtful, but these alternate names are listed where applicable and are preceded by "a.k.a." for "also known as."

Phantom teams, or teams that never actually played, are also listed here. In some cases, teams changed their names before ever playing a game under the names they had originally selected. In others, expansion teams or relocated teams never got to play before their entire leagues folded. Where one of these teams appears, the phrase *"did not play"* is added after the year in which it was intended to play.

Some teams were the result of a merger between two other clubs. Where this is the case, *"(**MERGED TEAM**)"* is followed by the complete history of *both* formerly separate franchises.

Italics indicate periods where a team played in a less significant or minor league, or where a team played independently or as an amateur squad, suspended operations, merged, or folded. A team name entirely in capital letters within a listing indicates a club that is currently active.

Consider the following example:

BROOKLYN AMERICANS
Quebec Bulldogs, Amateur Hockey Association, 1886–1908. Joined Eastern Canada Hockey Association, 1908–09. Joined Canadian Hockey Association, 1909.
Quebec Bulldogs (NHA 1910–17; NHL 1919–20)
(Suspended operations, 1917–19.)
Hamilton Tigers (NHL 1920–25)
New York Americans (H) (NHL 1925–41)
Brooklyn Americans (NHL 1941–42)
Folded, 1942.

This listing is for a hockey team called the Brooklyn Americans. The club started out as an amateur team in the Amateur Hockey Association as the Quebec Bulldogs. It played in that league from 1886–1908, then joined the Eastern Canada Hockey Association from 1908–09, and the Canadian Hockey Association in 1909. It became a major league team as the Quebec Bulldogs as a member of the National Hockey Association from 1910–17 and joined the National Hockey League from 1919–20. It suspended operations during those missing years of 1917–19. The team then became the Hamilton Tigers, then hockey's New York Americans, and finally the Brooklyn Americans, all still as a member of the NHL. Finally, in 1942, the team folded.

AKRON
(Ohio)

AKRON FIRESTONE NON-SKIDS
Akron Firestones, National Professional Basketball League (charter member), 1932–33. Independent, 1933–35. Midwest Basketball Conference, 1935–36. Akron Firestone Non-Skids, MBC, 1936–37.
Akron Firestone Non-Skids (NBL 1937–41)
a.k.a. Akron Firestones
Folded, 1941.

AKRON FIRESTONES
See *AKRON FIRESTONE NON-SKIDS*

AKRON GOODYEAR WINGFOOTS
Akron Goodyears, National Professional Basketball League, 1932–33. Independent, 1933–36. Akron Goodyear Regulars, Midwest Basketball Conference, 1936–37.
Akron Goodyear Wingfoots (NBL 1937–42)
a.k.a. Akron Goodyears
Folded, 1942.

AKRON GOODYEARS
See *AKRON GOODYEAR WINGFOOTS*

AKRON INDIANS
Akron Pros, independent, 1920.
Akron Pros (APFA 1920–21; NFL 1922)
Akron Indians (NFL 1923–26)
Folded, 1926.

AKRON PROS
See *AKRON INDIANS*

ALBANY
(New York)

ALBANY ATTACK
Albany Attack, began exhibition play, 1999.
ALBANY ATTACK (NLL 2000–present)

ALBANY CAPITALS
Albany Capitals (ASL3 1988–89; APSL 1990–91)
Folded, 1991.

ALBANY FIREBIRDS
ALBANY FIREBIRDS (AFL 1990–present)

ALBERTA
(Canada)

ALBERTA OILERS
See *EDMONTON OILERS*

ALTOONA
(Pennsylvania)

ALTOONA MOUNTAIN CITYS
See *ALTOONA UNIONS*

ALTOONA OTTOWAS
See *ALTOONA UNIONS*

ALTOONA PRIDE
See *ALTOONA UNIONS*

ALTOONA UNIONS
Altoona Unions (UA 1884)
   a.k.a. Altoona Mountain Citys
   a.k.a. Altoona Pride
   a.k.a. Altoona Ottowas
Independent during season, 1884.
Folded, post-1884.

AMERICA

TEAM AMERICA
U.S. National Team, independent, 1885–1982.
Team America (NASLo 1983)
U.S. National Team, independent, 1984–present.

ANAHEIM
(California)

ANAHEIM AMIGOS
See *UTAH STARS*

ANAHEIM ANGELS
Los Angeles Angels (AL 1961–64)
California Angels (AL 1965–96)
ANAHEIM ANGELS (AL 1997–present)

ANAHEIM BULLFROGS
Anaheim Bullfrogs (RHI 1993–97; MLRH 1998; RHI
   1999)
Folded, 1999.

ANAHEIM MIGHTY DUCKS
ANAHEIM MIGHTY DUCKS (NHL 1993–present)

ANAHEIM ORANGES
See *CALIFORNIA ORANGES*

ANAHEIM PIRANHAS
Las Vegas Sting (AFL 1995)
Anaheim Piranhas (AFL 1996–97)
Folded, 1997.

ANAHEIM SPLASH
Los Angeles United (CISL 1993)
Anaheim Splash (CISL 1994–97)
Folded, 1997.

ANDERSON
(Indiana)

ANDERSON DUFFEY PACKERS
See *ANDERSON PACKERS*

ANDERSON PACKERS
Anderson Chiefs, semipro, 1945–46.
Anderson Duffey Packers (NBL 1946–49)
Anderson Packers (NBA 1949–50)
Joined National Professional Basketball League, 1950–51.
Folded, 1951.

ARIZONA

ARIZONA CARDINALS
Morgan Athletic Club (Chicago), amateur, 1898. Chicago
   Normals, amateur, approximately 1899–1900. Racine
   Cardinals, amateur, 1901–05. Suspended operations,
   1906–12. Revived and continued as amateur team,
   1913–17. Suspended operations, 1918. Revived and
   continued as amateur team, 1919.
Racine Cardinals (APFA 1920–21)
Chicago Cardinals (NFL 1922–43)
Merged with Pittsburgh half of Phil-Pitt, 1944.
Card-Pitt (NFL 1944)
Split from Pittsburgh Steelers, 1945.
Chicago Cardinals (NFL 1945–59)
St. Louis Cardinals (F) (NFL 1960–88)
Phoenix Cardinals (NFL 1988–94)
ARIZONA CARDINALS (NFL 1994–present)

ARIZONA CONDORS
Arizona Condors (WSA 1989; APSL 1990)
Folded, 1990.

ARIZONA DIAMONDBACKS
ARIZONA DIAMONDBACKS (NL 1998–present)

ARIZONA OUTLAWS *(**MERGED TEAM**)*
Chicago Blitz (1) (USFL 1983)
Arizona Wranglers (2) (USFL 1984)
Merged with Oklahoma Outlaws, 1985.

Arizona Outlaws (USFL 1985)
Folded, 1985.

*****

Oklahoma Outlaws (USFL 1984)
Merged with Arizona Wranglers (2), 1985.
Arizona Outlaws (USFL 1985)
Folded, 1985.

ARIZONA RACQUETS
Phoenix Sunsets (TT 1982)
Arizona Racquets (TT 1983)
Folded, 1983.

ARIZONA RATTLERS
ARIZONA RATTLERS (AFL 1992–present)

ARIZONA SANDSHARKS
See *ARIZONA THUNDER*

ARIZONA THUNDER
Arizona SandSharks (CISL 1993–95, 1997)
(Suspended operations, 1996.)
ARIZONA THUNDER (PSA 1998; WISL 1999–present)

ARIZONA WRANGLERS (1)
See *CHICAGO BLITZ (2)*

ARIZONA WRANGLERS (2)
See *ARIZONA OUTLAWS*

ATLANTA
(Georgia)

ATLANTA APOLLOS
Atlanta Chiefs (S) (NPSLo 1967; NASLo 1968–72)
Atlanta Apollos (NASLo 1973)
Folded, 1973.

ATLANTA ATTACK
See *KANSAS CITY ATTACK*

ATLANTA BLACK CRACKERS
*Atlanta Black Crackers, minor Negro Southern League,
   1920–37.*
Atlanta Black Crackers (NAL 1938)
Folded, 1938.

ATLANTA BRAVES
Boston Red Stockings (1) (NA 1871–75)
   a.k.a. Boston Reds (1)

Boston Red Caps (NL 1876–82)
Boston Bostons (NL 1883–1906)
   a.k.a. Boston Beaneaters (1)
   a.k.a. Boston Nationals, 1901–06
Boston Doves (NL 1907–10)
   a.k.a. Boston Pilgrims (2)
Boston Heps (NL 1911)
   a.k.a. Boston Rustlers
Boston Braves (B) (NL 1912–35)
Boston Bees (NL 1936–40)
Boston Braves (B) (NL 1941–52)
Milwaukee Braves (NL 1953–65)
ATLANTA BRAVES (NL 1966–present)

ATLANTA CHIEFS (S)
See *ATLANTA APOLLOS*

ATLANTA CHIEFS (S/IS)
Colorado Caribous (NASLo 1978)
Atlanta Chiefs (S/IS) (NASLo 1979–81) and (NASLi
   1979–81)
Folded, 1981.

ATLANTA FALCONS
ATLANTA FALCONS (NFL 1966–present)

ATLANTA FIRE ANTS
See *OKLAHOMA COYOTES*

ATLANTA FLAMES
See *CALGARY FLAMES*

ATLANTA GLORY
Atlanta Glory (ABLw 1996–98)
Folded, 1998.

ATLANTA HAWKS
Buffalo Bisons (Bk3) (NBL 1946)
Tri-Cities Blackhawks (NBL 1946–49; NBA 1949–51)
Milwaukee Hawks (NBA 1951–55)
St. Louis Hawks (NBA 1955–68)
ATLANTA HAWKS (NBA 1968–present)

ATLANTA THRASHERS
ATLANTA THRASHERS (NHL 1999–present)

ATLANTA THUNDER
See *MILWAUKEE RACQUETEERS*

ATLANTIC CITY
(New Jersey)

ATLANTIC CITY BACHARACH GIANTS
Duvall Giants (Jacksonville), independent, pre-1916–22.
Atlantic City Bacharach Giants (ECL 1923–28; ANL
   1929; NNL2 1934)
(Independent, 1930–33.)
Folded, 1934.

ATLANTIC CITY SAND SNIPERS
Atlantic City Sand Snipers (ABL2 1936)
Folded during season, 1936.

(AZTECS)
(No location name: Orlando, Florida)

AZTECS
Aztecs (WRHL 1993)
Folded, 1993.

BALTIMORE
(Maryland)

BALTIMORE AMERICANS (1)
Baltimore Americans (1) (ASL2 1939–40)
Folded, 1940.

BALTIMORE AMERICANS (2)
Baltimore Americans (2) (ASL2 1941–42)
Folded, 1942.

BALTIMORE AMERICANS (3)
Baltimore Americans (3) (ASL2 1943–48)
Folded during 1948–49 season, 1948.

BALTIMORE BALTFEDS
See *BALTIMORE TERRAPINS*

BALTIMORE BANNERS
Baltimore Banners (WTT 1974)
Folded, 1974.

BALTIMORE BAYS (1)
Baltimore Bays (1) (NPSLo 1967; NASLo 1968–69)
Folded, 1969.

BALTIMORE BAYS (2)
Baltimore Stars (S) (ASL2 1972)
Baltimore Bays (2) (ASL2 1973)
Folded, 1973.

BALTIMORE BLACK SOX
Baltimore Black Sox, independent, 1916–22.
Baltimore Black Sox (ECL 1923–28; ANL 1929; NNL2
   1933, 1934)
(Independent, 1930–31, 1934.)
(Joined East-West Colored League, 1932.)
Folded, 1934.

BALTIMORE BLADES
Los Angeles Aces (WHA 1972 *did not play*)
Los Angeles Sharks (WHA 1972–74)
Michigan Stags (WHA 1974–75)
Baltimore Blades (WHA 1975)
Folded, 1975.

BALTIMORE BLAST
Houston Summit Soccer (MISL 1978–79)
Baltimore Blast (MISL 1980–90; MSL 1990–92)
Baltimore Spirit (NPSLi 1992–98)
BALTIMORE BLAST (NPSLi 1998–present)

BALTIMORE BULLETS (1)
Baltimore Bullets (1) (ABL2 1944–47; BAA 1947–49;
   NBA 1949–54)
Folded during 1954–55 season, 1954.

BALTIMORE BULLETS (2)
See *WASHINGTON WIZARDS*

BALTIMORE CANARIES
See *BALTIMORE LORD BALTIMORES*

BALTIMORE CANTON
See *BALTIMORE SOCCER CLUB*

BALTIMORE CFL COLTS
See *MONTREAL ALOUETTES (3)*

BALTIMORE CFLS
See *MONTREAL ALOUETTES (3)*

BALTIMORE CLAWS
Louisiana Buccaneers (ABA 1967 *did not play*)
New Orleans Buccaneers (ABA 1967–70)
Memphis Pros (ABA 1970–72)
Memphis Tams (ABA 1972–74)
Memphis Sounds (ABA 1974–75)

Baltimore Hustlers (ABA 1975 *did not play*)
Baltimore Claws (ABA 1975 *did not play*)
Folded before season, 1975.

BALTIMORE CLIPPERS
Visitation Triangles (Brooklyn), independent, 1918–21.
    Brooklyn Visitations, first Metropolitan League, 1921–
    28. Simultaneously joined first ABL (see below) during
    season, January 1928.
Brooklyn Visitations (ABL1 1928–31; ABL2 1933–36)
(Absorbed Washington Palace Five during season, 1928.)
(Joined second Metropolitan League, 1931–33.)
Paterson Visitations (ABL2 1936)
Brooklyn Visitations (ABL2 1936–39)
Baltimore Clippers (ABL2 1939–41)
    a.k.a. Baltimore Orioles (Bk2)
Folded, 1941.

BALTIMORE COLTS (1)
Miami Seahawks (AAFC 1946)
Baltimore Colts (1) (AAFC 1947–49; NFL 1950)
Folded, 1950.

BALTIMORE COLTS (2)
See *INDIANAPOLIS COLTS*

BALTIMORE COMETS
See *SAN DIEGO SOCKERS*

BALTIMORE ELITE GIANTS
Standard Giants (Nashville), independent, 1916–19.
    Joined minor Negro Southern League, 1920–29.
Nashville Elite Giants (NNL1 1930)
Cleveland Cubs (NNL1 1931)
Nashville Elite Giants (NSL 1932; NNL2 1933–34)
Columbus Elite Giants (NNL2 1935)
Washington Elite Giants (NNL2 1936–37)
Baltimore Elite Giants (NNL2 1938–48; NAL 1949–50)
Continued as member of minor NAL, 1951–55.
Folded, 1955.

BALTIMORE FLYERS
Baltimore St. Gerards (ASL2 1966–67)
Baltimore Flyers (ASL2 1967–68)
Folded, 1968.

BALTIMORE GERMANS
Baltimore Germans (ASL2 1938–39, 1940–41)
(Suspended operations, 1939–40.)
Folded, 1941.

BALTIMORE HUSTLERS
See *BALTIMORE CLAWS*

BALTIMORE LORD BALTIMORES
Baltimore Lord Baltimores (NA 1872–74)
    a.k.a. Baltimore Canaries
Folded during season, 1874.

BALTIMORE MARYLANDS
Baltimore Marylands (NA 1873)
Folded during season, 1873.

BALTIMORE MONUMENTALS
See *BALTIMORE UNIONS*

BALTIMORE ORIOLES (B1)
Baltimore Orioles (B1) (AA 1882–89, 1890–91; NL
    1892–99)
(Suspended operations during season, 1889. Joined At-
    lantic Association, beginning of 1890.)
Absorbed by Brooklyn Superbas, 1900.

BALTIMORE ORIOLES (B2)
See *NEW YORK YANKEES (B)*

BALTIMORE ORIOLES (B3)
Milwaukee Brewers, Western League (charter member),
    1894–95. Milwaukee Creams, WL, 1896–97. Milwau-
    kee Brewers, WL, 1898–99. Continued when WL be-
    came minor American League, 1900.
Milwaukee Brewers (4) (AL 1901)
St. Louis Browns (2) (AL 1902–53)
    a.k.a. St. Louis Ravens, 1906
BALTIMORE ORIOLES (B3) (AL 1954–present)

BALTIMORE ORIOLES (Bk1)
Baltimore Orioles (Bk1) (ABL1 1926–27)
Folded, 1927.

BALTIMORE ORIOLES (Bk2)
See *BALTIMORE CLIPPERS*

BALTIMORE POMPEI
Baltimore Rockets (ASL2 1953–57)
Baltimore Pompei (ASL2 1957–61)
Folded, 1961.

BALTIMORE RAVENS
Cleveland Browns (F1) (AAFC 1946–49; NFL 1950–96)
BALTIMORE RAVENS (NFL 1996–present)

BALTIMORE ROCKETS
See *BALTIMORE POMPEI*

BALTIMORE ST. GERARDS
See *BALTIMORE FLYERS*

BALTIMORE SOCCER CLUB
Baltimore Soccer Club (ASL2 1934–36)
Baltimore Canton (ASL2 1936–38)
Baltimore Soccer Club (ASL2 1938–48)
Folded during season, 1948.

BALTIMORE SPIRIT
See *BALTIMORE BLAST*

BALTIMORE STALLIONS
See *MONTREAL ALOUETTES (3)*

BALTIMORE STARS (F) *(**MERGED TEAM**)*
Philadelphia Stars (F) (USFL 1983–84)
Merged with Pittsburgh Maulers, 1985.
Baltimore Stars (F) (USFL 1985)
Folded, 1985.

*****

Pittsburgh Maulers (USFL 1984)
Merged with Philadelphia Stars (F), 1985.
Baltimore Stars (F) (USFL 1985)
Folded, 1985.

BALTIMORE STARS (S)
See *BALTIMORE BAYS (2)*

BALTIMORE TERRAPINS
Baltimore Terrapins (FL 1914–15)
    a.k.a. Baltimore Baltfeds
Folded, 1915.

BALTIMORE THUNDER
See *PITTSBURGH CROSSEFIRE*

BALTIMORE UNIONS
Baltimore Unions (UA 1884)
    a.k.a. Baltimore Monumentals
*Lancaster Ironsides, Eastern League, 1884–85. Bridge-
    port Giants, EL, during season, 1885–87. Joined Con-
    necticut State League (charter member), 1888.
    Stamford (Connecticut) during season, 1888.
Folded, 1888.*

BATTLE CREEK
(Michigan)

BATTLE CREEK BELLES
See *MUSKEGON BELLES*

BETHLEHEM
(Pennsylvania)

BETHLEHEM
Bethlehem (ASL2 1938–39)
Folded, 1939.

BETHLEHEM STEEL
*Bethlehem Steel, North American Foot Ball League, 1917–
    21.*
Philadelphia Field Club (1) (ASL1 1921–22)
Bethlehem Steel (ASL1 1922–28; ACL 1929–30)
*(Withdrew during season and joined second Eastern Pro-
    fessional Soccer League, 1928–29.)*
Folded, 1930.

BIRMINGHAM
(Alabama)

BIRMINGHAM AMERICANS
Birmingham Americans (WFL 1974)
Folded, 1974.

BIRMINGHAM BARRACUDAS
Birmingham Barracudas (CFL 1995)
Folded, 1995.

BIRMINGHAM BLACK BARONS
*Birmingham Black Barons, minor Negro Southern League,
    1920–23.*
Birmingham Black Barons (NNL1 1924–25, 1927–30;
    NAL 1937–38, 1940–50)
*(Rejoined minor NSL, 1926, 1931–36. Suspended opera-
    tions, 1939.)*
Continued as member of minor NAL, 1951–61.
Folded, 1961.

BIRMINGHAM BULLS
Ottawa Nationals (WHA 1972–73)
Toronto Toros (WHA 1973–76)

Birmingham Bulls (WHA 1976–78)
Folded, 1978.

BIRMINGHAM STALLIONS
Birmingham Stallions (USFL 1983–85)
Folded, 1985.

BIRMINGHAM VULCANS
Birmingham Vulcans (WFL 1975)
Folded during season, 1975.

(BLAST)
(No location name: Orlando, Florida)

BLAST
Blast (WRHL 1993)
Folded, 1993.

BOCA
(Buenos Aires, Argentina, in name only; actually played in Astoria, Queens, New York)

BOCA JUNIORS (**MERGED TEAM**)
Brooklyn Italians (ASL2 1956–61)
Merged with Inter Soccer Club (1), 1961.
Inter-Brooklyn Italians (ASL2 1961–62)
Inter Soccer Club (1) (ASL2 1962–63)
Boca Juniors (ASL2 1963–64)
Folded, 1964.

*****
Inter Soccer Club (1) (ASL2 1960–61)
Merged with Brooklyn Italians, 1961.
Inter-Brooklyn Italians (ASL2 1961–62)
Inter Soccer Club (1) (ASL2 1962–63)
Boca Juniors (ASL2 1963–64)
Folded, 1964.

BOSTON
(Massachusetts)

BOSTON
See *BOSTON BEARS (S)*

BOSTON AMERICANS
See *BOSTON RED SOX*

BOSTON ASTROS
See *WORCESTER ASTROS*

BOSTON BAYS
Boston Bays (TT 1984–86)
Folded, 1986.

BOSTON BEACONS
*Shamrock Rovers (Dublin, Ireland), independent, pre-
     1967.*
Boston Rovers (USA 1967)
Boston Beacons (NASLo 1968)
Folded, 1968.

BOSTON BEANEATERS (1)
See *ATLANTA BRAVES*

BOSTON BEANEATERS (2)
See *BOSTON RED STOCKINGS (2)*

BOSTON BEARS (F)
Boston Bears (F) (AFL3 1940)
Folded, 1940.

BOSTON BEARS (S)
Boston Wonder Workers (ASL1 1924–29)
*(Simultaneously joined first International Soccer League,
     1926.)*
Boston (ACL 1929)
Suspended operations during season, 1929–30.
Boston Bears (S) (ASL1 1931, 1931–33)
(Suspended operations during season, 1931.)
Folded, 1933.

BOSTON BEES
See *ATLANTA BRAVES*

BOSTON BLAZERS
New England Blazers (MILL 1989–91)
Boston Blazers (MILL 1992–97; NLL 1998 *did not play*)
Folded before season, 1998.

BOSTON BOLTS
Boston Bolts (ASL3 1988–89; APSL 1990)
Folded, 1990.

BOSTON BOSTONS
See *ATLANTA BRAVES*

BOSTON BRAVES (B)
See *ATLANTA BRAVES*

BOSTON BRAVES (F)
See *WASHINGTON REDSKINS*

BOSTON BREAKERS
See *PORTLAND BREAKERS*

BOSTON BRUINS
BOSTON BRUINS (NHL 1924–present)

BOSTON BULLDOGS (1)
Boston Bulldogs (1) (AFL1 1926)
Folded during season, 1926.

BOSTON BULLDOGS (2)
*Pottsville Maroons, independent Anthracite Football
    League, 1922–24.*
Pottsville Maroons (NFL 1925–28)
Boston Bulldogs (2) (NFL 1929)
Folded, 1929.

BOSTON BULLDOGS (3)
See *CHARLOTTE HORNETS (F)*

BOSTON BULLS
See *CHARLOTTE HORNETS (F)*

BOSTON CELTICS
BOSTON CELTICS (BAA 1946–49; NBA 1949–present)

BOSTON DOVES
See *ATLANTA BRAVES*

BOSTON HEPS
See *ATLANTA BRAVES*

BOSTON LOBSTERS
Boston Lobsters (WTT 1974–78)
Folded, 1978.

BOSTON METROS
Boston Metros (ASL2 1963–64)
Joined Eastern Professional Soccer Conference, 1964–65.
Folded, 1965.

BOSTON MINUTEMEN
Boston Minutemen (NASLo 1974–76)
Folded, 1976.

BOSTON NATIONALS
See *ATLANTA BRAVES*

BOSTON PATRIOTS
See *NEW ENGLAND PATRIOTS*

BOSTON PILGRIMS (1)
See *BOSTON RED SOX*

BOSTON PILGRIMS (2)
See *ATLANTA BRAVES*

BOSTON PLYMOUTH ROCKS
See *BOSTON RED SOX*

BOSTON PURITANS
See *BOSTON RED SOX*

BOSTON RED CAPS
See *ATLANTA BRAVES*

BOSTON RED SOX
*Boston Americans, minor American League (charter
    member), 1900.*
Boston Americans (AL 1901–06)
    a.k.a. Boston Somersets
    a.k.a. Boston Puritans
    a.k.a. Boston Plymouth Rocks
    a.k.a. Boston Speedboys
    a.k.a. Boston Pilgrims (1)
    a.k.a. Boston Red Stockings (3)
BOSTON RED SOX (AL 1907–present)

BOSTON RED STOCKINGS (1)
See *ATLANTA BRAVES*

BOSTON RED STOCKINGS (2)
Boston Red Stockings (2) (PL 1890; AA 1891)
    a.k.a. Boston Reds (3)
    a.k.a. Boston Beaneaters (2)
Folded, 1891.

BOSTON RED STOCKINGS (3)
See *BOSTON RED SOX*

BOSTON REDS (1)
See *ATLANTA BRAVES*

BOSTON REDS (2)
See *BOSTON UNIONS*

BOSTON REDS (3)
See *BOSTON RED STOCKINGS (2)*

BOSTON REDSKINS
See *WASHINGTON REDSKINS*

BOSTON ROVERS
See *BOSTON BEACONS*

BOSTON RUSTLERS
See *ATLANTA BRAVES*

BOSTON SHAMROCKS
Boston Shamrocks (AFL2 1936–37)
Folded, 1937.

BOSTON SOMERSETS
See *BOSTON RED SOX*

BOSTON SPEEDBOYS
See *BOSTON RED SOX*

BOSTON TIGERS
Boston Tigers (ASL2 1965–68)
Folded, 1968.

BOSTON TROJANS
Boston Trojans (ABL2 1934–35)
Folded, 1935.

BOSTON UNIONS
Boston Unions (UA 1884)
    a.k.a. Boston Reds (2)
Folded, 1884.

BOSTON WHIRLWINDS
Boston Whirlwinds (ABL1 1925)
Folded during season, 1925.

BOSTON WONDER WORKERS
See *BOSTON BEARS (S)*

BOSTON YANKS
See *DALLAS TEXANS (F1)*

BRIDGEPORT
(Connecticut)

BRIDGEPORT AER-A-SOLS
See *BRIDGEPORT ROESSLERS*

BRIDGEPORT BEARS
See *PHILADELPHIA FOOTBALL CLUB*

BRIDGEPORT HUNGARIA
See *NEWARK AMERICANS*

BRIDGEPORT NEWFIELD STEELERS
See *BRIDGEPORT ROESSLERS*

BRIDGEPORT ROESSLERS
Bridgeport Newfield Steelers (ABL2 1948–49)
Bridgeport Aer-A-Sols (ABL2 1949–51)
Bridgeport Roesslers (ABL2 1951–52)
Folded, 1952.

BRIGHTON
(East Sussex, England)

BRIGHTON TIGERS
Brighton Tigers (MLRH 1998)
Folded, 1998.

BRITISH COLUMBIA
(Canada)

BRITISH COLUMBIA LIONS
British Columbia Lions, Western Interprovincial Football
    Union, 1954–55.
BRITISH COLUMBIA LIONS (CFC 1956–57; CFL
    1958–present)

BRONX
(New York)

BRONX AMERICANS
Brooklyn Americans, second Metropolitan League, 1932.
    Brooklyn Hill House, ML, during season, 1932–33.
    Brooklyn Americans, ML, during season, 1933. Bronx
    Braves, ML, during season, 1933.
Bronx Americans (ABL2 1933–34)
Folded, 1934.

BRONX YANKEES
See *NEW YORK YANKEES (Bk)*

BROOKHATTAN
(Brooklyn and Manhattan, New York)

BROOKHATTAN
See *GALICIA-HONDURAS*

BROOKHATTAN-GALICIA
(Brooklyn and Manhattan, New York, and, in name only, Galicia, Spain; actually played in Brooklyn and Manhattan)

BROOKHATTAN-GALICIA
See *GALICIA-HONDURAS*

BROOKLYN
(New York)

BROOKLYN AMERICANS
Quebec Bulldogs, Amateur Hockey Association, 1886–1908. Joined Eastern Canada Hockey Association, 1908–09. Joined Canadian Hockey Association, 1909.
Quebec Bulldogs (NHA 1910–17; NHL 1919–20)
(Suspended operations, 1917–19.)
Hamilton Tigers (NHL 1920–25)
New York Americans (H) (NHL 1925–41)
Brooklyn Americans (NHL 1941–42)
Folded, 1942.

BROOKLYN ARCADIANS
Brooklyn Arcadians (ABL1 1925–26)
Folded during 1926–27 season, 1926.

BROOKLYN ATLANTICS (1)
Brooklyn Atlantics, amateur, 1855–71.
Brooklyn Atlantics (1) (NA 1872–75)
Folded, 1875.

BROOKLYN ATLANTICS (2)
See *LOS ANGELES DODGERS*

BROOKLYN BRIDEGROOMS
See *LOS ANGELES DODGERS*

BROOKLYN BROOKFEDS
See *BROOKLYN TIP-TOPS*

BROOKLYN CELTICS (Bk1)
See *NEW YORK CELTICS*

BROOKLYN CELTICS (Bk2)
New York Original Celtics (ABL2 1937–38)
Troy Haymakers (Bk) (ABL2 1938–39)
Troy Celtics (1) (ABL2 1939–40)
(Absorbed Kingston Colonials during season, 1939.)
Brooklyn Celtics (Bk2) (ABL2 1940–41)
Folded, 1941.

BROOKLYN CELTICS (S1)
See *ST. MARY'S CELTICS (1)*

BROOKLYN CELTICS (S2)
Brooklyn Celtics (S2) (ASL2 1940–41)
Folded, 1941.

BROOKLYN DODGERS (B)
See *LOS ANGELES DODGERS*

BROOKLYN DODGERS (F1)
See *BROOKLYN TIGERS (2)*

BROOKLYN DODGERS (F2)
See *BROOKLYN-NEW YORK YANKEES*

BROOKLYN EAGLES
See *HOUSTON EAGLES*

BROOKLYN ECKFORDS
Brooklyn Eckfords, amateur, 1855–71.
Brooklyn Eckfords (NA 1871–72)
(Joined NA in August 1871, but games erased from record because team did not join at start of season.)
Folded, 1872.

BROOKLYN FEDS
See *BROOKLYN TIP-TOPS*

BROOKLYN FOOTBALL CLUB
Brooklyn Football Club (ASL2 1933)
Folded during season, 1933.

BROOKLYN GLADIATORS
Brooklyn Gladiators (AA 1890)
a.k.a. Brooklyn Ridgewoods
Folded during season, 1890.

BROOKLYN GOTHAMS
Brooklyn Jewels, second Metropolitan League, 1931–33.
Brooklyn Jewels (ABL2 1933–34)

New York Jewels (ABL2 1934–36)
Brooklyn Jewels (ABL2 1936–37)
New Haven Jewels (ABL2 1937)
New York Jewels (ABL2 1937–41, 1942–43)
(Absorbed Jersey Reds during season, 1940. Suspended
  operations during season, 1941.)
New York Americans (Bk1) (ABL2 1943–44)
New York Westchesters (ABL2 1944–45)
   a.k.a. Westchester Indians
New York Gothams (Bk) (ABL2 1945–46)
Brooklyn Gothams (ABL2 1946–49)
Folded, 1949.

BROOKLYN GRAYS
See *LOS ANGELES DODGERS*

BROOKLYN HAKOAH
See *NEW YORK HAKOAH (1)*

BROOKLYN HARTFORDS
Hartford Dark Blues (NA 1874–75; NL 1876)
   a.k.a. Hartford Hartfords
Brooklyn Hartfords (NL 1877)
Folded, 1877.

BROOKLYN HISPANO
Brooklyn Hispano (ASL2 1933–57)
Folded, 1957.

BROOKLYN HORSE-LIONS *(**MERGED TEAM**)*
Brooklyn Horsemen (AFL1 1926)
Merged with Brooklyn Lions during season, 1926.
Brooklyn Horse-Lions (NFL 1926)
Folded, 1926.

*****

Brooklyn Lions (NFL 1926)
Merged with Brooklyn Horsemen during season, 1926.
Brooklyn Horse-Lions (NFL 1926)
Folded, 1926.

BROOKLYN HORSEMEN
See *BROOKLYN HORSE-LIONS*

BROOKLYN INDIANS (1)
See *WILMINGTON BOMBERS*

BROOKLYN INDIANS (2)
Brooklyn Indians (2) (ABL2 1943–44)
Folded during season, 1944.

BROOKLYN ITALIANS
See *BOCA JUNIORS*

BROOKLYN JEWELS
See *BROOKLYN GOTHAMS*

BROOKLYN LIONS
See *BROOKLYN HORSE-LIONS*

BROOKLYN RIDGEWOODS
See *BROOKLYN GLADIATORS*

BROOKLYN ROBINS
See *LOS ANGELES DODGERS*

BROOKLYN ROYAL GIANTS
Brooklyn Royal Giants, independent, 1905–22.
Brooklyn Royal Giants (ECL 1923–27)
Independent, 1928–43.
Folded, 1943.

BROOKLYN SUPERBAS
See *LOS ANGELES DODGERS*

BROOKLYN TIGERS (1)
See *ROCHESTER TIGERS*

BROOKLYN TIGERS (2)
St. Mary's Cadets (Dayton), independent, 1913–14. Day-
  ton Gym Cadets, independent, 1915. Dayton Triangles,
  independent, 1916–19.
Dayton Triangles (APFA 1920–21; NFL 1922–29)
Brooklyn Dodgers (F1) (NFL 1930–43)
Brooklyn Tigers (2) (NFL 1944)
Absorbed by Boston Yanks, 1945.

BROOKLYN TIP-TOPS
Brooklyn Brookfeds (FL 1914)
   a.k.a. Brooklyn Feds
Brooklyn Tip-Tops (FL 1914–15)
Folded, 1915.

BROOKLYN TROLLEY DODGERS
See *LOS ANGELES DODGERS*

BROOKLYN VISITATIONS
See *BALTIMORE CLIPPERS*

BROOKLYN WANDERERS (1)
See *NEW YORK AMERICANS (S)*

BROOKLYN WANDERERS (2)
Brooklyn Wanderers (2) (ASL1 1932–33)
Folded, 1933.

BROOKLYN WANDERERS (3)
Brooklyn Wanderers (3) (ASL2 1942–48)
Folded during season, 1948.

BROOKLYN WONDERS
Brooklyn Wonders (PL 1890)
Absorbed by Brooklyn Bridegrooms, 1891.

BROOKLYN-NEW YORK
(New York)

BROOKLYN-NEW YORK YANKEES *(**MERGED TEAM**)*
Brooklyn Dodgers (F2) (AAFC 1946–48)
Merged with New York Yankees (F3), 1949.
Brooklyn-New York Yankees (AAFC 1949)
Folded, 1949.

*****
New York Yankees (F3) (AAFC 1946–48)
Merged with Brooklyn Dodgers (F2), 1949.
Brooklyn-New York Yankees (AAFC 1949)
Folded, 1949.

BUFFALO
(New York)

BUFFALO ALL-AMERICANS
See *BUFFALO BISONS (F1)*

BUFFALO BANDITS
BUFFALO BANDITS (MILL 1992–97; NLL 1998–present)

BUFFALO BILLS (1)
Buffalo Bisons (F2) (AAFC 1946)
Buffalo Bills (1) (AAFC 1947–49)
Folded, 1949.

BUFFALO BILLS (2)
BUFFALO BILLS (2) (AFL4 1960–70; NFL 1970–present)

BUFFALO BISONS (B1)
Buffalo Bisons, International Association, 1878.

Buffalo Bisons (B1) (NL 1879–85)
Joined International League, 1886–90. Montreal, IL, during season, 1890. Grand Rapids, IL, during season, 1890. Quebec, IL, during season, 1890.
Folded, 1890.

BUFFALO BISONS (B2)
Buffalo Bisons (B2) (PL 1890)
Folded, 1890.

BUFFALO BISONS (Bk1)
See *BUFFALO GERMANS*

BUFFALO BISONS (Bk2)
Buffalo Bisons, independent, pre-1937.
Buffalo Bisons (Bk2) (NBL 1937–38)
Folded, 1938.

BUFFALO BISONS (Bk3)
See *ATLANTA HAWKS*

BUFFALO BISONS (F1)
Buffalo All-Americans, independent, pre-1920.
Buffalo All-Americans (APFA 1920–21; NFL 1922–23)
Buffalo Bisons (F1) (NFL 1924–25)
Buffalo Rangers (NFL 1926)
Buffalo Bisons (F1) (NFL 1927, 1929)
(Suspended operations during season, 1927, and 1928.)
Folded, 1929.

BUFFALO BISONS (F2)
See *BUFFALO BILLS (1)*

BUFFALO BLIZZARD
BUFFALO BLIZZARD (NPSLi 1992–present)

BUFFALO BLUES
Buffalo Buffeds (FL 1914)
Buffalo Blues (FL 1915)
  a.k.a. Buffalo Electrics
Folded, 1915.

BUFFALO BRAVES
See *LOS ANGELES CLIPPERS*

BUFFALO BUFFEDS
See *BUFFALO BLUES*

BUFFALO DESTROYERS
BUFFALO DESTROYERS (AFL 1999–present)

BUFFALO ELECTRICS
See *BUFFALO BLUES*

BUFFALO GERMANS
Buffalo Germans (ABL1 1925–26)
   a.k.a. Buffalo Bisons (Bk1)
Folded, 1926.

BUFFALO INDIANS
See *BUFFALO TIGERS*

BUFFALO RANGERS
See *BUFFALO BISONS (F1)*

BUFFALO SABRES
BUFFALO SABRES (NHL 1970–present)

BUFFALO STALLIONS
Buffalo Stallions (MISL 1979–84)
Folded, 1984.

BUFFALO STAMPEDE
Buffalo Stampede (RHI 1994–95)
Folded, 1995.

BUFFALO STORM
Buffalo Storm (USL 1984)
Folded, 1984.

BUFFALO TIGERS
Buffalo Indians (AFL3 1940)
Buffalo Tigers (AFL3 1941)
Folded, 1941.

BUFFALO WINGS (1)
Phoenix Cobras (RHI 1994–95)
Empire State Cobras (RHI 1996)
Buffalo Wings (1) (RHI 1997; MLRH 1998; RHI 1999)
Independent, 2000–present.

BUFFALO WINGS (2)
BUFFALO WINGS (2) (W-MLRH 2000–present)

CALGARY
(Alberta, Canada)

CALGARY BOOMERS
Memphis Rogues (S/IS) (NASLo 1978–80) and (NASLi
   1979–80)

Calgary Boomers (NASLo 1981) and (NASLi 1980–81)
Folded, 1981.

CALGARY BRONCOS
See *MINNESOTA FIGHTING SAINTS (2)*

CALGARY COWBOYS
Miami Screaming Eagles (WHA 1972 *did not play*)
Philadelphia Blazers (WHA 1972–73)
Vancouver Blazers (WHA 1973–75)
Calgary Cowboys (WHA 1975–77)
Folded, 1977.

CALGARY FLAMES
Atlanta Flames (NHL 1972–80)
CALGARY FLAMES (NHL 1980–present)

CALGARY RAD'Z
Calgary Rad'z (RHI 1993–94)
Folded, 1994.

CALGARY STAMPEDERS
*Calgary Bronks, Western Canada Rugby Football Union,
   1935. Continued when WCRFU became Western Interprovincial Football Union, 1936–40. Independent,
   1941–45. Calgary Stampeders, WIFU, 1946–55.*
CALGARY STAMPEDERS (CFC 1956–57; CFL 1958–
   present)

CALGARY TIGERS
Calgary Tigers (WCHL 1921–25; WHL 1925–26)
Folded, 1926.

CALIFORNIA

CALIFORNIA ANGELS
See *ANAHEIM ANGELS*

CALIFORNIA CLIPPERS
Oakland Clippers (NPSLo 1967)
California Clippers (NASLo 1968)
Folded, 1968.

CALIFORNIA EMPERORS
Hollywood Kickers (WSL 1986)
California Kickers (WSL 1987–88; WSA 1989)
California Emperors (APSL 1990)
Amateur, 1991.
Folded, post-1991.

CALIFORNIA GOLDEN SEALS
See *CLEVELAND BARONS*

CALIFORNIA KICKERS
See *CALIFORNIA EMPERORS*

CALIFORNIA ORANGES
Anaheim Oranges (WTT 1978)
Suspended operations, 1979–80.
California Oranges (TT 1981–83)
Folded, 1983.

CALIFORNIA SEALS
See *CLEVELAND BARONS*

CALIFORNIA SUNSHINE
California Sunshine (ASL2 1977–80)
Folded, 1980.

CALIFORNIA SURF
St. Louis Stars (S) (NPSLo 1967; NASLo 1968–77)
California Surf (NASLo 1978–81) and (NASLi 1979–81)
Folded, 1981.

CAMDEN
(New Jersey)

CAMDEN ATHLETICS
See *NEW BRITAIN MULES*

CAMDEN BREWERS
See *NEW BRITAIN MULES*

CAMDEN INDIANS
See *WILMINGTON BOMBERS*

CANTON
(Ohio)

CANTON BULLDOGS
*Canton Professionals, independent, 1911–14. Canton
    Bulldogs, independent, 1915–19.*
Canton Bulldogs (APFA 1920–21; NFL 1922–23, 1925–
    26)
(Suspended operations, 1924.)
Independent, 1927.
Folded, 1927.

CANTON INVADERS
See *COLUMBUS INVADERS*

CAPITAL
(Washington, D.C.)

CAPITAL BULLETS
See *WASHINGTON WIZARDS*

CARBONDALE
(Pennsylvania)

CARBONDALE ACES
Carbondale Aces (ABL2 1950–52)
Folded, 1952.

(CARD-PITT)
(No location name: Chicago, Illinois, and Pittsburgh, Pennsylvania)

CARD-PITT *(**MERGED TEAM**)*
See *ARIZONA CARDINALS* and *PITTSBURGH STEEL-
    ERS*

CAROLINA
(North Carolina)

CAROLINA COBRAS
CAROLINA COBRAS (AFL 2000–present)

CAROLINA COPPERHEADS
See *CAROLINA CRUSHERS*

CAROLINA COUGARS
See *UTAH ROCKIES*

CAROLINA CRUSHERS
Carolina Copperheads (MLRH 1997)
Merged with unnamed expansion team, 1998.
Carolina Crushers (MLRH 1998)
Folded, 1998.

CAROLINA HURRICANES
New England Whalers (WHA 1972–79)
Hartford Whalers (NHL 1979–97)
CAROLINA HURRICANES (NHL 1997–present)

CAROLINA LIGHTNIN'
See *CHARLOTTE GOLD*

CAROLINA PANTHERS
CAROLINA PANTHERS (NFL 1995–present)

CAROLINA VIPERS
Carolina Vipers (CISL 1994)
Folded, 1994.

CHARLOTTE
(North Carolina)

CHARLOTTE COBRAS
Charlotte Cobras (MILL 1996)
Folded, 1996.

CHARLOTTE EXPRESS
Charlotte Express (WTT 1994–95)
Folded, 1995.

CHARLOTTE GOLD
Carolina Lightnin' (ASL2 1981–83)
Charlotte Gold (USL 1984)
Folded, 1984.

CHARLOTTE HEAT
Charlotte Heat (TT 1987–91)
Folded, 1991.

CHARLOTTE HORNETS (Bk)
Charlotte Spirit (NBA 1988 *did not play*)
CHARLOTTE HORNETS (Bk) (NBA 1988–present)

CHARLOTTE HORNETS (F)
Boston Bulldogs (3) (WFL 1974 *did not play*)
Boston Bulls (WFL 1974 *did not play*)
New York Stars (WFL 1974)
Charlotte Stars (WFL 1974)
Charlotte Hornets (F) (WFL 1975)
Folded during season, 1975.

CHARLOTTE RAGE
Charlotte Rage (AFL 1992–96)
Folded, 1996.

CHARLOTTE SPIRIT
See *CHARLOTTE HORNETS (Bk)*

CHARLOTTE STARS
See *CHARLOTTE HORNETS (F)*

CHARLOTTE STING
CHARLOTTE STING (WNBA 1997–present)

CHICAGO
(Illinois)

CHICAGO ACES (1)
Chicago Aces (1) (WTT 1974)
Folded, 1974.

CHICAGO ACES (2)
See *CHICAGO FIRE (T)*

CHICAGO AMERICAN GEARS
Chicago American Gears (NBL 1944–47)
      a.k.a. Chicago Gears
Joined Professional Basketball League of America (charter member), 1947.
Folded during season, 1947.

CHICAGO AMERICAN GIANTS
Chicago American Giants, independent, 1911–19.
Chicago American Giants (NNL1 1920–31)
Cole's American Giants (NSL 1932; NNL2 1933–35)
Independent, 1936.
Chicago American Giants (NAL 1937–50)
Continued as member of minor NAL, 1951–54.
Folded, 1954.

CHICAGO AMERICANS
Chicago Americans (ASL2 1972)
Folded during season, 1972.

CHICAGO BABES
See *CHICAGO CUBS*

CHICAGO BEARS
Decatur Staleys, independent, 1919.
Decatur Staleys (APFA 1920)

Chicago Staleys (APFA 1921)
CHICAGO BEARS (NFL 1922–present)

CHICAGO BLACK HAWKS
See *CHICAGO BLACKHAWKS*

CHICAGO BLACKHAWKS
Chicago Black Hawks (NHL 1926–86)
CHICAGO BLACKHAWKS (NHL 1986–present)

CHICAGO BLITZ (1)
See *ARIZONA OUTLAWS*

CHICAGO BLITZ (2)
Arizona Wranglers (1) (USFL 1983)
Chicago Blitz (2) (USFL 1984)
Folded, 1984.

CHICAGO BLUESMEN
Chicago Bluesmen (RHI 1999)
Folded, 1999.

CHICAGO BRONCOS
See *CHICAGO CUBS*

CHICAGO BROWNS
See *PITTSBURGH STOGIES*

CHICAGO BRUINS (1)
See *CHICAGO STUDEBAKER FLYERS*

CHICAGO BRUINS (2)
Chicago Stags (BAA 1946–49; NBA 1949–50)
Chicago Bruins (2) (NBA 1950 *did not play*)
Folded before 1950–51 season, 1950.

CHICAGO BRUISERS
Chicago Bruisers (AFL 1987–89)
Folded, 1989.

CHICAGO BULLS (Bk)
CHICAGO BULLS (Bk) (NBA 1966–present)

CHICAGO BULLS (F)
Chicago Bulls (F) (AFL1 1926)
Folded, 1926.

CHICAGO CARDINALS
See *ARIZONA CARDINALS*

CHICAGO CATS
Chicago Cats (ASL2 1975–76)
Folded, 1976.

CHICAGO CHAMPIONS
See *CHICAGO STUDEBAKER FLYERS*

CHICAGO CHEETAHS
Chicago Cheetahs (RHI 1994–95)
Folded, 1995.

CHICAGO CHIFEDS
See *CHICAGO WHALES*

CHICAGO COLLEENS
Chicago Colleens (AAGPBL 1948)
Folded, 1948.

CHICAGO COLTS
See *CHICAGO CUBS*

CHICAGO CONDORS
Chicago Condors (ABLw 1998)
Folded during 1998–99 season, 1998.

CHICAGO COUGARS
Chicago Cougars (WHA 1972–75)
Folded, 1975.

CHICAGO COWBOYS
See *CHICAGO CUBS*

CHICAGO CUBS
Chicago White Stockings, amateur National Association,
    1870.
Chicago White Stockings (1) (NA 1871, 1874–75; NL
    1876–89)
(Suspended operations, 1872–73.)
    a.k.a. Chicago Remnants, 1874–89
Chicago Colts (NL 1890–97)
    a.k.a. Chicago Babes
    a.k.a. Chicago Cubs
    a.k.a. Chicago Rainmakers
    a.k.a. Chicago Recruits
(Absorbed Chicago Pirates, 1891.)
Chicago Orphans (NL 1898–1901)
    a.k.a. Chicago Cowboys
    a.k.a. Chicago Broncos
CHICAGO CUBS (NL 1902–present)

CHICAGO FIRE (F)
See *CHICAGO WINDS*

CHICAGO FIRE (S)
CHICAGO FIRE (S) (MLS 1998–present)

CHICAGO FIRE (T)
Chicago Aces (2) (TT 1982)
Chicago Fyre (TT 1983–85)
Chicago Fire (T) (TT 1986)
Folded, 1986.

CHICAGO FYRE
See *CHICAGO FIRE (T)*

CHICAGO GEARS
See *CHICAGO AMERICAN GEARS*

CHICAGO GIANTS
Chicago Giants, independent, 1905–19.
Chicago Giants (NNL1 1920–21)
Folded, 1921.

CHICAGO HORIZONS
Chicago Horizons (MISL 1980–81)
Folded, 1981.

CHICAGO HORNETS
Chicago Rockets (AAFC 1946–48)
Chicago Hornets (AAFC 1949)
Folded, 1949.

CHICAGO INVADERS
See *CHICAGO WHITE SOX*

CHICAGO MAJORS
Chicago Majors (ABL3 1961–62)
Folded during 1962–63 season, 1962.

CHICAGO MUSTANGS
Cagliari Calcio (Sardegna, Italy), independent, pre-1967.
Chicago Mustangs (USA 1967; NASLo 1968)
Joined National Soccer League, 1969.
Folded, post-1969.

CHICAGO ORPHANS
See *CHICAGO CUBS*

CHICAGO PACKERS
See *WASHINGTON WIZARDS*

CHICAGO PIRATES
Chicago Pirates (PL 1890)
Absorbed by Chicago Colts, 1891.

CHICAGO POWER
See *EDMONTON DRILLERS (IS)*

CHICAGO RAINMAKERS
See *CHICAGO CUBS*

CHICAGO RECRUITS
See *CHICAGO CUBS*

CHICAGO REMNANTS
See *CHICAGO CUBS*

CHICAGO ROCKETS
See *CHICAGO HORNETS*

CHICAGO SHOCCERS
Chicago Vultures (AISA 1984–85)
Chicago Shoccers (AISA 1985–87)
Folded, 1987.

CHICAGO SPURS
See *KANSAS CITY SPURS*

CHICAGO STAGS
See *CHICAGO BRUINS (2)*

CHICAGO STALEYS
See *CHICAGO BEARS*

CHICAGO STING
Chicago Sting (NASLo 1975–84) and (NASLi 1980–82;
    MISL 1982–83; NASLi 1983–84; MISL 1984–88)
Folded, 1988.

CHICAGO STUDEBAKER FLYERS
Chicago Bruins (1) (ABL1 1925–31; NBL 1939–42)
(Independent, 1931–39.)
Chicago Studebaker Flyers (NBL 1942–43)
    a.k.a. Chicago Studebakers
    a.k.a. Chicago Champions
Folded, 1943.

CHICAGO STUDEBAKERS
See *CHICAGO STUDEBAKER FLYERS*

CHICAGO TIGERS
Chicago Tigers, independent, pre-1920.
Chicago Tigers (APFA 1920)
Folded, 1920.

CHICAGO UNIQUES
See *CHICAGO WHITE SOX*

CHICAGO VULTURES
See *CHICAGO SHOCCERS*

CHICAGO WHALES
Chicago Chifeds (FL 1914)
Chicago Whales (FL 1915)
Folded, 1915.

CHICAGO WHITE SOX
Sioux City Cornhuskers (Iowa), Western League, 1894. St.
Paul Saints, WL, 1895–99. Chicago Invaders when WL
became minor American League, 1900.
Chicago Invaders (AL 1901–03)
 a.k.a. Chicago White Stockings (2)
Chicago Uniques (AL 1904)
CHICAGO WHITE SOX (AL 1904–present)

CHICAGO WHITE STOCKINGS (1)
See *CHICAGO CUBS*

CHICAGO WHITE STOCKINGS (2)
See *CHICAGO WHITE SOX*

CHICAGO WINDS
Chicago Fire (F) (WFL 1974)
Suspended operations during season, 1974.
Chicago Winds (WFL 1975)
Folded during season, 1975.

CHICAGO ZEPHYRS
See *WASHINGTON WIZARDS*

CINCINNATI
(Ohio)

CINCINNATI BENGALS (1)
Cincinnati Bengals (1) (AFL2 1937; AFL3 1940–41)
(Independent, 1938. Joined American Professional Foot-
ball League, 1939.)
Folded, 1941.

CINCINNATI BENGALS (2)
CINCINNATI BENGALS (2) (AFL4 1968–70; NFL
 1970–present)

CINCINNATI BUCKEYES
See *CLEVELAND BUCKEYES*

CINCINNATI CELTS
Cincinnati Celts, independent, 1914–20.
Cincinnati Celts (APFA 1921)
Independent, 1922.
Folded, 1922.

CINCINNATI CLOWNS
See *INDIANAPOLIS CLOWNS*

CINCINNATI COMELLOS
Richmond King Clothiers, independent, pre-1937.
Richmond King Clothiers (NBL 1937–38)
 a.k.a. Richmond Kings
Cincinnati Comellos (NBL 1938)
Folded, 1938.

CINCINNATI COMETS
Cincinnati Comets (ASL2 1972–75)
Folded, 1975.

CINCINNATI CUBANS
See *CUBAN STARS (WEST)*

CINCINNATI KELLYS
See *CINCINNATI PORKERS*

CINCINNATI KIDS
Cincinnati Kids (MISL 1978–79)
Folded, 1979.

CINCINNATI KILLERS
See *CINCINNATI PORKERS*

CINCINNATI OUTLAW REDS
Cincinnati Outlaw Reds (UA 1884)
Folded, 1884.

CINCINNATI PORKERS
Cincinnati Porkers (AA 1891)
 a.k.a. Cincinnati Kellys
 a.k.a. Cincinnati Killers
Folded during season, 1891.

CINCINNATI RED STOCKINGS
See *CINCINNATI REDS (B)*

CINCINNATI REDLEGS
See *CINCINNATI REDS (B)*

CINCINNATI REDS (B)
*Cincinnati Resolutes, amateur National Association,
     1866–67. Cincinnati Red Stockings, amateur NA,
     1868–70. Suspended operations, 1871–75.*
Cincinnati Red Stockings (NL 1876–77)
Cincinnati Reds (B) (NL 1878–80)
*Independent, 1881. Cincinnati Stars during season, 1881.
     Cincinnati Buckeyes during season, 1881.*
Cincinnati Red Stockings (AA 1882–89)
Cincinnati Reds (B) (NL 1890–1943)
Cincinnati Redlegs (NL 1944–45)
Cincinnati Reds (B) (NL 1946–52)
Cincinnati Redlegs (NL 1953–58)
CINCINNATI REDS (B) (NL 1959–present)

CINCINNATI REDS (F)
See *ST. LOUIS GUNNERS*

CINCINNATI ROCKERS
Cincinnati Rockers (AFL 1992–93)
Folded, 1993.

CINCINNATI ROYALS
See *SACRAMENTO KINGS*

CINCINNATI SILVERBACKS
Dayton Dynamo (AISA 1988–90; NPSLi 1990–95)
Cincinnati Silverbacks (NPSLi 1995–98)
Folded, 1998.

CINCINNATI STINGERS
Cincinnati Stingers (WHA 1975–79)
Folded, 1979.

CINCINNATI TIGERS
*Claybrook Tigers (Arkansas), independent, 1934. Joined
     minor Negro Southern League, 1935–36.*
Cincinnati Tigers (NAL 1937)
Folded, 1937.

CLEVELAND
(Ohio)

CLEVELAND ALLMEN TRANSFERS
Cleveland Allmen Transfers (NBL 1944–46)
Folded, 1946.

CLEVELAND BARONS
California Seals (NHL 1967)
Oakland Seals (NHL 1967–70)
California Golden Seals (NHL 1970–76)
Cleveland Barons (NHL 1976–78)
Absorbed by Minnesota North Stars, 1978.

CLEVELAND BEARS
See *JACKSONVILLE RED CAPS*

CLEVELAND BLUEBIRDS
See *CLEVELAND INDIANS (B)*

CLEVELAND BLUES (1)
Cleveland Blues (1) (NL 1879–84)
Folded, 1884.

CLEVELAND BLUES (2)
See *CLEVELAND SPIDERS*

CLEVELAND BLUES (3)
See *CLEVELAND INDIANS (B)*

CLEVELAND BRASS
See *CLEVELAND CHASE BRASSMEN*

CLEVELAND BRONCHOS
See *CLEVELAND INDIANS (B)*

CLEVELAND BROWNS (B)
Cleveland Browns (B) (NNL1 1924)
Folded, 1924.

CLEVELAND BROWNS (F1)
See *BALTIMORE RAVENS*

CLEVELAND BROWNS (F2)
CLEVELAND BROWNS (F2) (NFL 1999–present)

CLEVELAND BUCKEYES
Cincinnati Buckeyes (NAL 1942)
Cleveland Buckeyes (NAL 1943–48)
Louisville Buckeyes (NAL 1949)

Cleveland Buckeyes (NAL 1950)
Folded during season, 1950.

CLEVELAND BULLDOGS
Cleveland Indians (F2) (NFL 1923)
Cleveland Bulldogs (NFL 1924–25, 1927)
(Suspended operations, 1926.)
Folded, 1927.

CLEVELAND CAVALIERS
CLEVELAND CAVALIERS (NBA 1970–present)

CLEVELAND CHASE BRASSMEN
Cleveland Chase Brassmen (NBL 1943–44)
   a.k.a. Cleveland Brass
Folded, 1944.

CLEVELAND COBRAS
See *GEORGIA GENERALS*

CLEVELAND CRUNCH
CLEVELAND CRUNCH (MISL 1989–90; MSL 1990–
   92; NPSLi 1992–present)

CLEVELAND CRUSADERS
See *MINNESOTA FIGHTING SAINTS (2)*

CLEVELAND CUBS
See *BALTIMORE ELITE GIANTS*

CLEVELAND ELITES
Cleveland Elites (NNL1 1926)
Folded during season, 1926.

CLEVELAND FORCE
Cleveland Force (MISL 1978–88)
Folded, 1988.

CLEVELAND FOREST CITYS
Cleveland Forest Citys, independent, 1869–70.
Cleveland Forest Citys (NA 1871–72)
Folded during season, 1872.

CLEVELAND GIANTS
Cleveland Giants (NNL2 1933)
Folded, 1933.

CLEVELAND HORNETS
Cleveland Hornets (NNL1 1927)
Folded, 1927.

CLEVELAND INDIANS (B)
Cleveland Lake Shores, minor American League (charter
   member), 1900.
Cleveland Bluebirds (AL 1901)
   a.k.a. Cleveland Blues (3)
Cleveland Bronchos (AL 1902)
Cleveland Naps (AL 1903–11)
Cleveland Molly McGuires (AL 1912–14)
CLEVELAND INDIANS (B) (AL 1915–present)

CLEVELAND INDIANS (F1)
Cleveland Tigers, independent, 1919.
Cleveland Tigers (APFA 1920)
Cleveland Indians (F1) (APFA 1921)
Folded, 1921.

CLEVELAND INDIANS (F2)
See *CLEVELAND BULLDOGS*

CLEVELAND INDIANS (F3)
Cleveland Indians (F3) (NFL 1931)
Folded, 1931.

CLEVELAND INFANTS
Cleveland Infants (PL 1890)
Folded, 1890.

CLEVELAND MOLLY McGUIRES
See *CLEVELAND INDIANS (B)*

CLEVELAND NAPS
See *CLEVELAND INDIANS (B)*

CLEVELAND NETS
Cleveland Nets (WTT 1974–77)
Folded, 1977.

CLEVELAND PANTHERS
Cleveland Panthers (AFL1 1926)
Folded, 1926.

CLEVELAND PIPERS
Cleveland Pipers, National Industrial League, by at least
   1959–61.
Cleveland Pipers (ABL3 1961–62)
Folded, 1962.

CLEVELAND RAMS
See *ST. LOUIS RAMS*

CLEVELAND REBELS
Cleveland Rebels (BAA 1946–47)
Folded, 1947.

CLEVELAND RED SOX
Cleveland Red Sox (NNL2 1934)
Folded, 1934.

CLEVELAND ROCKERS
CLEVELAND ROCKERS (WNBA 1997–present)

CLEVELAND ROSENBLUMS
Cleveland Rosenblums (ABL1 1925–30)
Folded during season, 1930.

CLEVELAND SPIDERS
Cleveland Blues (2) (AA 1887–88)
Cleveland Spiders (NL 1889–99)
Absorbed by St. Louis Cardinals (B), 1900.

CLEVELAND STARS
See *GEORGIA GENERALS*

CLEVELAND STOKERS
*Stoke City (Stoke-on-Trent, Stafford, England), independ-
    ent, pre-1967.*
Cleveland Stokers (USA 1967; NASLo 1968)
Folded, 1968.

CLEVELAND TATE STARS
Cleveland Tate Stars (NNL1 1922)
Folded, 1922.

CLEVELAND THUNDERBOLTS
Columbus Thunderbolts (AFL 1991)
Cleveland Thunderbolts (AFL 1992–94)
Folded, 1994.

CLEVELAND TIGERS
See *CLEVELAND INDIANS (F1)*

CLEVELAND WHITE HORSES
See *DETROIT EAGLES*

COBALT
(Ontario, Canada)

COBALT SILVER KINGS
Cobalt Silver Kings (NHA 1909–11)
Folded, 1911.

COLE'S
(Robert J. Cole, Chicago, Illinois)

COLE'S AMERICAN GIANTS
See *CHICAGO AMERICAN GIANTS*

(COLOMBO)
(No location name: Staten Island, New York)

COLOMBO
Colombo (ASL2 1959–60)
Folded, 1960.

COLORADO

COLORADO AVALANCHE
San Francisco Sharks (WHA 1972 *did not play*)
Quebec Nordiques (WHA 1972–79; NHL 1979–95)
COLORADO AVALANCHE (NHL 1995–present)

COLORADO CARIBOUS
See *ATLANTA CHIEFS (S/IS)*

COLORADO FOXES
Colorado Foxes (APSL 1990–94)
*Continued when APSL became A-League, 1995–97. San
    Diego Flash, A-League, 1998–present.*

COLORADO INFERNO
Colorado Inferno (MLRH 1999 *did not play*)
Joined Major League Roller Hockey—AAA, 2000–present.

COLORADO RAPIDS
COLORADO RAPIDS (MLS 1996–present)

COLORADO ROCKIES (B)
COLORADO ROCKIES (B) (NL 1993–present)

COLORADO ROCKIES (H)
See *NEW JERSEY DEVILS*

COLORADO XPLOSION
Colorado Xplosion (ABLw 1996–98)
Folded during 1998–99 season, 1998.

COLUMBUS
(Ohio)

COLUMBUS ATHLETIC SUPPLY
Columbus Athletic Supply, Midwest Basketball Conference, 1936–37.
Columbus Athletic Supply (NBL 1937–38)
Folded, 1938.

COLUMBUS BLUE BIRDS
Columbus Blue Birds (NNL2 1933)
Folded during season, 1933.

COLUMBUS BLUE JACKETS
COLUMBUS BLUE JACKETS (NHL 2000–present)

COLUMBUS BUCKEYES (1)
Columbus Buckeyes (1) (AA 1883–84)
    a.k.a. Columbus Colts (1)
    a.k.a. Columbus Senators
Folded, 1884.

COLUMBUS BUCKEYES (2)
Columbus Buckeyes (2) (AA 1889–91)
    a.k.a. Columbus Colts (2)
    a.k.a. Columbus Solons
Folded, 1891.

COLUMBUS BUCKEYES (3)
Columbus Buckeyes (3) (NNL1 1921)
Folded, 1921.

COLUMBUS BULLIES
Columbus Bullies, minor league team, approximately 1939. Joined American Professional Football League, 1939.
Columbus Bullies (AFL3 1940–41)
Folded, 1941.

COLUMBUS CAPITALS
Columbus Capitals (AISA 1984–86)
Folded, 1986.

COLUMBUS COLTS (1)
See *COLUMBUS BUCKEYES (1)*

COLUMBUS COLTS (2)
See *COLUMBUS BUCKEYES (2)*

COLUMBUS CREW
COLUMBUS CREW (MLS 1996–present)

COLUMBUS ELITE GIANTS
See *BALTIMORE ELITE GIANTS*

COLUMBUS HAWKS
Columbus Hawks (MLRH 1998)
Folded, 1998.

COLUMBUS INVADERS
Canton Invaders (AISA 1984–90; NPSLi 1990–96)
Columbus Invaders (NPSLi 1996–97)
Absorbed by Montreal Impact, 1997.

COLUMBUS MAGIC
Columbus Magic (ASL2 1979–80)
Folded, 1980.

COLUMBUS PANHANDLES
See *COLUMBUS TIGERS*

COLUMBUS QUEST
Columbus Quest (ABLw 1996–98)
Folded during 1998–99 season, 1998.

COLUMBUS SENATORS
See *COLUMBUS BUCKEYES (1)*

COLUMBUS SOLONS
See *COLUMBUS BUCKEYES (2)*

COLUMBUS THUNDERBOLTS
See *CLEVELAND THUNDERBOLTS*

COLUMBUS TIGERS
Columbus Panhandles, independent, 1904–19.
Columbus Panhandles (APFA 1920–21; NFL 1922)
Columbus Tigers (NFL 1923–26)
Folded, 1926.

COLUMBUS TURFS
Columbus Turfs (NSL 1932)
Folded, 1932.

CONNECTICUT

CONNECTICUT BICENTENNIALS
See *EDMONTON DRILLERS (S/IS)*

CONNECTICUT COASTERS
See *SACRAMENTO RIVER RATS*

CONNECTICUT COYOTES
Connecticut Coyotes (AFL 1995–96)
Folded, 1996.

CONNECTICUT WILDCATS
See *CONNECTICUT YANKEES*

CONNECTICUT YANKEES
Northeast United (ASL2 1972)
Connecticut Wildcats (ASL2 1973–74)
Connecticut Yankees (ASL2 1975–78)
Folded, 1978.

CORPUS CHRISTI
(Texas)

CORPUS CHRISTI ADVANTAGE
Corpus Christi Advantage (TT 1986)
Folded, 1986.

(COSMOS)
(No location name: New York, New York)

COSMOS
See *NEW YORK COSMOS*

CUBAN
(Cuba in name only; actually played in USA)

CUBAN STARS
See *CUBAN STARS (WEST)*

CUBAN STARS (EAST)
*Cuban Stars (East), independent, 1916. Havana Stars,
    independent, 1917. Cuban Stars (East), independent,
    1918–22.*

Cuban Stars (East) (ECL 1923–28; ANL 1929)
Folded, 1929.

CUBAN STARS (WEST)
Cuban Stars, independent, 1907–19.
Cuban Stars (NNL1 1920)
Cincinnati Cubans (NNL1 1921)
Cuban Stars (NNL1 1922)
Cuban Stars (West) (NNL1 1923–30)
Folded, 1930.

D.C.
(District of Columbia)

D.C. UNITED
D.C. UNITED (MLS 1996–present)

DALLAS
(Texas)

DALLAS AMERICANS
Dallas Americans (ASL2 1983; USL 1984–85)
Folded, 1985.

DALLAS BURN
DALLAS BURN (MLS 1996–present)

DALLAS CHAPARRALS
See *SAN ANTONIO SPURS*

DALLAS COWBOYS
DALLAS COWBOYS (NFL 1960–present)

DALLAS EXPRESS
See *LOS ANGELES CLIPPERS*

DALLAS MAVERICKS (Bk)
DALLAS MAVERICKS (Bk) (NBA 1980–present)

DALLAS MAVERICKS (IS)
See *DALLAS SIDEKICKS*

DALLAS SIDEKICKS
New Jersey Rockets (MISL 1981–82)
Suspended operations, 1982–84.
Dallas Sidekicks (MISL 1984–89)
Dallas Mavericks (IS) (MISL 1989–90; MSL 1990–92)

DALLAS SIDEKICKS (CISL 1993–97; PSA 1998;
    WISL 1999–present)

DALLAS STALLIONS
Dallas Stallions (RHI 1999)
Folded, 1999.

DALLAS STARS (H)
Minnesota North Stars (NHL 1967–93)
(Absorbed Cleveland Barons, 1978.)
DALLAS STARS (H) (NHL 1993–present)

DALLAS STARS (T)
Dallas Stars (T) (TT 1982–83)
Folded, 1983.

DALLAS TEXANS (AF)
Dallas Texans (AF) (AFL 1990–95)
Folded, 1995.

DALLAS TEXANS (F1)
Boston Yanks (NFL 1944–48)
(Absorbed Brooklyn Tigers [2], 1945.)
New York Bulldogs (NFL 1949)
New York Yanks (NFL 1950–51)
Dallas Texans (F1) (NFL 1952)
Folded, 1952.

DALLAS TEXANS (F2)
See *KANSAS CITY CHIEFS*

DALLAS TORNADO
Dundee United (Angus, Scotland), independent, pre-1967.
Dallas Tornado (USA 1967; NASLo 1968–81) and
    (NASLi 1980–81)
Folded, 1981.

DARBY
(Pennsylvania)

DARBY DAISIES
    See *HILLDALE*

DAYTON
(Ohio)

DAYTON AEROS
See *HOUSTON AEROS*

DAYTON DYNAMO
See *CINCINNATI SILVERBACKS*

DAYTON MARCOS
Dayton Marcos, independent, 1919.
Dayton Marcos (NNL1 1920, 1926)
(Suspended operations, 1921. Independent, 1922–25.)
Folded during season, 1926.

DAYTON METROPOLITANS
*Dayton Metropolitans, a.k.a. Dayton Metros, Midwest
    Basketball Conference (charter member), 1935–37.*
Dayton Metropolitans (NBL 1937–38)
    a.k.a. Dayton Metros
Folded, 1938.

DAYTON METROS
See *DAYTON METROPOLITANS*

DAYTON RENS
*New York Renaissance Five, a.k.a. New York Rens, inde-
    pendent, pre-1949.*
Dayton Rens (NBL 1949)
Folded, 1949.

DAYTON TRIANGLES
See *BROOKLYN TIGERS (2)*

DECATUR
(Illinois)

DECATUR STALEYS
See *CHICAGO BEARS*

DELAWARE

DELAWARE SMASH
New Jersey Stars (TT 1987–91; WTT 1992–95)
DELAWARE SMASH (WTT 1996–present)

DELAWARE WINGS
Delaware Wings (ASL2 1972–74)
Folded, 1974.

DENVER
(Colorado)

DENVER AVALANCHE
See *TACOMA STARS (1)*

DENVER BRONCOS
DENVER BRONCOS (AFL4 1960–70; NFL 1970–present)

DENVER DAREDEVILS
Denver DareDevils (RHI 1996)
Folded, 1996.

DENVER DYNAMITE
See *FLORIDA BOBCATS*

DENVER DYNAMOS
See *MINNESOTA KICKS*

DENVER GOLD
Denver Gold (USFL 1983–85)
Folded, 1985.

DENVER LARKS
See *DENVER NUGGETS (2)*

DENVER NUGGETS (1)
Denver Safeway-Piggly Wigglys, Amateur Athletic Union, 1935. Denver Safeway Stores, AAU, 1936–38. Denver Nuggets, AAU, 1939–40. Denver American Legion, AAU, 1941–44. Denver Ambrose Jellymakers, AAU, 1945–46. Denver Nuggets, AAU, 1947–48.
Denver Nuggets (1) (NBL 1948–49; NBA 1949–50)
Denver Frontier Refiners, National Professional Basketball League, 1950. Evansville Agogans, NPBL, during season, 1950–51.
Folded, 1951.

DENVER NUGGETS (2)
Denver Larks (ABA 1967 *did not play*)
Denver Rockets (ABA 1967–74)
DENVER NUGGETS (2) (ABA 1974–76; NBA 1976–present)

DENVER RACQUETS
See *PHOENIX RACQUETS*

DENVER ROCKETS
See *DENVER NUGGETS (2)*

DENVER SPURS
See *OTTAWA CIVICS*

DENVER THUNDER
Illinois Thunder (NPSLi 1990–92)
Denver Thunder (NPSLi 1992–93)
Folded, 1993.

DETROIT
(Michigan)

DETROIT CARDINALS
Detroit Cardinals (ABL1 1927–28)
Folded during season, 1928.

DETROIT COUGARS (H)
See *DETROIT RED WINGS*

DETROIT COUGARS (S)
Glentoran Football Club (Belfast, Antrim, Northern Ireland), independent, pre-1967.
Detroit Cougars (S) (USA 1967; NASLo 1968)
Folded, 1968.

DETROIT DRIVE
See *GRAND RAPIDS RAMPAGE*

DETROIT EAGLES
Warren Penn Oilers, Midwest Basketball Conference, 1936–37.
Warren Penn Oilers (NBL 1937–38)
a.k.a. Warren Penns
Cleveland White Horses (NBL 1938–39)
Detroit Eagles (NBL 1939–41)
Folded, 1941.

DETROIT EXPRESS (S)
Detroit Express (S) (ASL2 1981–83)
Folded, 1983.

DETROIT EXPRESS (S/IS)
See *WASHINGTON DIPLOMATS (2)*

DETROIT FALCONS (Bk)
Detroit Falcons (Bk) (BAA 1946–47)
Folded, 1947.

DETROIT FALCONS (H)
See *DETROIT RED WINGS*

DETROIT FURY
DETROIT FURY (AFL 2001–present)

DETROIT GEMS
See *LOS ANGELES LAKERS*

DETROIT HERALDS
Detroit Heralds, independent, 1913–19.
Detroit Heralds (APFA 1920)
Folded, 1920.

DETROIT LIGHTNING
See *KANSAS CITY COMETS*

DETROIT LIONS
*Portsmouth Presidents, independent, 1926. Portsmouth
    Shoe-Steels, independent, 1927. Portsmouth Spartans,
    independent, 1928–29.*
Portsmouth Spartans (NFL 1930–33)
DETROIT LIONS (NFL 1934–present)

DETROIT LOVES
Detroit Loves (WTT 1974)
Folded, 1974.

DETROIT MOTOR CITY MUSTANGS
Detroit Motor City Mustangs (RHI 1995)
Folded, 1995.

DETROIT MUSTANGS
Detroit Soccer Club (ASL2 1972)
Detroit Mustangs (ASL2 1972–73)
Folded, 1973.

DETROIT NEON
See *DETROIT SAFARI*

DETROIT PANTHERS
See *DETROIT WOLVERINES (F)*

DETROIT PISTONS
Fort Wayne Zollner Pistons, independent, 1939–41.
Fort Wayne Zollner Pistons (NBL 1941–49)

Fort Wayne Pistons (NBA 1949–57)
DETROIT PISTONS (NBA 1957–present)

DETROIT PULASKI POST FIVE
Detroit Pulaski Post Five (ABL1 1925–26)
Folded during 1926–27 season, 1926.

DETROIT RACERS
Detroit Racers (RHI 1999 *did not play*)
Folded before season, 1999.

DETROIT RED WINGS
Detroit Cougars (H) (NHL 1926–29)
Detroit Falcons (H) (NHL 1929–32)
DETROIT RED WINGS (NHL 1932–present)

DETROIT ROCKERS
DETROIT ROCKERS (NPSLi 1990–present)

DETROIT SAFARI
Detroit Neon (CISL 1994–96)
Detroit Safari (CISL 1997)
Folded, 1997.

DETROIT SHOCK
DETROIT SHOCK (WNBA 1998–present)

DETROIT SOCCER CLUB
See *DETROIT MUSTANGS*

DETROIT STARS
Detroit Stars, independent, 1919.
Detroit Stars (NNL1 1920–31; NNL2 1933; NAL 1937)
(Independent, 1932. Suspended operations, 1934–36.)
*Continued as member of minor NAL, 1938–57. Detroit
    Clowns, minor NAL, 1958. Detroit Stars, minor NAL,
    1959. Detroit-New Orleans Stars, minor NAL, 1960–
    61.*
Folded, 1961.

DETROIT TIGERS (B)
*Detroit Wolverines, minor American League (charter
    member), 1900.*
DETROIT TIGERS (B) (AL 1901–present)

DETROIT TIGERS (F)
Detroit Tigers (F) (APFA 1921)
Folded, 1921.

DETROIT TURBOS
Detroit Turbos (MILL 1989–94)
Folded, 1994.

DETROIT VAGABOND KINGS
Detroit Vagabond Kings (NBL 1948–49)
Folded, 1949.

DETROIT WHEELS
Detroit Wheels (WFL 1974)
Folded during season, 1974.

DETROIT WOLVERINES (B)
Detroit Wolverines (B) (NL 1881–88)
Folded, 1888.

DETROIT WOLVERINES (F)
Detroit Panthers (NFL 1925–26)
Suspended operations, 1927.
Detroit Wolverines (F) (NFL 1928)
Absorbed by New York Giants (F2), 1929.

DULUTH
(Minnesota)

DULUTH ESKIMOS
Duluth Kelleys, independent, 1920–22.
Duluth Kelleys (NFL 1923–25)
Duluth Eskimos (NFL 1926–27)
Folded, 1927.

DULUTH KELLEYS
See *DULUTH ESKIMOS*

EAST LIVERPOOL
(Ohio)

EAST LIVERPOOL PANTHERS
East Liverpool Panthers (ABL1 1925 *did not play*)
Folded before season, 1925.

EDMONTON
(Alberta, Canada)

EDMONTON BRICKMEN
Edmonton Brickmen, minor league team, pre-1985.

Edmonton Brickmen (WSL 1986)
*Joined Canadian Soccer League (charter member), 1987–
90.*
Folded, 1990.

EDMONTON DRILLERS (IS)
Chicago Power (AISA 1988–90; NPSLi 1990–96)
EDMONTON DRILLERS (IS) (NPSLi 1996–present)

EDMONTON DRILLERS (S/IS)
Hartford Bicentennials (NASLo 1975–76)
Connecticut Bicentennials (NASLo 1977)
Oakland Stompers (NASLo 1978)
Edmonton Drillers (S/IS) (NASLo 1979–82) and (NASLi
1980–82)
Folded, 1982.

EDMONTON ESKIMOS (F)
*Edmonton Rugby Foot-ball Club, independent rugby team,
1907. Edmonton Eskimaux, independent, 1908–10.
Edmonton Eskimos, independent, 1910. Joined Western Canada Rugby Football Union, 1911–35. Continued when WCRFU became Western Interprovincial
Football Union, 1936–40. Independent, 1941–48. Rejoined WIFU, 1949–55.*
EDMONTON ESKIMOS (F) (CFC 1956–57; CFL 1958–
present)

EDMONTON ESKIMOS (H)
Edmonton Eskimos (H) (WCHL 1921–25; WHL 1925–
26)
Folded, 1926.

EDMONTON OIL KINGS
See *EDMONTON OILERS*

EDMONTON OILERS
Edmonton Oil Kings (WHA 1972 *did not play*)
Alberta Oilers (WHA 1972–73)
EDMONTON OILERS (WHA 1973–79; NHL 1979–pre-
sent)

EDMONTON SLED DOGS
See *TORONTO WAVE*

EL PASO-JUAREZ
**(El Paso, Texas, and Ciudad Juarez,
Chihuahua, Mexico)**

EL PASO-JUAREZ GAMECOCKS
El Paso-Juarez Gamecocks (USL 1985)
Folded, 1985.

ELIZABETH
(New Jersey)

ELIZABETH BRAVES
See *HARTFORD HURRICANES*

ELIZABETH FALCONS
See *FALCONS-WARSAW*

ELIZABETH POLISH FALCONS
See *FALCONS-WARSAW*

ELIZABETH RESOLUTES
Elizabeth Resolutes (NA 1873)
Folded, 1873.

ELMIRA
(New York)

ELMIRA COLONELS
Elmira Colonels (ABL2 1951–53)
Folded, 1953.

EMPIRE STATE
(New York)

EMPIRE STATE COBRAS
See *BUFFALO WINGS (1)*

ENGLISH
(England)

ENGLISH LIONS
English Lions (MLRH 1997)
Folded, 1997.

EVANSVILLE
(Indiana)

EVANSVILLE CRIMSON GIANTS
Evansville Crimson Giants (APFA 1921; NFL 1922)
*(Independent during season, 1921; APFA record erased
    from final standings.)*
Folded, 1922.

(EXPRESS)
(No location name: Orlando, Florida)

EXPRESS
Express (WRHL 1993)
Folded, 1993.

(FALCONS SOCCER CLUB)
(No location name: Elizabeth, New Jersey)

FALCONS SOCCER CLUB
See *FALCONS-WARSAW*

(FALCONS-WARSAW)
(No location name: Elizabeth, New Jersey)

FALCONS-WARSAW
Elizabeth Falcons (ASL2 1954–56)
Elizabeth Polish Falcons (ASL2 1956–58)
Elizabeth Falcons (ASL2 1958–59)
Falcons Soccer Club (ASL2 1959–62)
Falcons-Warsaw (ASL2 1962–64)
Folded, 1964.

FALL RIVER
(Massachusetts)

FALL RIVER ASTROS
See *WORCESTER ASTROS*

FALL RIVER FOOTBALL CLUB (1)
See *NEW BEDFORD WHALERS (2)*

FALL RIVER FOOTBALL CLUB (2)
Fall River Football Club (2) (ASL1 1932–33)
Folded, 1933.

FALL RIVER MARKSMEN
See *NEW YORK YANKEES (S)*

FALL RIVER SOCCER CLUB
Fall River Soccer Club (ASL2 1957–63)
Folded, 1963.

FALL RIVER UNITED
See *NEW YORK YANKEES (S)*

FLEISHER
(Fleisher Yarn Company, Philadelphia, Pennsylvania)

FLEISHER YARN
Fleisher Yarn, independent, pre-1923.
Fleisher Yarn (ASL1 1924–25)
Folded, 1925.

FLINT
(Michigan)

FLINT CHEMICALS
See *FLINT DOW A.C.'S*

FLINT DOW A.C.'S
Pittsburgh Raiders (NBL 1944–45)
Youngstown Bears (NBL 1945–47)
Midland Dow A.C.'s (NBL 1947)
    a.k.a. Midland Chemicals
Flint Dow A.C.'s (NBL 1947–48)

a.k.a. Flint Chemicals
Folded, 1948.

FLORIDA

FLORIDA BLAZERS
See *SAN ANTONIO WINGS*

FLORIDA BOBCATS
Denver Dynamite (AFL 1987, 1989–91)
(Suspended operations, 1988.)
Sacramento Attack (AFL 1992)
Miami Hooters (AFL 1993–95)
FLORIDA BOBCATS (AFL 1996–present)

FLORIDA BREAKERS
See *MINNESOTA FIGHTING SAINTS (2)*

FLORIDA FLAMINGOS
Florida Flamingos (WTT 1974)
Folded, 1974.

FLORIDA HAMMERHEADS
Florida Hammerheads (RHI 1993–94)
Folded, 1994.

FLORIDA JACKALS
Orlando Jackals (RHI 1996–97)
Suspended operations, 1998.
Miami Jackals (RHI 1999 *did not play*)
Florida Jackals (RHI 1999 *did not play*)
Folded before season, 1999.

FLORIDA MARLINS
FLORIDA MARLINS (NL 1993–present)

FLORIDA PANTHERS
FLORIDA PANTHERS (NHL 1993–present)

FLORIDA SUNS
See *SAN ANTONIO WINGS*

FLORIDA THUNDERCATS (IS)
Florida ThunderCats (IS) (NPSLi 1998–99)
Folded, 1999.

FLORIDA THUNDERCATS (RH)
See *PHILADELPHIA THUNDERCATS*

FLORIDA TWIST
Florida Twist (WTT 1993–95)
Folded, 1995.

(FLORIDIANS)
(No location name: Florida)

FLORIDIANS
Minnesota Muskies (ABA 1967–68)
Miami Floridians (ABA 1968–70)
Floridians (ABA 1970–72)
Folded, 1972.

FORT LAUDERDALE
(Florida)

FORT LAUDERDALE STRIKERS (S)
Fort Lauderdale Strikers (S) (ASL3 1988–89; APSL
  1990–94)
(Absorbed Orlando Lions, 1991.)
Folded, 1994.

FORT LAUDERDALE STRIKERS (S/IS)
See *MINNESOTA STRIKERS*

FORT LAUDERDALE SUN
See *SOUTH FLORIDA SUN*

FORT WAYNE
(Indiana)

FORT WAYNE CASEYS
See *FORT WAYNE HOOSIERS*

FORT WAYNE DAISIES
Minneapolis Millerettes (AAGPBL 1944)
Fort Wayne Daisies (AAGPBL 1945–54)
Folded, 1954.

FORT WAYNE FLAMES
See *INDIANA KICK*

FORT WAYNE GENERAL ELECTRICS
Fort Wayne General Electrics, Midwest Basketball Con-
  ference, 1936–37.

Fort Wayne General Electrics (NBL 1937–38)
Folded, 1938.

FORT WAYNE GUARDS
See *FORT WAYNE HOOSIERS*

FORT WAYNE HOOSIERS
Fort Wayne Caseys (ABL1 1925–26)
Fort Wayne Hoosiers (ABL1 1926–31)
  a.k.a. Fort Wayne Guards
Folded, 1931.

FORT WAYNE KEKIONGAS
Fort Wayne Kekiongas (NA 1871)
Folded during season, 1871.

FORT WAYNE PISTONS
See *DETROIT PISTONS*

FORT WAYNE ZOLLNER PISTONS
See *DETROIT PISTONS*

FORT WORTH
(Texas)

FORT WORTH CAVALRY
Fort Worth Cavalry (AFL 1994)
Folded, 1994.

FRANKFORD
(Pennsylvania)

FRANKFORD YELLOW JACKETS
See *PHILADELPHIA EAGLES*

FRESNO
(California)

FRESNO SUN-NETS
Fresno Sun-Nets (TT 1988–89)
Folded, 1989.

(FURY)
(No location name: Orlando, Florida)

FURY
Fury (WRHL 1993)
Folded, 1993.

GALICIA
(Spain in name only; actually played in Brooklyn and Manhattan, New York)

GALICIA
See *GALICIA-HONDURAS*

GALICIA-HONDURAS
(Spain and Honduras in name only; actually played in Brooklyn and Manhattan, New York)

GALICIA-HONDURAS
New York Brookhattan (ASL1 1933)
Brookhattan (ASL2 1933–56)
Brookhattan-Galicia (ASL2 1956–58)
Galicia (ASL2 1958–61)
Merged with independent Honduras, 1961.
Galicia-Honduras (ASL2 1961–62)
Folded, 1962.

GARY
(Indiana)

GARY TIGERS
See *INDIANA TIGERS*

GEORGIA

GEORGIA GENERALS
Cleveland Stars (ASL2 1972–73)
Cleveland Cobras (ASL2 1974–81)
Georgia Generals (ASL2 1982)
Folded, 1982.

GLENS FALLS-SARATOGA
(Glens Falls and Saratoga Springs, New York)

GLENS FALLS-SARATOGA
New York Harlem Yankees (ABL2 1949–50)
Saratoga Harlem Yankees (ABL2 1950–52)
Glens Falls-Saratoga (ABL2 1952–53)
Folded during season, 1953.

GOLDEN BAY
(San Francisco Bay, California)

GOLDEN BAY EARTHQUAKES
See *SAN FRANCISCO BAY BLACKHAWKS*

GOLDEN GATE
(San Francisco Bay, California)

GOLDEN GATE GALES
Golden Gate Gales (ASL2 1980)
Folded, 1980.

(GOLDEN GATERS)
(No location name: San Francisco Bay, California)

GOLDEN GATERS
See *OAKLAND BREAKERS*

GOLDEN STATE
(California)

GOLDEN STATE WARRIORS
Philadelphia Warriors (2) (BAA 1946–49; NBA 1949–62)
San Francisco Warriors (NBA 1962–71)
GOLDEN STATE WARRIORS (NBA 1971–present)

GRAND RAPIDS
(Michigan)

GRAND RAPIDS CHICKS
Milwaukee Chicks (AAGPBL 1944)

Grand Rapids Chicks (AAGPBL 1945–54)
Folded, 1954.

GRAND RAPIDS RAMPAGE
Detroit Drive (AFL 1988–93)
Massachusetts Marauders (AFL 1994)
Suspended operations, 1995–97.
GRAND RAPIDS RAMPAGE (AFL 1998–present)

GREEN BAY
(Wisconsin)

GREEN BAY BLUES
See *GREEN BAY PACKERS*

GREEN BAY PACKERS
Acme Packers (Green Bay), independent, 1919–20.
Green Bay Packers (APFA 1921)
Green Bay Blues (NFL 1922)
GREEN BAY PACKERS (NFL 1922–present)

GUILDFORD
(Surrey, England)

BEAST OF GUILDFORD
Beast of Guildford (MLRH 1998)
Folded, 1998.

HAILEYBURY
(Ontario, Canada)

HAILEYBURY COMETS
Haileybury Comets (NHA 1909–11)
Folded, 1911.

(HAKOAH ALL-STARS)
(No location name: New York, New York)

HAKOAH ALL-STARS
See *NEW YORK HAKOAH (1)*

HAMILTON
(Ontario, Canada)

HAMILTON HAMMERS
See *TORONTO WAVE*

HAMILTON TIGER-CATS
Hamilton Tigers, independent rugby team, 1869–83.
Joined Ontario Rugby Football Union, 1883–1907.
Joined Interprovincial Rugby Football Union, 1907–
14. Merged with Hamilton Alerts, remaining Hamilton
Tigers, 1914. Continued in IRFU, 1914–42. Suspended
operations, 1942–45. Revived in IRFU, 1946–49.
Merged with Hamilton Wildcats (formerly Hamilton
Flying Wildcats of Royal Canadian Air Force), 1950,
and changed name to Hamilton Tiger-Cats. Continued
in IRFU, 1950–55.
HAMILTON TIGER-CATS (CFC 1956–57; CFL 1958–
present)

HAMILTON TIGERS
See *BROOKLYN AMERICANS*

HAMMOND
(Indiana)

HAMMOND CALUMET BUCCANEERS
Hammond Calumet Buccaneers (NBL 1948–49)
Folded, 1949.

HAMMOND CIESAR ALL-AMERICANS
Whiting Ciesar All-Americans, Midwest Basketball Con-
ference, 1936–37.
Whiting Ciesar All-Americans (NBL 1937–38)
Hammond Ciesar All-Americans (NBL 1938–41)
Folded, 1941.

HAMMOND HOOSIERS
See *HAMMOND PROS*

HAMMOND INDIANS
See *HAMMOND PROS*

HAMMOND PROS
Hammond Pros, a.k.a. Hammond Bobcats, independent,
1919.
Hammond Pros (APFA 1920–21; NFL 1922–26)
    a.k.a. Hammond Hoosiers
    a.k.a. Hammond Indians

a.k.a. Hammond Tigers
Folded during season, 1926.

HAMMOND TIGERS
See *HAMMOND PROS*

HARRISBURG
(Pennsylvania)

HARRISBURG GIANTS
Harrisburg Giants, independent, 1922–23.
Harrisburg Giants (ECL 1924–27)
Folded, 1927.

HARRISBURG HEAT
HARRISBURG HEAT (NPSLi 1991--present)

HARRISBURG SENATORS
Harrisburg Senators (ABL2 1942–43)
Folded, 1943.

HARRISBURG-ST. LOUIS
(Pennsylvania and Missouri)

HARRISBURG-ST. LOUIS STARS
St. Louis Stars (B2) (NAL 1937, 1939)
(Suspended operations, 1938.)
Independent, 1940.
New Orleans-St. Louis Stars (NAL 1941)
Suspended operations, 1942.
Harrisburg-St. Louis Stars (NNL2 1943)
Folded during season, 1943.

HARRISON
(New Jersey)

HARRISON SOCCER CLUB
Kearny Erie AA, North American Foot Ball League, pre-1921.
Harrison Soccer Club (ASL1 1921–23)
Folded, 1923.

HARTFORD
(Connecticut)

HARTFORD AMERICANS
Hartford Americans (ASL1 1927)
Folded during season, 1927.

HARTFORD BICENTENNIALS
See *EDMONTON DRILLERS (S/IS)*

HARTFORD BLUES
Waterbury Blues (Connecticut), independent, by at least 1924–25. Hartford Blues, independent, during season, 1925.
Hartford Blues (NFL 1926)
Folded, 1926.

HARTFORD DARK BLUES
See *BROOKLYN HARTFORDS*

HARTFORD FOXFORCE
HARTFORD FOXFORCE (WTT 2000–present)

HARTFORD HARTFORDS
See *BROOKLYN HARTFORDS*

HARTFORD HELLIONS
See *LAS VEGAS AMERICANS*

HARTFORD HURRICANES
Elizabeth Braves (ABL2 1946–47)
Hartford Hurricanes (ABL2 1947–50)
Folded, 1950.

HARTFORD KINGS
Hartford Soccer Club (ASL2 1964–66)
Hartford Kings (ASL2 1966–67)
Hartford Soccer Club (ASL2 1967–68)
Hartford Kings (ASL2 1968)
Folded, 1968.

HARTFORD SOCCER CLUB
See *HARTFORD KINGS*

HARTFORD WHALERS
See *CAROLINA HURRICANES*

HAWAII

HAWAII CHIEFS
See *LONG BEACH CHIEFS*

HAWAII LEIS
Hawaii Leis (WTT 1974–76)
Folded, 1976.

TEAM HAWAII
See *TULSA ROUGHNECKS*

(HAWAIIANS)
(No location name: Hawaii)

HAWAIIANS
Honolulu Hawaiians (WFL 1974)
Hawaiians (WFL 1975)
Folded during season, 1975.

HERNE BAY
(Kent, England)

HERNE BAY GULLS
Herne Bay Gulls (MLRH 1998)
Folded, 1998.

HERSHEY
(Pennsylvania)

HERSHEY IMPACT
Hershey Impact (AISA 1988–90; NPSLi 1990–91)
Folded, 1991.

HILLDALE
(Darby, Pennsylvania)

HILLDALE
Hilldale, independent, 1910–22.
Hilldale (ECL 1923–27; ANL 1929)
   a.k.a. Hilldale Giants
   a.k.a. Hilldale Daisies
   a.k.a. Darby Daisies
(Suspended operations, 1928.)

Independent, 1930–31. Joined East-West League, 1932.
Folded, 1932.

HILLDALE DAISIES
See *HILLDALE*

HILLDALE GIANTS
See *HILLDALE*

HOLLYWOOD
(California)

HOLLYWOOD KICKERS
See *CALIFORNIA EMPERORS*

HOLYOKE
(Massachusetts)

HOLYOKE FALCOS
Holyoke Falcos (ASL1 1921–22)
Folded, 1922.

HOMESTEAD
(Pennsylvania)

HOMESTEAD GRAYS
See *WASHINGTON HOMESTEAD GRAYS*

HONOLULU
(Hawaii)

HONOLULU HAWAIIANS
See *HAWAIIANS*

HOUSTON
(Texas)

HOUSTON AEROS
Dayton Aeros (WHA 1972 *did not play*)
Houston Aeros (WHA 1972–78)
Folded, 1978.

HOUSTON ASTRO-KNOTS
Houston Astro-Knots (TT 1982–83)
Folded, 1983.

HOUSTON ASTROS
Houston Colt .45s (NL 1962–64)
HOUSTON ASTROS (NL 1965–present)

HOUSTON COLT .45S
See *HOUSTON ASTROS*

HOUSTON COMETS
HOUSTON COMETS (WNBA 1997–present)

HOUSTON DYNAMOS
Houston Dynamos (USL 1984)
Folded, 1984.

HOUSTON E-Z RIDERS
Houston E-Z Riders (WTT 1974)
Folded, 1974.

HOUSTON EAGLES *(**MERGED TEAM**)*
Newark Dodgers, independent, 1933.
Newark Dodgers (NNL2 1934–35)
Merged with Brooklyn Eagles, 1936.
Newark Eagles (NNL2 1936–48)
Houston Eagles (NAL 1949–50)
Folded, 1950.

*****

Brooklyn Eagles (NNL2 1935)
Merged with Newark Dodgers, 1936.
Newark Eagles (NNL2 1936–48)
Houston Eagles (NAL 1949–50)
Folded, 1950.

HOUSTON GAMBLERS
Houston Gamblers (USFL 1984–85)
Folded, 1985.

HOUSTON HOTSHOTS
HOUSTON HOTSHOTS (CISL 1994–97; WISL 1999–
    present)
(Suspended operations, 1998.)

HOUSTON HURRICANE
Houston Hurricane (NASLo 1978–80)
Folded, 1980.

HOUSTON MAVERICKS
See *UTAH ROCKIES*

HOUSTON OILERS
See *TENNESSEE TITANS*

HOUSTON ROCKETS
San Diego Rockets (NBA 1967–71)
HOUSTON ROCKETS (NBA 1971–present)

HOUSTON STARS
*Bangu AC (Rio de Janeiro, Brazil), independent, pre-
    1967.*
Houston Stars (USA 1967; NASLo 1968)
Folded, 1968.

HOUSTON SUMMIT SOCCER
See *BALTIMORE BLAST*

HOUSTON TEXANS (1)
See *SHREVEPORT STEAMER*

HOUSTON TEXANS (2)
HOUSTON TEXANS (2) (NFL 2002–present)

HOUSTON THUNDERBEARS
Texas Terror (AFL 1996–97)
HOUSTON THUNDERBEARS (AFL 1998–present)

(HUNGARIAN AMERICANS)
(No location name: New Brunswick, New Jersey)

HUNGARIAN AMERICANS
Hungarian Americans (ASL2 1963–68)
Folded, 1968.

IDAHO

IDAHO SNEAKERS
IDAHO SNEAKERS (WTT 1994–present)

ILLINOIS

ILLINOIS THUNDER
See *DENVER THUNDER*

INDIANA

INDIANA FEVER
INDIANA FEVER (WNBA 2000–present)

INDIANA KICK
Fort Wayne Flames (AISA 1986–89)
Indiana Kick (AISA 1989–90)
Folded, 1990.

INDIANA LOVES (1)
Indiana Loves (1) (WTT 1975–78)
Folded, 1978.

INDIANA LOVES (2)
Indiana Loves (2) (TT 1983)
Folded, 1983.

INDIANA PACERS
INDIANA PACERS (ABA 1967–76; NBA 1976–present)

INDIANA TIGERS
Gary Tigers (ASL2 1973)
Indiana Tigers (ASL2 1974)
Folded, 1974.

INDIANA TWISTERS
Indianapolis Twisters (CISL 1996)
Indiana Twisters (CISL 1997)
Folded, 1997.

INDIANA
(Indiana Flooring Company, New York, New York)

INDIANA FLOORING
See *NEW YORK GIANTS (S2)*

INDIANAPOLIS
(Indiana)

INDIANAPOLIS ABC'S
Birmingham Giants, independent, 1904–13. West Baden Sprudels (Indiana), independent, 1914. Indianapolis ABC's, independent, 1915–19.
Indianapolis ABC's (NNL1 1920–24, 1925–26, 1931; NSL 1932; NAL 1938–39)

(Suspended operations during season, 1924, and 1927–30, 1933–37.)
Folded during season, 1939.

INDIANAPOLIS ALL-AMERICANS
See *INDIANAPOLIS JETS*

INDIANAPOLIS ATHLETICS
Indianapolis Athletics (NAL 1937)
Folded, 1937.

INDIANAPOLIS BLUES
See *INDIANAPOLIS HOOSIERS (2)*

INDIANAPOLIS BROWNS
See *INDIANAPOLIS HOOSIERS (1)*

INDIANAPOLIS CLOWNS
Miami Clowns, independent, pre-1943. Ethiopian Clowns, independent, pre-1943.
Cincinnati Clowns (NAL 1943)
Indianapolis-Cincinnati Clowns (NAL 1944)
Cincinnati Clowns (NAL 1945)
Indianapolis Clowns (NAL 1946–50)
Independent, 1951–75.
Folded, 1975.

INDIANAPOLIS COLTS
Baltimore Colts (2) (NFL 1953–84)
INDIANAPOLIS COLTS (NFL 1984–present)

INDIANAPOLIS CRAWFORDS
Crawford Colored Giants (Pittsburgh), independent, 1931–32.
Pittsburgh Crawfords (NNL2 1933–38)
Suspended operations, 1939.
Toledo Crawfords (NAL 1939)
Indianapolis Crawfords (NAL 1940)
Folded, 1940.

INDIANAPOLIS DAREDEVILS
Rhode Island Oceaneers (ASL2 1974–76)
New England Oceaneers (ASL2 1977)
Indianapolis Daredevils (ASL2 1978–79)
Folded, 1979.

INDIANAPOLIS FEDERALS
See *NEWARK PEPPERS*

INDIANAPOLIS HOOFEDS
See *NEWARK PEPPERS*

INDIANAPOLIS HOOSIERFEDS
See *NEWARK PEPPERS*

INDIANAPOLIS HOOSIERS (1)
Indianapolis Hoosiers (1) (NL 1878)
  a.k.a. Indianapolis Browns
Folded, 1878.

INDIANAPOLIS HOOSIERS (2)
Indianapolis Hoosiers (2) (AA 1884)
  a.k.a. Indianapolis Blues
Folded, 1884.

INDIANAPOLIS HOOSIERS (3)
St. Louis Maroons (2) (UA 1884; NL 1885–86)
Indianapolis Hoosiers (3) (NL 1887–89)
Folded, 1889.

INDIANAPOLIS HOOSIERS (4)
See *NEWARK PEPPERS*

INDIANAPOLIS JETS
Indianapolis Kautsky ACs, independent, 1931–32. Indian-
  apolis Kautskys, National Professional Basketball
  League (charter member), 1932–33. Independent,
  1933–35. Midwest Basketball Conference (charter
  member), 1935–37.
Indianapolis Kautskys (NBL 1937–38, 1939–40, 1941–
  42, 1945–46, 1947–48)
  a.k.a. Indianapolis All-Americans
(Suspended operations, 1938–39, 1942–45, 1946–47. In-
  dependent, 1940–41.)
Indianapolis Jets (BAA 1948–49)
Folded, 1949.

INDIANAPOLIS KAUTSKYS
See *INDIANAPOLIS JETS*

INDIANAPOLIS OLYMPIANS
Indianapolis Olympians (NBA 1949–53)
Folded, 1953.

INDIANAPOLIS RACERS
Indianapolis Racers (WHA 1974–78)
Folded during season, 1978.

INDIANAPOLIS TWISTERS
See *INDIANA TWISTERS*

INDIANAPOLIS-CINCINNATI
(Indiana and Ohio)

INDIANAPOLIS-CINCINNATI CLOWNS
See *INDIANAPOLIS CLOWNS*

INTER
(International; played in New York, New York)

INTER SOCCER CLUB (1)
See *BOCA JUNIORS*

INTER SOCCER CLUB (2)
See *NEW YORK INTER*

INTER-BROOKLYN
(International-Brooklyn; played in New York)

INTER-BROOKLYN ITALIANS
See *BOCA JUNIORS*

IOWA

IOWA BARNSTORMERS
IOWA BARNSTORMERS (AFL 1995–present)

(IRISH-AMERICANS)
(No location name: Kearny, New Jersey)

IRISH-AMERICANS
Irish-Americans (ASL2 1949–51)
  a.k.a. Kearny Celtic
Folded, 1951.

J & P
(J & P Coats Manufacturing Company, Pawtucket, Rhode Island)

J & P COATS
See *PAWTUCKET RANGERS*

JACKSONVILLE
(Florida)

JACKSONVILLE BULLS
Jacksonville Bulls (USFL 1984–85)
Folded, 1985.

JACKSONVILLE EXPRESS
Jacksonville Express (WFL 1975)
Folded during season, 1975.

JACKSONVILLE GENERALS
Jacksonville Generals (AISA 1988)
Folded, 1988.

JACKSONVILLE JAGUARS
JACKSONVILLE JAGUARS (NFL 1995–present)

JACKSONVILLE RED CAPS
Jacksonville Red Caps (NAL 1938)
Suspended operations during season, 1938.
Cleveland Bears (NAL 1939–40)
Jacksonville Red Caps (NAL 1941–42)
Folded during season, 1942.

JACKSONVILLE SHARKS
Jacksonville Sharks (WFL 1974)
Folded during season, 1974.

JACKSONVILLE TEA MEN
New England Tea Men (NASLo 1978–80) and (NASLi 1979–80)
Jacksonville Tea Men (NASLo 1981–82; ASL2 1983; USL 1984) and (NASLi 1980–82)
Folded, 1984.

JERSEY
(New Jersey)

JERSEY KNIGHTS
See *SAN DIEGO MARINERS*

JERSEY REDS
Union City Redlegs, independent, 1925–31. Union City Reds, second Metropolitan League, 1931–33.
Union City Reds (ABL2 1933–34)
Jersey Reds (ABL2 1934–40)
Absorbed by New York Jewels during season, 1940.

JERSEY CITY
(New Jersey)

JERSEY CITY
Jersey City (ASL1 1929)
Folded, 1929.

JERSEY CITY ATOMS
See *LANCASTER ROSES*

JERSEY CITY CELTICS
Jersey City Celtics (ASL1 1921)
Folded during season, 1921.

KALAMAZOO
(Michigan)

KALAMAZOO KANGAROOS
Kalamazoo Kangaroos (AISA 1984–86)
Folded, 1986.

KALAMAZOO LASSIES
Muskegon Lassies (AAGPBL 1946–49)
Kalamazoo Lassies (AAGPBL 1950–54)
Folded, 1954.

KANKAKEE
(Illinois)

KANKAKEE GALLAGHER TROJANS
Kankakee Gallagher Trojans, independent, pre-1937.
Kankakee Gallagher Trojans (NBL 1937–38)
Folded, 1938.

KANSAS CITY
(Missouri)

KANSAS CITY ATHLETICS
See *OAKLAND ATHLETICS*

KANSAS CITY ATTACK
Atlanta Attack (AISA 1989–90; NPSLi 1990–91)
KANSAS CITY ATTACK (NPSLi 1991–present)

KANSAS CITY BLUES (B)
See *KANSAS CITY COWBOYS (B3)*

KANSAS CITY BLUES (F)
See *KANSAS CITY COWBOYS (F)*

KANSAS CITY CHIEFS
Dallas Texans (F2) (AFL4 1960–62)
KANSAS CITY CHIEFS (AFL4 1963–70; NFL 1970–present)

KANSAS CITY COMETS
Detroit Lightning (MISL 1979–80)
San Francisco Fog (MISL 1980–81)
Kansas City Comets (MISL 1981–90; MSL 1990–91)
Folded, 1991.

KANSAS CITY COWBOYS (B1)
See *KANSAS CITY UNIONS*

KANSAS CITY COWBOYS (B2)
Kansas City Cowboys (B2) (NL 1886)
Folded, 1886.

KANSAS CITY COWBOYS (B3)
Kansas City Cowboys (B3) (AA 1888–89)
   a.k.a. Kansas City Blues (B)
Folded, 1889.

KANSAS CITY COWBOYS (F)
Kansas City Blues (F) (NFL 1923–24)

Kansas City Cowboys (F) (NFL 1925–26)
Folded, 1926.

KANSAS CITY EXPLORERS
KANSAS CITY EXPLORERS (WTT 1993–present)

KANSAS CITY KINGS
See *SACRAMENTO KINGS*

KANSAS CITY MONARCHS
Kansas City Monarchs (NNL1 1920–27, 1929–30; NAL 1937–50)
(Suspended operations, 1928, 1931–37.)
Continued as member of minor NAL, 1951–61.
Folded, 1961.

KANSAS CITY PACKERS
Kansas City Packers (FL 1914–15)
Folded, 1915.

KANSAS CITY ROYALS
KANSAS CITY ROYALS (AL 1969–present)

KANSAS CITY SCOUTS
See *NEW JERSEY DEVILS*

KANSAS CITY SPURS
Chicago Spurs (NPSLo 1967)
Kansas City Spurs (NASLo 1968–70)
Folded, 1970.

KANSAS CITY STEERS
Kansas City Steers (ABL3 1961–62)
Folded during 1962–63 season, 1962.

KANSAS CITY UNIONS
Kansas City Unions (UA 1884)
   a.k.a. Kansas City Cowboys (B1)
Folded, 1884.

KANSAS CITY WIZ
See *KANSAS CITY WIZARDS*

KANSAS CITY WIZARDS
Kansas City Wiz (MLS 1996)
KANSAS CITY WIZARDS (MLS 1997–present)

KANSAS CITY-OMAHA
(Missouri and Nebraska)

KANSAS CITY-OMAHA KINGS
See *SACRAMENTO KINGS*

KEARNY
(New Jersey)

KEARNY AMERICANS
Kearny Americans (ASL2 1944–46, 1947–49)
(Suspended operations, 1946–47.)
Folded, 1949.

KEARNY CELTIC
See *IRISH-AMERICANS*

KEARNY CELTICS
Kearny Irish-Americans (ASL2 1933–38)
Newark Irish (ASL2 1938–41, 1941–42)
(Suspended operations, 1941.)
Newark Celtics (ASL2 1942–43)
Kearny Celtics (ASL2 1943–49)
Folded, 1949.

KEARNY IRISH-AMERICANS
See *KEARNY CELTICS*

KEARNY SCOTS
See *SCOTS-AMERICANS*

KENOSHA
(Wisconsin)

KENOSHA COMETS
Kenosha Comets (AAGPBL 1943–51)
Folded, 1951.

KENOSHA MAROONS
Toledo Maroons (NFL 1922–23)
Kenosha Maroons (NFL 1924)
Folded, 1924.

KENTUCKY

KENTUCKY COLONELS
Kentucky Colonels (ABA 1967–76)
Folded, 1976.

KEOKUK
(Iowa)

KEOKUK WESTERNS
Keokuk Westerns (NA 1875)
Folded during season, 1875.

KINGSTON
(New York)

KINGSTON COLONIALS
Kingston Colonials (ABL2 1935–39)
Absorbed by Troy Celtics (1) during season, 1939.

LANCASTER
(Pennsylvania)

LANCASTER ROSES
Jersey City Atoms (ABL2 1946–48)
Lancaster Roses (ABL2 1948)
Folded, 1948.

LAS VEGAS
(Nevada)

LAS VEGAS AMERICANS
Hartford Hellions (MISL 1979–81)
Memphis Americans (MISL 1981–84)
Las Vegas Americans (MISL 1984–85)
Folded, 1985.

LAS VEGAS COYOTES
Las Vegas Coyotes (RHI 1999)
Folded, 1999.

LAS VEGAS DUSTDEVILS
Las Vegas DustDevils (CISL 1994–95)
Folded, 1995.

LAS VEGAS FLASH
See *UTAH SUN DOGS*

LAS VEGAS POSSE
Las Vegas Posse (CFL 1994)
Folded, 1994.

LAS VEGAS QUICKSILVERS
See *SAN DIEGO SOCKERS*

LAS VEGAS SEAGULLS
Las Vegas Seagulls (ASL2 1979)
Folded, 1979.

LAS VEGAS STING
See *ANAHEIM PIRANHAS*

LONDON
(England)

LONDON LASERS
London Lasers (MLRH 1997)
Folded, 1997.

LONDON LIONS
London Lions (MLRH 1998)
Folded, 1998.

LONDON UNITED
London United (WISL 1999 *did not play*)
*Withdrew with England's Professional Indoor Football
    League before season, 1999. Folded with PIFL before
    season, 1999.*

LONG BEACH
(California)

LONG BEACH BREAKERS
Long Beach Breakers (TT 1984)
Folded, 1984.

LONG BEACH CHIEFS
Hawaii Chiefs (ABL3 1961–62)

Long Beach Chiefs (ABL3 1962)
Folded during 1962–63 season, 1962.

LONG BEACH STINGRAYS
Long Beach StingRays (ABLw 1997–98)
Folded, 1998.

LONG ISLAND
(New York)

LONG ISLAND JAWZ
Long Island Jawz (RHI 1996)
Folded, 1996.

LOS ANGELES
(California)

LOS ANGELES ACES
See *BALTIMORE BLADES*

LOS ANGELES ANGELS
See *ANAHEIM ANGELS*

LOS ANGELES AVENGERS
LOS ANGELES AVENGERS (AFL 2000–present)

LOS ANGELES AZTECS
Los Angeles Aztecs (NASLo 1974–81) and (NASLi
    1979–81)
Folded, 1981.

LOS ANGELES BLADES
Los Angeles Blades (RHI 1993–97)
Folded, 1997.

LOS ANGELES BUCCANEERS
Los Angeles Buccaneers (NFL 1926)
Folded, 1926.

LOS ANGELES BULLDOGS
Los Angeles Bulldogs, independent, 1936.
Los Angeles Bulldogs (AFL2 1937)
*Independent, 1938. Joined American Professional Foot-
    ball League, 1939. Joined Pacific Coast Professional
    Football League (charter member), 1940–46.*
Folded, approximately 1946.

LOS ANGELES CHARGERS
See *SAN DIEGO CHARGERS*

LOS ANGELES CLIPPERS
Buffalo Braves (NBA 1970–78)
Dallas Express (NBA 1978 *did not play*)
San Diego Clippers (NBA 1978–84)
LOS ANGELES CLIPPERS (NBA 1984–present)

LOS ANGELES COBRAS
Los Angeles Cobras (AFL 1988)
Folded, 1988.

LOS ANGELES DODGERS
*Brooklyn Atlantics, Eastern Association, 1881–82. Joined
   Inter-State League, 1883.*
Brooklyn Atlantics (2) (AA 1884–88)
   a.k.a. Brooklyn Grays
Brooklyn Bridegrooms (AA 1889; NL 1890–98)
(Absorbed Brooklyn Wonders, 1891.)
Brooklyn Superbas (NL 1899–1910)
(Absorbed Baltimore Orioles [B1], 1900.)
Brooklyn Trolley Dodgers (NL 1911)
Brooklyn Dodgers (B) (NL 1911–13)
Brooklyn Robins (NL 1914–31)
Brooklyn Dodgers (B) (NL 1932–57)
LOS ANGELES DODGERS (NL 1958–present)

LOS ANGELES DONS
Los Angeles Dons (AAFC 1946–49)
Folded, 1949.

LOS ANGELES EXPRESS
Los Angeles Express (USFL 1983–85)
Folded, 1985.

LOS ANGELES GALAXY
LOS ANGELES GALAXY (MLS 1996–present)

LOS ANGELES HEAT
Los Angeles Heat (WSL 1986–88; WSA 1989; APSL
   1990)
Folded, 1990.

LOS ANGELES HOT RODS
Los Angeles Hot Rods (AFL 1998 *did not play*)
Folded before season, 1998.

LOS ANGELES JETS
Los Angeles Jets (ABL3 1961–62)
Folded during season, 1962.

LOS ANGELES KINGS
LOS ANGELES KINGS (NHL 1967–present)

LOS ANGELES LAKERS
Detroit Gems (NBL 1946–47)
Minneapolis Lakers (NBL 1947–48; BAA 1948–49; NBA
   1949–60)
LOS ANGELES LAKERS (NBA 1960–present)

LOS ANGELES LAZERS
Philadelphia Fever (MISL 1978–82)
Los Angeles Lazers (MISL 1982–89)
Folded, 1989.

LOS ANGELES RAIDERS
See *OAKLAND RAIDERS*

LOS ANGELES RAMS
See *ST. LOUIS RAMS*

LOS ANGELES SALSA
Los Angeles Salsa (APSL 1993–94)
Folded, 1994.

LOS ANGELES SHARKS
See *BALTIMORE BLADES*

LOS ANGELES SKYHAWKS
Los Angeles Skyhawks (ASL2 1976–79)
Folded, 1979.

LOS ANGELES SPARKS
LOS ANGELES SPARKS (WNBA 1997–present)

LOS ANGELES STARS
See *UTAH STARS*

LOS ANGELES STRINGS
Los Angeles Strings (WTT 1974–78; TT 1981–91; WTT
   1992–93)
(Suspended operations, 1979–80.)
Folded, 1993.

LOS ANGELES TOROS
See *SAN DIEGO TOROS*

LOS ANGELES UNITED
See *ANAHEIM SPLASH*

LOS ANGELES WILDCATS
Los Angeles Wildcats (AFL1 1926)
Folded, 1926.

LOS ANGELES WINGS
Los Angeles Wings (AFL 1992 *did not play*)
Folded before season, 1992.

LOS ANGELES WOLVES
Wolverhampton Wanderers (Stafford, England), inde-
pendent, pre-1967.
Los Angeles Wolves (USA 1967; NASLo 1968)
Folded, 1968.

LOUISIANA

LOUISIANA BUCCANEERS
See *BALTIMORE CLAWS*

LOUISVILLE
(Kentucky)

LOUISVILLE BLACK CAPS
Louisville Black Caps (NSL 1932)
Folded during season, 1932.

LOUISVILLE BRECKS
Floyd and Brecks (Louisville), independent, 1907–20.
Louisville Brecks (APFA 1921; NFL 1922–23)
(Independent during season, 1921; APFA record erased
from final standings.)
Folded, 1923.

LOUISVILLE BUCKEYES
See *CLEVELAND BUCKEYES*

LOUISVILLE COLONELS (B)
Louisville Eclipse (AA 1882–84)
Louisville Colonels (B) (AA 1885–91; NL 1892–99)
   a.k.a. Louisville Cyclones
Absorbed by Pittsburgh Pirates (B), 1900.

LOUISVILLE COLONELS (F)
Louisville Colonels (F) (NFL 1926)
Folded during season, 1926.

LOUISVILLE CYCLONES
See *LOUISVILLE COLONELS (B)*

LOUISVILLE ECLIPSE
See *LOUISVILLE COLONELS (B)*

LOUISVILLE GRAYS
Louisville Grays (NL 1876–77)
Folded, 1877.

LOUISVILLE THUNDER
Louisville Thunder (AISA 1984–87)
Folded, 1987.

LOUISVILLE WHITE SOX
Louisville White Sox (NNL1 1931)
Folded, 1931.

LUDLOW
(Massachusetts)

LUDLOW ASTROS
See *WORCESTER ASTROS*

LUDLOW LUSITANO
Ludlow Soccer Club (ASL2 1955–57)
Ludlow Lusitano (ASL2 1957–58)
Minor league team, 1958–97. Western Massachusetts Pio-
neers, D3 Pro League as part of United Systems of In-
dependent Soccer Leagues, 1998. Continued when
USISL became United Soccer Leagues, 1999–present.

LUDLOW SOCCER CLUB
See *LUDLOW LUSITANO*

MANCHESTER
(Connecticut)

MANCHESTER BRITISH AMERICANS
Manchester British Americans (ABL2 1951–53)
Folded, 1953.

MANCHESTER
(Greater Manchester, England)

MANCHESTER LIGHTNING
See *MANCHESTER MAGIC*

MANCHESTER MAGIC
Manchester Lightning (WISL 1999 *did not play*)
Manchester Magic (WISL 1999 *did not play*)
*Withdrew with England's Professional Indoor Football
    League before season, 1999. Folded with PIFL before
    season, 1999.*

MANCHESTER STORM
Manchester Storm (MLRH 1997)
Folded, 1997.

MANCHESTER TRIBE
Manchester Tribe (MLRH 1998)
Folded, 1998.

MARYLAND

MARYLAND BAYS
Maryland Bays (ASL3 1988–89; APSL 1990–91)
(Absorbed Washington Stars, 1991.)
Folded, 1991.

MARYLAND COMMANDOS
See *WASHINGTON COMMANDOS*

MASSACHUSETTS

MASSACHUSETTS MARAUDERS
See *GRAND RAPIDS RAMPAGE*

MEMPHIS
(Tennessee)

MEMPHIS AMERICANS
See *LAS VEGAS AMERICANS*

MEMPHIS GRIZZLIES
Toronto Northmen (WFL 1974 *did not play*)
Memphis Southmen (WFL 1974–75)

Memphis Grizzlies (WFL 1975 *did not play*)
Folded during season, 1975.

MEMPHIS MAD DOGS
Memphis Mad Dogs (CFL 1995)
Folded, 1995.

MEMPHIS PHARAOHS
See *OKLAHOMA WRANGLERS*

MEMPHIS PROS
See *BALTIMORE CLAWS*

MEMPHIS RED SOX
Memphis Red Sox, independent, 1923.
Memphis Red Sox (NNL1 1924, 1925, 1927, 1929–30;
    NSL 1932; NAL 1937–41, 1943–50)
*(Suspended operations during season, 1924, 1928, 1931,
    1942. Joined minor Negro Southern League, 1926,
    1933–36.)*
Continued as member of minor NAL, 1951–59.
Folded, 1959.

MEMPHIS ROGUES (IS)
Memphis Storm (AISA 1986–89)
Memphis Rogues (IS) (AISA 1989–90)
Folded, 1990.

MEMPHIS ROGUES (S/IS)
See *CALGARY BOOMERS*

MEMPHIS SHOWBOATS
Memphis Showboats (USFL 1984–85)
Folded, 1985.

MEMPHIS SOUNDS
See *BALTIMORE CLAWS*

MEMPHIS SOUTHMEN
See *MEMPHIS GRIZZLIES*

MEMPHIS STORM
See *MEMPHIS ROGUES (IS)*

MEMPHIS TAMS
See *BALTIMORE CLAWS*

MEXICO

MEXICO TOROS
Mexico Toros (CISL 1995)
Folded, 1995.

MIAMI
(Florida)

MIAMI AMERICANS
New Jersey Schaefer Brewers (ASL2 1972)
New Jersey Brewers (ASL2 1973–75)
New Jersey Americans (S) (ASL2 1976–79)
Miami Americans (ASL2 1980)
Folded, 1980.

MIAMI BREAKERS (1)
See *WELLINGTON ACES*

MIAMI BREAKERS (2)
Miami Beach Breakers (2) (TT 1990)
Miami Breakers (2) (TT 1991)
Folded, 1991.

MIAMI DOLPHINS
MIAMI DOLPHINS (AFL4 1966–70;
    NFL 1970–present)

MIAMI FLORIDIANS
See *FLORIDIANS*

MIAMI FREEDOM
Miami Sharks (ASL3 1988–89)
Miami Freedom (APSL 1990–92)
Folded, 1992.

MIAMI FUSION
MIAMI FUSION (MLS 1998–present)

MIAMI GATOS
See *MINNESOTA STRIKERS*

MIAMI HEAT
MIAMI HEAT (NBA 1988–present)

MIAMI HOOTERS
See *FLORIDA BOBCATS*

MIAMI JACKALS
See *FLORIDA JACKALS*

MIAMI SCREAMING EAGLES
See *CALGARY COWBOYS*

MIAMI SEAHAWKS
See *BALTIMORE COLTS (1)*

MIAMI SHARKS
See *MIAMI FREEDOM*

MIAMI SOL
MIAMI SOL (WNBA 2000–present)

MIAMI TOROS
See *MINNESOTA STRIKERS*

MIAMI BEACH
(Florida)

MIAMI BEACH BREAKERS (1)
See *WELLINGTON ACES*

MIAMI BEACH BREAKERS (2)
See *MIAMI BREAKERS (2)*

MICHIGAN

MICHIGAN BLAST
Michigan North Americans (MLRH 1998 *did not play*)
Port Huron North Americans (MLRH 1998)
Michigan Blast (MLRH 1999 *did not play*)
Folded before season, 1999.

MICHIGAN NORTH AMERICANS
See *MICHIGAN BLAST*

MICHIGAN PANTHERS
Michigan Panthers (USFL 1983–84)
Absorbed by Oakland Invaders, 1985.

MICHIGAN STAGS
See *BALTIMORE BLADES*

MIDDLETOWN
(Connecticut)

MIDDLETOWN GUARDS
Middletown Guards (ABL2 1951–53)
Folded during season, 1953.

MIDDLETOWN MANSFIELDS
Middletown Mansfields, amateur, 1871.
Middletown Mansfields (NA 1872)
Folded during season, 1872.

MIDLAND
(Michigan)

MIDLAND CHEMICALS
See *FLINT DOW A.C.'S*

MIDLAND DOW A.C.'S
See *FLINT DOW A.C.'S*

MILWAUKEE
(Wisconsin)

MILWAUKEE ALL-STARS
Oshkosh All-Stars, independent, pre-1937.
Oshkosh All-Stars (NBL 1937–49)
Milwaukee All-Stars (NBA 1949 *did not play*)
Folded before season, 1949.

MILWAUKEE BADGERS
Milwaukee Badgers (NFL 1922–26)
Independent during season, 1926–27.
Folded, 1927.

MILWAUKEE BEARS
Milwaukee Bears (NNL1 1923)
Folded during season, 1923.

MILWAUKEE BRAVES
See *ATLANTA BRAVES*

MILWAUKEE BREWERS (1)
See *MILWAUKEE GRAYS (1)*

MILWAUKEE BREWERS (2)
See *MILWAUKEE CREAM CITYS (2)*

MILWAUKEE BREWERS (3)
Milwaukee Brewers, first Western League, 1891.
Milwaukee Brewers (3) (AA 1891)
Returned to first Western League, 1892.
Folded during season, 1892.

MILWAUKEE BREWERS (4)
See *BALTIMORE ORIOLES (B3)*

MILWAUKEE BREWERS (5)
Seattle Pilots (AL 1969)
MILWAUKEE BREWERS (5) (AL 1970–97; NL 1998–
    present)

MILWAUKEE BUCKS
MILWAUKEE BUCKS (NBA 1968–present)

MILWAUKEE CHICKS
See *GRAND RAPIDS CHICKS*

MILWAUKEE CHIEFS
Milwaukee Chiefs (AFL3 1940–41)
Folded, 1941.

MILWAUKEE CREAM CITYS (1)
See *MILWAUKEE GRAYS (1)*

MILWAUKEE CREAM CITYS (2)
Milwaukee, Northwestern League, 1884.
Milwaukee Cream Citys (2) (UA 1884)
    a.k.a. Milwaukee Grays (2)
    a.k.a. Milwaukee Brewers (2)
Folded during season, 1884.

MILWAUKEE DEUCE
See *MILWAUKEE RACQUETEERS*

MILWAUKEE GRAYS (1)
Milwaukee Grays (1) (NL 1878)
    a.k.a. Milwaukee Cream Citys (1)
    a.k.a. Milwaukee Brewers (1)
Folded, 1878.

MILWAUKEE GRAYS (2)
See *MILWAUKEE CREAM CITYS (2)*

MILWAUKEE HAWKS
See *ATLANTA HAWKS*

MILWAUKEE MUSTANGS
MILWAUKEE MUSTANGS (AFL 1995–present)

MILWAUKEE RACQUETEERS
Atlanta Thunder (TT 1991; WTT 1992–96)
Milwaukee Deuce (WTT 1997 *did not play*)
Milwaukee Racqueteers (WTT 1997)
Folded, 1997.

MILWAUKEE WAVE
MILWAUKEE WAVE (AISA 1984–90; NPSLi 1990–
    present)

MINNEAPOLIS
(Minnesota)

MINNEAPOLIS LAKERS
See *LOS ANGELES LAKERS*

MINNEAPOLIS MARINES
Minneapolis Marines, independent, 1917–20.
Minneapolis Marines (APFA 1921; NFL 1922–24)
*(Independent during season, 1921; APFA record erased
    from final standings.)*
Folded, 1924.

MINNEAPOLIS MILLERETTES
See *FORT WAYNE DAISIES*

MINNEAPOLIS REDJACKETS
Minneapolis Redjackets (NFL 1929–30)
Folded, 1930.

MINNESOTA

MINNESOTA ARCTIC BLAST
Minnesota Arctic Blast (RHI 1994, 1996)
(Suspended operations, 1995.)
Folded, 1996.

MINNESOTA BLUE OX (1)
Minnesota Blue Ox (1) (RHI 1995)
Folded, 1995.

MINNESOTA BLUE OX (2)
Minnesota Blue Ox (2) (RHI 1999)
Folded, 1999.

MINNESOTA BUCKSKINS
Minnesota Buckskins (WTT 1974)
Folded, 1974.

MINNESOTA FIGHTING PIKE
Minnesota Fighting Pike (AFL 1996)
Folded, 1996.

MINNESOTA FIGHTING SAINTS (1)
Minnesota Fighting Saints (1) (WHA 1972–76)
Folded during season, 1976.

MINNESOTA FIGHTING SAINTS (2)
Calgary Broncos (WHA 1972 *did not play*)
Cleveland Crusaders (WHA 1972–76)
Florida Breakers (WHA 1976 *did not play*)
Minnesota Fighting Saints (2) (WHA 1976–77)
Folded during season, 1977.

MINNESOTA KICKS
Denver Dynamos (NASLo 1974–75)
Minnesota Kicks (NASLo 1976–81) and (NASLi 1979–
    81)
Folded, 1981.

MINNESOTA LYNX
MINNESOTA LYNX (WNBA 1999–present)

MINNESOTA MUSKIES
See *FLORIDIANS*

MINNESOTA NORTH STARS
See *DALLAS STARS (H)*

MINNESOTA PENGUINS
Minnesota Penguins (WTT 1993)
Folded, 1993.

MINNESOTA PIPERS
See *PITTSBURGH CONDORS*

MINNESOTA STRIKERS
Washington Brittanica (ASL2 1967)
Washington Darts (ASL2 1968–69; NASLo 1970–71)
Miami Gatos (NASLo 1972)
Miami Toros (NASLo 1973–76)
Fort Lauderdale Strikers (S/IS) (NASLo 1977–83) and
    (NASLi 1979–81)
Minnesota Strikers (NASLo 1984) and (MISL 1984–88)
Folded, 1988.

MINNESOTA TIMBERWOLVES
MINNESOTA TIMBERWOLVES (NBA 1989–present)

MINNESOTA TWINS
Washington Senators, minor American League (charter
*   member), 1900.*
Washington Senators (B3) (AL 1901–04)
Washington Nationals (5) (AL 1905–56)
Washington Senators (B3) (AL 1957–60)
MINNESOTA TWINS (AL 1961–present)

MINNESOTA VIKINGS
MINNESOTA VIKINGS (NFL 1961–present)

MINNESOTA WILD
MINNESOTA WILD (NHL 2000–present)

MONROE
(Louisiana)

MONROE MONARCHS
Monroe Monarchs, independent, by at least 1930–31.
Monroe Monarchs (NSL 1932)
Joined Texas-Oklahoma-Louisiana Negro League, 1933–
*   35.*
Folded, 1935.

MONTERREY
(Nuevo Leon, Mexico)

MONTERREY LA RAZA
MONTERREY LA RAZA (CISL 1993–97; WISL 1999–
    present)
(Suspended operations, 1998.)

MONTGOMERY
(Alabama)

MONTGOMERY GREY SOX
Montgomery Grey Sox (NSL 1932)
Folded, 1932.

MONTREAL
(Quebec, Canada)

MONTREAL ALOUETTES (1)
Montreal Alouettes, Western Interprovincial Football
*   Union, 1946–55.*
Montreal Alouettes (1) (CFC 1956–57; CFL 1958–80)
Folded, 1980.

MONTREAL ALOUETTES (2)
Montreal Concordes (CFL 1981–85)
Montreal Alouettes (2) (CFL 1986–87)
Folded, 1987.

MONTREAL ALOUETTES (3)
Baltimore CFL Colts (CFL 1994 *did not play*)
Baltimore CFLs (CFL 1994–95)
Baltimore Stallions (CFL 1995)
MONTREAL ALOUETTES (3) (CFL 1996–present)

MONTREAL CANADIENS
MONTREAL CANADIENS (NHA 1909–17; NHL
    1917–present)
    a.k.a. Montreal Habs, 1915–at least 1935

MONTREAL CONCORDES
See *MONTREAL ALOUETTES (2)*

MONTREAL EXPOS
MONTREAL EXPOS (NL 1969–present)

MONTREAL HABS
See *MONTREAL CANADIENS*

MONTREAL IMPACT
Montreal Supra, Canadian Soccer League, 1988–92.
Montreal Impact (APSL 1993–94) and (NPSLi 1997–
    2000)
(Continued when APSL became A-League, 1995–98,
*   2000–present.)*
(Absorbed Columbus Invaders, 1997.)

MONTREAL MANIC
Philadelphia Fury (NASLo 1978–80)
Montreal Manic (NASLo 1981–83) and (NASLi 1981–
    82)
Folded, 1983.

MONTREAL MAROONS
Montreal Maroons (NHL 1924–38)
Folded, 1938.

MONTREAL OLYMPIQUE
Montreal Olympique (NASLo 1971–73)
Folded, 1973.

MONTREAL ROADRUNNERS
Montreal Roadrunners (RHI 1994–97)
Folded, 1997.

MONTREAL SHAMROCKS
Montreal Crystals, Amateur Hockey Association, 1886–
approximately 1908. Montreal Shamrocks, Eastern
Canada Hockey Association, 1908–09. Joined
Canadian Hockey Association, 1909. Left when league
folded, 1909.
Montreal Shamrocks (NHA 1909–11)
Folded, 1911.

MONTREAL WANDERERS
Montreal Wanderers, Federal Amateur Hockey League,
1903–08. Joined Eastern Canada Hockey Association,
1908–09.
Montreal Wanderers (NHA 1909–17; NHL 1917–18)
Folded, 1918.

MUNCIE
(Indiana)

MUNCIE FLYERS
Congerville Flyers (Illinois), independent, 1919.
Muncie Flyers (APFA 1920–21)
Folded during season, 1921.

MUSKEGON
(Michigan)

MUSKEGON BELLES
Racine Belles (AAGPBL 1943–50)
Battle Creek Belles (AAGPBL 1951–52)
Muskegon Belles (AAGPBL 1953)
Folded, 1953.

MUSKEGON LASSIES
See *KALAMAZOO LASSIES*

NASHVILLE
(Tennessee)

NASHVILLE DIAMONDS
Nashville Diamonds (ASL2 1982)
Folded, 1982.

NASHVILLE ELITE GIANTS
See *BALTIMORE ELITE GIANTS*

NASHVILLE KATS
NASHVILLE KATS (AFL 1997–present)

NASHVILLE NOISE
Nashville Noise (ABLw 1998)
Folded during 1998–99 season, 1998.

NASHVILLE PREDATORS
NASHVILLE PREDATORS (NHL 1998–present)

NEW BEDFORD
(Massachusetts)

NEW BEDFORD WHALERS (1)
New Bedford Whalers, Southern New England Soccer
League, pre-1924.
New Bedford Whalers (1) (ASL1 1924–29; ACL 1929–
30; ASL1 1931)
(Simultaneously joined first International Soccer League,
1926.)
(Joined second Eastern Professional Soccer League dur-
ing season, 1929.)
Absorbed by Fall River Football Club (1), 1931.

NEW BEDFORD WHALERS (2)
Providence Clamdiggers (ASL1 1924–28)
Providence Gold Bugs (ASL1 1928–29; ACL 1929–30)
Fall River Football Club (1) (ASL1 1931)
(Absorbed New Bedford Whalers [1] during season,
1931.)
Absorbed New York Yankees (S), 1931.
New Bedford Whalers (2) (ASL1 1931–33)
Folded, 1933.

NEW BRITAIN
(Connecticut)

NEW BRITAIN JACKAWAYS
See *NEW BRITAIN MULES*

NEW BRITAIN MULES *(**MERGED TEAM**)*
Hoboken Lisas (New Jersey), second Metropolitan
   League, 1931–33.
North Hudson Thourots (ABL2 1933)
Camden Brewers (ABL2 1933–34)
   a.k.a. Camden Athletics
New Britain Palaces (ABL2 1934)
New Britain Jackaways (ABL2 1934–35)
Merged with Newark Mules during season, 1935.
New Britain Mules (ABL2 1935)
Folded, 1935.

*****
Newark Bears (Bk) (ABL2 1933–34)
   a.k.a. Newark Joe Fays
Newark Mules (ABL2 1934–35)
Merged with New Britain Jackaways during season, 1935.
New Britain Mules (ABL2 1935)
Folded, 1935.

NEW BRITAIN PALACES
See *NEW BRITAIN MULES*

NEW ENGLAND
(USA)

NEW ENGLAND BLAZERS
See *BOSTON BLAZERS*

NEW ENGLAND BLIZZARD
New England Blizzard (ABLw 1996–98)
Folded during 1998–99 season, 1998.

NEW ENGLAND OCEANEERS
See *INDIANAPOLIS DAREDEVILS*

NEW ENGLAND PATRIOTS
Boston Patriots (AFL4 1960–70)
NEW ENGLAND PATRIOTS (NFL 1970–present)

NEW ENGLAND REVOLUTION
NEW ENGLAND REVOLUTION (MLS 1996–present)

NEW ENGLAND SEA WOLVES
New York CityHawks (AFL 1997–98)
NEW ENGLAND SEA WOLVES (AFL 1999–present)

NEW ENGLAND SHARKS
New England Sharks (ASL2 1981)
Folded, 1981.

NEW ENGLAND STEAMROLLERS
New England Steamrollers (AFL 1988)
Folded, 1988.

NEW ENGLAND STINGERS
See *OTTAWA WHEELS*

NEW ENGLAND TEA MEN
See *JACKSONVILLE TEA MEN*

NEW ENGLAND WHALERS
See *CAROLINA HURRICANES*

NEW HAVEN
(Connecticut)

NEW HAVEN ELM CITYS
New Haven Elm Citys (NA 1875)
   a.k.a. New Haven New Havens
Folded during season, 1875.

NEW HAVEN JEWELS
See *BROOKLYN GOTHAMS*

NEW HAVEN NEW HAVENS
See *NEW HAVEN ELM CITYS*

NEW JERSEY

NEW JERSEY AMERICANS (Bk)
See *NEW JERSEY NETS*

NEW JERSEY AMERICANS (S)
See *MIAMI AMERICANS*

NEW JERSEY BREWERS
See *MIAMI AMERICANS*

NEW JERSEY DEVILS
Kansas City Scouts (NHL 1974–76)

Colorado Rockies (H) (NHL 1976–82)
NEW JERSEY DEVILS (NHL 1982–present)

NEW JERSEY EAGLES
New Jersey Eagles (ASL3 1988–89; APSL 1990)
Folded, 1990.

NEW JERSEY FREIGHTERS
See *NEW JERSEY NETS*

NEW JERSEY GENERALS
New Jersey Generals (USFL 1983–85)
Folded, 1985.

NEW JERSEY NETS
New Jersey Freighters (ABA 1967 *did not play*)
New Jersey Americans (Bk) (ABA 1967–68)
New York Americans (Bk2) (ABA 1968–69)
New York Nets (ABA 1969–76; NBA 1976–77)
NEW JERSEY NETS (NBA 1977–present)

NEW JERSEY RED DOGS
NEW JERSEY RED DOGS (AFL 1997–present)

NEW JERSEY ROCKETS
See *DALLAS SIDEKICKS*

NEW JERSEY ROCKIN' ROLLERS
See *NEW YORK/NEW JERSEY ROCKIN' ROLLERS*

NEW JERSEY SAINTS
See *NEW YORK SAINTS*

NEW JERSEY SCHAEFER BREWERS
See *MIAMI AMERICANS*

NEW JERSEY STARS
See *DELAWARE SMASH*

NEW MEXICO

NEW MEXICO CHILIES
New Mexico Chilies (APSL 1990)
Folded, 1990.

NEW ORLEANS
(Louisiana)

NEW ORLEANS BREAKERS
See *PORTLAND BREAKERS*

NEW ORLEANS BUCCANEERS
See *BALTIMORE CLAWS*

NEW ORLEANS JAZZ
See *UTAH JAZZ*

NEW ORLEANS NIGHT
New Orleans Night (AFL 1991–92)
Folded, 1992.

NEW ORLEANS SAINTS
NEW ORLEANS SAINTS (NFL 1967–present)

NEW ORLEANS-ST. LOUIS
(Louisiana and Missouri)

NEW ORLEANS-ST. LOUIS STARS
See *HARRISBURG-ST. LOUIS STARS*

NEW WESTMINSTER
(British Columbia, Canada)

NEW WESTMINSTER ROYALS
See *PORTLAND ROSEBUDS (1)*

NEW YORK

NEW YORK OTBZZ
See *SCHENECTADY COUNTY ELECTRICS*

NEW YORK
(New York)

NEW YORK AMERICANS (Bk1)
See *BROOKLYN GOTHAMS*

NEW YORK AMERICANS (Bk2)
See *NEW JERSEY NETS*

NEW YORK AMERICANS (F)
New York Yankees (F2) (AFL2 1936–37; AFL3 1940)
(Independent, 1938–39.)
New York Americans (F) (AFL3 1941)
Folded, 1941.

NEW YORK AMERICANS (H)
See *BROOKLYN AMERICANS*

NEW YORK AMERICANS (S)
Brooklyn Wanderers (1) (ASL1 1922–29; ACL 1929–30; ASL1 1931)
(Simultaneously joined first International Soccer League, 1926.)
New York Americans (S) (ASL1 1931–33; ASL2 1933–56)
Absorbed by New York Hakoah (2), 1956.

NEW YORK APOLLO
See *NEW YORK UNITED*

NEW YORK APPLES
New York Sets (WTT 1974–76)
New York Apples (WTT 1977–78)
Folded, 1978.

NEW YORK ARROWS
See *NEW YORK EXPRESS*

NEW YORK BLACK YANKEES
Harlem Stars (New York), independent, 1931. New York Black Yankees, independent, 1932–35.
New York Black Yankees (NNL2 1936–48)
Independent, 1949–50.
Folded, 1950.

NEW YORK BRICKLEY'S GIANTS
New York Brickley's Giants (APFA 1921)
   a.k.a. New York Giants (F1)
New York Giants, independent, 1922–23.
Folded, 1923.

NEW YORK BROOKHATTAN
See *GALICIA-HONDURAS*

NEW YORK BULLDOGS
See *DALLAS TEXANS (F1)*

NEW YORK CELTICS
Brooklyn Celtics (Bk1) (ABL1 1926–27)
New York Celtics (ABL1 1927–28, 1929)
(Suspended operations, 1928–29.)
Folded during 1929–30 season, 1929.

NEW YORK CITYHAWKS
See *NEW ENGLAND SEA WOLVES*

NEW YORK COSMOS
New York Cosmos (NASLo 1971–76)
Cosmos (NASLo 1977–78)
New York Cosmos (NASLo 1979–84) and (NASLi 1981–82, 1983–84; MISL 1984–85)
Independent during season, 1985.
Folded, 1985.

NEW YORK CUBANS
New York Cubans (NNL2 1935–36, 1939–48; NAL 1949–50)
(Suspended operations, 1937–38.)
Folded, 1950.

NEW YORK EAGLES
New York Eagles (ASL2 1978–79, 1981)
(Suspended operations, 1980.)
Folded, 1981.

NEW YORK EXPRESS
New York Arrows (MISL 1978–84)
Suspended operations, 1984–86.
New York Express (MISL 1986–87)
Folded during season, 1987.

NEW YORK FIELD CLUB (1)
New York Field Club, North American Foot Ball League, 1916–21.
New York Field Club (1) (ASL1 1921–24)
Folded, 1924.

NEW YORK FIELD CLUB (2)
New York Field Club (2) (ASL1 1932–33)
Folded, 1933.

NEW YORK FLASH
New York Flash, began exhibition play, 1999.
NEW YORK FLASH (W-MLRH 2000–present)

NEW YORK GENERALS
New York Generals (NPSLo 1967; NASLo 1968)
Folded, 1968.

NEW YORK GIANTS (B1)
See *SAN FRANCISCO GIANTS*

NEW YORK GIANTS (B2)
New York Giants (B2) (PL 1890)
Absorbed by New York Giants (B1), 1891.

NEW YORK GIANTS (F1)
See *NEW YORK BRICKLEY'S GIANTS*

NEW YORK GIANTS (F2)
NEW YORK GIANTS (F2) (NFL 1925–present)
(Absorbed Detroit Wolverines [F], 1929.)

NEW YORK GIANTS (S1)
See *NEW YORK YANKEES (S)*

NEW YORK GIANTS (S2)
Indiana Flooring (New York), independent, pre-1924.
Indiana Flooring (ASL1 1924–27)
New York Nationals (1) (ASL1 1927–29; ACL 1929–30)
New York Giants (S2) (ACL 1930; ASL1 1931–32)
Folded, 1932.

NEW YORK GOLDEN BLADES
See *SAN DIEGO MARINERS*

NEW YORK GOTHAMS (B)
See *SAN FRANCISCO GIANTS*

NEW YORK GOTHAMS (Bk)
See *BROOKLYN GOTHAMS*

NEW YORK GREEKS
See *NEW YORK UNITED*

NEW YORK GREEN STOCKINGS
See *SAN FRANCISCO GIANTS*

NEW YORK HAKOAH (1)
Brooklyn Hakoah (ASL1 1929)
*Merged with New York Hakoahs from second Eastern
     Professional Soccer League, 1929.*
Hakoah All-Stars (ACL 1929–30)
New York Hakoah (1) (ASL1 1931–33)
Folded, 1933.

NEW YORK HAKOAH (2)
See *NEW YORK HAKOAH-AMERICANS*

NEW YORK HAKOAH-AMERICANS
New York Hakoah (2) (ASL2 1948–62)

(Absorbed New York Americans [S], 1956.)
New York Hakoah-Americans (ASL2 1962–64)
Folded, 1964.

NEW YORK HAKOAHS
New York Hakoahs (ABL1 1928–29)
Folded, 1929.

NEW YORK HAMPTONS
NEW YORK HAMPTONS (WTT 2000–present)

NEW YORK HARLEM YANKEES
See *GLENS FALLS-SARATOGA*

NEW YORK HIGHLANDERS
See *NEW YORK YANKEES (B)*

NEW YORK HILLTOPPERS
See *NEW YORK YANKEES (B)*

NEW YORK INTER
Inter Soccer Club (2) (ASL2 1965–66)
New York Inter (ASL2 1966–69)
Folded, 1969.

NEW YORK INVADERS
See *NEW YORK YANKEES (B)*

NEW YORK ISLANDERS
NEW YORK ISLANDERS (NHL 1972–present)

NEW YORK JETS
New York Titans (AFL4 1960–62)
NEW YORK JETS (AFL4 1963–70; NFL 1970–present)

NEW YORK JEWELS
See *BROOKLYN GOTHAMS*

NEW YORK KICK
New York Kick (NPSLi 1990–91)
Folded, 1991.

NEW YORK KNICKERBOCKERS
NEW YORK KNICKERBOCKERS (BAA 1946–49;
   NBA 1949–present)

NEW YORK KNIGHTS
New York Knights (AFL 1988)
Folded, 1988.

NEW YORK LIBERTY
NEW YORK LIBERTY (WNBA 1997–present)

NEW YORK LINCOLN GIANTS
New York Lincoln Giants, independent, 1911–22.
New York Lincoln Giants (ECL 1923–26, 1928; ANL
   1929)
(Independent, 1927.)
Independent, 1930.
Folded, 1930.

NEW YORK METROPOLITANS
New York Metropolitans, independent, 1880. Joined East-
   ern Association, 1881. Independent, 1882.
New York Metropolitans (AA 1883–87)
   a.k.a. New York Mets (1)
Folded, 1887.

NEW YORK METS (1)
See *NEW YORK METROPOLITANS*

NEW YORK METS (2)
NEW YORK METS (2) (NL 1962–present)

NEW YORK MUTUALS
New York Mutuals, independent, 1857–70.
New York Mutuals (NA 1871–75; NL 1876)
Folded, 1876.

NEW YORK NATIONALS (1)
See *NEW YORK GIANTS (S2)*

NEW YORK NATIONALS (2)
New York Nationals (2) (USL 1984)
Folded, 1984.

NEW YORK NETS
See *NEW JERSEY NETS*

NEW YORK ORIGINAL CELTICS
See *BROOKLYN CELTICS (Bk2)*

NEW YORK RAIDERS
See *SAN DIEGO MARINERS*

NEW YORK RANGERS
NEW YORK RANGERS (NHL 1926–present)

NEW YORK RIOT
New York Riot (MLRH 1997–98)
Folded, 1998.

NEW YORK SAINTS
New Jersey Saints (EPBLL 1987–88)
NEW YORK SAINTS (MILL 1989–97; NLL 1998–pres-
   ent)

NEW YORK SETS
See *NEW YORK APPLES*

NEW YORK SKYLINERS
CA Cerro (Montevideo, Uruguay), independent, pre-1967.
New York Skyliners (USA 1967)
Folded, 1967.

NEW YORK SOCCER CLUB
See *NEW YORK YANKEES (S)*

NEW YORK STARS
See *CHARLOTTE HORNETS (F)*

NEW YORK TAPERS
See *PHILADELPHIA TAPERS*

NEW YORK TITANS
See *NEW YORK JETS*

NEW YORK UNITED
New York Greeks, independent, by at least 1967–70.
New York Greeks (ASL2 1971–72)
New York Apollo (ASL2 1973–79)
New York United (ASL2 1980–81)
Folded, 1981.

NEW YORK WESTCHESTERS
See *BROOKLYN GOTHAMS*

NEW YORK YANKEES (B)
Baltimore Orioles, minor American League (charter mem-
   ber), 1900.
Baltimore Orioles (B2) (AL 1901–02)
New York Highlanders (AL 1903–12)
   a.k.a. New York Hilltoppers
   a.k.a. New York Invaders
NEW YORK YANKEES (B) (AL 1913–present)

NEW YORK YANKEES (Bk)
Bronx Yankees (ABL2 1937)
New York Yankees (Bk) (ABL2 1937–38)
Folded during season, 1938.

NEW YORK YANKEES (F1)
New York Yankees (F1) (AFL1 1926; NFL 1927–28)
Folded, 1928.

NEW YORK YANKEES (F2)
See *NEW YORK AMERICANS (F)*

NEW YORK YANKEES (F3)
See *BROOKLYN-NEW YORK YANKEES*

NEW YORK YANKEES (S) *(**MERGED TEAM**)*
Fall River United (ASL1 1921–22)
Fall River Marksmen (ASL1 1922–29; ACL 1929–30)
Merged with New York Soccer Club, 1931.
New York Yankees (S) (ASL1 1931)
Absorbed by Fall River Football Club (1), 1931.

*****
Paterson Silk Sox (ASL1 1922–23)
New York Giants (S1) (ASL1 1923–28; ACL 1929–30)
(Joined second Eastern Professional Soccer League during season, 1928–29.)
New York Soccer Club (ACL 1930)
Merged with Fall River Marksmen, 1930.
New York Yankees (S) (ASL1 1931)
Absorbed by Fall River Football Club (1), 1931.

NEW YORK YANKS
See *DALLAS TEXANS (F1)*

NEW YORK-NEW JERSEY

NEW YORK-NEW JERSEY METROSTARS
NEW YORK-NEW JERSEY METROSTARS (MLS 1996–present)

NEW YORK/NEW JERSEY

NEW YORK/NEW JERSEY ROCKIN' ROLLERS
New Jersey Rockin' Rollers (RHI 1994–97)
Suspended operations, 1997–98.
New York/New Jersey Rockin' Rollers (RHI 1999 *did not play*)
Folded before season, 1999.

NEWARK
(New Jersey)

NEWARK
See *NEWARK AMERICANS*

NEWARK AMERICANS
Newark, second Eastern Professional Soccer League, 1928–29.
Bridgeport Hungaria (ACL 1929)
Newark (ACL 1929–30)
Newark Americans (ACL 1930; ASL1 1931–32)
Folded, 1932.

NEWARK BEARS (Bk)
See *NEW BRITAIN MULES*

NEWARK BEARS (F)
Newark Bears (F) (AFL1 1926)
Independent during season, 1926.
Folded, 1926.

NEWARK BOBCATS
Newark Bobcats (ABL2 1946–47)
Folded, 1947.

NEWARK CELTICS
See *KEARNY CELTICS*

NEWARK DODGERS
See *HOUSTON EAGLES*

NEWARK EAGLES
See *HOUSTON EAGLES*

NEWARK FALCOS
Newark Falcos (ASL2 1964–67)
Folded during season, 1967.

NEWARK FEDS
See *NEWARK PEPPERS*

NEWARK GERMANS
Newark Germans (ASL2 1933–36)
Folded, 1936.

NEWARK IRISH
See *KEARNY CELTICS*

NEWARK JERSEYMEN
See *NEWARK PEPPERS*

NEWARK JOE FAYS
See *NEW BRITAIN MULES*

NEWARK MULES
See *NEW BRITAIN MULES*

NEWARK NEWFEDS
See *NEWARK PEPPERS*

NEWARK PEPPERS
Indianapolis Federals, minor Federal League (charter member), 1913.
Indianapolis Federals (FL 1914)
    a.k.a. Indianapolis Hoosiers (4)
    a.k.a. Indianapolis Hoosierfeds
    a.k.a. Indianapolis Hoofeds
Newark Peppers (FL 1915)
    a.k.a. Newark Peps
    a.k.a. Newark Feds
    a.k.a. Newark Newfeds
    a.k.a. Newark Jerseymen
Folded, 1915.

NEWARK PEPS
See *NEWARK PEPPERS*

NEWARK PORTUGUESE
Newark Portuguese (ASL2 1951–63, 1964–68)
(Suspended operations, 1963–64.)
Folded, 1968.

NEWARK SITCH
Newark Ukrainian Sitch (ASL2 1962–64, 1965–68)
(Suspended operations, 1964–65.)
Newark Sitch (ASL2 1969–70)
Folded, 1970.

NEWARK SKEETERS
Newark Skeeters (ASL1 1923–28)
Joined second Eastern Professional Soccer League, 1928.
Folded, 1928.

NEWARK STARS
Newark Stars (ECL 1926)
Folded during season, 1926.

NEWARK TORNADOES
Orange Tornadoes (NFL 1929)
Newark Tornadoes (NFL 1930)
Folded, 1930.

NEWARK UKRAINIAN SITCH
See *NEWARK SITCH*

NEWCASTLE
(Newcastle-Upon-Tyne, Tyne and Wear, England)

NEWCASTLE GEORDIES
Newcastle Geordies (WISL 1999 *did not play*)
Withdrew with England's Professional Indoor Football League before season, 1999. Folded with PIFL before season, 1999.

NEWPORT BEACH
(California)

NEWPORT BEACH DUKES
Newport Beach Dukes (TT 1990–91; WTT 1992–94)
Folded, 1994.

NORTH HUDSON
(Hudson County, New Jersey)

NORTH HUDSON THOUROTS
See *NEW BRITAIN MULES*

NORTHEAST
(USA)

NORTHEAST UNITED
See *CONNECTICUT YANKEES*

NORTHERN
(Canada)

NORTHERN FUSILIERS
228th Battalion of the Northern Fusiliers (Toronto), military team, pre-1916.
Northern Fusiliers (NHA 1916–17)
Military unit shipped to France during season, 1917.

OAKLAND
(California)

<u>OAKLAND ACES</u>
Oakland Aces (TT 1985–86)
Folded, 1986.

<u>OAKLAND AMERICANS</u>
See *VIRGINIA SQUIRES*

<u>OAKLAND ATHLETICS</u>
Philadelphia Athletics, minor American League (charter member), 1900.
Philadelphia Athletics (4) (AL 1901–54)
Kansas City Athletics (AL 1955–67)
OAKLAND ATHLETICS (AL 1968–present)

<u>OAKLAND BREAKERS</u>
Golden Gaters (WTT 1974–78)
Suspended operations, 1979–80.
Oakland Breakers (TT 1981–82)
Folded, 1982.

<u>OAKLAND BUCCANEERS</u>
Oakland Buccaneers (ASL2 1976)
Folded, 1976.

<u>OAKLAND CLIPPERS</u>
See *CALIFORNIA CLIPPERS*

<u>OAKLAND INVADERS</u>
Oakland Invaders (USFL 1983–85)
(Absorbed Michigan Panthers, 1985.)
Folded, 1985.

<u>OAKLAND OAKS (1)</u>
San Francisco Saints (ABL3 1961–62)
Oakland Oaks (1) (ABL3 1962)
Folded during 1962–63 season, 1962.

<u>OAKLAND OAKS (2)</u>
See *VIRGINIA SQUIRES*

<u>OAKLAND RAIDERS</u>
Oakland Raiders (AFL4 1960–70; NFL 1970–82)
Los Angeles Raiders (NFL 1982–95)
OAKLAND RAIDERS (NFL 1995–present)

<u>OAKLAND SEALS</u>
See *CLEVELAND BARONS*

<u>OAKLAND SKATES</u>
Oakland Skates (RHI 1993–96)
Folded, 1996.

<u>OAKLAND STOMPERS</u>
See *EDMONTON DRILLERS (S/IS)*

OKLAHOMA

<u>OKLAHOMA COYOTES</u>
Atlanta Fire Ants (RHI 1994)
Oklahoma Coyotes (RHI 1995–96)
Folded, 1996.

<u>OKLAHOMA OUTLAWS</u>
See *ARIZONA OUTLAWS*

<u>OKLAHOMA WRANGLERS</u>
Memphis Pharaohs (AFL 1995–96)
Portland Forest Dragons (AFL 1997–99)
OKLAHOMA WRANGLERS (AFL 2000–present)

OKLAHOMA CITY
(Oklahoma)

<u>OKLAHOMA CITY SLICKERS</u>
See *OKLAHOMA CITY STAMPEDE*

<u>OKLAHOMA CITY STAMPEDE</u>
Oklahoma City Slickers (ASL2 1982–83)
Oklahoma City Stampede (USL 1984)
Folded, 1984.

(OLYMPIA)
(No location name: New Britain, Connecticut)

<u>OLYMPIA</u>
Olympia (ASL2 1965–67)
Folded, 1967.

ONTARIO
(Canada)

ONTARIO RAIDERS
See *TORONTO ROCK*

OORANG
(Oorang Dog Kennels, LaRue, Ohio)

OORANG INDIANS
Oorang Indians (NFL 1922–23)
Folded, 1923.

ORANGE
(New Jersey)

ORANGE TORNADOES
See *NEWARK TORNADOES*

ORLANDO
(Florida)

ORLANDO JACKALS
See *FLORIDA JACKALS*

ORLANDO LIONS
Orlando Lions (ASL3 1988–89; APSL 1990)
Absorbed by Fort Lauderdale Strikers (S), 1991.

ORLANDO MAGIC
ORLANDO MAGIC (NBA 1989–present)

ORLANDO MIRACLE
ORLANDO MIRACLE (WNBA 1999–present)

ORLANDO PREDATORS
ORLANDO PREDATORS (AFL 1991–present)

ORLANDO RENEGADES
Washington Federals (USFL 1983–84)
Orlando Renegades (USFL 1985)
Folded, 1985.

ORLANDO ROLLERGATORS
See *TORONTO WAVE*

ORLANDO SURGE
Orlando Surge (MLRH 1998)
Folded, 1998.

OSHAWA
(Ontario, Canada)

OSHAWA OUTLAWS
Oshawa Outlaws (MLRH 1998 *did not play*)
Folded before season, 1998.

OSHKOSH
(Wisconsin)

OSHKOSH ALL-STARS
See *MILWAUKEE ALL-STARS*

OTTAWA
(Ontario, Canada)

OTTAWA CIVICS
Denver Spurs (WHA 1975–76)
Ottawa Civics (WHA 1976)
Folded during season, 1976.

OTTAWA LOGGERS
See *OTTAWA WHEELS*

OTTAWA NATIONALS
See *BIRMINGHAM BULLS*

OTTAWA ROUGH RIDERS
Ottawa Rough Riders, Interprovincial Rugby Football Union, 1907–23. Merged with St. Brigit's Club and became Ottawa Senators, IRFU, 1924–25. Ottawa Rough Riders, IRFU, 1926–55.
Ottawa Rough Riders (CFC 1956–57; CFL 1958–96)
Folded, 1996.

OTTAWA SENATORS (1)
See *ST. LOUIS EAGLES (H)*

OTTAWA SENATORS (2)
OTTAWA SENATORS (2) (NHL 1992–present)

OTTAWA WHEELS
New England Stingers (RHI 1994)
Ottawa Loggers (RHI 1995–97)
Ottawa Wheels (RHI 1997)
Folded, 1997.

PASSAIC
(New Jersey)

PASSAIC BENGAL TIGERS
See *TRENTON TIGERS*

PASSAIC RED DEVILS
Paterson Panthers (ABL2 1935)
Trenton Bengals (2) (ABL2 1935–36)
    a.k.a. Trenton Moose (2)
Passaic Red Devils (ABL2 1936)
    a.k.a. Passaic Reds
Folded, 1936.

PASSAIC REDS
See *PASSAIC RED DEVILS*

PASSON
(Harry Passon, Philadelphia, Pennsylvania)

PASSON PHILLIES
See *PHILADELPHIA PASSON*

PATERSON
(New Jersey)

PATERSON CALEDONIANS
Paterson Caledonians (ASL2 1936–38, 1939–41)
(Suspended operations, 1938–39.)
Folded, 1941.

PATERSON CRESCENTS (1)
Paterson Crescents (1) (ABL1 1929–30)
Folded during season, 1930.

PATERSON CRESCENTS (2)
Washington Capitol's (ABL2 1944)
Paterson Crescents (2) (ABL2 1945–51)
Folded, 1951.

PATERSON PANTHERS
See *PASSAIC RED DEVILS*

PATERSON SILK SOX
See *NEW YORK YANKEES (S)*

PATERSON VISITATIONS
See *BALTIMORE CLIPPERS*

PATERSON WHIRLWINDS
Paterson Whirlwinds (ABL1 1928–29)
Folded, 1929.

PAWTUCKET
(Rhode Island)

PAWTUCKET RANGERS
*J & P Coats, Southern New England Soccer League
    (charter member), 1914–21.*
J & P Coats (ASL1 1921–29)
Pawtucket Rangers (ASL1 1929; ACL 1929–30; ASL1
    1931–33)
Folded, 1933.

PAWTUCKET SLATERS
Pawtucket Slaters (ABL2 1952–53)
Folded, 1953.

PENN-JERSEY
(Pennsylvania and New Jersey)

PENN-JERSEY SPIRIT
Penn-Jersey Spirit (APSL 1990–91)
Folded, 1991.

PENNSYLVANIA

PENNSYLVANIA POSSE
Pennsylvania Posse (MLRH 1997–98)
Folded, 1998.

PENNSYLVANIA STONERS
Pennsylvania Stoners (ASL2 1979–83)
Folded, 1983.

PEORIA
(Illinois)

PEORIA REDWINGS
Peoria Redwings (AAGPBL 1946–51)
Folded, 1951.

(PHIL-PITT)
(No location name: Philadelphia and Pittsburgh, Pennsylvania)

PHIL-PITT *(**MERGED TEAM**)*
See *PHILADELPHIA EAGLES* and *PITTSBURGH STEELERS*

PHILADELPHIA
(Pennsylvania)

PHILADELPHIA
Philadelphia (ASL1 1928–29)
Folded, 1929.

PHILADELPHIA AMERICANS
See *UHRIK TRUCKERS*

PHILADELPHIA ATHLETICS (1)
Philadelphia Athletics, independent, 1860–70.
Philadelphia Athletics (1) (NA 1871–75; NL 1876)
Folded, 1876.

PHILADELPHIA ATHLETICS (2)
Philadelphia Athletics (2) (AA 1882–90)
Folded, 1890.

PHILADELPHIA ATHLETICS (3)
Philadelphia Quakers (B2) (PL 1890)
Philadelphia Athletics (3) (AA 1891)
Folded, 1891.

PHILADELPHIA ATHLETICS (4)
See *OAKLAND ATHLETICS*

PHILADELPHIA ATOMS
Philadelphia Atoms (NASLo 1973–76)
Folded, 1976.

PHILADELPHIA BELL
Philadelphia Bell (WFL 1974–75)
Folded during season, 1975.

PHILADELPHIA BLAZERS
See *CALGARY COWBOYS*

PHILADELPHIA BLUE JAYS
See *PHILADELPHIA PHILLIES (B2)*

PHILADELPHIA BULLDOGS
Philadelphia Bulldogs (RHI 1994–96)
Folded, 1996.

PHILADELPHIA CELTIC
Philadelphia Celtic (ASL1 1927)
Folded during season, 1927.

PHILADELPHIA CENTENNIALS
Philadelphia Centennials (NA 1875)
Folded during season, 1875.

PHILADELPHIA COLONIALS
See *PHILADELPHIA SPHAS*

PHILADELPHIA EAGLES
Loyola Athletic Club (Frankford), independent, 1909–11.
Frankford Yellow Jackets, independent, 1912–23.
Frankford Yellow Jackets (NFL 1924–31)
Suspended operations, 1932.
Philadelphia Eagles (NFL 1933–42)
Merged with Pittsburgh Steelers, 1943.
Phil-Pitt (NFL 1943)
a.k.a. Steagles
Split from Pittsburgh half of Card-Pitt, 1944.
PHILADELPHIA EAGLES (NFL 1944–present)

PHILADELPHIA FEVER
See *LOS ANGELES LAZERS*

PHILADELPHIA FIELD CLUB (1)
See *BETHLEHEM STEEL*

PHILADELPHIA FIELD CLUB (2)
Philadelphia Field Club (2) (ASL1 1922–27)
Folded, 1927.

PHILADELPHIA FILLIES
See *PHILADELPHIA PHILLIES (B2)*

PHILADELPHIA FLYERS
PHILADELPHIA FLYERS (NHL 1967–present)

PHILADELPHIA FOOTBALL CLUB
Bridgeport Bears (ASL1 1929)
Philadelphia Football Club (ASL1 1929)
Folded during season, 1929.

PHILADELPHIA FREEDOMS
Philadelphia Freedoms (WTT 1974)
Folded, 1974.

PHILADELPHIA FURY
See *MONTREAL MANIC*

PHILADELPHIA GERMAN-AMERICANS
See *UHRIK TRUCKERS*

PHILADELPHIA GERMANS
See *UHRIK TRUCKERS*

PHILADELPHIA HEBREWS
See *PHILADELPHIA SPHAS*

PHILADELPHIA KEYSTONES
Philadelphia Keystones (UA 1884)
Independent semipro team during season, 1884.
Folded, post-1884.

PHILADELPHIA KIXX
PHILADELPHIA KIXX (NPSLi 1996–present)

PHILADELPHIA NATIONALS (B)
See *PHILADELPHIA PHILLIES (B2)*

PHILADELPHIA NATIONALS (S)
Philadelphia Nationals (S) (ASL2 1941–53)
Folded during season, 1953.

PHILADELPHIA PASSON
Philadelphia Passon (ASL2 1936–41)
    a.k.a. Passon Phillies
Folded, 1941.

PHILADELPHIA PEARLS
See *PHILADELPHIA PHILLIES (B1)*

PHILADELPHIA PHILADELPHIAS
See *PHILADELPHIA PHILLIES (B1)*

PHILADELPHIA PHILLIES (B1)
Philadelphia Philadelphias (NA 1873)

    a.k.a. Philadelphia White Stockings
    a.k.a. Philadelphia Whites
Philadelphia Pearls (NA 1874)
Philadelphia Phillies (B1) (NA 1875)
Folded, 1875.

PHILADELPHIA PHILLIES (B2)
Philadelphia Nationals (B) (NL 1883–89)
    a.k.a. Philadelphia Quakers (B1)
Philadelphia Fillies (NL 1890)
Philadelphia Phillies (B2) (NL 1890–1943)
Philadelphia Blue Jays (NL 1944–45)
PHILADELPHIA PHILLIES (B2) (NL 1946–present)

PHILADELPHIA PHILLIES (Bk)
See *PHILADELPHIA WARRIORS (1)*

PHILADELPHIA QUAKERS (B1)
See *PHILADELPHIA PHILLIES (B2)*

PHILADELPHIA QUAKERS (B2)
See *PHILADELPHIA ATHLETICS (3)*

PHILADELPHIA QUAKERS (Bk)
See *PHILADELPHIA WARRIORS (1)*

PHILADELPHIA QUAKERS (F)
Union A.A. of Phoenixville (Pennsylvania), independent,
    by at least 1920. Philadelphia Quakers, independent,
    1921–25.
Philadelphia Quakers (F) (AFL1 1926)
Folded, 1926.

PHILADELPHIA QUAKERS (H)
Pittsburgh Yellow Jackets, amateur, pre-1924.
Pittsburgh Pirates (H) (NHL 1925–30)
Philadelphia Quakers (H) (NHL 1930–31)
Folded, 1931.

PHILADELPHIA RAGE
Richmond Rage (ABLw 1996–97)
Philadelphia Rage (ABLw 1997–98)
Folded during 1998–99 season, 1998.

PHILADELPHIA SEVENTY-SIXERS
Syracuse Nationals (NBL 1946–49; NBA 1949–63)
PHILADELPHIA SEVENTY-SIXERS (NBA 1963–present)

PHILADELPHIA SPARTANS (1)
Philadelphia Spartans (1) (NPSLo 1967)
Folded, 1967.

PHILADELPHIA SPARTANS (2)
Philadelphia Spartans (2) (ASL2 1969–73)
Folded, 1973.

PHILADELPHIA SPHAS
Philadelphia Sphas, independent, 1918–31. Joined Eastern League, 1931–33.
Philadelphia Hebrews (ABL2 1933–37)
Philadelphia Sphas (ABL2 1937–49)
  a.k.a. Philadelphia Colonials, 1939–40
Folded, 1949.

PHILADELPHIA STARS (B)
Philadelphia Stars, independent, 1933.
Philadelphia Stars (B) (NNL2 1934–48; NAL 1949–50)
Folded, 1950.

PHILADELPHIA STARS (F)
See *BALTIMORE STARS (F)*

PHILADELPHIA STING
Philadelphia Sting (MLRH 1998)
Folded, 1998.

PHILADELPHIA TAPERS
Washington Capitols (3) (ABL3 1961–62)
New York Tapers (ABL3 1962)
Philadelphia Tapers (ABL3 1962)
Folded during 1962–63 season, 1962.

PHILADELPHIA THUNDERCATS
Florida ThunderCats, began exhibition play, 1999.
Florida ThunderCats (RH) (W-MLRH 2000 *did not play*)
PHILADELPHIA THUNDERCATS (W-MLRH 2000–present)

PHILADELPHIA TIGERS
Philadelphia Tigers (ECL 1928)
Folded, 1928.

PHILADELPHIA UKRAINIAN NATIONALS
Philadelphia Ukrainian Nationals (ASL2 1957–64, 1965–70)
(Suspended operations, 1964–65.)
Joined German-American League, 1971.
Folded, post-1971.

PHILADELPHIA WARRIORS (1)
Philadelphia Phillies (Bk) (ABL1 1926–27)
  a.k.a. Philadelphia Quakers (Bk)
Philadelphia Warriors (1) (ABL1 1927–28)
  a.k.a. Philadelphia Quakers (Bk)
Folded, 1928.

PHILADELPHIA WARRIORS (2)
See *GOLDEN STATE WARRIORS*

PHILADELPHIA WHITE STOCKINGS
See *PHILADELPHIA PHILLIES (B1)*

PHILADELPHIA WHITES
See *PHILADELPHIA PHILLIES (B1)*

PHILADELPHIA WINGS
PHILADELPHIA WINGS (EPBLL 1987–88; MILL 1989–97; NLL 1998–present)

PHOENIX
(Arizona)

PHOENIX CARDINALS
See *ARIZONA CARDINALS*

PHOENIX COBRAS
See *BUFFALO WINGS (1)*

PHOENIX COYOTES
Winnipeg Jets (WHA 1972–79; NHL 1979–96)
PHOENIX COYOTES (NHL 1996–present)

PHOENIX FIRE
Phoenix Fire (ASL2 1980 *did not play*)
Folded before season, 1980.

PHOENIX INFERNO
See *PHOENIX PRIDE*

PHOENIX MERCURY
PHOENIX MERCURY (WNBA 1997–present)

PHOENIX PRIDE
Phoenix Inferno (MISL 1980–83)
Phoenix Pride (MISL 1983–84)
Folded, 1984.

PHOENIX RACQUETS
Denver Racquets (WTT 1974)

Phoenix Racquets (WTT 1975–78)
Folded, 1978.

PHOENIX ROADRUNNERS
Phoenix Roadrunners (WHA 1974–77)
Folded, 1977.

PHOENIX SMASH
Phoenix Smash (WTT 1992–94)
Folded, 1994.

PHOENIX SUNS
PHOENIX SUNS (NBA 1968–present)

PHOENIX SUNSETS
See *ARIZONA RACQUETS*

PITTSBURGH
(Pennsylvania)

PITTSBURGH ALLEGHENIES
See *PITTSBURGH PIRATES (B)*

PITTSBURGH AMERICANS
Pittsburgh Americans (AFL2 1936–37)
Folded, 1937.

PITTSBURGH BULLS
Pittsburgh Bulls (MILL 1990–93)
(Absorbed part of Washington Wave, 1990.)
Folded, 1993.

PITTSBURGH BURGHERS
Pittsburgh Burghers (PL 1890)
Absorbed by Pittsburgh Innocents, 1891.

PITTSBURGH CANONS
Pittsburgh Canons (ASL2 1972)
Folded, 1972.

PITTSBURGH CONDORS
Pittsburgh Pipers (ABA 1967–68)
Minnesota Pipers (ABA 1968–69)
Pittsburgh Pipers (ABA 1969–70)
Pittsburgh Pioneers (ABA 1970 *did not play*)
Pittsburgh Condors (ABA 1970–72)
Folded, 1972.

PITTSBURGH CRAWFORDS
See *INDIANAPOLIS CRAWFORDS*

PITTSBURGH CROSSEFIRE
Baltimore Thunder (EPBLL 1987–88; MILL 1989–97;
    NLL 1998–99)
(Absorbed part of Washington Wave, 1990.)
PITTSBURGH CROSSEFIRE (NLL 2000–present)

PITTSBURGH GLADIATORS
See *TAMPA BAY STORM*

PITTSBURGH INNOCENTS
See *PITTSBURGH PIRATES (B)*

PITTSBURGH IRONMEN
Pittsburgh Ironmen (BAA 1946–47)
Folded, 1947.

PITTSBURGH KEYSTONES
Pittsburgh Keystones (NNL1 1922)
Folded, 1922.

PITTSBURGH MAULERS
See *BALTIMORE STARS (F)*

PITTSBURGH MINERS
Pittsburgh Miners (ASL2 1975)
Folded, 1975.

PITTSBURGH PENGUINS
PITTSBURGH PENGUINS (NHL 1967–present)

PITTSBURGH PHANTOMS (RH)
Pittsburgh Phantoms (RH) (RHI 1994)
Folded, 1994.

PITTSBURGH PHANTOMS (S)
Pittsburgh Phantoms (S) (NPSLo 1967)
Folded, 1967.

PITTSBURGH PIONEERS
See *PITTSBURGH CONDORS*

PITTSBURGH PIPERS
See *PITTSBURGH CONDORS*

PITTSBURGH PIRATES (B)
Pittsburgh Alleghenies (AA 1882–86; NL 1887–89)
Pittsburgh Innocents (NL 1890)
PITTSBURGH PIRATES (B) (NL 1891–present)

(Absorbed Pittsburgh Burghers, 1891.)
(Absorbed Louisville Colonels [B], 1899.)

PITTSBURGH PIRATES (Bk)
Pittsburgh Pirates, independent, pre-1937.
Pittsburgh Pirates (Bk) (NBL 1937–39)
Folded, 1939.

PITTSBURGH PIRATES (F)
See *PITTSBURGH STEELERS*

PITTSBURGH PIRATES (H)
See *PHILADELPHIA QUAKERS (H)*

PITTSBURGH PITTSFEDS
See *PITTSBURGH REBELS*

PITTSBURGH RAIDERS
See *FLINT DOW A.C.'S*

PITTSBURGH REBELS
Pittsburgh Pittsfeds, minor Federal League (charter member), 1913.
Pittsburgh Pittsfeds (FL 1914)
Pittsburgh Rebels (FL 1914–15)
Folded, 1915.

PITTSBURGH RENAISSANCES
Pittsburgh Renaissances (ABL3 1961–62)
    a.k.a. Pittsburgh Rens
Folded during 1962–63 season, 1962.

PITTSBURGH RENS
See *PITTSBURGH RENAISSANCES*

PITTSBURGH SPIRIT
Pittsburgh Spirit (MISL 1978–80, 1981–86)
(Suspended operations, 1980–81.)
Folded, 1986.

PITTSBURGH STEELERS
Pittsburgh Pirates (F) (NFL 1933–40)
Pittsburgh Steelers (NFL 1941–42)
Merged with Philadelphia Eagles, 1943.
Phil-Pitt (NFL 1943)
    a.k.a. Steagles
Split from Philadelphia Eagles and merged with Chicago Cardinals, 1944.
Card-Pitt (NFL 1944)
Split from Chicago Cardinals, 1945.
PITTSBURGH STEELERS (NFL 1945–present)

PITTSBURGH STINGERS
Pittsburgh Stingers (CISL 1994–95)
Folded, 1995.

PITTSBURGH STOGIES
Chicago Browns (UA 1884)
Pittsburgh Stogies (UA 1884)
Folded, 1884.

PITTSBURGH TRIANGLES
Pittsburgh Triangles (WTT 1974–76)
Folded, 1976.

PORT HURON
(Michigan)

PORT HURON NORTH AMERICANS
See *MICHIGAN BLAST*

PORTLAND
(Oregon)

FOOTBALL CLUB PORTLAND
See *PORTLAND TIMBERS (S)*

PORTLAND BREAKERS
Boston Breakers (USFL 1983)
New Orleans Breakers (USFL 1984)
Portland Breakers (USFL 1985)
Folded, 1985.

PORTLAND CAPITALS
Regina Capitals (WCHL 1921–25)
Portland Capitals (WHL 1925–26)
    a.k.a. Portland Rosebuds (2)
Folded, 1926.

PORTLAND FIRE
PORTLAND FIRE (WNBA 2000–present)

PORTLAND FOREST DRAGONS
See *OKLAHOMA WRANGLERS*

PORTLAND PANTHERS
Portland Panthers (TT 1988–89)
Folded, 1989.

PORTLAND POWER
Portland Power (ABLw 1996–98)
Folded during 1998–99 season, 1998.

PORTLAND PRIDE
See *PORTLAND PYTHONS*

PORTLAND PYTHONS
Portland Pride (CISL 1993–97)
Portland Pythons (PSA 1998; WISL 1999)
Folded, 1999.

PORTLAND RAGE
Portland Rage (RHI 1993–94)
Folded, 1994.

PORTLAND ROSEBUDS (1)
New Westminster Royals (PCHA 1912–14)
Portland Rosebuds (1) (PCHA 1914–17)
     a.k.a. Portland Uncle Sams
Folded, 1917.

PORTLAND ROSEBUDS (2)
See *PORTLAND CAPITALS*

PORTLAND STORM
See *PORTLAND THUNDER*

PORTLAND THUNDER
Portland Storm (WFL 1974)
Portland Thunder (WFL 1975)
Folded during season, 1975.

PORTLAND TIMBERS (S)
Football Club Portland (WACS 1985; WSL 1986–88)
Portland Timbers (S) (WSA 1989; APSL 1990)
Folded, 1990.

PORTLAND TIMBERS (S/IS)
Portland Timbers (S/IS) (NASLo 1975–82) and (NASLi
     1980–82)
Folded, 1982.

PORTLAND TRAIL BLAZERS
PORTLAND TRAIL BLAZERS (NBA 1970–present)

PORTSMOUTH
(Ohio)

PORTSMOUTH SPARTANS
See *DETROIT LIONS*

POTTSVILLE
(Pennsylvania)

POTTSVILLE MAROONS
See *BOSTON BULLDOGS (2)*

PRAGUE
(Czechoslovakia in name only; actually played in USA)

PRAGUE
Prague (ASL1 1933)
Folded, 1933.

PROVIDENCE
(Rhode Island)

PROVIDENCE CLAMDIGGERS
See *NEW BEDFORD WHALERS (2)*

PROVIDENCE GOLD BUGS
See *NEW BEDFORD WHALERS (2)*

PROVIDENCE GRAYS
Providence Grays (NL 1878–85)
     a.k.a. Providence Rhode Islanders
Folded, 1885.

PROVIDENCE RHODE ISLANDERS
See *PROVIDENCE GRAYS*

PROVIDENCE STEAM ROLLER
*Providence, independent, 1916. Providence Steam Roller
     during season, 1916–24.*
Providence Steam Roller (NFL 1925–31)
Independent, 1932.
Folded, 1932.

PROVIDENCE STEAMROLLERS
Providence Steamrollers (BAA 1946–49)
Folded, 1949.

QUEBEC
(Quebec, Canada)

QUEBEC BULLDOGS
See *BROOKLYN AMERICANS*

QUEBEC NORDIQUES
See *COLORADO AVALANCHE*

QUEENS
(New York)

QUEENS BOHEMIANS
Queens Bohemians (ASL1 1932–33)
Folded, 1933.

RACINE
(Racine Avenue, Chicago, Illinois)

RACINE CARDINALS
See *ARIZONA CARDINALS*

RACINE
(Wisconsin)

RACINE BELLES
See *MUSKEGON BELLES*

RACINE LEGION
See *RACINE TORNADOES*

RACINE TORNADOES
Racine Legion, independent, 1915–21.
Racine Legion (NFL 1922–24)
Suspended operations, 1925.
Racine Tornadoes (NFL 1926)
Folded during season, 1926.

RALEIGH
(North Carolina)

RALEIGH EDGE
Raleigh Edge (TT 1990–91; WTT 1992–93)
Folded, 1993.

REGINA
(Saskatchewan, Canada)

REGINA CAPITALS
See *PORTLAND CAPITALS*

RENFREW
(Ontario, Canada)

RENFREW CREAMERY KINGS
See *RENFREW MILLIONAIRES*

RENFREW MILLIONAIRES
Renfrew Millionaires, Eastern Canada Hockey Association, 1909.
Renfrew Millionaires (NHA 1909–12)
    a.k.a. Renfrew Creamery Kings
Folded, 1912.

RHODE ISLAND

RHODE ISLAND OCEANEERS
See *INDIANAPOLIS DAREDEVILS*

RICHMOND
(Indiana)

RICHMOND KING CLOTHIERS
See *CINCINNATI COMELLOS*

RICHMOND KINGS
See *CINCINNATI COMELLOS*

RICHMOND
(Virginia)

RICHMOND RAGE
See *PHILADELPHIA RAGE*

RICHMOND VIRGINIANS
Richmond Virginians, Eastern League, pre-1884.
Richmond Virginians (AA 1884)
Joined Virginia League, 1885–86.
Folded, 1886.

ROCHESTER
(New York)

ROCHESTER BRAVES
Syracuse Braves (AFL2 1936)
Rochester Braves (AFL2 1936)
Folded during season, 1936.

ROCHESTER BRONCOS
See *ROCHESTER HOP-BITTERS*

ROCHESTER CENTRALS
Rochester Centrals, independent, 1905–25.
Rochester Centrals (ABL1 1925–31)
Folded, 1931.

ROCHESTER FLASH
Rochester Flash (ASL2 1981–82; USL 1984)
(Suspended operations, 1983.)
Folded, 1984.

ROCHESTER HOP-BITTERS
Rochester Hop-Bitters (AA 1890)
    a.k.a. Rochester Broncos
*Joined International League, 1891. Joined Eastern
    League, 1892.*
Folded, 1892.

ROCHESTER JEFFERSONS
Rochester Jeffersons, independent, 1908–19.
Rochester Jeffersons (APFA 1920–21; NFL 1922–25)
Folded, 1925.

ROCHESTER KNIGHTHAWKS
ROCHESTER KNIGHTHAWKS (MILL 1995–97; NLL
    1998–present)

ROCHESTER LANCERS
Rochester Lancers (ASL2 1967–69; NASLo 1970–80)
Folded, 1980.

ROCHESTER ROYALS
See *SACRAMENTO KINGS*

ROCHESTER TIGERS
Rochester Tigers, independent, 1935.
Brooklyn Tigers (1) (AFL2 1936)
Rochester Tigers (AFL2 1936–37)
Folded, 1937.

ROCK ISLAND
(Illinois)

ROCK ISLAND INDEPENDENTS
Rock Island Independents, independent, 1911–19.
Rock Island Independents (APFA 1920–21; NFL 1922–
    25; AFL1 1926)
Independent during season, 1926–27.
Folded, 1927.

ROCKFORD
(Illinois)

ROCKFORD FOREST CITYS
Rockford Forest Citys, amateur, 1865–70.
Rockford Forest Citys (NA 1871)
Folded, 1871.

ROCKFORD PEACHES
Rockford Peaches (AAGPBL 1943–54)
Folded, 1954.

ROMA
(Rome, Italy, in name only; actually played in Paterson, New Jersey)

ROMA SOCCER CLUB
Roma Soccer Club (ASL2 1964–68)
Folded, 1968.

SACRAMENTO
(California)

SACRAMENTO ATTACK
See *FLORIDA BOBCATS*

SACRAMENTO CAPITALS
SACRAMENTO CAPITALS (TT 1986–91; WTT 1992–present)

SACRAMENTO GOLD
Sacramento Spirits (ASL2 1976–77)
Sacramento Gold (ASL2 1978–80)
Folded, 1980.

SACRAMENTO GOLD MINERS
See *SAN ANTONIO TEXANS*

SACRAMENTO KINGS
Rochester Seagrams, independent, 1923–32. Joined District Basketball Association, 1932–33. Joined District Basketball League, 1933–36. Independent, 1936–42. Rochester Eber Seagrams, independent, 1942–43. Rochester Pros, independent, 1943–45.
Rochester Royals (NBL 1945–48; BAA 1948–49; NBA 1949–58)
Cincinnati Royals (NBA 1958–72)
Kansas City-Omaha Kings (NBA 1972–75)
Kansas City Kings (NBA 1975–85)
SACRAMENTO KINGS (NBA 1985–present)

SACRAMENTO KNIGHTS
SACRAMENTO KNIGHTS (CISL 1993–97; PSA 1998; WISL 1999–present)

SACRAMENTO MONARCHS
SACRAMENTO MONARCHS (WNBA 1997–present)

SACRAMENTO RIVER RATS
Connecticut Coasters (RHI 1993)
Sacramento River Rats (RHI 1994–97)
Folded, 1997.

SACRAMENTO SENATORS
Sacramento Senators (WSA 1989)
Folded, 1989.

SACRAMENTO SPIRITS
See *SACRAMENTO GOLD*

ST. LOUIS
(Missouri)

ST. LOUIS ACES
ST. LOUIS ACES (WTT 1994–present)

ST. LOUIS ALL-STARS
St. Louis All-Stars (NFL 1923)
Folded, 1923.

ST. LOUIS AMBUSH
Tulsa Ambush (NPSLi 1991–92)
St. Louis Ambush (NPSLi 1992–2000)
Folded, 2000.

ST. LOUIS BLUES
ST. LOUIS BLUES (NHL 1967–present)

ST. LOUIS BOMBERS
St. Louis Bombers (BAA 1946–49; NBA 1949–50)
Folded, 1950.

ST. LOUIS BROWN STOCKINGS (1)
St. Louis Brown Stockings (1) (NA 1875; NL 1876–77)
Folded, 1877.

ST. LOUIS BROWN STOCKINGS (2)
See *ST. LOUIS CARDINALS (B)*

ST. LOUIS BROWNIES
See *ST. LOUIS TERRIERS*

ST. LOUIS BROWNS (1)
See *ST. LOUIS CARDINALS (B)*

ST. LOUIS BROWNS (2)
See *BALTIMORE ORIOLES (B3)*

ST. LOUIS CARDINALS (B)
St. Louis Brown Stockings, amateur, 1881.
St. Louis Brown Stockings (2) (AA 1882)
St. Louis Browns (1) (AA 1883–91; NL 1892–98)
   a.k.a. St. Louis Maroons (1)
St. Louis Perfectos (NL 1899)
Absorbed Cleveland Spiders, 1900.
ST. LOUIS CARDINALS (B) (NL 1900–present)

ST. LOUIS CARDINALS (F)
See *ARIZONA CARDINALS*

ST. LOUIS EAGLES (H)
Ottawa Silver Seven, amateur, 1884–85. Ottawa Generals,
  Amateur Hockey Association, 1886–1908. Ottawa
  Senators, Eastern Canada Hockey Association, 1908–
  09. Joined Canadian Hockey Association, 1909.
Ottawa Senators (1) (NHA 1909–17; NHL 1917–31,
  1932–34)
(Suspended operations, 1931–32.)
St. Louis Eagles (H) (NHL 1934–35)
Folded, 1935.

ST. LOUIS EAGLES (T)
See *ST. LOUIS SLIMS*

ST. LOUIS FROGS
St. Louis Mules (ASL2 1972)
St. Louis Frogs (ASL2 1972)
Folded, 1972.

ST. LOUIS GIANTS
St. Louis Giants, independent, 1909–19.
St. Louis Giants (NNL1 1920–21)
Folded, 1921.

ST. LOUIS GUNNERS
(In part St. Louis Gunners, independent, 1931–33.)
Cincinnati Reds (F) (NFL 1933–34)
Merged with independent St. Louis Gunners, 1934.
St. Louis Gunners (NFL 1934)
Minor league team, 1935–40.
Folded, 1940.

ST. LOUIS HAWKS
See *ATLANTA HAWKS*

ST. LOUIS MAROONS (1)
See *ST. LOUIS CARDINALS (B)*

ST. LOUIS MAROONS (2)
See *INDIANAPOLIS HOOSIERS (3)*

ST. LOUIS MINERS
See *ST. LOUIS TERRIERS*

ST. LOUIS MULES
See *ST. LOUIS FROGS*

ST. LOUIS PERFECTOS
See *ST. LOUIS CARDINALS (B)*

ST. LOUIS RAMS
Cleveland Rams (AFL2 1936; NFL 1937–42, 1944–45)

(Suspended operations, 1943.)
Los Angeles Rams (NFL 1946–95)
ST. LOUIS RAMS (NFL 1995–present)

ST. LOUIS RAVENS
See *BALTIMORE ORIOLES (B3)*

ST. LOUIS RED STOCKINGS
St. Louis Red Stockings, amateur, 1873–74.
St. Louis Red Stockings (NA 1875)
    a.k.a. St. Louis Reds
Amateur during season, 1875.
Folded, post-1875.

ST. LOUIS REDS
See *ST. LOUIS RED STOCKINGS*

ST. LOUIS SLIMS
St. Louis Eagles (T) (TT 1984)
St. Louis Slims (TT 1985)
Folded, 1985.

ST. LOUIS SLOUFEDS
See *ST. LOUIS TERRIERS*

ST. LOUIS SPIRIT
St. Louis Storm (MISL 1989–90)
St. Louis Spirit (MSL 1990–92)
Folded, 1992.

ST. LOUIS STAMPEDE
St. Louis Stampede (AFL 1995–96)
Folded, 1996.

ST. LOUIS STARS (B1)
St. Louis Stars (B1) (NNL1 1922–31)
Folded, 1931.

ST. LOUIS STARS (B2)
See *HARRISBURG-ST. LOUIS STARS*

ST. LOUIS STARS (S)
See *CALIFORNIA SURF*

ST. LOUIS STEAMERS (1)
St. Louis Steamers (1) (MISL 1979–88)
Folded, 1988.

ST. LOUIS STEAMERS (2)
ST. LOUIS STEAMERS (2) (WISL 2000–present)

ST. LOUIS STORM
See *ST. LOUIS SPIRIT*

ST. LOUIS TERRIERS
St. Louis Terriers (FL 1914–15)
    a.k.a. St. Louis Brownies
    a.k.a. St. Louis Miners
    a.k.a. St. Louis Sloufeds
Folded, 1915.

ST. LOUIS VIPERS
St. Louis Vipers (RHI 1993–97, 1999)
(Suspended operations, 1998.)
Folded, 1999.

SPIRITS OF ST. LOUIS
See *UTAH ROCKIES*

ST. MARY'S
(St. Mary's Church, Brooklyn, New York)

ST. MARY'S CELTICS (1)
Brooklyn Celtics (S1) (ASL2 1933–35)
St. Mary's Celtics (1) (ASL2 1935–40)
Folded, 1940.

ST. MARY'S CELTICS (2)
St. Mary's Celtics (2) (ASL2 1941–42)
Folded, 1942.

ST. PAUL
(Minnesota)

ST. PAUL SAINTS
St. Paul Apostles, Northwestern League (charter member),
    1884.
St. Paul Saints (UA 1884)
    a.k.a. St. Paul Whitecaps
Folded, 1884.

ST. PAUL WHITECAPS
See *ST. PAUL SAINTS*

SALT LAKE
(Salt Lake City, Utah)

SALT LAKE STING
Salt Lake Sting (APSL 1990–91)
Folded during season, 1991.

SAN ANTONIO
(Texas)

SAN ANTONIO FORCE
San Antonio Force (AFL 1992)
Folded, 1992.

SAN ANTONIO GUNSLINGERS (Bk)
See *SAN ANTONIO SPURS*

SAN ANTONIO GUNSLINGERS (F)
San Antonio Gunslingers (F) (USFL 1984–85)
Folded, 1985.

SAN ANTONIO RACQUETS
San Antonio Racquets (TT 1985–91; WTT 1992–94)
Folded, 1994.

SAN ANTONIO SPURS
Dallas Chaparrals (ABA 1967–70)
Texas Chaparrals (ABA 1970–71)
Dallas Chaparrals (ABA 1971–73)
San Antonio Gunslingers (Bk) (ABA 1973 *did not play*)
SAN ANTONIO SPURS (ABA 1973–76; NBA 1976–
    present)

SAN ANTONIO TEXANS
Sacramento Gold Miners (CFL 1994)
San Antonio Texans (CFL 1995)
Folded, 1995.

SAN ANTONIO THUNDER
See *TULSA ROUGHNECKS*

SAN ANTONIO WINGS
Washington Ambassadors (WFL 1974 *did not play*)
Virginia Ambassadors (WFL 1974 *did not play*)
Florida Suns (WFL 1974 *did not play*)
Florida Blazers (WFL 1974)

San Antonio Wings (WFL 1975)
Folded during season, 1975.

SAN DIEGO
(California)

SAN DIEGO BARRACUDAS
San Diego Barracudas (RHI 1993–96)
Folded, 1996.

SAN DIEGO BUDS
San Diego Friars (WTT 1975–78; TT 1981–83)
(Suspended operations, 1979–80.)
San Diego Buds (TT 1984–85)
Folded, 1985.

SAN DIEGO CHARGERS
Los Angeles Chargers (AFL4 1960)
SAN DIEGO CHARGERS (AFL4 1961–70; NFL 1970–
    present)

SAN DIEGO CLIPPERS
See *LOS ANGELES CLIPPERS*

SAN DIEGO CONQUISTADORS
See *SAN DIEGO SAILS*

SAN DIEGO FRIARS
See *SAN DIEGO BUDS*

SAN DIEGO JAWS
See *SAN DIEGO SOCKERS*

SAN DIEGO MARINERS
New York Raiders (WHA 1972–73)
New York Golden Blades (WHA 1973)
Jersey Knights (WHA 1973–74)
San Diego Mariners (WHA 1974–77)
Folded, 1977.

SAN DIEGO NOMADS
San Diego Nomads (WSL 1986–88; WSA 1989; APSL
    1990)
Amateur, 1991.
Folded, post-1991.

SAN DIEGO PADRES
SAN DIEGO PADRES (NL 1969–present)

SAN DIEGO ROCKETS
See *HOUSTON ROCKETS*

SAN DIEGO SAILS
San Diego Conquistadors (ABA 1972–75)
San Diego Sails (ABA 1975)
Folded during 1975–76 season, 1975.

SAN DIEGO SOCKERS
Baltimore Comets (NASLo 1974–75)
San Diego Jaws (NASLo 1976)
Las Vegas Quicksilvers (NASLo 1977)
SAN DIEGO SOCKERS (NASLo 1978–84) and (NASLi
    1980–82; MISL 1982–83; NASLi 1983–84; MISL
    1984–90; MSL 1990–92; CISL 1993–96; WISL 2001–
    present)
(Suspended operations, 1997–2000.)

SAN DIEGO TOROS
Los Angeles Toros (NPSLo 1967)
San Diego Toros (NASLo 1968)
Folded, 1968.

SAN FRANCISCO
(California)

SAN FRANCISCO FOG
See *KANSAS CITY COMETS*

SAN FRANCISCO FORTY-NINERS
SAN FRANCISCO FORTY-NINERS (AAFC 1946–49;
    NFL 1950–present)

SAN FRANCISCO GALES
*ADO (Den Haag [The Hague], Zuid Holland, Nether-
    lands), independent, pre-1967.*
San Francisco Gales (USA 1967)
Absorbed by Vancouver Royals, 1968.

SAN FRANCISCO GIANTS
Troy Trojans (NL 1879–82)
New York Gothams (B) (NL 1883–84)
    a.k.a. New York Green Stockings
New York Giants (B1) (NL 1885–1957)
(Absorbed New York Giants [B2], 1891.)
SAN FRANCISCO GIANTS (NL 1958–present)

SAN FRANCISCO SAINTS
See *OAKLAND OAKS (1)*

SAN FRANCISCO SHARKS
See *COLORADO AVALANCHE*

SAN FRANCISCO WARRIORS
See *GOLDEN STATE WARRIORS*

SAN FRANCISCO BAY
(California)

SAN FRANCISCO BAY BLACKHAWKS
San Jose Earthquakes (S/IS) (NASLo 1974–82) and (NASLi 1980–82)
Golden Bay Earthquakes (NASLo 1983–84) and (MISL 1982–83; NASLi 1983–84)
San Jose Earthquakes (S/IS) (WACS 1985; WSL 1986–88)
San Francisco Bay Blackhawks (WSA 1989; APSL 1990–92)
Folded, 1992.

SAN JOSE
(California)

SAN JOSE CLASH
See *SAN JOSE EARTHQUAKES (S)*

SAN JOSE EARTHQUAKES (S)
San Jose Clash (MLS 1996–99)
SAN JOSE EARTHQUAKES (S) (MLS 2000–present)

SAN JOSE EARTHQUAKES (S/IS)
See *SAN FRANCISCO BAY BLACKHAWKS*

SAN JOSE GRIZZLIES
San Jose Grizzlies (CISL 1994–95)
Folded, 1995.

SAN JOSE LASERS
San Jose Lasers (ABLw 1996–98)
Folded during 1998–99 season, 1998.

SAN JOSE RHINOS
San Jose Rhinos (RHI 1994–97, 1999)
(Suspended operations, 1998.)
Folded, 1999.

SAN JOSE SABERCATS
SAN JOSE SABERCATS (AFL 1995–present)

SAN JOSE SHARKS
SAN JOSE SHARKS (NHL 1991–present)

SANTA BARBARA
(California)

REAL SANTA BARBARA
Real Santa Barbara (WSA 1989; APSL 1990)
Folded, 1990.

SANTA BARBARA CONDORS
Santa Barbara Condors (ASL2 1977)
Folded during season, 1977.

SARATOGA
(Saratoga Springs, New York)

SARATOGA HARLEM YANKEES
See *GLENS FALLS-SARATOGA*

SASKATCHEWAN
(Canada)

SASKATCHEWAN ROUGHRIDERS
Regina Rugby Club, Saskatchewan Rugby Football Union, 1910. Joined Canada Rugby Football Union, 1911–23. Regina Roughriders, CRFU, 1924–35. Joined newly renamed Western Interprovincial Football Union, 1936–45. Saskatchewan Roughriders, WIFU, 1946–55. (Name change became legal in 1950.)
SASKATCHEWAN ROUGHRIDERS (CFC 1956–57; CFL 1958–present)

SASKATOON
(Saskatchewan, Canada)

SASKATOON CRESCENTS
See *SASKATOON SHEIKS*

SASKATOON SHEIKS
Saskatoon Crescents, independent, 1920–21.
Saskatoon Crescents (WCHL 1921–23)
Saskatoon Sheiks (WCHL 1923–25; WHL 1925–26)
Independent, 1926–approximately 1932. Member of Prairie League, at least 1932–33.
Folded, post-1933.

SCHENECTADY
(New York)

SCHENECTADY PACKERS
Schenectady Packers (ABL2 1949)
Folded during season, 1949.

SCHENECTADY YANKEES
Schenectady Yankees (ABL2 1951–52)
Folded, 1952.

SCHENECTADY COUNTY
(New York)

SCHENECTADY COUNTY ELECTRICS
New York OTBzz (WTT 1995–98)
SCHENECTADY COUNTY ELECTRICS (WTT 1999–present)

SCOTLAND

SCOTLAND EAGLES
Scotland Eagles (MLRH 1997)
Folded, 1997.

(SCOTS-AMERICANS)
(No location name: Kearny, New Jersey)

SCOTS-AMERICANS
Kearny Scots (ASL2 1933–44, 1946–47, 1949–51)
(Suspended operations, 1944–46, 1947–49.)
Scots-Americans (ASL2 1951–53)
Folded, 1953.

SCRANTON
(Pennsylvania)

SCRANTON MINERS
Scranton Miners (ABL2 1947, 1948–53)
(Suspended operations during season, 1947–48.)
Folded, 1953.

SEA-PORT
(Seattle-Portland, Washington and Oregon)

SEA-PORT CASCADES
See *SEATTLE CASCADES*

SEATTLE
(Washington)

FOOTBALL CLUB SEATTLE
See *SEATTLE STORM (S)*

SEATTLE CASCADES
Sea-Port Cascades (WTT 1977)
Seattle Cascades (WTT 1978)
Folded, 1978.

SEATTLE MARINERS
SEATTLE MARINERS (AL 1977–present)

SEATTLE METROPOLITANS
Seattle Metropolitans (PCHA 1916–24)
Folded, 1924.

SEATTLE PILOTS
See *MILWAUKEE BREWERS (5)*

SEATTLE REIGN
Seattle Reign (ABLw 1996–98)
Folded during 1998–99 season, 1998.

SEATTLE SEADOGS
Seattle SeaDogs (CISL 1995–97)
Folded, 1997.

SEATTLE SEAHAWKS
SEATTLE SEAHAWKS (NFL 1976–present)

SEATTLE SOUNDERS (S)
Seattle Sounders (S) (APSL 1994)
Continued when APSL became A-League, 1995–present.

SEATTLE SOUNDERS (S/IS)
Seattle Sounders (S/IS) (NASLo 1974–83) and (NASLi 1980–82)
Folded, 1983.

SEATTLE STORM (Bk)
SEATTLE STORM (Bk) (WNBA 2000–present)

SEATTLE STORM (S)
Football Club Seattle (WACS 1985)
Seattle Storm (S) (WSL 1986–88; WSA 1989; APSL 1990)
Folded, 1990.

SEATTLE SUPERSONICS
SEATTLE SUPERSONICS (NBA 1967–present)

SHAWSHEEN
(Shawsheen County, Massachusetts)

SHAWSHEEN INDIANS
Shawsheen Indians (ASL1 1925–26)
Folded during season, 1926.

SHEBOYGAN
(Wisconsin)

SHEBOYGAN RED SKINS
Sheboygan Red Skins (NBL 1938–49; NBA 1949–50)
Joined National Professional Basketball League, 1950–51. Folded, 1951.

SHEFFIELD
(South Yorkshire, England)

SHEFFIELD STRIKERS
Sheffield Strikers (WISL 1999 *did not play*)
Withdrew with England's Professional Indoor Football League before season, 1999. Folded with PIFL before season, 1999.

SHREVEPORT
(Louisiana)

SHREVEPORT PIRATES
Shreveport Pirates (CFL 1994–95)
Folded, 1995.

SHREVEPORT STEAMER
Houston Texans (1) (WFL 1974)
Shreveport Steamer (WFL 1974–75)
Folded during season, 1975.

SOUTH BEND
(Indiana)

SOUTH BEND BLUE SOX
South Bend Blue Sox (AAGPBL 1943–54)
Folded, 1954.

SOUTH CAROLINA

SOUTH CAROLINA FIRE ANTS
South Carolina Fire Ants (MLRH 1998)
Folded, 1998.

SOUTH FLORIDA
(Florida)

SOUTH FLORIDA BREAKERS
See *WELLINGTON ACES*

SOUTH FLORIDA SUN
Fort Lauderdale Sun (USL 1984)
South Florida Sun (USL 1985)
Folded, 1985.

SOUTHERN CALIFORNIA
(California)

SOUTHERN CALIFORNIA LAZERS
Southern California Lazers (ASL2 1978)
Folded, 1978.

SOUTHERN CALIFORNIA SUN
Southern California Sun (WFL 1974–75)
Folded during season, 1975.

(SOVIETS)
(No location name: Soviet Union)

SOVIETS
Soviets (WTT 1977)
Folded, 1977.

SPOKANE
(Washington)

SPOKANE CANARIES
See *VICTORIA COUGARS*

SPRINGFIELD
(Illinois)

SPRINGFIELD SALLIES
Springfield Sallies (AAGPBL 1948)
Folded, 1948.

SPRINGFIELD
(Massachusetts)

SPRINGFIELD BABES
Springfield Babes (ASL1 1926)
Folded during season, 1926.

SPRINGFIELD
(Missouri)

SPRINGFIELD LASERS
SPRINGFIELD LASERS (WTT 1996–present)

STAPLETON
(Staten Island, New York)

STAPLETON STAPES
See *STATEN ISLAND STAPES*

STATEN ISLAND
(New York)

STATEN ISLAND STAPES
Staten Island Stapletons, independent, 1915–28.
Staten Island Stapletons (NFL 1929–30)
Staten Island Stapes (NFL 1931–32)
    a.k.a. Stapleton Stapes
Independent, 1933.
Folded, 1933.

STATEN ISLAND STAPLETONS
See *STATEN ISLAND STAPES*

(STEAGLES)
(No location name: Philadelphia and Pittsburgh, Pennsylvania)

STEAGLES *(**MERGED TEAM**)*
See *PHILADELPHIA EAGLES* and *PITTSBURGH STEELERS*

SUN BELT
(Southeastern USA; played in New Orleans, Louisiana)

SUN BELT NETS
Sun Belt Nets (WTT 1978)
Folded, 1978.

SWINDON
(Wiltshire, England)

SWINDON SCREAMING EAGLES
Swindon Screaming Eagles (MLRH 1998)
Folded, 1998.

SYRACUSE
(New York)

SYRACUSE ALL-AMERICANS
Syracuse All-Americans (ABL1 1929–30)
Folded during season, 1930.

SYRACUSE BRAVES
See *ROCHESTER BRAVES*

SYRACUSE NATIONALS
See *PHILADELPHIA SEVENTY-SIXERS*

SYRACUSE SCORPIONS
Syracuse Scorpions (ASL2 1969–71)
Folded, 1971.

SYRACUSE SMASH
SYRACUSE SMASH (NLL 1998–present)

SYRACUSE STARS (1)
Syracuse Stars, International League, 1878.
Syracuse Stars (1) (NL 1879)
Folded, 1879.

SYRACUSE STARS (2)
Syracuse Stars, New York State League (charter member),
    1885. Joined International League, 1886–87. Joined
    International Association (charter member), 1888–89.
Syracuse Stars (2) (AA 1890)
Joined Eastern Association (charter member), 1891–92.
    Utica during season, 1892.
Folded, 1892.

SYRACUSE SUNS
Syracuse Suns (ASL2 1973–74)
Folded, 1974.

TACOMA
(Washington)

TACOMA STARS (1)
Denver Avalanche (MISL 1980–82)
Suspended operations, 1982–83.
Tacoma Stars (1) (MISL 1983–88)
Folded, 1988.

TACOMA STARS (2)
Tacoma Stars (2) (MISL 1988–90; MSL 1990–92)
Folded, 1992.

TACOMA TIDES
Tacoma Tides (ASL2 1976)
Folded, 1976.

TAMPA BAY
(Florida)

TAMPA BAY ACTION
Tampa Bay Action (WTT 1992)
Folded, 1992.

TAMPA BAY BANDITS
Tampa Bay Bandits (USFL 1983–85)
Folded, 1985.

TAMPA BAY BUCCANEERS
TAMPA BAY BUCCANEERS (NFL 1976–present)

TAMPA BAY DEVIL RAYS
TAMPA BAY DEVIL RAYS (AL 1998–present)

TAMPA BAY LIGHTNING
TAMPA BAY LIGHTNING (NHL 1992–present)

TAMPA BAY MUTINY
TAMPA BAY MUTINY (MLS 1996–present)

TAMPA BAY ROLLIN' THUNDER
Tampa Bay Rollin' Thunder (MLRH 1998)
Folded, 1998.

TAMPA BAY ROWDIES (IS)
Tampa Bay Rowdies (IS) (AISA 1986–87)
Folded, 1987.

TAMPA BAY ROWDIES (S)
Tampa Bay Rowdies (S) (ASL3 1988–89; APSL 1990–
    93)
Folded, 1993.

TAMPA BAY ROWDIES (S/IS)
Tampa Bay Rowdies (S/IS) (NASLo 1975–84) and
    (NASLi 1979–82, 1983–84)
Folded, 1984.

TAMPA BAY STORM
Pittsburgh Gladiators (AFL 1987–90)
TAMPA BAY STORM (AFL 1991–present)

TAMPA BAY TERROR
Tampa Bay Terror (NPSLi 1995–97)
Folded, 1997.

TAMPA BAY TRITONS
Tampa Bay Tritons (RHI 1994)
Folded, 1994.

TENNESSEE

TENNESSEE OILERS
See *TENNESSEE TITANS*

TENNESSEE TITANS
Houston Oilers (AFL4 1960–70; NFL 1970–97)
Tennessee Oilers (NFL 1997–99)
TENNESSEE TITANS (NFL 1999–present)

TEXAS

TEXAS CHAPARRALS
See *SAN ANTONIO SPURS*

TEXAS RANGERS
Washington Senators (B4) (AL 1961–71)
TEXAS RANGERS (AL 1972–present)

TEXAS TERROR
See *HOUSTON THUNDERBEARS*

(TITANS)
(No location name: Orlando, Florida)

TITANS
Titans (WRHL 1993)
Folded, 1993.

TODD
(Todd Shipyards, Brooklyn, New York)

TODD SHIPYARDS
Todd Shipyards (ASL1 1921–22)
Folded, 1922.

TOLEDO
(Ohio)

TOLEDO BLUE STOCKINGS
Toledo Blue Stockings, Northwestern League (charter member), 1883.
Toledo Blue Stockings (AA 1884)
Folded, 1884.

TOLEDO CHEVIES
See *TOLEDO JIM WHITE CHEVROLETS*

TOLEDO CRAWFORDS
See *INDIANAPOLIS CRAWFORDS*

TOLEDO JEEPS
See *WATERLOO HAWKS*

TOLEDO JIM WHITE CHEVROLETS
Toledo Jim White Chevrolets (NBL 1941–42)
 a.k.a. Toledo Chevies
Folded during 1942–43 season, 1942.

TOLEDO MAROONS
See *KENOSHA MAROONS*

TOLEDO MAUMEES
Toledo Maumees (AA 1890)
Folded, 1890.

TOLEDO PRIDE
Toledo Pride (AISA 1986–87)
Folded, 1987.

TOLEDO RED MAN TOBACCOS
Toledo Red Man Tobaccos (ABL1 1930–31)
Folded, 1931.

TOLEDO TIGERS
Toledo Tigers (NNL1 1923)
Folded during season, 1923.

TONAWANDA
(New York)

TONAWANDA KARDEX
All-Tonawanda Lumberjacks, a.k.a. All-Tonawandas, independent, 1920.
Tonawanda Kardex (APFA 1921)
    a.k.a. Tonawanda Lumbermen
Folded, 1921.

TONAWANDA LUMBERMEN
See *TONAWANDA KARDEX*

TORONTO
(Ontario, Canada)

TORONTO ARENAS
See *TORONTO MAPLE LEAFS*

TORONTO ARGONAUTS
Argonaut Rowing Club, 1872–82. Toronto Argonauts, Ontario Rugby Football Union, 1883–1906. Joined Interprovincial Rugby Football Union, 1907–55.
TORONTO ARGONAUTS (CFC 1956–57; CFL 1958–present)

TORONTO BLIZZARD (1)
Metros Croatia, independent, 1956–70.
Toronto Metros (NASLo 1971–74)
Merged with semipro Croatia, 1975.
Toronto Metros-Croatia (NASLo 1975–81) and (NASLi 1980–82)
Toronto Blizzard (1) (NASLo 1982–84)
Joined Canadian National Soccer League, 1985.
Folded, post-1985.

TORONTO BLIZZARD (2)
Toronto Blizzard, Canadian Soccer League (charter member), 1987–92.
Toronto Blizzard (2) (APSL 1993)
Folded, 1993.

TORONTO BLUE JAYS
TORONTO BLUE JAYS (AL 1977–present)

TORONTO BLUESHIRTS
Toronto Blueshirts (NHA 1912–17)
Folded, 1917.

TORONTO CITY
Hibernian Football Club (Edinburgh, Scotland), independent, pre-1967.
Toronto City (USA 1967)
Folded, 1967.

TORONTO FALCONS
Toronto Falcons (NPSLo 1967; NASLo 1968)
Folded, 1968.

TORONTO FORCE
Toronto Torpedoes (MLRH 1998)
Toronto Force (MLRH 1999 *did not play*)
Folded before season, 1999.

TORONTO HUSKIES
Toronto Huskies (BAA 1946–47)
Folded, 1947.

TORONTO MAPLE LEAFS
Toronto Arenas, independent, 1916–17.
Toronto Arenas (NHL 1917–19)
Toronto St. Patricks (NHL 1919–26)
TORONTO MAPLE LEAFS (NHL 1926–present)

TORONTO METROS
See *TORONTO BLIZZARD (1)*

TORONTO METROS-CROATIA
See *TORONTO BLIZZARD (1)*

TORONTO NORTHMEN
See *MEMPHIS GRIZZLIES*

TORONTO ONTARIOS
See *TORONTO SHAMROCKS*

TORONTO PLANETS
Toronto Planets (RHI 1993)
Folded, 1993.

TORONTO RAPTORS
TORONTO RAPTORS (NBA 1995–present)

TORONTO ROCK
Ontario Raiders (NLL 1998)
TORONTO ROCK (NLL 1998–present)

TORONTO ROCKETS
*North York Rockets (Ontario), Canadian Soccer League
    (charter member), 1987–92. Canadian National Soc-
    cer League (semipro), 1993.*
Toronto Rockets (APSL 1994)
Folded, 1994.

TORONTO ST. PATRICKS
See *TORONTO MAPLE LEAFS*

TORONTO SHAMROCKS
Toronto Tecumsehs (NHA 1912–13)
Toronto Ontarios (NHA 1913–14)
Toronto Shamrocks (NHA 1914–16)
Folded, 1916.

TORONTO SHOOTING STARS
Toronto Shooting Stars (NPSLi 1996–97)
Folded, 1997.

TORONTO TECUMSEHS
See *TORONTO SHAMROCKS*

TORONTO THUNDERHAWKS
TORONTO THUNDERHAWKS (NPSLi 2000–present)

TORONTO TOROS
See *BIRMINGHAM BULLS*

TORONTO TORPEDOES
See *TORONTO FORCE*

TORONTO WAVE
Edmonton Sled Dogs (RHI 1994)
Orlando RollerGators (RHI 1995)
Suspended operations, 1996.
Hamilton Hammers (RHI 1997 *did not play*)
Toronto Wave (RHI 1997 *did not play*)
Folded before season, 1997.

TORONTO-BUFFALO
(Ontario, Canada, and New York)

TORONTO-BUFFALO ROYALS
Toronto-Buffalo Royals (WTT 1974)
Folded, 1974.

TRENTON
(New Jersey)

TRENTON AMERICANS
Trenton Americans (ASL2 1953–55)
Folded, 1955.

TRENTON ATHLETICS
Trenton Athletics (ASL2 1948–51)
Folded, 1951.

TRENTON BENGALS (1)
See *TRENTON ROYAL BENGALS*

TRENTON BENGALS (2)
See *PASSAIC RED DEVILS*

TRENTON HIGHLANDERS
Trenton Highlanders (ASL2 1938–39)
Folded, 1939.

TRENTON MOOSE (1)
Trenton Moose, Eastern League, 1932–33.
Trenton Moose (1) (ABL2 1933–34)
Folded, 1934.

TRENTON MOOSE (2)
See *PASSAIC RED DEVILS*

TRENTON ROYAL BENGALS
Trenton Royal Bengals (ABL1 1928–29)
    a.k.a. Trenton Bengals (1)
Folded, 1929.

TRENTON TIGERS
Passaic Bengal Tigers (ABL2 1941)
Trenton Tigers (ABL2 1941–50)
Folded, 1950.

TRI-CITIES
(Davenport, Iowa; Moline, Illinois; and Rock Island, Illinois)

TRI-CITIES BLACKHAWKS
See *ATLANTA HAWKS*

TROY
(New York)

TROY CELTICS (1)
See *BROOKLYN CELTICS (Bk2)*

TROY CELTICS (2)
Troy Celtics (2) (ABL2 1946–47)
Folded, 1947.

TROY HAYMAKERS (B)
Union of Troy, a.k.a. Troy Haymakers, amateur National Association, approximately 1869–70.
Troy Haymakers (B) (NA 1871–72)
Folded during season, 1872.

TROY HAYMAKERS (Bk)
See *BROOKLYN CELTICS (Bk2)*

TROY TROJANS
See *SAN FRANCISCO GIANTS*

TULSA
(Oklahoma)

TULSA AMBUSH
See *ST. LOUIS AMBUSH*

TULSA ROUGHNECKS
San Antonio Thunder (NASLo 1975–76)
Team Hawaii (NASLo 1977)
Tulsa Roughnecks (NASLo 1978–84) and (NASLi 1979–82, 1983–84)
Folded, 1984.

TULSA TORNADOES
Tulsa Tornadoes (USL 1985)
Folded, 1985.

(TURBOS)
(No location name: Orlando, Florida)

TURBOS
Turbos (WRHL 1993)
Folded, 1993.

(TYPHOON)
(No location name: Orlando, Florida)

TYPHOON
Typhoon (WRHL 1993)
Folded, 1993.

UHRIK
(Uhrik Trucking Company, Philadelphia, Pennsylvania)

UHRIK TRUCKERS
Philadelphia Rifle Club, independent, 1920s–32. First German Soccer Club, independent, 1933.
Philadelphia Germans (ASL2 1933–41)
   a.k.a. Philadelphia German-Americans
Philadelphia Americans (ASL2 1941–53)
Uhrik Truckers (ASL2 1953–65)
Folded, 1965.

UNION CITY
(New Jersey)

UNION CITY REDS
See *JERSEY REDS*

UTAH

UTAH FREEZZ
UTAH FREEZZ (WISL 1999–present)

UTAH GOLDEN SPIKERS
Utah Pioneers (ASL2 1976)
Utah Golden Spikers (ASL2 1976)
Folded, 1976.

UTAH JAZZ
New Orleans Jazz (NBA 1974–79)
UTAH JAZZ (NBA 1979–present)

UTAH PIONEERS
See *UTAH GOLDEN SPIKERS*

UTAH ROCKIES
Houston Mavericks (ABA 1967–69)
Carolina Cougars (ABA 1969–74)
Spirits of St. Louis (ABA 1974–76)
Utah Rockies (ABA 1976 *did not play*)
Folded before 1976–77 season, 1976.

UTAH ROLLERBEES
See *UTAH SUN DOGS*

UTAH STARS
Anaheim Amigos (ABA 1967–68)
Los Angeles Stars (ABA 1968–70)
Utah Stars (ABA 1970–75)
Folded during 1975–76 season, 1975.

UTAH STARZZ
UTAH STARZZ (WNBA 1997–present)

UTAH SUN DOGS
Utah Rollerbees (RHI 1993)
Las Vegas Flash (RHI 1994)
Utah Rollerbees (RHI 1995 *did not play*)
Suspended operations, 1995–98.
Utah Sun Dogs (RHI 1999 *did not play*)
Folded before season, 1999.

UTICA
(New York)

UTICA PROS
Utica Pros (ABL2 1950–51)
Folded, 1951.

VAIL
(Colorado)

VAIL EAGLES
Vail Eagles (WTT 1992)
Folded, 1992.

VANCOUVER
(British Columbia, Canada)

VANCOUVER BLAZERS
See *CALGARY COWBOYS*

VANCOUVER CANUCKS
VANCOUVER CANUCKS (NHL 1970–present)

VANCOUVER EIGHTY-SIXERS
Vancouver Eighty-Sixers, Canadian Soccer League
  (charter member), 1987–92.
Vancouver Eighty-Sixers (APSL 1993–94)
Continued when APSL became A-League, 1995–present.

VANCOUVER GRIZZLIES
Vancouver Mounties (NBA 1995 *did not play*)
VANCOUVER GRIZZLIES (NBA 1995–present)

VANCOUVER MAROONS
Vancouver Millionaires (PCHA 1912–24)
Vancouver Maroons (WCHL 1924–25; WHL 1925–26)
Folded, 1926.

VANCOUVER MILLIONAIRES
See *VANCOUVER MAROONS*

VANCOUVER MOUNTIES
See *VANCOUVER GRIZZLIES*

VANCOUVER ROYAL CANADIANS
See *VANCOUVER ROYALS*

VANCOUVER ROYALS
Sunderland Football Club (Durham, England), independ-
  ent, pre-1967.
Vancouver Royal Canadians (USA 1967)
Absorbed San Francisco Gales, 1968.
Vancouver Royals (NASLo 1968)
Folded, 1968.

VANCOUVER VOODOO
Vancouver VooDoo (RHI 1993–96)
Folded, 1996.

VANCOUVER WHITECAPS
Vancouver Whitecaps (NASLo 1974–84) and (NASLi
    1980–82, 1983–84)
Folded, 1984.

VICTORIA
(British Columbia, Canada)

VICTORIA ARISTOCRATS
See *VICTORIA COUGARS*

VICTORIA COUGARS
Victoria Senators (PCHA 1912–13)
Victoria Aristocrats (PCHA 1913–16)
Spokane Canaries (PCHA 1916–17)
Victoria Senators (PCHA 1917–19)
Victoria Cougars (PCHA 1919–24; WCHL 1924–25;
    WHL 1925–26)
Folded, 1926.

VICTORIA RIPTIDE
Victoria Riptide (WACS 1985)
Independent, 1986.
Folded, post-1986.

VICTORIA SENATORS
See *VICTORIA COUGARS*

VIRGINIA

VIRGINIA AMBASSADORS
See *SAN ANTONIO WINGS*

VIRGINIA CAPITOL CAVALIERS
See *WASHINGTON CAVALIERS*

VIRGINIA SQUIRES
Oakland Americans (ABA 1967 *did not play*)
Oakland Oaks (2) (ABA 1967–69)
Washington Capitols (4) (ABA 1969–70)
Virginia Squires (ABA 1970–76)
Folded, 1976.

VIRGINIA VULTURES
Virginia Vultures (MLRH 1998)
Folded, 1998.

VIRGINIA WINGS
Virginia Wings, began exhibition play, 1999.
VIRGINIA WINGS (W-MLRH 2000–present)

WARREN
(Pennsylvania)

WARREN PENN OILERS
See *DETROIT EAGLES*

WARREN PENNS
See *DETROIT EAGLES*

WASHINGTON
(District of Columbia)

WASHINGTON AMBASSADORS
See *SAN ANTONIO WINGS*

WASHINGTON BLACK SENATORS
Washington Black Senators (NNL2 1938)
Folded during season, 1938.

WASHINGTON BREWERS
Washington Heurichs (ABL2 1938–39)
Washington Heurich Brewers (ABL2 1939–40)
Washington Brewers (ABL2 1940–42)
Folded, 1942.

WASHINGTON BRITTANICA
See *MINNESOTA STRIKERS*

WASHINGTON BULLETS
See *WASHINGTON WIZARDS*

WASHINGTON CAPITALS
WASHINGTON CAPITALS (NHL 1974–present)

WASHINGTON CAPITOL'S
See *PATERSON CRESCENTS (2)*

WASHINGTON CAPITOLS (1)
Washington Capitols (1) (BAA 1946–49; NBA 1949–51)
Folded during season, 1951.

WASHINGTON CAPITOLS (2)
Washington Capitols (2) (ABL2 1951–52)
Folded, 1952.

WASHINGTON CAPITOLS (3)
See *PHILADELPHIA TAPERS*

WASHINGTON CAPITOLS (4)
See *VIRGINIA SQUIRES*

WASHINGTON CAVALIERS
Virginia Capitol Cavaliers (ASL2 1971)
Washington Cavaliers (ASL2 1972)
Folded, 1972.

WASHINGTON COMMANDOS
Washington Commandos (AFL 1987)
Suspended operations, 1988.
Maryland Commandos (AFL 1989)
Washington Commandos (AFL 1990)
Folded, 1990.

WASHINGTON DARTS
See *MINNESOTA STRIKERS*

WASHINGTON DIPLOMATS (1)
Washington Diplomats (1) (NASLo 1974–80)
Folded, 1980.

WASHINGTON DIPLOMATS (2)
Detroit Express (S/IS) (NASLo 1978–80) and (NASLi
    1979–81)
Washington Diplomats (2) (NASLo 1981)
Folded, 1981.

WASHINGTON DIPLOMATS (3)
Washington Diplomats (3) (ASL3 1988–89; APSL 1990)
Folded, 1990.

WASHINGTON ELITE GIANTS
See *BALTIMORE ELITE GIANTS*

WASHINGTON FEDERALS
See *ORLANDO RENEGADES*

WASHINGTON HEURICH BREWERS
See *WASHINGTON BREWERS*

WASHINGTON HEURICHS
See *WASHINGTON BREWERS*

WASHINGTON LAUNDRYMEN
See *WASHINGTON PALACE FIVE*

WASHINGTON MYSTICS
WASHINGTON MYSTICS (WNBA 1998–present)

WASHINGTON NATIONALS (1)
See *WASHINGTON OLYMPICS*

WASHINGTON NATIONALS (2)
Washington Nationals, amateur, 1859–71.
Washington Nationals (2) (NA 1872–73, 1875)
    a.k.a. Washington Washingtons
(Amateur, 1874.)
Folded during season, 1875.

WASHINGTON NATIONALS (3)
Washington Nationals (3) (AA 1884)
Folded during season, 1884.

WASHINGTON NATIONALS (4)
Washington Nationals (4) (UA 1884)
    a.k.a. Washington Quicksteps
Joined Eastern League, 1885.
Folded, 1885.

WASHINGTON NATIONALS (5)
See *MINNESOTA TWINS*

WASHINGTON OLYMPICS
Washington Olympics, amateur, 1867–70.
Washington Olympics (NA 1871–72)
    a.k.a. Washington Nationals (1)
Folded during season, 1872.

WASHINGTON PALACE FIVE
Washington Palace Five (ABL1 1925–28)
    a.k.a. Washington Laundrymen
    a.k.a. Washington Palacians
Absorbed by Brooklyn Visitations (1) during season, 1928.

WASHINGTON PALACIANS
See *WASHINGTON PALACE FIVE*

WASHINGTON POTOMACS
Washington Potomacs, independent, 1923.
Washington Potomacs (ECL 1924)
Folded, 1924.

WASHINGTON POWER
Washington Power (MLRH 1997–98)
Folded, 1998.

WASHINGTON PROS
Washington Pros (APFA 1921)
   a.k.a. Washington Senators (F)
Independent, 1922.
Folded, 1922.

WASHINGTON QUICKSTEPS
See *WASHINGTON NATIONALS (4)*

WASHINGTON REDSKINS
Boston Braves (F) (NFL 1932)
Boston Redskins (NFL 1933–36)
WASHINGTON REDSKINS (NFL 1937–present)

WASHINGTON SENATORS (B1)
See *WASHINGTON STATESMEN (1)*

WASHINGTON SENATORS (B2)
See *WASHINGTON STATESMEN (2)*

WASHINGTON SENATORS (B3)
See *MINNESOTA TWINS*

WASHINGTON SENATORS (B4)
See *TEXAS RANGERS*

WASHINGTON SENATORS (F)
See *WASHINGTON PROS*

WASHINGTON SPIN
Washington Spin, began exhibition play, 1999.
WASHINGTON SPIN (W-MLRH 2000–present)

WASHINGTON STARS
Washington Stars (ASL3 1988–89; APSL 1990)
Absorbed by Maryland Bays, 1991.

WASHINGTON STATESMEN (1)
Washington Statesmen (1) (NL 1886–89)
   a.k.a. Washington Senators (B1)
Folded, 1889.

WASHINGTON STATESMEN (2)
Washington Statesmen (2) (AA 1891; NL 1892–99)
   a.k.a. Washington Senators (B2)
Folded, 1899.

WASHINGTON WARTHOGS
Washington Warthogs (CISL 1994–97)
Folded, 1997.

WASHINGTON WASHINGTONS
See *WASHINGTON NATIONALS (2)*

WASHINGTON WAVE
Washington Wave (EPBLL 1987–88; MILL 1989)
Absorbed by Baltimore Thunder and Pittsburgh Bulls, 1990.

WASHINGTON WHIPS
Aberdeen Football Club (Aberdeen, Scotland), independent, pre-1967.
Washington Whips (USA 1967; NASLo 1968)
Folded, 1968.

WASHINGTON WIZARDS
Chicago Packers (NBA 1961–62)
Chicago Zephyrs (NBA 1962–63)
Baltimore Bullets (2) (NBA 1963–73)
Capital Bullets (NBA 1973–74)
Washington Bullets (NBA 1974–97)
WASHINGTON WIZARDS (NBA 1997–present)

WASHINGTON HOMESTEAD
(District of Columbia and Pennsylvania; actually played only in Washington)

WASHINGTON HOMESTEAD GRAYS
Homestead Blue Ribbon, independent, pre-1912. Murdock Grays, independent, pre-1912–28.
Homestead Grays (ANL 1929)
Independent, 1930–34.
Washington Homestead Grays (NNL2 1935–48)
Independent, 1949–50.
Folded, 1950.

WATERLOO
(Iowa)

WATERLOO HAWKS
Toledo Jeeps (NBL 1946–48)
Waterloo Hawks (NBL 1948–49; NBA 1949–50)

Joined National Professional Basketball League, 1950–51. Folded, 1951.

(WAVE)
(No location name: Orlando, Florida)

WAVE
Wave (WRHL 1993)
Folded, 1993.

WELLINGTON
(Florida)

WELLINGTON ACES
Miami Beach Breakers (1) (TT 1985–86)
Miami Breakers (1) (TT 1987)
South Florida Breakers (TT 1988)
Wellington Aces (TT 1989–91)
Folded, 1991.

WESTCHESTER
(Westchester County, New York)

WESTCHESTER INDIANS
See *BROOKLYN GOTHAMS*

WHITING
(Indiana)

WHITING CIESAR ALL-AMERICANS
See *HAMMOND CIESAR ALL-AMERICANS*

WICHITA
(Kansas)

WICHITA ADVANTAGE
Wichita Advantage (TT 1991; WTT 1992–95)
Folded, 1995.

WICHITA WINGS
WICHITA WINGS (MISL 1979–90; MSL 1990–92; NPSLi 1992–present)

WILKES-BARRE
(Pennsylvania)

WILKES-BARRE BARONS (1)
Wilkes-Barre Barons (1) (ABL2 1938–40)
Folded, 1940.

WILKES-BARRE BARONS (2)
Wilkes-Barre Barons (2) (ABL2 1947–53)
Folded, 1953.

WILMINGTON
(Delaware)

WILMINGTON BLUE BOMBERS
See *WILMINGTON BOMBERS*

WILMINGTON BOMBERS
Wilmington Blue Bombers (ABL2 1941–42)
Camden Indians (ABL2 1942–43)
Brooklyn Indians (1) (ABL2 1943)
Wilmington Blue Bombers (ABL2 1943–44)
Wilmington Bombers (ABL2 1944–47)
Folded, 1947.

WILMINGTON QUICKSTEPS
Wilmington Delawareans, Eastern League, 1884.
Wilmington Quicksteps (UA 1884)
Folded during season, 1884.

WINNIPEG
(Manitoba, Canada)

WINNIPEG BLUE BOMBERS
Winnipeg Rugby Football Club, independent, 1880–1929. Winnipegs, independent, 1930–32. Merged with St. John's to form Winnipeg Pegs, independent, 1933–35. Winnipeg Blue Bombers, newly renamed Western Interprovincial Football Union (charter member), 1936–55.

WINNIPEG BLUE BOMBERS (CFC 1956–57; CFL 1958–present)

WINNIPEG JETS
See *PHOENIX COYOTES*

WORCESTER
(Massachusetts)

WORCESTER ASTROS
Ludlow Astros (ASL2 1967)
Fall River Astros (ASL2 1968)
Boston Astros (ASL2 1969–74)
Worcester Astros (ASL2 1975)
Folded, 1975.

WORCESTER BROWN STOCKINGS
See *WORCESTER RUBY LEGS*

WORCESTER RUBY LEGS
Worcester Ruby Legs (NL 1880–82)
  a.k.a. Worcester Brown Stockings
Folded, 1882.

YONKERS
(New York)

YONKERS CHIEFS
Yonkers Chiefs (ABL2 1946–47)
Folded, 1947.

YOUNGSTOWN
(Ohio)

YOUNGSTOWN BEARS
See *FLINT DOW A.C.'S*

Part 2

The Leagues

In this section, teams are listed according to the leagues in which they played. The leagues themselves are listed according to sport in the order of baseball, football, basketball, hockey, soccer, indoor soccer, arena football, tennis, roller hockey, and lacrosse. Within each sport, the leagues are listed in chronological order according to first year of operation. Leagues which changed their names are listed only once under all names, but the appropriate years are cited for each name. An example is the American Professional Football Association (1920–1921)/National Football League (1922–present).

Franchises are listed in alphabetical order according to the *first* name used by each franchise, and according to the first year of *major league* operation. Each team is listed according to all the names it used in that league (for example, the Kansas City Scouts/Colorado Rockies/New Jersey Devils). The years of its existence in that league are given next. The years are not broken down according to team name (which years as the Scouts, for instance, which as the Rockies, and which as the Devils). For that information, refer to Part 1. If a team played in more than one league, notations are given below the team name in italics. If the team changed names when it switched leagues, that information is also provided.

Teams that merged into a single franchise are indicated by superscripted numbers. For example, the Arizona Wranglers and the Oklahoma Outlaws merged to form the Arizona Outlaws. The teams are listed as Arizona Wranglers/Arizona Outlaws[1] and Oklahoma Outlaws/Arizona Outlaws[1]. Thus, while the name Arizona Outlaws appears twice, the reader will know that there were not two teams called the Arizona Outlaws, but one. If two teams merged and later split, the numbers will indicate which team name

or names were in use during the merger (for example, Philadelphia Eagles/Phil-Pitt[1]/Steagles[1]/Philadelphia Eagles, and Pittsburgh Steelers/Phil-Pitt[1]/Steagles[1]/Card-Pitt, etc.).

A double slash ("//") indicates that a team played in another league for a time, then returned to the league in question. For example, in the National League, the Cincinnati Reds are listed like this: Cincinnati Red Stockings/Cincinnati Reds//Cincinnati Reds/Cincinnati Redlegs, etc. Notice the double slash between the first and second "Cincinnati Reds." In this case, the team left the National League to play in the American Association as the Cincinnati Red Stockings, then returned to the National League as the Cincinnati Reds later on. A double slash is also used if a slash is part of the team's name (for example, the New Jersey Rockin' Rollers//New York/New Jersey Rockin' Rollers).

Some leagues actually continued as minor leagues after their major league run. For example, baseball's Negro American League played until 1961, but once the white major leagues were integrated, they began to siphon its talent, and the NAL is not considered to have been of major league caliber after 1950. Only the years of major league operation are presented here.

In a few cases, teams may appear with years which postdate a league's collapse. In such an instance, a team may have formed or changed names in preparation for a certain season, and the entire league folded or suspended operations before the season actually occurred. For example, Major League Roller Hockey did not operate in 1999. The Colorado Inferno had been formed for that season, so they are listed as a 1999 team even though there was no 1999 season.

NATIONAL ASSOCIATION
(1871–1875)

FRANCHISE	YEARS
Baltimore Lord Baltimores/Baltimore Canaries	1872–1874
Baltimore Marylands	1873
Boston Red Stockings/Boston Reds *Joined National League as Boston Red Caps, 1876.*	1871–1875
Brooklyn Atlantics	1872–1875
Brooklyn Eckfords	1871–1872
Chicago White Stockings/Chicago Remnants *Joined National League, 1876.*	1871, 1874–1875
Cleveland Forest Citys	1871–1872
Elizabeth Resolutes	1873
Fort Wayne Kekiongas	1871
Hartford Dark Blues/Hartford Hartfords *Joined National League, 1876.*	1874–1875
Keokuk Westerns	1875
Middletown Mansfields	1872
New Haven Elm Citys/New Haven New Havens	1875
New York Mutuals *Joined National League, 1876.*	1871–1875
Philadelphia Athletics *Joined National League, 1876.*	1871–1875
Philadelphia Centennials	1875
Philadelphia Philadelphias/Philadelphia White Stockings/Philadelphia Whites/Philadelphia Pearls/Philadelphia Phillies	1873–1875

FRANCHISE	YEARS
Rockford Forest Citys	1871
St. Louis Brown Stockings *Joined National League, 1876.*	1875
St. Louis Red Stockings/St. Louis Reds	1875
Troy Haymakers	1871–1872
Washington Nationals/Washington Washingtons	1872–1873, 1875
Washington Olympics/Washington Nationals	1871–1872

NATIONAL LEAGUE
(1876–PRESENT)

FRANCHISE	YEARS
Arizona Diamondbacks	1998–present
Baltimore Orioles *From American Association.* *Absorbed by Brooklyn Superbas, 1900.*	1892–1899
Boston Red Caps/Boston Bostons/Boston Beaneaters/Boston Nationals/Boston Doves/ Boston Pilgrims/Boston Heps/Boston Rustlers/ Boston Braves/Boston Bees/Boston Braves/ Milwaukee Braves/Atlanta Braves *From National Association as Boston Reds.*	1876–present
Brooklyn Bridegrooms/Brooklyn Superbas/ Brooklyn Trolley Dodgers/Brooklyn Dodgers/ Brooklyn Robins/Brooklyn Dodgers/Los Angeles Dodgers *From American Association.*	1890–present
Buffalo Bisons	1879–1885

FRANCHISE	YEARS
Chicago White Stockings/Chicago Remnants/ Chicago Colts/Chicago Babes/Chicago Cubs/ Chicago Rainmakers/Chicago Recruits/Chicago Orphans/Chicago Cowboys/Chicago Broncos/ Chicago Cubs	1876–present
From National Association.	
Cincinnati Red Stockings/Cincinnati Reds// Cincinnati Reds/Cincinnati Redlegs/Cincinnati Reds/Cincinnati Redlegs/Cincinnati Reds	1876–1880, 1890–present
Joined American Association as Cincinnati Red Stockings, 1882. *From American Association as Cincinnati Red Stockings, 1890.*	
Cleveland Blues	1879–1884
Cleveland Spiders	1889–1899
From American Association as Cleveland Blues. *Absorbed by St. Louis Cardinals, 1900.*	
Colorado Rockies	1993–present
Detroit Wolverines	1881–1888
Florida Marlins	1993–present
Hartford Dark Blues/Hartford Hartfords/Brooklyn Hartfords	1876–1877
From National Association.	
Houston Colt .45s/Houston Astros	1962–present
Indianapolis Hoosiers/Indianapolis Browns	1878
Kansas City Cowboys	1886
Louisville Colonels/Louisville Cyclones	1892–1899
From American Association. *Absorbed by Pittsburgh Pirates, 1900.*	
Louisville Grays	1876–1877
Milwaukee Brewers	1998–present
From American League.	
Milwaukee Grays/Milwaukee Cream Citys/ Milwaukee Brewers	1878

FRANCHISE	YEARS
Montreal Expos	1969–present
New York Mets	1962–present
New York Mutuals *From National Association.*	1876
Philadelphia Athletics *From National Association.*	1876
Philadelphia Nationals/Philadelphia Quakers/ Philadelphia Fillies/Philadelphia Phillies/ Philadelphia Blue Jays/Philadelphia Phillies	1883–present
Pittsburgh Alleghenies/Pittsburgh Innocents/ Pittsburgh Pirates	1887–present
Providence Grays/Providence Rhode Islanders	1878–1885
St. Louis Brown Stockings *From National Association.*	1876–1877
St. Louis Browns/St. Louis Maroons/St. Louis Perfectos/St. Louis Cardinals *From American Association.*	1892–present
St. Louis Maroons/Indianapolis Hoosiers *From Union Association.*	1885–1889
San Diego Padres	1969–present
Syracuse Stars	1879
Troy Trojans/New York Gothams/New York Green Stockings/New York Giants/San Francisco Giants	1879–present
Washington Statesmen/Washington Senators	1886–1889
Washington Statesmen/Washington Senators *From American Association.*	1892–1899
Worcester Ruby Legs/Worcester Brown Stockings	1880–1882

AMERICAN ASSOCIATION
(1882–1891)

FRANCHISE	YEARS
Baltimore Orioles *Joined National League, 1892.*	1882–1889, 1890–1891
Boston Red Stockings/Boston Reds/Boston Beaneaters *From Players League.*	1891
Brooklyn Atlantics/Brooklyn Grays/Brooklyn Bridegrooms *Joined National League, 1890.*	1884–1889
Brooklyn Gladiators/Brooklyn Ridgewoods	1890
Cincinnati Porkers/Cincinnati Kellys/Cincinnati Killers	1891
Cincinnati Red Stockings *From National League as Cincinnati Reds.* *Joined National League as Cincinnati Reds, 1890.*	1882–1889
Cleveland Blues *Joined National League as Cleveland Spiders, 1889.*	1887–1888
Columbus Buckeyes/Columbus Colts/Columbus Senators	1883–1884
Columbus Buckeyes/Columbus Colts/Columbus Solons	1889–1891
Indianapolis Hoosiers/Indianapolis Blues	1884
Kansas City Cowboys/Kansas City Blues	1888–1889
Louisville Eclipse/Louisville Colonels/Louisville Cyclones *Joined National League, 1892.*	1882–1891
Milwaukee Brewers	1891
New York Metropolitans/New York Mets	1883–1887

FRANCHISE	YEARS
Philadelphia Athletics	1882–1890
Philadelphia Athletics *From Players League as Philadelphia Quakers.*	1891
Pittsburgh Alleghenies *Joined National League, 1887.*	1882–1886
Richmond Virginians	1884
Rochester Hop-Bitters/Rochester Broncos	1890
St. Louis Brown Stockings/St. Louis Browns/ St. Louis Maroons *Joined National League, 1892.*	1882–1891
Syracuse Stars	1890
Toledo Blue Stockings	1884
Toledo Maumees	1890
Washington Nationals	1884
Washington Statesmen/Washington Senators *Joined National League, 1892.*	1891

UNION ASSOCIATION
(1884)

FRANCHISE	YEARS
Altoona Unions/Altoona Mountain Citys/Altoona Pride/Altoona Ottowas	1884
Baltimore Unions/Baltimore Monumentals	1884
Boston Unions/Boston Reds	1884
Chicago Browns/Pittsburgh Stogies	1884

FRANCHISE	YEARS
Cincinnati Outlaw Reds	1884
Kansas City Unions/Kansas City Cowboys	1884
Milwaukee Cream Citys/Milwaukee Grays/ Milwaukee Brewers	1884
Philadelphia Keystones	1884
St. Louis Maroons *Joined National League, 1885.*	1884
St. Paul Saints/St. Paul Whitecaps	1884
Washington Nationals/Washington Quicksteps	1884
Wilmington Quicksteps	1884

PLAYERS LEAGUE
(1890)

FRANCHISE	YEARS
Boston Red Stockings/Boston Reds/Boston Beaneaters *Joined American Association, 1891.*	1890
Brooklyn Wonders *Absorbed by Brooklyn Bridegrooms in National League, 1891.*	1890
Buffalo Bisons	1890
Chicago Pirates *Absorbed by Chicago Colts in National League, 1891.*	1890
Cleveland Infants	1890

FRANCHISE	YEARS
New York Giants *Absorbed by New York Giants in National League, 1891.*	1890
Philadelphia Quakers *Joined American Association as Philadelphia Athletics, 1891.*	1890
Pittsburgh Burghers *Absorbed by Pittsburgh Innocents in National League, 1891.*	1890

AMERICAN LEAGUE
(1901–PRESENT)

FRANCHISE	YEARS
Baltimore Orioles/New York Highlanders/New York Hilltoppers/New York Invaders/New York Yankees	1901–present
Boston Americans/Boston Somersets/Boston Puritans/Boston Plymouth Rocks/Boston Speedboys/Boston Pilgrims/Boston Red Stockings/Boston Red Sox	1901–present
Chicago Invaders/Chicago White Stockings/Chicago Uniques/Chicago White Sox	1901–present
Cleveland Bluebirds/Cleveland Blues/Cleveland Bronchos/Cleveland Naps/Cleveland Molly McGuires/Cleveland Indians	1901–present
Detroit Tigers	1901–present
Kansas City Royals	1969–present
Los Angeles Angels/California Angels/Anaheim Angels	1961–present
Milwaukee Brewers/St. Louis Ravens/St. Louis Browns/Baltimore Orioles	1901–present

FRANCHISE	YEARS
Philadelphia Athletics/Kansas City Athletics/ Oakland Athletics	1901–present
Seattle Mariners	1977–present
Seattle Pilots/Milwaukee Brewers *Joined National League, 1998.*	1969–1997
Tampa Bay Devil Rays	1998–present
Toronto Blue Jays	1977–present
Washington Senators/Texas Rangers	1961–present
Washington Senators/Washington Nationals/ Washington Senators/Minnesota Twins	1901–present

FEDERAL LEAGUE
(1914–1915)

FRANCHISE	YEARS
Baltimore Terrapins/Baltimore Baltfeds	1914–1915
Brooklyn Brookfeds/Brooklyn Feds/Brooklyn Tip-Tops	1914–1915
Buffalo Buffeds/Buffalo Blues/Buffalo Electrics	1914–1915
Chicago Chifeds/Chicago Whales	1914–1915
Indianapolis Federals/Indianapolis Hoosiers/ Indianapolis Hoosierfeds/Indianapolis Hoofeds/ Newark Peppers/Newark Peps/Newark Feds/ Newark Newfeds/Newark Jerseymen	1914–1915
Kansas City Packers	1914–1915

FRANCHISE	YEARS
Pittsburgh Pittsfeds/Pittsburgh Rebels	1914–1915
St. Louis Terriers/St. Louis Brownies/St. Louis Miners/St. Louis Sloufeds	1914–1915

NEGRO NATIONAL LEAGUE *(FIRST)*
(1920–1931)

FRANCHISE	YEARS
Birmingham Black Barons *Joined Negro American League, 1937.*	1924–1925, 1927–1930
Chicago American Giants *Joined Negro Southern League as Cole's American Giants, 1932.*	1920–1931
Chicago Giants	1920–1921
Cleveland Browns	1924
Cleveland Elites	1926
Cleveland Hornets	1927
Cleveland Tate Stars	1922
Columbus Buckeyes	1921
Cuban Stars/Cincinnati Cubans/Cuban Stars/Cuban Stars (West)	1920–1930
Dayton Marcos	1920, 1926
Detroit Stars *Joined second Negro National League, 1933.*	1920–1931
Indianapolis ABC's *Joined Negro Southern League, 1932.*	1920–1924, 1925–1926, 1931

FRANCHISE	YEARS
Kansas City Monarchs *Joined Negro American League, 1937.*	1920–1927, 1929–1930
Louisville White Sox	1931
Memphis Red Sox *Joined Negro Southern League, 1932.*	1924, 1925, 1927, 1929–1930
Milwaukee Bears	1923
Nashville Elite Giants/Cleveland Cubs *Joined Negro Southern League as Nashville Elite Giants, 1932.*	1930–1931
Pittsburgh Keystones	1922
St. Louis Giants	1920–1921
St. Louis Stars *Joined Negro American League, 1937.*	1922–1931
Toledo Tigers	1923

EASTERN COLORED LEAGUE
(1923–1928)

FRANCHISE	YEARS
Atlantic City Bacharach Giants *Joined American Negro League, 1929.*	1923–1928
Baltimore Black Sox *Joined American Negro League, 1929.*	1923–1928
Brooklyn Royal Giants	1923–1927
Cuban Stars (East) *Joined American Negro League, 1929.*	1923–1928
Harrisburg Giants	1924–1927

FRANCHISE	YEARS
Hilldale/Hilldale Giants/Hilldale Daisies/Darby Daisies *Joined American Negro League, 1929.*	1923–1927
New York Lincoln Giants *Joined American Negro League, 1929.*	1923–1926, 1928
Newark Stars	1926
Philadelphia Tigers	1928
Washington Potomacs	1924

(League folded during season, 1928.)

AMERICAN NEGRO LEAGUE
(1929)

FRANCHISE	YEARS
Atlantic City Bacharach Giants *From Eastern Colored League.* *Joined second Negro National League, 1934.*	1929
Baltimore Black Sox *From Eastern Colored League.* *Joined second Negro National League, 1933.*	1929
Cuban Stars (East) *From Eastern Colored League.*	1929
Hilldale/Hilldale Giants/Hilldale Daisies/Darby Daisies *From Eastern Colored League.*	1929
Homestead Grays *Joined second Negro National League as* *Washington Homestead Grays, 1935.*	1929
New York Lincoln Giants *From Eastern Colored League.* *Joined second Negro National League, 1935.*	1929

NEGRO SOUTHERN LEAGUE
(1932)

FRANCHISE	YEARS
Cole's American Giants	1932
From first Negro National League as Chicago American Giants.	
Joined second Negro National League, 1933.	
Columbus Turfs	1932
Indianapolis ABC's	1932
From first Negro National League.	
Joined Negro American League, 1938.	
Louisville Black Caps	1932
Memphis Red Sox	1932
From first Negro National League.	
Joined Negro American League, 1937.	
Monroe Monarchs	1932
Montgomery Grey Sox	1932
Nashville Elite Giants	1932
From first Negro National League as Cleveland Cubs.	
Joined second Negro National League, 1933.	

NEGRO NATIONAL LEAGUE *(SECOND)*
(1933–1948)

FRANCHISE	YEARS
Atlantic City Bacharach Giants	1934
From American Negro League.	
Baltimore Black Sox	1933, 1934
From American Negro League.	

FRANCHISE	YEARS
Brooklyn Eagles/Newark Eagles[1] *Joined Negro American League as Houston Eagles, 1949.*	1935–1948
Cleveland Giants	1933
Cleveland Red Sox	1934
Cole's American Giants *From Negro Southern League.* *Joined Negro American League as Chicago American Giants, 1937.*	1933–1935
Columbus Blue Birds	1933
Detroit Stars *From first Negro National League.* *Joined Negro American League, 1937.*	1933
Harrisburg-St. Louis Stars *From Negro American League as New Orleans-St. Louis Stars.*	1943
Nashville Elite Giants/Columbus Elite Giants/ Washington Elite Giants/Baltimore Elite Giants *From Negro Southern League.* *Joined Negro American League, 1949.*	1933–1948
New York Black Yankees	1936–1948
New York Cubans *Joined Negro American League, 1949.*	1935–1936, 1939–1948
Newark Dodgers/Newark Eagles[1] *Joined Negro American League as Houston Eagles, 1949.*	1934–1948
Philadelphia Stars *Joined Negro American League, 1949.*	1934–1948
Pittsburgh Crawfords *Joined Negro American League as Toledo Crawfords, 1939.*	1933–1938
Washington Black Senators	1938
Washington Homestead Grays *From American Negro League as Homestead Grays.*	1935–1948

NEGRO AMERICAN LEAGUE
(1937–1950)

FRANCHISE	YEARS
Atlanta Black Crackers	1938
Baltimore Elite Giants *From second Negro National League.*	1949–1950
Birmingham Black Barons *From first Negro National League.*	1937–1938, 1940–1950
Chicago American Giants *From second Negro National League as Cole's American Giants.*	1937–1950
Cincinnati Buckeyes/Cleveland Buckeyes/ Louisville Buckeyes/Cleveland Buckeyes	1942–1950
Cincinnati Clowns/Indianapolis-Cincinnati Clowns/Cincinnati Clowns/Indianapolis Clowns	1943–1950
Cincinnati Tigers	1937
Detroit Stars *From second Negro National League.*	1937
Houston Eagles *From second Negro National League as Newark Eagles.*	1949–1950
Indianapolis ABC's *From Negro Southern League.*	1938–1939
Indianapolis Athletics	1937
Jacksonville Red Caps/Cleveland Bears/ Jacksonville Red Caps	1938–1942
Kansas City Monarchs *From second Negro National League.*	1937–1950
Memphis Red Sox *From Negro Southern League.*	1937–1941, 1943–1950
New York Cubans *From second Negro National League.*	1949–1950

FRANCHISE	YEARS
Philadelphia Stars *From second Negro National League.*	1949–1950
St. Louis Stars/New Orleans-St. Louis Stars *From first Negro National League.* *Joined second Negro National League as Har-* *risburg-St. Louis Stars, 1943.*	1937, 1939, 1941
Toledo Crawfords/Indianapolis Crawfords *From second Negro National League as Pitts-* *burgh Crawfords.*	1939–1940

(Continued as minor league through 1962.)

ALL-AMERICAN GIRLS
PROFESSIONAL BASEBALL LEAGUE
(1943–1954)

FRANCHISE	YEARS
Chicago Colleens	1948
Kenosha Comets	1943–1951
Milwaukee Chicks/Grand Rapids Chicks	1944–1954
Minneapolis Millerettes/Fort Wayne Daisies	1944–1954
Muskegon Lassies/Kalamazoo Lassies	1946–1954
Peoria Redwings	1946–1951
Racine Belles/Battle Creek Belles/Muskegon Belles	1943–1953
Rockford Peaches	1943–1954
South Bend Blue Sox	1943–1954
Springfield Sallies	1948

AMERICAN PROFESSIONAL FOOTBALL ASSOCIATION
(1920–1921)

NATIONAL FOOTBALL LEAGUE
(1922–PRESENT)

FRANCHISE	YEARS
Akron Pros/Akron Indians	1920–1926
Atlanta Falcons	1966–present
Baltimore Colts *From All-America Football Conference.*	1950
Baltimore Colts/Indianapolis Colts	1953–present
Boston Braves/Boston Redskins/Washington Redskins	1932–present
Boston Yanks/New York Bulldogs/New York Yanks/Dallas Texans	1944–1952
Brooklyn Lions/Brooklyn Horse-Lions *In part from first American Football League as Brooklyn Horsemen.*	1926
Buffalo All-Americans/Buffalo Bisons/Buffalo Rangers/Buffalo Bisons	1920–1927, 1929
Buffalo Bills *From fourth American Football League.*	1970–present
Canton Bulldogs	1920–1923, 1925–1926
Carolina Panthers	1995–present
Chicago Tigers	1920
Cincinnati Bengals *From fourth American Football League.*	1970–present
Cincinnati Celts	1921

FRANCHISE	YEARS
Cincinnati Reds/St. Louis Gunners	1933–1934
Cleveland Browns	1999–present
Cleveland Browns/Baltimore Ravens *From All-America Football Conference.*	1950–present
Cleveland Indians	1931
Cleveland Indians/Cleveland Bulldogs	1923–1925, 1927
Cleveland Rams/Los Angeles Rams/St. Louis Rams *From second American Football League.*	1937–1942, 1944–present
Cleveland Tigers/Cleveland Indians	1920–1921
Columbus Panhandles/Columbus Tigers	1920–1926
Dallas Cowboys	1960–present
Dayton Triangles/Brooklyn Dodgers/Brooklyn Tigers *Absorbed by Boston Yanks, 1945.*	1920–1944
Decatur Staleys/Chicago Staleys/Chicago Bears	1920–present
Denver Broncos *From fourth American Football League.*	1970–present
Detroit Heralds	1920
Detroit Panthers/Detroit Wolverines *Absorbed by New York Giants, 1929.*	1925–1926, 1928
Detroit Tigers	1921
Duluth Kelleys/Duluth Eskimos	1923–1927
Evansville Crimson Giants	1921–1922
Frankford Yellow Jackets/Philadelphia Eagles/ Phil-Pitt[1]/Steagles[1]/Philadelphia Eagles	1924–1931, 1933–present
Green Bay Packers/Green Bay Blues/Green Bay Packers	1921–present

FRANCHISE	YEARS
Hammond Pros/Hammond Hoosiers/Hammond Indians/Hammond Tigers	1920–1926
Hartford Blues	1926
Houston Oilers/Tennessee Oilers/Tennessee Titans *From fourth American Football League.*	1970–present
Houston Texans	2002–present
Jacksonville Jaguars	1995–present
Kansas City Blues/Kansas City Cowboys	1923–1926
Kansas City Chiefs *From fourth American Football League.*	1970–present
Los Angeles Buccaneers	1926
Louisville Brecks	1921–1923
Louisville Colonels	1926
Miami Dolphins *From fourth American Football League.*	1970–present
Milwaukee Badgers	1922–1926
Minneapolis Marines	1921–1924
Minneapolis Redjackets	1929–1930
Minnesota Vikings	1961–present
Muncie Flyers	1920–1921
New England Patriots *From fourth American Football League as Boston Patriots.*	1970–present
New Orleans Saints	1967–present
New York Brickley's Giants/New York Giants	1921
New York Giants	1925–present
New York Jets *From fourth American Football League.*	1970–present

FRANCHISE	YEARS
New York Yankees *From first American Football League.*	1927–1928
Oakland Raiders/Los Angeles Raiders/Oakland Raiders *From fourth American Football League.*	1970–present
Oorang Indians	1922–1923
Orange Tornadoes/Newark Tornadoes	1929–1930
Pittsburgh Pirates/Pittsburgh Steelers/Phil-Pitt[1]/Steagles[1]/Card-Pitt[2]/Pittsburgh Steelers	1933–present
Portsmouth Spartans/Detroit Lions	1930–present
Pottsville Maroons/Boston Bulldogs	1925–1929
Providence Steam Roller	1925–1931
Racine Cardinals/Chicago Cardinals/Card-Pitt[2]/Chicago Cardinals/St. Louis Cardinals/Phoenix Cardinals/Arizona Cardinals	1920–present
Racine Legion/Racine Tornadoes	1922–1924, 1926
Rochester Jeffersons	1920–1925
Rock Island Independents *Joined first American Football League, 1926.*	1920–1925
St. Louis All-Stars	1923
San Diego Chargers *From fourth American Football League.*	1970–present
San Francisco 49ers *From All-America Football Conference.*	1950–present
Seattle Seahawks	1976–present
Staten Island Stapletons/Staten Island Stapes/Stapleton Stapes	1929–1932
Tampa Bay Buccaneers	1976–present
Toledo Maroons/Kenosha Maroons	1922–1924

FRANCHISE	YEARS
Tonawanda Kardex/Tonawanda Lumbermen	1921
Washington Pros/Washington Senators	1921

AMERICAN FOOTBALL LEAGUE *(FIRST)*
(1926)

FRANCHISE	YEARS
Boston Bulldogs	1926
Brooklyn Horsemen *Joined National Football League in merger with Brooklyn Lions as part of Brooklyn Horse-Lions, 1926.*	1926
Chicago Bulls	1926
Cleveland Panthers	1926
Los Angeles Wildcats	1926
New York Yankees *Joined National Football League, 1927.*	1926
Newark Bears	1926
Philadelphia Quakers	1926
Rock Island Independents *From National Football League.*	1926

AMERICAN FOOTBALL LEAGUE *(SECOND)*
(1936–1937)

FRANCHISE	YEARS
Boston Shamrocks	1936–1937
Brooklyn Tigers/Rochester Tigers	1936–1937
Cincinnati Bengals *Joined third American Football League, 1940.*	1937
Cleveland Rams *Joined National Football League, 1937.*	1936
Los Angeles Bulldogs	1937
New York Yankees	1936–1937
Pittsburgh Americans	1936–1937
Syracuse Braves/Rochester Braves	1936

AMERICAN FOOTBALL LEAGUE *(THIRD)*
(1940–1941)

FRANCHISE	YEARS
Boston Bears	1940
Buffalo Indians/Buffalo Tigers	1940–1941
Cincinnati Bengals *From second American Football League.*	1940–1941
Columbus Bullies	1940–1941
Milwaukee Chiefs	1940–1941
New York Yankees/New York Americans	1940–1941

ALL-AMERICA FOOTBALL CONFERENCE
(1946–1949)

FRANCHISE	YEARS
Brooklyn Dodgers/Brooklyn-New York Yankees[1]	1946–1949
Buffalo Bisons/Buffalo Bills	1946–1949
Chicago Rockets/Chicago Hornets	1946–1949
Cleveland Browns *Joined National Football League, 1950.*	1946–1949
Los Angeles Dons	1946–1949
Miami Seahawks/Baltimore Colts *Joined National Football League, 1950.*	1946–1949
New York Yankees/Brooklyn-New York Yankees[1]	1946–1949
San Francisco 49ers *Joined National Football League, 1950.*	1946–1949

CANADIAN FOOTBALL COUNCIL
(1956–1957)

CANADIAN FOOTBALL LEAGUE
(1958–PRESENT)

FRANCHISE	YEARS
Baltimore CFL Colts/Baltimore CFLs/Baltimore Stallions/Montreal Alouettes	1994–present
Birmingham Barracudas	1995
British Columbia Lions	1956–present

FRANCHISE	YEARS
Calgary Stampeders	1956–present
Edmonton Eskimos	1956–present
Hamilton Tiger-Cats	1956–present
Las Vegas Posse	1994
Memphis Mad Dogs	1995
Montreal Alouettes	1956–1980
Montreal Concordes/Montreal Alouettes	1981–1987
Ottawa Rough Riders	1956–1996
Sacramento Gold Miners/San Antonio Texans	1994–1995
Saskatchewan Roughriders	1956–present
Shreveport Pirates	1994–1995
Toronto Argonauts	1956–present
Winnipeg Blue Bombers	1956–present

AMERICAN FOOTBALL LEAGUE *(FOURTH)*
(1960–1970)

FRANCHISE	YEARS
Boston Patriots *Joined National Football League as New England Patriots, 1970.*	1960–1970
Buffalo Bills *Joined National Football League, 1970.*	1960–1970
Cincinnati Bengals *Joined National Football League, 1970.*	1968–1970

FRANCHISE	YEARS
Dallas Texans/Kansas City Chiefs *Joined National Football League, 1970.*	1960–1970
Denver Broncos *Joined National Football League, 1970.*	1960–1970
Houston Oilers *Joined National Football League, 1970.*	1960–1970
Los Angeles Chargers/San Diego Chargers *Joined National Football League, 1970.*	1960–1970
Miami Dolphins *Joined National Football League, 1970.*	1966–1970
New York Titans/New York Jets *Joined National Football League, 1970.*	1960–1970
Oakland Raiders *Joined National Football League, 1970.*	1960–1970

WORLD FOOTBALL LEAGUE
(1974–1975)

FRANCHISE	YEARS
Birmingham Americans	1974
Birmingham Vulcans	1975
Boston Bulldogs/Boston Bulls/New York Stars/ Charlotte Stars/Charlotte Hornets	1974–1975
Chicago Fire/Chicago Winds	1974–1975
Detroit Wheels	1974
Honolulu Hawaiians/Hawaiians	1974–1975
Houston Texans/Shreveport Steamer	1974–1975

FRANCHISE	YEARS
Jacksonville Express	1975
Jacksonville Sharks	1974
Philadelphia Bell	1974–1975
Portland Storm/Portland Thunder	1974–1975
Southern California Sun	1974–1975
Toronto Northmen/Memphis Southmen/Memphis Grizzlies	1974–1975
Washington Ambassadors/Virginia Ambassadors/Florida Suns/Florida Blazers/San Antonio Wings	1974–1975

UNITED STATES FOOTBALL LEAGUE
(1983–1985)

FRANCHISE	YEARS
Arizona Wranglers/Chicago Blitz	1983–1984
Birmingham Stallions	1983–1985
Boston Breakers/New Orleans Breakers/Portland Breakers	1983–1985
Chicago Blitz/Arizona Wranglers/Arizona Outlaws[1]	1983–1985
Denver Gold	1983–1985
Houston Gamblers	1984–1985
Jacksonville Bulls	1984–1985
Los Angeles Express	1983–1985
Memphis Showboats	1984–1985

FRANCHISE	YEARS
Michigan Panthers *Absorbed by Oakland Invaders, 1985.*	1983–1984
New Jersey Generals	1983–1985
Oakland Invaders	1983–1985
Oklahoma Outlaws/Arizona Outlaws[1]	1984–1985
Philadelphia Stars/Baltimore Stars[2]	1983–1985
Pittsburgh Maulers/Baltimore Stars[2]	1984–1985
San Antonio Gunslingers	1984–1985
Tampa Bay Bandits	1983–1985
Washington Federals/Orlando Renegades	1983–1985

(League folded during season, 1985.)

AMERICAN BASKETBALL LEAGUE *(FIRST)*
(1925–1931)

FRANCHISE	YEARS
Baltimore Orioles	1926–1927
Boston Whirlwinds	1925
Brooklyn Arcadians	1925–1926
Brooklyn Celtics/New York Celtics	1926–1928, 1929
Brooklyn Visitations *Joined second American Basketball League,* *1933.*	1928–1931
Buffalo Germans/Buffalo Bisons	1925–1926
Chicago Bruins *Joined National Basketball League, 1939.*	1925–1931

FRANCHISE	YEARS
Cleveland Rosenblums	1925–1930
Detroit Cardinals	1927–1928
Detroit Pulaski Post Five	1925–1926
East Liverpool Panthers	1925
Fort Wayne Caseys/Fort Wayne Hoosiers/Fort Wayne Guards	1925–1931
New York Hakoahs	1928–1929
Paterson Crescents	1929–1930
Paterson Whirlwinds	1928–1929
Philadelphia Phillies/Philadelphia Quakers/Philadelphia Warriors	1926–1928
Rochester Centrals	1925–1931
Syracuse All-Americans	1929–1930
Toledo Red Man Tobaccos	1930–1931
Trenton Royal Bengals/Trenton Bengals	1928–1929
Washington Palace Five/Washington Laundry-men/Washington Palacians *Absorbed by Brooklyn Visitations, 1928.*	1925–1928

AMERICAN BASKETBALL LEAGUE *(SECOND)*
(1933–1953)

FRANCHISE	YEARS
Atlantic City Sand Snipers	1936
Baltimore Bullets *Joined Basketball Association of America, 1947.*	1944–1947
Boston Trojans	1934–1935
Bridgeport Newfield Steelers/Bridgeport Aer-A-Sols/Bridgeport Roesslers	1948–1952
Bronx Americans	1933–1934
Bronx Yankees/New York Yankees	1937–1938
Brooklyn Indians	1943–1944
Brooklyn Jewels/New York Jewels/Brooklyn Jewels/New Haven Jewels/New York Jewels/New York Americans/New York Westchesters/Westchester Indians/New York Gothams/Brooklyn Gothams	1933–1941, 1942–1949
Brooklyn Visitations/Paterson Visitations/Brooklyn Visitations/Baltimore Clippers/Baltimore Orioles *From first American Basketball League.*	1933–1941
Carbondale Aces	1950–1952
Elizabeth Braves/Hartford Hurricanes	1946–1950
Elmira Colonels	1951–1953
Harrisburg Senators	1942–1943
Jersey City Atoms/Lancaster Roses	1946–1948
Kingston Colonials *Absorbed by Troy Celtics, 1939.*	1935–1939
Manchester British Americans	1951–1953

FRANCHISE	YEARS
Middletown Guards	1951–1953
New York Harlem Yankees/Saratoga Harlem Yankees/Glens Falls-Saratoga	1949–1953
New York Original Celtics/Troy Haymakers/Troy Celtics/Brooklyn Celtics	1937–1941
Newark Bears/Newark Joe Fays/Newark Mules/ New Britain Mules[1]	1933–1935
Newark Bobcats	1946–1947
North Hudson Thourots/Camden Brewers/Camden Athletics/New Britain Palaces/New Britain Jacka-ways/New Britain Mules[1]	1933–1935
Passaic Bengal Tigers/Trenton Tigers	1941–1950
Paterson Panthers/Trenton Bengals/Trenton Moose/Passaic Red Devils/Passaic Reds	1935–1936
Pawtucket Slaters	1952–1953
Philadelphia Hebrews/Philadelphia Colonials/ Philadelphia Sphas	1933–1949
Schenectady Packers	1949
Schenectady Yankees	1951–1952
Scranton Miners	1947, 1948–1953
Trenton Moose	1933–1934
Troy Celtics	1946–1947
Union City Reds/Jersey Reds Absorbed by New York Jewels, 1940.	1933–1940
Utica Pros	1950–1951
Washington Capitol's/Paterson Crescents	1944–1951
Washington Capitols	1951–1952
Washington Heurichs/Washington Heurich Brew-ers/Washington Brewers	1938–1942

FRANCHISE	YEARS
Wilkes-Barre Barons	1938–1940
Wilkes-Barre Barons	1947–1953
Wilmington Blue Bombers/Camden Indians/ Brooklyn Indians/Wilmington Blue Bombers/ Wilmington Bombers	1941–1947
Yonkers Chiefs	1946–1947

NATIONAL BASKETBALL LEAGUE
(1937–1949)

FRANCHISE	YEARS
Akron Firestone Non-Skids/Akron Firestones	1937–1941
Akron Goodyear Wingfoots/Akron Goodyears	1937–1942
Anderson Duffey Packers *Joined National Basketball Association as Anderson Packers, 1949.*	1946–1949
Buffalo Bisons	1937–1938
Buffalo Bisons/Tri-Cities Blackhawks *Joined National Basketball Association, 1949.*	1946–1949
Chicago American Gears/Chicago Gears	1944–1947
Chicago Bruins/Chicago Studebaker Flyers/ Chicago Studebakers/Chicago Champions *From first American Basketball League.*	1939–1943
Cleveland Allmen Transfers	1944–1946
Cleveland Chase Brassmen/Cleveland Brass	1943–1944
Columbus Athletic Supply	1937–1938
Dayton Metropolitans/Dayton Metros	1937–1938

FRANCHISE	YEARS
Dayton Rens	1949
Denver Nuggets *Joined National Basketball Association, 1949.*	1948–1949
Detroit Gems/Minneapolis Lakers *Joined Basketball Association of America,* *1948.*	1946–1948
Detroit Vagabond Kings	1948–1949
Fort Wayne General Electrics	1937–1938
Fort Wayne Zollner Pistons *Joined National Basketball Association as Fort* *Wayne Pistons, 1949.*	1941–1949
Hammond Calumet Buccaneers	1948–1949
Indianapolis Kautskys/Indianapolis All-Americans *Joined Basketball Association of America as* *Indianapolis Jets, 1948.*	1937–1938, 1939– 1940, 1941–1942, 1945–1946, 1947–1948
Kankakee Gallagher Trojans	1937–1938
Oshkosh All-Stars *Joined National Basketball Association as* *Milwaukee All-Stars, 1949.*	1937–1949
Pittsburgh Pirates	1937–1939
Pittsburgh Raiders/Youngstown Bears/Midland Dow A.C.'s/Midland Chemicals/Flint Dow A.C.'s/ Flint Chemicals	1944–1948
Richmond King Clothiers/Richmond Kings/ Cincinnati Comellos	1937–1938
Rochester Royals *Joined Basketball Association of America,* *1948.*	1945–1948
Sheboygan Red Skins *Joined National Basketball Association, 1949.*	1938–1949
Syracuse Nationals *Joined National Basketball Association, 1949.*	1946–1949

FRANCHISE	YEARS
Toledo Jeeps/Waterloo Hawks *Joined National Basketball Association, 1949.*	1946–1949
Toledo Jim White Chevrolets/Toledo Chevies	1941–1942
Warren Penn Oilers/Warren Penns/Cleveland White Horses/Detroit Eagles	1937–1941
Whiting Ciesar All-Americans/Hammond Ciesar All-Americans	1937–1941

BASKETBALL ASSOCIATION OF AMERICA
(1946–1949)

NATIONAL BASKETBALL ASSOCIATION
(1949–PRESENT)

FRANCHISE	YEARS
Anderson Packers *From National Basketball League as Anderson Duffey Packers.*	1949–1950
Baltimore Bullets	1947–1954
Boston Celtics	1946–present
Buffalo Braves/Dallas Express/San Diego Clippers/Los Angeles Clippers	1970–present
Charlotte Spirit/Charlotte Hornets	1988–present
Chicago Bulls	1966–present
Chicago Packers/Chicago Zephyrs/Baltimore Bullets/Capital Bullets/Washington Bullets/Washington Wizards	1961–present
Chicago Stags/Chicago Bruins	1946–1950

FRANCHISE	YEARS
Cleveland Cavaliers	1970–present
Cleveland Rebels	1946–1947
Dallas Mavericks	1980–present
Denver Nuggets *From National Basketball League.*	1949–1950
Denver Nuggets *From American Basketball Association.*	1976–present
Detroit Falcons	1946–1947
Fort Wayne Pistons/Detroit Pistons *From National Basketball League as Fort* *Wayne Zollner Pistons.*	1949–present
Indiana Pacers *From American Basketball Association.*	1976–present
Indianapolis Jets *From National Basketball League as Indian-* *apolis Kautskys.*	1948–1949
Indianapolis Olympians	1949–1953
Miami Heat	1988–present
Milwaukee All-Stars *From National Basketball League as Oshkosh* *All-Stars.*	1949
Milwaukee Bucks	1968–present
Minneapolis Lakers/Los Angeles Lakers *From National Basketball League.*	1948–present
Minnesota Timberwolves	1989–present
New Orleans Jazz/Utah Jazz	1974–present
New York Knickerbockers	1946–present
New York Nets/New Jersey Nets *From American Basketball Association.*	1976–present
Orlando Magic	1989–present

FRANCHISE	YEARS
Philadelphia Warriors/San Francisco Warriors/ Golden State Warriors	1946–present
Phoenix Suns	1968–present
Pittsburgh Ironmen	1946–1947
Portland Trail Blazers	1970–present
Providence Steamrollers	1946–1949
Rochester Royals/Cincinnati Royals/Kansas City-Omaha Kings/Kansas City Kings/Sacramento Kings *From National Basketball League.*	1948–present
St. Louis Bombers	1946–1950
San Antonio Spurs *From American Basketball Association.*	1976–present
San Diego Rockets/Houston Rockets	1967–present
Seattle SuperSonics	1967–present
Sheboygan Red Skins *From National Basketball League.*	1949–1950
Syracuse Nationals/Philadelphia 76ers *From National Basketball League.*	1949–present
Toronto Huskies	1946–1947
Toronto Raptors	1995–present
Tri-Cities Blackhawks/Milwaukee Hawks/ St. Louis Hawks/Atlanta Hawks *From National Basketball League.*	1949–present
Vancouver Mounties/Vancouver Grizzlies	1995–present
Washington Capitols	1946–1951
Waterloo Hawks *From National Basketball League.*	1949–1950

AMERICAN BASKETBALL LEAGUE *(THIRD)*
(1961–1962)

FRANCHISE	YEARS
Chicago Majors	1961–1962
Cleveland Pipers	1961–1962
Hawaii Chiefs/Long Beach Chiefs	1961–1962
Kansas City Steers	1961–1962
Los Angeles Jets	1961–1962
Pittsburgh Renaissances/Pittsburgh Rens	1961–1962
San Francisco Saints/Oakland Oaks	1961–1962
Washington Capitols/New York Tapers/ Philadelphia Tapers	1961–1962

(League folded during 1962–63 season on December 31, 1962.)

AMERICAN BASKETBALL ASSOCIATION
(1967–1976)

FRANCHISE	YEARS
Anaheim Amigos/Los Angeles Stars/Utah Stars	1967–1975
Dallas Chaparrals/Texas Chaparrals/Dallas Chaparrals/San Antonio Gunslingers/San Antonio Spurs *Joined National Basketball Association, 1976.*	1967–1976
Denver Larks/Denver Rockets/Denver Nuggets *Joined National Basketball Association, 1976.*	1967–1976
Houston Mavericks/Carolina Cougars/Spirits of St. Louis/Utah Rockies	1967–1976

FRANCHISE	YEARS
Indiana Pacers *Joined National Basketball Association, 1976.*	1967–1976
Kentucky Colonels	1967–1976
Louisiana Buccaneers/New Orleans Buccaneers/ Memphis Pros/Memphis Tams/Memphis Sounds/ Baltimore Hustlers/Baltimore Claws	1967–1975
Minnesota Muskies/Miami Floridians/Floridians	1967–1972
New Jersey Freighters/New Jersey Americans/ New York Americans/New York Nets *Joined National Basketball Association, 1976.*	1967–1976
Oakland Americans/Oakland Oaks/Washington Capitols/Virginia Squires	1967–1976
Pittsburgh Pipers/Minnesota Pipers/Pittsburgh Pipers/Pittsburgh Pioneers/Pittsburgh Condors	1967–1972
San Diego Conquistadors/San Diego Sails	1972–1975

AMERICAN BASKETBALL LEAGUE *(WOMEN'S)*
(1996–1998)

FRANCHISE	YEARS
Atlanta Glory	1996–1998
Chicago Condors	1998
Colorado Xplosion	1996–1998
Columbus Quest	1996–1998
Long Beach StingRays	1997–1998
Nashville Noise	1998
New England Blizzard	1996–1998

FRANCHISE	YEARS
Portland Power	1996–1998
Richmond Rage/Philadelphia Rage	1996–1998
San Jose Lasers	1996–1998
Seattle Reign	1996–1998

(League folded during 1998–99 season on December 22, 1998.)

WOMEN'S NATIONAL BASKETBALL ASSOCIATION
(1997–PRESENT)

FRANCHISE	YEARS
Charlotte Sting	1997–present
Cleveland Rockers	1997–present
Detroit Shock	1998–present
Houston Comets	1997–present
Indiana Fever	2000–present
Los Angeles Sparks	1997–present
Miami Sol	2000–present
Minnesota Lynx	1999–present
New York Liberty	1997–present
Orlando Miracle	1999–present
Phoenix Mercury	1997–present
Portland Fire	2000–present
Sacramento Monarchs	1997–present

FRANCHISE	YEARS
Seattle Storm	2000–present
Utah Starzz	1997–present
Washington Mystics	1998–present

NATIONAL HOCKEY ASSOCIATION
(1909–1917)

FRANCHISE	YEARS
Cobalt Silver Kings	1909–1911
Haileybury Comets	1909–1911
Montreal Habs/Montreal Canadiens *Joined National Hockey League, 1917.*	1909–1917
Montreal Shamrocks	1909–1911
Montreal Wanderers *Joined National Hockey League, 1917.*	1909–1917
Northern Fusiliers	1916–1917
Ottawa Senators *Joined National Hockey League, 1917.*	1909–1917
Quebec Bulldogs *Joined National Hockey League, 1919.*	1910–1917
Renfrew Millionaires/Renfrew Creamery Kings	1909–1912
Toronto Blueshirts	1912–1917
Toronto Tecumsehs/Toronto Ontarios/Toronto Shamrocks	1912–1916

PACIFIC COAST HOCKEY ASSOCIATION
(1912–1924)

FRANCHISE	YEARS
New Westminster Royals/Portland Rosebuds/Portland Uncle Sams	1912–1917
Seattle Metropolitans	1916–1924
Vancouver Millionaires *Joined Western Canada Hockey League as Vancouver Maroons, 1924.*	1912–1924
Victoria Senators/Victoria Aristocrats/Spokane Canaries/Victoria Senators/Victoria Cougars *Joined Western Canada Hockey League, 1924.*	1912–1924

NATIONAL HOCKEY LEAGUE
(1917–PRESENT)

FRANCHISE	YEARS
Anaheim Mighty Ducks	1993–present
Atlanta Flames/Calgary Flames	1972–present
Atlanta Thrashers	1999–present
Boston Bruins	1924–present
Buffalo Sabres	1970–present
California Seals/Oakland Seals/California Golden Seals/Cleveland Barons *Absorbed by Minnesota North Stars, 1978.*	1967–1978
Chicago Black Hawks/Chicago Blackhawks	1926–present
Columbus Blue Jackets	2000–present

FRANCHISE	YEARS
Detroit Cougars/Detroit Falcons/Detroit Red Wings	1926–present
Edmonton Oilers *From World Hockey Association.*	1979–present
Florida Panthers	1993–present
Hartford Whalers/Carolina Hurricanes *From World Hockey Association as New England Whalers.*	1979–present
Kansas City Scouts/Colorado Rockies/New Jersey Devils	1974–present
Los Angeles Kings	1967–present
Minnesota North Stars/Dallas Stars	1967–present
Minnesota Wild	2000–present
Montreal Habs/Montreal Canadiens *From National Hockey Association.*	1917–present
Montreal Maroons	1924–1938
Montreal Wanderers *From National Hockey Association.*	1917–1918
Nashville Predators	1998–present
New York Islanders	1972–present
New York Rangers	1926–present
Ottawa Senators	1992–present
Ottawa Senators/St. Louis Eagles *From National Hockey Association.*	1917–1931, 1932–1935
Philadelphia Flyers	1967–present
Pittsburgh Penguins	1967–present
Pittsburgh Pirates/Philadelphia Quakers	1925–1931

FRANCHISE	YEARS
Quebec Bulldogs/Hamilton Tigers/New York Americans/Brooklyn Americans *From National Hockey Association.*	1919–1942
Quebec Nordiques/Colorado Avalanche *From World Hockey Association.*	1979–present
St. Louis Blues	1967–present
San Jose Sharks	1991–present
Tampa Bay Lightning	1992–present
Toronto Arenas/Toronto St. Patricks/Toronto Maple Leafs	1917–present
Vancouver Canucks	1970–present
Washington Capitals	1974–present
Winnipeg Jets/Phoenix Coyotes *From World Hockey Association.*	1979–present

WESTERN CANADA HOCKEY LEAGUE
(1921–1925)

WESTERN HOCKEY LEAGUE
(1925–1926)

FRANCHISE	YEARS
Calgary Tigers	1921–1926
Edmonton Eskimos	1921–1926
Regina Capitals/Portland Capitals/Portland Rosebuds	1921–1926
Saskatoon Crescents/Saskatoon Sheiks	1921–1926

FRANCHISE	YEARS
Vancouver Maroons *From Pacific Coast Hockey Association as* *Vancouver Millionaires.*	1924–1926
Victoria Cougars *From Pacific Coast Hockey Association.*	1924–1926

WORLD HOCKEY ASSOCIATION
(1972–1979)

FRANCHISE	YEARS
Calgary Broncos/Cleveland Crusaders/Florida Breakers/Minnesota Fighting Saints	1972–1977
Chicago Cougars	1972–1975
Cincinnati Stingers	1975–1979
Dayton Aeros/Houston Aeros	1972–1978
Denver Spurs/Ottawa Civics	1975–1976
Edmonton Oil Kings/Alberta Oilers/Edmonton Oilers *Joined National Hockey League, 1979.*	1972–1979
Indianapolis Racers	1974–1978
Los Angeles Aces/Los Angeles Sharks/Michigan Stags/Baltimore Blades	1972–1975
Miami Screaming Eagles/Philadelphia Blazers/ Vancouver Blazers/Calgary Cowboys	1972–1977
Minnesota Fighting Saints	1972–1976
New England Whalers *Joined National Hockey League as Hartford* *Whalers, 1979.*	1972–1979

FRANCHISE	YEARS
New York Raiders/New York Golden Blades/ Jersey Knights/San Diego Mariners	1972–1977
Ottawa Nationals/Toronto Toros/Birmingham Bulls	1972–1978
Phoenix Roadrunners	1974–1977
San Francisco Sharks/Quebec Nordiques *Joined National Hockey League, 1979.*	1972–1979
Winnipeg Jets *Joined National Hockey League, 1979.*	1972–1979

AMERICAN SOCCER LEAGUE *(FIRST)*
(1921–1929, 1931–1933)

ATLANTIC COAST LEAGUE
(1929–1930)

FRANCHISE	YEARS
Boston Wonder Workers/Boston/Boston Bears	1924–1929, 1931, 1931–1933
Bridgeport Bears/Philadelphia Football Club	1929
Bridgeport Hungaria/Newark/Newark Americans	1929–1932
Brooklyn Hakoah/Hakoah All-Stars/New York Hakoah	1929–1933
Brooklyn Wanderers	1932–1933
Brooklyn Wanderers/New York Americans *Joined second American Soccer League, 1933.*	1922–1933
Fall River Football Club	1932–1933

FRANCHISE	YEARS
Fall River United/Fall River Marksmen/New York Yankees[1] *Absorbed by Fall River Football Club, 1931.*	1921–1931
Fleisher Yarn	1924–1925
Harrison Soccer Club	1921–1923
Hartford Americans	1927
Holyoke Falcos	1921–1922
Indiana Flooring/New York Nationals/New York Giants	1924–1932
J & P Coats/Pawtucket Rangers	1921–1933
Jersey City	1929
Jersey City Celtics	1921
New Bedford Whalers *Absorbed by Fall River Football Club, 1931.*	1924–1929, 1929–1931
New York Brookhattan *Joined second American Soccer League as Brookhattan, 1933.*	1933
New York Field Club	1921–1924
New York Field Club	1932–1933
Newark Skeeters	1923–1928
Paterson Silk Sox/New York Giants/New York Soccer Club/New York Yankees[1] *Absorbed by Fall River Football Club, 1931.*	1922–1928, 1929–1931
Philadelphia	1928–1929
Philadelphia Celtic	1927
Philadelphia Field Club	1922–1927
Philadelphia Field Club/Bethlehem Steel	1921–1928, 1929–1930
Prague	1933

FRANCHISE	YEARS
Providence Clamdiggers/Providence Gold Bugs/ Fall River Football Club/New Bedford Whalers	1924–1933
Queens Bohemians	1932–1933
Shawsheen Indians	1925–1926
Springfield Babes	1926
Todd Shipyards	1921–1922

AMERICAN SOCCER LEAGUE *(SECOND)*
(1933–1983)

FRANCHISE	YEARS
Baltimore Americans	1939–1940
Baltimore Americans	1941–1942
Baltimore Americans	1943–1948
Baltimore Germans	1938–1939, 1940–1941
Baltimore Rockets/Baltimore Pompei	1953–1961
Baltimore St. Gerards/Baltimore Flyers	1966–1968
Baltimore Soccer Club/Baltimore Canton/ Baltimore Soccer Club	1934–1948
Baltimore Stars/Baltimore Bays	1972–1973
Bethlehem	1938–1939
Boston Metros	1963–1964
Boston Tigers	1965–1968

FRANCHISE	YEARS

Brookhattan/Brookhattan-Galicia/Galicia/
Galicia-Honduras
    From first American Soccer League as New
    York Brookhattan.
	1933–1962

Brooklyn Celtics	1940–1941
Brooklyn Celtics/St. Mary's Celtics	1933–1940
Brooklyn Football Club	1933
Brooklyn Hispano	1933–1957
Brooklyn Italians/Inter-Brooklyn Italians[1]/Inter Soccer Club[1]/Boca Juniors[1]	1956–1964
Brooklyn Wanderers	1942–1948
California Sunshine	1977–1980

Carolina Lightnin'
    Joined United Soccer League as Charlotte
    Gold, 1984.
	1981–1983

Chicago Americans	1972
Chicago Cats	1975–1976
Cincinnati Comets	1972–1975
Cleveland Stars/Cleveland Cobras/Georgia Generals	1972–1982
Colombo	1959–1960
Columbus Magic	1979–1980
Dallas Americans *Joined United Soccer League, 1984.*	1983
Delaware Wings	1972–1974
Detroit Express	1981–1983
Detroit Soccer Club/Detroit Mustangs	1972–1973

FRANCHISE	YEARS
Elizabeth Falcons/Elizabeth Polish Falcons/ Elizabeth Falcons/Falcons Soccer Club/Falcons-Warsaw	1954–1964
Fall River Soccer Club	1957–1963
Gary Tigers/Indiana Tigers	1973–1974
Golden Gate Gales	1980
Hartford Soccer Club/Hartford Kings/Hartford Soccer Club/Hartford Kings	1964–1968
Hungarian Americans	1963–1968
Inter Soccer Club/Inter-Brooklyn Italians[1]/Inter Soccer Club[1]/Boca Juniors[1]	1960–1964
Inter Soccer Club/New York Inter	1965–1969
Irish-Americans/Kearny Celtic	1949–1951
Jacksonville Tea Men	1983
From outdoor North American Soccer League. Joined United Soccer League, 1984.	
Kearny Americans	1944–1946, 1947–1949
Kearny Irish-Americans/Newark Irish/Newark Celtics/Kearny Celtics	1933–1941, 1941–1949
Kearny Scots/Scots-Americans	1933–1944, 1946–1947, 1949–1953
Las Vegas Seagulls	1979
Los Angeles Skyhawks	1976–1979
Ludlow Astros/Fall River Astros/Boston Astros/ Worcester Astros	1967–1975
Ludlow Soccer Club/Ludlow Lusitano	1955–1958
Nashville Diamonds	1982
New England Sharks	1981

FRANCHISE	YEARS
New Jersey Schaefer Brewers/New Jersey Brewers/New Jersey Americans/Miami Americans	1972–1980
New York Americans *From first American Soccer League.* *Absorbed by New York Hakoah, 1956.*	1933–1956
New York Eagles	1978–1979, 1981
New York Greeks/New York Apollo/New York United	1971–1981
New York Hakoah/New York Hakoah-Americans	1948–1964
Newark Falcos	1964–1967
Newark Germans	1933–1936
Newark Portuguese	1951–1963, 1964–1968
Newark Ukrainian Sitch/Newark Sitch	1962–1964, 1965–1970
Northeast United/Connecticut Wildcats/Connecticut Yankees	1972–1978
Oakland Buccaneers	1976
Oklahoma City Slickers *Joined United Soccer League as Oklahoma* *City Stampede, 1984.*	1982–1983
Olympia	1965–1967
Paterson Caledonians	1936–1938, 1939–1941
Pennsylvania Stoners	1979–1983
Philadelphia Germans/Philadelphia German-Americans/Philadelphia Americans/Uhrik Truckers	1933–1965
Philadelphia Nationals	1941–1953
Philadelphia Passon/Passon Phillies	1936–1941
Philadelphia Spartans	1969–1973
Philadelphia Ukrainian Nationals	1957–1964, 1965–1970

FRANCHISE	YEARS
Phoenix Fire	1980
Pittsburgh Canons	1972
Pittsburgh Miners	1975
Rhode Island Oceaneers/New England Oceaneers/Indianapolis Daredevils	1974–1979
Rochester Flash *Joined United Soccer League, 1984.*	1981–1982
Rochester Lancers *Joined outdoor North American Soccer League, 1970.*	1967–1969
Roma Soccer Club	1964–1968
Sacramento Spirits/Sacramento Gold	1976–1980
St. Louis Mules/St. Louis Frogs	1972
St. Mary's Celtics	1941–1942
Santa Barbara Condors	1977
Southern California Lazers	1978
Syracuse Scorpions	1969–1971
Syracuse Suns	1973–1974
Tacoma Tides	1976
Trenton Americans	1953–1955
Trenton Athletics	1948–1951
Trenton Highlanders	1938–1939
Utah Pioneers/Utah Golden Spikers	1976
Virginia Capitol Cavaliers/Washington Cavaliers	1971–1972
Washington Brittanica/Washington Darts *Joined outdoor North American Soccer League, 1970.*	1967–1969

UNITED SOCCER ASSOCIATION
(1967)

FRANCHISE	YEARS
Boston Rovers *Joined outdoor North American Soccer League as Boston Beacons, 1968.*	1967
Chicago Mustangs *Joined outdoor North American Soccer League, 1968.*	1967
Cleveland Stokers *Joined outdoor North American Soccer League, 1968.*	1967
Dallas Tornado *Joined outdoor North American Soccer League, 1968.*	1967
Detroit Cougars *Joined outdoor North American Soccer League, 1968.*	1967
Houston Stars *Joined outdoor North American Soccer League, 1968.*	1967
Los Angeles Wolves *Joined outdoor North American Soccer League, 1968.*	1967
New York Skyliners	1967
San Francisco Gales *Absorbed by Vancouver Royals in outdoor North American Soccer League, 1968.*	1967
Toronto City	1967
Vancouver Royal Canadians *Joined outdoor North American Soccer League as Vancouver Royals, 1968.*	1967
Washington Whips *Joined outdoor North American Soccer League, 1968.*	1967

NATIONAL PROFESSIONAL SOCCER LEAGUE *(OUTDOOR)*
(1967)

FRANCHISE	YEARS
Atlanta Chiefs *Joined outdoor North American Soccer League, 1968.*	1967
Baltimore Bays *Joined outdoor North American Soccer League, 1968.*	1967
Chicago Spurs *Joined outdoor North American Soccer League as Kansas City Spurs, 1968.*	1967
Los Angeles Toros *Joined outdoor North American Soccer League as San Diego Toros, 1968.*	1967
New York Generals *Joined outdoor North American Soccer League, 1968.*	1967
Oakland Clippers *Joined outdoor North American Soccer League as California Clippers, 1968.*	1967
Philadelphia Spartans	1967
Pittsburgh Phantoms	1967
St. Louis Stars *Joined outdoor North American Soccer League, 1968.*	1967
Toronto Falcons *Joined outdoor North American Soccer League, 1968.*	1967

NORTH AMERICAN SOCCER LEAGUE *(OUTDOOR)*
(1968–1984)

FRANCHISE	YEARS
Atlanta Chiefs/Atlanta Apollos *From outdoor National Professional Soccer League.*	1968–1973
Baltimore Bays *From outdoor National Professional Soccer League.*	1968–1969
Baltimore Comets/San Diego Jaws/Las Vegas Quicksilvers/San Diego Sockers *Simultaneously joined indoor North American Soccer League, 1980, 1983. Simultaneously joined Major Indoor Soccer League, 1982. Joined Major Indoor Soccer League, 1984.*	1974–1984
Boston Beacons *From United Soccer Association as Boston Rovers.*	1968
Boston Minutemen	1974–1976
California Clippers *From outdoor National Professional Soccer League as Oakland Clippers.*	1968
Chicago Mustangs *From United Soccer Association.*	1968
Chicago Sting *Simultaneously joined indoor North American Soccer League, 1980, 1983. Joined Major Indoor Soccer League, 1984.*	1975–1984
Cleveland Stokers *From United Soccer Association.*	1968
Colorado Caribous/Atlanta Chiefs *Simultaneously joined indoor North American Soccer League, 1979.*	1978–1981

FRANCHISE	YEARS
Dallas Tornado *From United Soccer Association.* *Simultaneously joined indoor North American* *Soccer League, 1980.*	1968–1981
Denver Dynamos/Minnesota Kicks *Simultaneously joined indoor North American* *Soccer League, 1979.*	1974–1981
Detroit Cougars *From United Soccer Association.*	1968
Detroit Express/Washington Diplomats *Simultaneously joined indoor North American* *Soccer League, 1979.*	1978–1981
Hartford Bicentennials/Connecticut Bicentennials/ Oakland Stompers/Edmonton Drillers *Simultaneously joined indoor North American* *Soccer League, 1980.*	1975–1982
Houston Hurricane	1978–1980
Houston Stars *From United Soccer Association.*	1968
Kansas City Spurs *From outdoor National Professional Soccer* *League as Chicago Spurs.*	1968–1970
Los Angeles Aztecs *Simultaneously joined indoor North American* *Soccer League, 1979.*	1974–1981
Los Angeles Wolves *From United Soccer Association.*	1968
Memphis Rogues/Calgary Boomers *Simultaneously joined indoor North American* *Soccer League, 1979.*	1978–1981
Montreal Olympique	1971–1973
New England Tea Men/Jacksonville Tea Men *Simultaneously joined indoor North American* *Soccer League, 1979.* *Joined United Soccer League, 1984.*	1978–1982

FRANCHISE	**YEARS**
New York Cosmos/Cosmos/New York Cosmos	1971–1984
Simultaneously joined indoor North American Soccer League, 1981, 1983.	
Joined Major Indoor Soccer League, 1984.	
New York Generals	1968
From outdoor National Professional Soccer League.	
Philadelphia Atoms	1973–1976
Philadelphia Fury/Montreal Manic	1978–1983
Simultaneously joined indoor North American Soccer League, 1981.	
Portland Timbers	1975–1982
Simultaneously joined indoor North American Soccer League, 1980.	
Rochester Lancers	1970–1980
From second American Soccer League.	
St. Louis Stars/California Surf	1968–1981
From outdoor National Professional Soccer League.	
Simultaneously joined indoor North American Soccer League, 1979.	
San Antonio Thunder/Team Hawaii/Tulsa Rough-necks	1975–1984
Simultaneously joined indoor North American Soccer League, 1979, 1983.	
San Diego Toros	1968
From outdoor National Professional Soccer League as Los Angeles Toros.	
San Jose Earthquakes/Golden Bay Earthquakes	1974–1984
Simultaneously joined indoor North American Soccer League, 1980, 1983. Simultaneously joined Major Indoor Soccer League, 1982. Joined Western Alliance Challenge Series as San Jose Earthquakes, 1985.	
Seattle Sounders	1974–1983
Simultaneously joined indoor North American Soccer League, 1980.	

FRANCHISE	YEARS
Tampa Bay Rowdies *Simultaneously joined indoor North American Soccer League, 1979, 1983.*	1975–1984
Team America	1983
Toronto Falcons *From outdoor National Professional Soccer League.*	1968
Toronto Metros/Toronto Metros-Croatia/Toronto Blizzard *Simultaneously joined indoor North American Soccer League, 1980.*	1971–1984
Vancouver Royals *From United Soccer Association as Vancouver Royal Canadians.*	1968
Vancouver Whitecaps *Simultaneously joined indoor North American Soccer League, 1980, 1983.*	1974–1984
Washington Darts/Miami Gatos/Miami Toros/ Fort Lauderdale Strikers/Minnesota Strikers *From second American Soccer League as Washington Brittanica. Simultaneously joined indoor North American Soccer League, 1979. Joined Major Indoor Soccer League, 1984.*	1970–1984
Washington Diplomats	1974–1980
Washington Whips *From United Soccer Association.*	1968

UNITED SOCCER LEAGUE
(1984–1985)

FRANCHISE	YEARS
Buffalo Storm	1984
Charlotte Gold *From second American Soccer League as* *Carolina Lightnin'.*	1984
Dallas Americans *From second American Soccer League.*	1984–1985
El Paso-Juarez Gamecocks	1985
Fort Lauderdale Sun/South Florida Sun	1984–1985
Houston Dynamos	1984
Jacksonville Tea Men *From outdoor North American Soccer League.*	1984
New York Nationals	1984
Oklahoma City Stampede *From second American Soccer League as* *Oklahoma City Slickers.*	1984
Rochester Flash *From second American Soccer League.*	1984
Tulsa Tornadoes	1985

WESTERN ALLIANCE CHALLENGE SERIES
(1985)

WESTERN SOCCER LEAGUE
(1986–1988)

WESTERN SOCCER ALLIANCE
(1989)

FRANCHISE	YEARS
Arizona Condors *Joined American Professional Soccer League, 1990.*	1989
Edmonton Brickmen	1986
Football Club Portland/Portland Timbers *Joined American Professional Soccer League, 1990.*	1985–1989
Football Club Seattle/Seattle Storm *Joined American Professional Soccer League, 1990.*	1985–1989
Hollywood Kickers/California Kickers *Joined American Professional Soccer League as California Emperors, 1990.*	1986–1989
Los Angeles Heat *Joined American Professional Soccer League, 1990.*	1986–1989
Real Santa Barbara *Joined American Professional Soccer League, 1990.*	1989
Sacramento Senators	1989
San Diego Nomads *Joined American Professional Soccer League, 1990.*	1986–1989

FRANCHISE	YEARS
San Jose Earthquakes/San Francisco Bay Black-hawks *From outdoor North American Soccer League as Golden Bay Earthquakes.* *Joined American Professional Soccer League, 1990.*	1985–1989
Victoria Riptide	1985

AMERICAN SOCCER LEAGUE *(THIRD)*
(1988–1989)

FRANCHISE	YEARS
Albany Capitals *Joined American Professional Soccer League, 1990.*	1988–1989
Boston Bolts *Joined American Professional Soccer League, 1990.*	1988–1989
Fort Lauderdale Strikers *Joined American Professional Soccer League, 1990.*	1988–1989
Maryland Bays *Joined American Professional Soccer League, 1990.*	1988–1989
Miami Sharks *Joined American Professional Soccer League as Miami Freedom, 1990.*	1988–1989
New Jersey Eagles *Joined American Professional Soccer League, 1990.*	1988–1989
Orlando Lions *Joined American Professional Soccer League, 1990.*	1988–1989

FRANCHISE	YEARS
Tampa Bay Rowdies *Joined American Professional Soccer League, 1990.*	1988–1989
Washington Diplomats *Joined American Professional Soccer League, 1990.*	1988–1989
Washington Stars *Joined American Professional Soccer League, 1990.*	1988–1989

AMERICAN PROFESSIONAL SOCCER LEAGUE
(1990–1994)

FRANCHISE	YEARS
Albany Capitals *From third American Soccer League.*	1990–1991
Arizona Condors *From Western Soccer Alliance.*	1990
Boston Bolts *From third American Soccer League.*	1990
California Emperors *From Western Soccer Alliance as California Kickers.*	1990
Colorado Foxes	1990–1994
Fort Lauderdale Strikers *From third American Soccer League.*	1990–1994
Los Angeles Heat *From Western Soccer Alliance.*	1990
Los Angeles Salsa	1993–1994
Maryland Bays *From third American Soccer League.*	1990–1991

FRANCHISE	**YEARS**
Miami Freedom *From third American Soccer League as Miami Sharks.*	1990–1992
Montreal Impact *Joined indoor National Professional Soccer League, 1997.*	1993–1994
New Jersey Eagles *From third American Soccer League.*	1990
New Mexico Chilies	1990
Orlando Lions *From third American Soccer League.* *Absorbed by Fort Lauderdale Strikers, 1991.*	1990
Penn-Jersey Spirit	1990–1991
Portland Timbers *From Western Soccer Alliance.*	1990
Real Santa Barbara *From Western Soccer Alliance.*	1990
Salt Lake Sting	1990–1991
San Diego Nomads *From Western Soccer Alliance.*	1990
San Francisco Bay Blackhawks *From Western Soccer Alliance.*	1990–1992
Seattle Sounders	1994
Seattle Storm *From Western Soccer Alliance.*	1990
Tampa Bay Rowdies *From third American Soccer League.*	1990–1993
Toronto Blizzard	1993
Toronto Rockets	1994
Vancouver 86ers	1993–1994

FRANCHISE	YEARS
Washington Diplomats *From third American Soccer League.*	1990
Washington Stars *From third American Soccer League.* *Absorbed by Maryland Bays, 1991.*	1990

(Became minor A-League, 1995–present)

MAJOR LEAGUE SOCCER
(1996–PRESENT)

FRANCHISE	YEARS
Chicago Fire	1998–present
Colorado Rapids	1996–present
Columbus Crew	1996–present
D.C. United	1996–present
Dallas Burn	1996–present
Kansas City Wiz/Kansas City Wizards	1996–present
Los Angeles Galaxy	1996–present
Miami Fusion	1998–present
New England Revolution	1996–present
New York-New Jersey MetroStars	1996–present
San Jose Clash/San Jose Earthquakes	1996–present
Tampa Bay Mutiny	1996–present

MAJOR INDOOR SOCCER LEAGUE
(1978–1990)

MAJOR SOCCER LEAGUE
(1990–1992)

FRANCHISE	YEARS
Buffalo Stallions	1979–1984
Chicago Horizons	1980–1981
Chicago Sting *From indoor North American Soccer League (and simultaneously from outdoor North American Soccer League). (Joined indoor North American Soccer League [and simultaneously joined outdoor North American Soccer League], 1983.)*	1982–1983, 1984–1988
Cincinnati Kids	1978–1979
Cleveland Crunch *Joined indoor National Professional Soccer League, 1992.*	1989–1992
Cleveland Force	1978–1988
Denver Avalanche/Tacoma Stars	1980–1982, 1983–1988
Detroit Lightning/San Francisco Fog/Kansas City Comets	1979–1991
Golden Bay Earthquakes *Simultaneously from outdoor North American Soccer League as San Jose Earthquakes.*	1982–1983
Hartford Hellions/Memphis Americans/Las Vegas Americans	1979–1985
Houston Summit Soccer/Baltimore Blast *Joined indoor National Professional Soccer League as Baltimore Spirit, 1992.*	1978–1992
Minnesota Strikers *From outdoor North American Soccer League.*	1984–1988

FRANCHISE	YEARS
New Jersey Rockets/Dallas Sidekicks/Dallas Mavericks *Joined Continental Indoor Soccer League as Dallas Sidekicks, 1993.*	1981–1982, 1984–1992
New York Arrows/New York Express	1978–1984, 1986–1987
New York Cosmos *From outdoor North American Soccer League.*	1984–1985
Philadelphia Fever/Los Angeles Lazers	1978–1989
Phoenix Inferno/Phoenix Pride	1980–1984
Pittsburgh Spirit	1978–1980, 1981–1986
St. Louis Steamers	1979–1988
St. Louis Storm/St. Louis Spirit	1989–1992
San Diego Sockers *Simultaneously from outdoor North American Soccer League.* *Joined Continental Indoor Soccer League, 1993.*	1982–1983, 1984–1992
Tacoma Stars	1988–1992
Wichita Wings *Joined indoor National Professional Soccer League, 1992.*	1979–1992

NORTH AMERICAN SOCCER LEAGUE *(INDOOR)*
(1979–1982, 1983–1984)

FRANCHISE	YEARS
Atlanta Chiefs *Simultaneously from outdoor North American Soccer League.*	1979–1981
California Surf *Simultaneously from outdoor North American Soccer League.*	1979–1981
Chicago Sting *Simultaneously from outdoor North American Soccer League.* *(Joined Major Indoor Soccer League [and simultaneously joined outdoor North American Soccer League], 1982.)* *Joined Major Indoor Soccer League, 1984.*	1980–1982, 1983–1984
Dallas Tornado *Simultaneously from outdoor North American Soccer League.*	1980–1981
Detroit Express *Simultaneously from outdoor North American Soccer League.*	1979–1981
Edmonton Drillers *Simultaneously from outdoor North American Soccer League.*	1980–1982
Fort Lauderdale Strikers *Simultaneously from outdoor North American Soccer League.*	1979–1981
Los Angeles Aztecs *Simultaneously from outdoor North American Soccer League.*	1979–1981
Memphis Rogues/Calgary Boomers *Simultaneously from outdoor North American Soccer League.*	1979–1981
Minnesota Kicks *Simultaneously from outdoor North American Soccer League.*	1979–1981

FRANCHISE	YEARS
Montreal Manic *Simultaneously from outdoor North American* *Soccer League.*	1981–1982
New England Tea Men/Jacksonville Tea Men *Simultaneously from outdoor North American* *Soccer League.*	1979–1982
New York Cosmos *Simultaneously from outdoor North American* *Soccer League.*	1981–1982, 1983–1984
Portland Timbers *Simultaneously from outdoor North American* *Soccer League.*	1980–1982
San Diego Sockers *Simultaneously from outdoor North American* *Soccer League.* *Joined Major Indoor Soccer League, 1984.*	1980–1982, 1983–1984
San Jose Earthquakes/Golden Bay Earthquakes *Simultaneously from outdoor North American* *Soccer League.*	1980–1982, 1983–1984
Seattle Sounders *Simultaneously from outdoor North American* *Soccer League.*	1980–1982
Tampa Bay Rowdies *Simultaneously from outdoor North American* *Soccer League.*	1979–1982, 1983–1984
Toronto Metros-Croatia *Simultaneously from outdoor North American* *Soccer League.*	1980–1982
Tulsa Roughnecks *Simultaneously from outdoor North American* *Soccer League.*	1979–1982, 1983–1984
Vancouver Whitecaps *Simultaneously from outdoor North American* *Soccer League.*	1980–1982, 1983–1984

AMERICAN INDOOR SOCCER ASSOCIATION
(1984–1990)

NATIONAL PROFESSIONAL SOCCER LEAGUE *(INDOOR)*
(1990–PRESENT)

FRANCHISE	YEARS
Atlanta Attack/Kansas City Attack	1989–present
Baltimore Spirit/Baltimore Blast *From Major Soccer League as Baltimore Blast.*	1992–present
Buffalo Blizzard	1992–present
Canton Invaders/Columbus Invaders *Absorbed by Montreal Impact, 1997.*	1984–1997
Chicago Power/Edmonton Drillers	1988–present
Chicago Vultures/Chicago Shoccers	1984–1987
Cleveland Crunch *From Major Soccer League.*	1992–present
Columbus Capitals	1984–1986
Dayton Dynamo/Cincinnati Silverbacks	1988–1998
Detroit Rockers	1990–present
Florida ThunderCats	1998–1999
Fort Wayne Flames/Indiana Kick	1986–1990
Harrisburg Heat	1991–present
Hershey Impact	1988–1991
Illinois Thunder/Denver Thunder	1990–1993
Jacksonville Generals	1988
Kalamazoo Kangaroos	1984–1986

FRANCHISE	YEARS
Louisville Thunder	1984–1987
Memphis Storm/Memphis Rogues	1986–1990
Milwaukee Wave	1984–present
Montreal Impact *From American Professional Soccer League.*	1997–2000
New York Kick	1990–1991
Philadelphia Kixx	1996–present
Tampa Bay Rowdies	1986–1987
Tampa Bay Terror	1995–1997
Toledo Pride	1986–1987
Toronto Shooting Stars	1996–1997
Toronto ThunderHawks	2000–present
Tulsa Ambush/St. Louis Ambush	1991–2000
Wichita Wings *From Major Soccer League.*	1992–present

CONTINENTAL INDOOR SOCCER LEAGUE
(1993–1997)

FRANCHISE	YEARS
Arizona SandSharks *Joined Premier Soccer Alliance as Arizona* *Thunder, 1998.*	1993–1995, 1997
Carolina Vipers	1994

FRANCHISE	YEARS
Dallas Sidekicks *From Major Soccer League as Dallas Mavericks.* *Joined Premier Soccer Alliance, 1998.*	1993–1997
Detroit Neon/Detroit Safari	1994–1997
Houston Hotshots *Joined World Indoor Soccer League, 1999.*	1994–1997
Indianapolis Twisters/Indiana Twisters	1996–1997
Las Vegas DustDevils	1994–1995
Los Angeles United/Anaheim Splash	1993–1997
Mexico Toros	1995
Monterrey La Raza *Joined World Indoor Soccer League, 1999.*	1993–1997
Pittsburgh Stingers	1994–1995
Portland Pride *Joined Premier Soccer Alliance as Portland Pythons, 1998.*	1993–1997
Sacramento Knights *Joined Premier Soccer Alliance, 1998.*	1993–1997
San Diego Sockers *From Major Soccer League.* *Joined World Indoor Soccer League, 2001.*	1993–1996
San Jose Grizzlies	1994–1995
Seattle SeaDogs	1995–1997
Washington Warthogs	1994–1997

PREMIER SOCCER ALLIANCE
(1998)

WORLD INDOOR SOCCER LEAGUE
(1999–PRESENT)

FRANCHISE	YEARS
Arizona Thunder *From Continental Indoor Soccer League as Arizona SandSharks.*	1998–present
Dallas Sidekicks *From Continental Indoor Soccer League.*	1998–present
Houston Hotshots *From Continental Indoor Soccer League.*	1999–present
London United	1999
Manchester Lightning/Manchester Magic	1999
Monterrey La Raza *From Continental Indoor Soccer League.*	1999–present
Newcastle Geordies	1999
Portland Pythons *From Continental Indoor Soccer League as Portland Pride.*	1998–1999
Sacramento Knights *From Continental Indoor Soccer League.*	1998–present
St. Louis Steamers	2000–present
San Diego Sockers *From Continental Indoor Soccer League.*	2001–present
Sheffield Strikers	1999
Utah Freezz	1999–present

ARENA FOOTBALL LEAGUE
(1987–PRESENT)

FRANCHISE	YEARS
Albany Firebirds	1990–present
Arizona Rattlers	1992–present
Buffalo Destroyers	1999–present
Carolina Cobras	2000–present
Charlotte Rage	1992–1996
Chicago Bruisers	1987–1989
Cincinnati Rockers	1992–1993
Columbus Thunderbolts/Cleveland Thunderbolts	1991–1994
Connecticut Coyotes	1995–1996
Dallas Texans	1990–1995
Denver Dynamite/Sacramento Attack/Miami Hooters/Florida Bobcats	1987, 1989–present
Detroit Drive/Massachusetts Marauders/Grand Rapids Rampage	1988–1994, 1998–present
Detroit Fury	2001–present
Fort Worth Cavalry	1994
Iowa Barnstormers	1995–present
Las Vegas Sting/Anaheim Piranhas	1995–1997
Los Angeles Avengers	2000–present
Los Angeles Cobras	1988
Los Angeles Hot Rods	1998
Los Angeles Wings	1992

FRANCHISE	YEARS
Memphis Pharaohs/Portland Forest Dragons/ Oklahoma Wranglers	1995–present
Milwaukee Mustangs	1995–present
Minnesota Fighting Pike	1996
Nashville Kats	1997–present
New England Steamrollers	1988
New Jersey Red Dogs	1997–present
New Orleans Night	1991–1992
New York CityHawks/New England Sea Wolves	1997–present
New York Knights	1988
Orlando Predators	1991–present
Pittsburgh Gladiators/Tampa Bay Storm	1987–present
St. Louis Stampede	1995–1996
San Antonio Force	1992
San Jose SaberCats	1995–present
Texas Terror/Houston ThunderBears	1996–present
Washington Commandos/Maryland Commandos/ Washington Commandos	1987, 1989–1990

WORLD TEAMTENNIS
(1974–1978, 1992–PRESENT)

TEAMTENNIS
(1981–1991)

FRANCHISE	YEARS
Anaheim Oranges/California Oranges	1978, 1981–1983
Atlanta Thunder/Milwaukee Deuce/Milwaukee Racqueteers	1991–1997
Baltimore Banners	1974
Boston Bays	1984–1986
Boston Lobsters	1974–1978
Charlotte Express	1994–1995
Charlotte Heat	1987–1991
Chicago Aces	1974
Chicago Aces/Chicago Fyre/Chicago Fire	1982–1986
Cleveland Nets	1974–1977
Corpus Christi Advantage	1986
Dallas Stars	1982–1983
Denver Racquets/Phoenix Racquets	1974–1978
Detroit Loves	1974
Florida Flamingos	1974
Florida Twist	1993–1995
Fresno Sun-Nets	1988–1989
Golden Gaters/Oakland Breakers	1974–1978, 1981–1982
Hartford FoxForce	2000–present

FRANCHISE	YEARS
Hawaii Leis	1974–1976
Houston Astro-Knots	1982–1983
Houston E-Z Riders	1974
Idaho Sneakers	1994–present
Indiana Loves	1975–1978
Indiana Loves	1983
Kansas City Explorers	1993–present
Long Beach Breakers	1984
Los Angeles Strings	1974–1978, 1981–1993
Miami Beach Breakers/Miami Breakers	1990–1991
Miami Beach Breakers/Miami Breakers/South Florida Breakers/Wellington Aces	1985–1991
Minnesota Buckskins	1974
Minnesota Penguins	1993
New Jersey Stars/Delaware Smash	1987–present
New York Hamptons	2000–present
New York OTBzz/Schenectady County Electrics	1995–present
New York Sets/New York Apples	1974–1978
Newport Beach Dukes	1990–1994
Oakland Aces	1985–1986
Philadelphia Freedoms	1974
Phoenix Smash	1992–1994
Phoenix Sunsets/Arizona Racquets	1982–1983
Pittsburgh Triangles	1974–1976
Portland Panthers	1988–1989

FRANCHISE	YEARS
Raleigh Edge	1990–1993
Sacramento Capitals	1986–present
St. Louis Aces	1994–present
St. Louis Eagles/St. Louis Slims	1984–1985
San Antonio Racquets	1985–1994
San Diego Friars/San Diego Buds	1975–1978, 1981–1985
Sea-Port Cascades/Seattle Cascades	1977–1978
Soviets	1977
Springfield Lasers	1996–present
Sun Belt Nets	1978
Tampa Bay Action	1992
Toronto-Buffalo Royals	1974
Vail Eagles	1992
Wichita Advantage	1991–1995

WORLD ROLLER HOCKEY LEAGUE
(1993)

FRANCHISE	YEARS
Aztecs	1993
Blast	1993
Express	1993
Fury	1993

FRANCHISE	YEARS
Titans	1993
Turbos	1993
Typhoon	1993
Wave	1993

ROLLER HOCKEY INTERNATIONAL
(1993–1997, 1999)

FRANCHISE	YEARS
Anaheim Bullfrogs *Joined Major League Roller Hockey, 1998.* *From Major League Roller Hockey, 1999.*	1993–1997, 1999
Atlanta Fire Ants/Oklahoma Coyotes	1994–1996
Buffalo Stampede	1994–1995
Calgary Rad'z	1993–1994
Chicago Bluesmen	1999
Chicago Cheetahs	1994–1995
Connecticut Coasters/Sacramento River Rats	1993–1997
Dallas Stallions	1999
Denver DareDevils	1996
Detroit Motor City Mustangs	1995
Detroit Racers	1999
Edmonton Sled Dogs/Orlando RollerGators/ Hamilton Hammers/Toronto Wave	1994–1995, 1997
Florida Hammerheads	1993–1994

FRANCHISE	YEARS
Las Vegas Coyotes	1999
Long Island Jawz	1996
Los Angeles Blades	1993–1997
Minnesota Arctic Blast	1994, 1996
Minnesota Blue Ox	1995
Minnesota Blue Ox	1999
Montreal Roadrunners	1994–1997
New England Stingers/Ottawa Loggers/Ottawa Wheels	1994–1997
New Jersey Rockin' Rollers//New York/New Jersey Rockin' Rollers	1994–1997, 1999
Oakland Skates	1993–1996
Orlando Jackals/Miami Jackals/Florida Jackals	1996–1997, 1999
Philadelphia Bulldogs	1994–1996
Phoenix Cobras/Empire State Cobras/Buffalo Wings *Joined Major League Roller Hockey, 1998.* *From Major League Roller Hockey, 1999.*	1994–1997, 1999
Pittsburgh Phantoms	1994
Portland Rage	1993–1994
St. Louis Vipers	1993–1997, 1999
San Diego Barracudas	1993–1996
San Jose Rhinos	1994–1997, 1999
Tampa Bay Tritons	1994
Toronto Planets	1993

FRANCHISE	YEARS
Utah Rollerbees/Las Vegas Flash/Utah Rollerbees/ Utah Sun Dogs	1993–1995, 1999
Vancouver VooDoo	1993–1996

MAJOR LEAGUE ROLLER HOCKEY
(1997–1998)

FRANCHISE	YEARS
Anaheim Bullfrogs *From Roller Hockey International.* *Joined Roller Hockey International, 1999.*	1998
Beast of Guildford	1998
Brighton Tigers	1998
Buffalo Wings *From Roller Hockey International.* *Joined Roller Hockey International, 1999.*	1998
Carolina Copperheads/Carolina Crushers	1997–1998
Colorado Inferno	1999
Columbus Hawks	1998
English Lions	1997
Herne Bay Gulls	1998
London Lasers	1997
London Lions	1998
Manchester Storm	1997
Manchester Tribe	1998

FRANCHISE	YEARS
Michigan North Americans/Port Huron North Americans/Michigan Blast	1998–1999
New York Riot	1997–1998
Orlando Surge	1998
Oshawa Outlaws	1998
Pennsylvania Posse	1997–1998
Philadelphia Sting	1998
Scotland Eagles	1997
South Carolina Fire Ants	1998
Swindon Screaming Eagles	1998
Tampa Bay Rollin' Thunder	1998
Toronto Torpedoes/Toronto Force	1998–1999
Virginia Vultures	1998
Washington Power	1997–1998

WOMEN'S MAJOR LEAGUE ROLLER HOCKEY
(2000–PRESENT)

FRANCHISE	YEARS
Buffalo Wings	2000–present
Florida ThunderCats/Philadelphia ThunderCats	2000–present
New York Flash	2000–present
Virginia Wings	2000–present
Washington Spin	2000–present

EAGLE PRO BOX LACROSSE LEAGUE
(1987–1988)

MAJOR INDOOR LACROSSE LEAGUE
(1989–1997)

FRANCHISE	YEARS
Baltimore Thunder *Joined National Lacrosse League, 1998.*	1987–1997
Buffalo Bandits *Joined National Lacrosse League, 1998.*	1992–1997
Charlotte Cobras	1996
Detroit Turbos	1989–1994
New England Blazers/Boston Blazers *Joined National Lacrosse League, 1998.*	1989–1997
New Jersey Saints/New York Saints *Joined National Lacrosse League, 1998.*	1987–1997
Philadelphia Wings *Joined National Lacrosse League, 1998.*	1987–1997
Pittsburgh Bulls	1990–1993
Rochester Knighthawks *Joined National Lacrosse League, 1998.*	1995–1997
Washington Wave *Absorbed by Baltimore Thunder and Pittsburgh Bulls, 1990.*	1987–1989

NATIONAL LACROSSE LEAGUE
(1998–PRESENT)

FRANCHISE	YEARS
Albany Attack	2000–present
Baltimore Thunder/Pittsburgh CrosseFire *From Major Indoor Lacrosse League.*	1998–present
Boston Blazers *From Major Indoor Lacrosse League.*	1998
Buffalo Bandits *From Major Indoor Lacrosse League.*	1998–present
New York Saints *From Major Indoor Lacrosse League.*	1998–present
Ontario Raiders/Toronto Rock	1998–present
Philadelphia Wings *From Major Indoor Lacrosse League.*	1998–present
Rochester Knighthawks *From Major Indoor Lacrosse League.*	1998–present
Syracuse Smash	1998–present

Part 3

Team Names

This section features an alphabetical listing of every team name ever used in the major leagues. Each name is accompanied with a list of location names which were used in conjunction with it. In some cases, a team may have used the same team name with two or more different location names (for example, if the franchise moved to a new city at some point). Asterisks or, where there is more than one for a particular name, superscripted numbers identify different location names which formed the same franchise. Each location name is followed by the abbreviation for the sport in which the team played ("AF" for arena football, "B" for baseball, "Bk" for basketball, "F" for football, "H" for hockey, "IS" for indoor soccer, "L" for lacrosse, "RH" for roller hockey, "S" for soccer, and "T" for tennis). Consider the following partial example:

TIGERS

Brooklyn[1]	F
Brooklyn	F
Detroit	B
Detroit	F
Gary[2]	S
Indiana[2]	S
Philadelphia	B
Rochester[1]	F

There were two distinct football teams called the Brooklyn Tigers. The first Brooklyn Tigers and the Rochester Tigers (each marked with a "1") were the same team, while the Gary Tigers and Indiana Tigers (each marked with a "2") were also the same team. The rest were individual, distinct franchises.

The names used by teams were not always nicknames (like "Bandits," "Tigers," etc.). Some teams simply went by "Soccer Club," "Football Club," "Field Club," etc. Those names are listed here as applicable. Some teams used no name at all (such as a team called Boston, a team called Newark, etc.). These clubs are listed first under "(NO NAME)." Some teams bore the names of the companies which sponsored them (i.e., J & P Coats, Fleisher Yarn). While these names certainly do not qualify as nicknames like "Tigers" or even names like "Soccer Club," for the sake of consistency they are listed similarly. So J & P Coats can be found under "COATS," Fleisher Yarn under "YARN," etc.

A few clubs used a team name but no location name (such as a team simply called the Blast), and these names are accompanied with the notation "(no location name)."

The team names appear here in capital letters. The two teams which used the name "DAREDEVILS," however, actually used it in slightly different fashion from one another. The Indianapolis Daredevils used one capital *D* in their official name, while the Denver DareDevils used two.

This section identifies only the sport in which each team played. For further information on any team, refer to Part 1.

(NO NAME)			
Bethlehem	S		
Boston	S		
Brookhattan*	S		
Brookhattan-Galicia*	S		
Galicia*	S		
Galicia-Honduras*	S		
Glens Falls-Saratoga	Bk		
Hilldale	B		
Jersey City	S		
Newark	S		
Philadelphia	S		
Prague	S		

ABC'S		
Indianapolis	B	

ACES		
Carbondale	Bk	

Chicago	T	
Chicago	T	
Los Angeles	H	
Oakland	T	
St. Louis	T	
Wellington	T	

ACTION		
Tampa Bay	T	

ADVANTAGE		
Corpus Christi	T	
Wichita	T	

AER-A-SOLS		
Bridgeport	Bk	

AEROS		
Dayton*	H	
Houston*	H	

ALL-AMERICANS		
Buffalo	F	
Indianapolis	Bk	
Syracuse	Bk	

ALL-STARS		
Milwaukee*	Bk	
Oshkosh*	Bk	
St. Louis	F	

ALLEGHENIES		
Pittsburgh	B	

181

ALLMEN TRANSFERS
Cleveland   Bk

ALOUETTES
Montreal   F
Montreal   F
Montreal   F

AMBASSADORS
Virginia*   F
Washington*   F

AMBUSH
St. Louis*   IS
Tulsa*   IS

AMERICAN GEARS
Chicago   Bk

AMERICAN GIANTS
Chicago*   B
Cole's*   B

AMERICANS
Baltimore   S
Baltimore   S
Baltimore   S
Birmingham   F
Boston   B
Bronx   Bk
Brooklyn[1]   H
Chicago   S
Dallas   S
Hartford   S
Kearny   S
Las Vegas[2]   IS
Memphis[2]   IS
Miami[3]   S
New Jersey[4]   Bk
New Jersey[3]   S
New York   Bk
New York[4]   Bk
New York   F
New York[1]   H
New York   S
Newark   S
Oakland   Bk
Philadelphia   S
Pittsburgh   F
Trenton   S

AMIGOS
Anaheim   Bk

ANGELS
Anaheim*   B
California*   B
Los Angeles*   B

APOLLO
New York   S

APOLLOS
Atlanta   S

APPLES
New York   T

ARCADIANS
Brooklyn   Bk

ARCTIC BLAST
Minnesota   RH

ARENAS
Toronto   H

ARGONAUTS
Toronto   F

ARISTOCRATS
Victoria   H

ARROWS
New York   IS

ASTRO-KNOTS
Houston   T

ASTROS
Boston*   S
Fall River*   S
Houston   B
Ludlow*   S
Worcester*   S

ATHLETIC SUPPLY
Columbus   Bk

ATHLETICS
Camden   Bk
Indianapolis   B
Kansas City*   B

Oakland*   B
Philadelphia   B
Philadelphia   B
Philadelphia   B
Philadelphia*   B
Trenton   S

ATLANTICS
Brooklyn   B
Brooklyn   B

ATOMS
Jersey City   Bk
Philadelphia   S

ATTACK
Albany   L
Atlanta*   IS
Kansas City*   IS
Sacramento   AF

AVALANCHE
Colorado   H
Denver   IS

AVENGERS
Los Angeles   AF

AZTECS
(no location name) RH
Los Angeles   S/IS

BABES
Chicago   B
Springfield   S

BACHARACH GIANTS
Atlantic City   B

BADGERS
Milwaukee   F

BALTFEDS
Baltimore   B

BANDITS
Buffalo   L
Tampa Bay   F

BANNERS
Baltimore   T

BARNSTORMERS		
Iowa	AF	
BARONS		
Cleveland	H	
Wilkes-Barre	Bk	
Wilkes-Barre	Bk	
BARRACUDAS		
Birmingham	F	
San Diego	RH	
BAYS		
Baltimore	S	
Baltimore	S	
Boston	T	
Maryland	S	
BEACONS		
Boston	S	
BEANEATERS		
Boston	B	
Boston	B	
BEARS		
Boston	F	
Boston	S	
Bridgeport	S	
Chicago	F	
Cleveland	B	
Milwaukee	B	
Newark	Bk	
Newark	F	
Youngstown	Bk	
BEAST		
Guildford	RH	
BEES		
Boston	B	
BELL		
Philadelphia	F	
BELLES		
Battle Creek*	B	
Muskegon*	B	
Racine*	B	

BENGAL TIGERS		
Passaic	Bk	
BENGALS		
Cincinnati	F	
Cincinnati	F	
Trenton	Bk	
Trenton	Bk	
BICENTENNIALS		
Connecticut*	S	
Hartford*	S	
BILLS		
Buffalo	F	
Buffalo	F	
BISONS		
Buffalo	B	
Buffalo	B	
Buffalo	Bk	
Buffalo	Bk	
Buffalo	Bk	
Buffalo	F	
Buffalo	F	
BLACK BARONS		
Birmingham	B	
BLACK CAPS		
Louisville	B	
BLACK CRACKERS		
Atlanta	B	
BLACK HAWKS		
Chicago	H	
BLACK SENATORS		
Washington	B	
BLACK SOX		
Baltimore	B	
BLACK YANKEES		
New York	B	
BLACKHAWKS		
Chicago	H	
San Francisco Bay	S	
Tri-Cities	Bk	

BLADES		
Baltimore	H	
Los Angeles	RH	
BLAST		
(no location name)	RH	
Baltimore	IS	
Michigan	RH	
BLAZERS		
Boston[1]	L	
Florida	F	
New England[1]	L	
Philadelphia[2]	H	
Vancouver[2]	H	
BLITZ		
Chicago	F	
Chicago	F	
BLIZZARD		
Buffalo	IS	
New England	Bk	
Toronto	S	
Toronto	S	
BLUE BIRDS		
Columbus	B	
BLUE BOMBERS		
Wilmington	Bk	
Winnipeg	F	
BLUE JACKETS		
Columbus	H	
BLUE JAYS		
Philadelphia	B	
Toronto	B	
BLUE OX		
Minnesota	RH	
Minnesota	RH	
BLUE SOX		
South Bend	B	
BLUE STOCKINGS		
Toledo	B	

BLUEBIRDS		
Cleveland	B	
BLUES		
Buffalo	B	
Cleveland	B	
Cleveland	B	
Cleveland	B	
Green Bay	F	
Hartford	F	
Indianapolis	B	
Kansas City	B	
Kansas City	F	
St. Louis	H	
BLUESHIRTS		
Toronto	H	
BLUESMEN		
Chicago	RH	
BOBCATS		
Florida	AF	
Newark	Bk	
BOHEMIANS		
Queens	S	
BOLTS		
Boston	S	
BOMBERS		
St. Louis	Bk	
Wilmington	Bk	
BOOMERS		
Calgary	S/IS	
BOSTONS		
Boston	B	
BRASS		
Cleveland	Bk	
BRAVES		
Atlanta[1]	B	
Boston[1]	B	
Boston	F	
Buffalo	Bk	
Elizabeth	Bk	
Milwaukee[1]	B	

Rochester[2]	F	
Syracuse[2]	F	
BREAKERS		
Boston[1]	F	
Florida	H	
Long Beach	T	
Miami[2]	T	
Miami[3]	T	
Miami Beach[2]	T	
Miami Beach[3]	T	
New Orleans[1]	F	
Oakland	T	
Portland[1]	F	
South Florida[2]	T	
BRECKS		
Louisville	F	
BREWERS		
Camden	Bk	
Milwaukee	B	
Milwaukee	B	
Milwaukee	B	
Milwaukee	B	
Milwaukee	B	
New Jersey	S	
Washington	Bk	
BRICKLEY'S GIANTS		
New York	F	
BRICKMEN		
Edmonton	S	
BRIDEGROOMS		
Brooklyn	B	
BRITISH AMERICANS		
Manchester	Bk	
BRITTANICA		
Washington	S	
BRONCHOS		
Cleveland	B	
BRONCOS		
Calgary	H	
Chicago	B	

Denver	F	
Rochester	B	
BROOKFEDS		
Brooklyn	B	
BROOKHATTAN		
New York	S	
BROWN STOCKINGS		
St. Louis	B	
St. Louis	B	
Worcester	B	
BROWNIES		
St. Louis	B	
BROWNS		
Chicago	B	
Cleveland	B	
Cleveland	F	
Cleveland	F	
Indianapolis	B	
St. Louis	B	
St. Louis	B	
BRUINS		
Boston	H	
Chicago	Bk	
Chicago	Bk	
BRUISERS		
Chicago	AF	
BUCCANEERS		
Los Angeles	F	
Louisiana*	Bk	
New Orleans*	Bk	
Oakland	S	
Tampa Bay	F	
BUCKEYES		
Cincinnati*	B	
Cleveland*	B	
Columbus	B	
Columbus	B	
Columbus	B	
Louisville*	B	
BUCKS		
Milwaukee	Bk	

BUCKSKINS		
Minnesota	T	
BUDS		
San Diego	T	
BUFFEDS		
Buffalo	B	
BULLDOGS		
Boston	F	
Boston	F	
Boston	F	
Canton	F	
Cleveland	F	
Los Angeles	F	
New York	F	
Philadelphia	RH	
Quebec	H	
BULLETS		
Baltimore	Bk	
Baltimore*	Bk	
Capital*	Bk	
Washington*	Bk	
BULLFROGS		
Anaheim	RH	
BULLIES		
Columbus	F	
BULLS		
Birmingham	H	
Boston	F	
Chicago	Bk	
Chicago	F	
Jacksonville	F	
Pittsburgh	L	
BURGHERS		
Pittsburgh	B	
BURN		
Dallas	S	
CALEDONIANS		
Paterson	S	
CALUMET BUCCANEERS		
Hammond	Bk	

CANADIENS		
Montreal	H	
CANARIES		
Baltimore	B	
Spokane	H	
CANONS		
Pittsburgh	S	
CANTON		
Baltimore	S	
CANUCKS		
Vancouver	H	
CAPITALS		
Albany	S	
Columbus	IS	
Portland*	H	
Regina*	H	
Sacramento	T	
Washington	H	
CAPITOL CAVALIERS		
Virginia	S	
CAPITOL'S		
Washington	Bk	
CAPITOLS		
Washington	Bk	
Washington	Bk	
Washington	Bk	
Washington	Bk	
CARD-PITT		
(no location name)	F	
CARDINALS		
Arizona*	F	
Chicago*	F	
Detroit	Bk	
Phoenix*	F	
Racine*	F	
St. Louis	B	
St. Louis*	F	
CARIBOUS		
Colorado	S	

CASCADES		
Sea-Port*	T	
Seattle*	T	
CASEYS		
Fort Wayne	Bk	
CATS		
Chicago	S	
CAVALIERS		
Cleveland	Bk	
Washington	S	
CAVALRY		
Fort Worth	AF	
CELTIC		
Kearny	S	
Philadelphia	S	
CELTICS		
Boston	Bk	
Brooklyn[1]	Bk	
Brooklyn[2]	Bk	
Brooklyn[3]	S	
Brooklyn	S	
Jersey City	S	
Kearny[4]	S	
New York[1]	Bk	
Newark[4]	S	
St. Mary's[3]	S	
St. Mary's	S	
Troy[2]	Bk	
Troy	Bk	
CELTS		
Cincinnati	F	
CENTENNIALS		
Philadelphia	B	
CENTRALS		
Rochester	Bk	
CFL COLTS		
Baltimore	F	
CFLS		
Baltimore	F	

CHAMPIONS
   Chicago   Bk

CHAPARRALS
   Dallas*   Bk
   Texas*   Bk

CHARGERS
   Los Angeles*   F
   San Diego*   F

CHASE BRASSMEN
   Cleveland   Bk

CHEETAHS
   Chicago   RH

CHEMICALS
   Flint*   Bk
   Midland*   Bk

CHEVIES
   Toledo   Bk

CHICKS
   Grand Rapids*   B
   Milwaukee*   B

CHIEFS
   Atlanta   S
   Atlanta   S/IS
   Hawaii*   Bk
   Kansas City   F
   Long Beach*   Bk
   Milwaukee   F
   Yonkers   Bk

CHIFEDS
   Chicago   B

CHILIES
   New Mexico   S

CIESAR ALL-AMERICANS
   Hammond*   Bk
   Whiting*   Bk

CITY
   Toronto   S

CITYHAWKS
   New York   AF

CIVICS
   Ottawa   H

CLAMDIGGERS
   Providence   S

CLASH
   San Jose   S

CLAWS
   Baltimore   Bk

CLIPPERS
   Baltimore   Bk
   California[1]   S
   Los Angeles[2] Bk
   Oakland[1]   S
   San Diego[2]   Bk

CLOWNS
   Cincinnati*   B
   Indianapolis*   B
   Indianapolis-Cincinnati*
                      B

COASTERS
   Connecticut   RH

COATS
   J & P   S

COBRAS
   Carolina   AF
   Charlotte   L
   Cleveland   S
   Empire State* RH
   Los Angeles   AF
   Phoenix*   RH

COLLEENS
   Chicago   B

COLOMBO
   (no location name) S

COLONELS
   Elmira   Bk
   Kentucky   Bk

   Louisville   B
   Louisville   F

COLONIALS
   Kingston   Bk
   Philadelphia   Bk

COLT .45S
   Houston   B

COLTS
   Baltimore   F
   Baltimore*   F
   Chicago   B
   Columbus   B
   Columbus   B
   Indianapolis*   F

COMELLOS
   Cincinnati   Bk

COMETS
   Baltimore   S
   Cincinnati   S
   Haileybury   H
   Houston   Bk
   Kansas City   IS
   Kenosha   B

COMMANDOS
   Maryland*   AF
   Washington*   AF

CONCORDES
   Montreal   F

CONDORS
   Arizona   S
   Chicago   Bk
   Pittsburgh   Bk
   Santa Barbara S

CONQUISTADORS
   San Diego   Bk

COPPERHEADS
   Carolina   RH

COSMOS
   (no location name)* S
   New York*   S/IS

COUGARS	
Carolina	Bk
Chicago	H
Detroit	H
Detroit	S
Victoria	H
COWBOYS	
Calgary	H
Chicago	B
Dallas	F
Kansas City	B
Kansas City	B
Kansas City	B
Kansas City	F
COYOTES	
Connecticut	AF
Las Vegas	RH
Oklahoma	RH
Phoenix	H
CRAWFORDS	
Indianapolis*	B
Pittsburgh*	B
Toledo*	B
CREAM CITYS	
Milwaukee	B
Milwaukee	B
CREAMERY KINGS	
Renfrew	H
CRESCENTS	
Paterson	Bk
Paterson	Bk
Saskatoon	H
CREW	
Columbus	S
CRIMSON GIANTS	
Evansville	F
CROSSEFIRE	
Pittsburgh	L
CRUNCH	
Cleveland	IS

CRUSADERS	
Cleveland	H
CRUSHERS	
Carolina	RH
CUBANS	
Cincinnati	B
New York	B
CUBS	
Chicago	B
Cleveland	B
CYCLONES	
Louisville	B
DAISIES	
Darby*	B
Fort Wayne	B
Hilldale*	B
DAREDEVILS	
Denver	RH
Indianapolis	S
DARK BLUES	
Hartford	B
DARTS	
Washington	S
DESTROYERS	
Buffalo	AF
DEUCE	
Milwaukee	T
DEVIL RAYS	
Tampa Bay	B
DEVILS	
New Jersey	H
DIAMONDBACKS	
Arizona	B
DIAMONDS	
Nashville	S
DIPLOMATS	
Washington	S

Washington	S
Washington	S
DODGERS	
Brooklyn*	B
Brooklyn	F
Brooklyn	F
Los Angeles*	B
Newark	B
DOLPHINS	
Miami	F
DONS	
Los Angeles	F
DOVES	
Boston	B
DOW A.C.'S	
Flint*	Bk
Midland*	Bk
DRILLERS	
Edmonton	IS
Edmonton	S/IS
DRIVE	
Detroit	AF
DUFFEY PACKERS	
Anderson	Bk
DUKES	
Newport Beach	T
DUSTDEVILS	
Las Vegas	IS
DYNAMITE	
Denver	AF
DYNAMO	
Dayton	IS
DYNAMOS	
Denver	S
Houston	S
E-Z RIDERS	
Houston	T

EAGLES		Edmonton	F		Philadelphia	S	
Brooklyn*	B	Edmonton	H		Philadelphia	S	
Detroit	Bk						
Houston*	B	**EXPLORERS**			**FIGHTING PIKE**		
New Jersey	S	Kansas City	T		Minnesota	AF	
New York	S						
Newark*	B	**EXPOS**			**FIGHTING SAINTS**		
Philadelphia	F	Montreal	B		Minnesota	H	
St. Louis	H				Minnesota	H	
St. Louis	T	**EXPRESS**					
Scotland	RH	(no location name)	RH		**FILLIES**		
Vail	T	Charlotte	T		Philadelphia	B	
		Dallas	Bk				
EARTHQUAKES		Detroit	S		**FIRE**		
Golden Bay*	S/IS	Detroit	S/IS		Chicago	F	
San Jose	S	Jacksonville	F		Chicago	S	
San Jose*	S/IS	Los Angeles	F		Chicago	T	
		New York	IS		Phoenix	S	
ECKFORDS					Portland	Bk	
Brooklyn	B	**FALCONS**					
		Atlanta	F		**FIRE ANTS**		
ECLIPSE		Detroit	Bk		Atlanta	RH	
Louisville	B	Detroit	H		South Carolina	RH	
		Elizabeth	S				
EDGE		Toronto	S		**FIREBIRDS**		
Raleigh	T				Albany	AF	
		FALCONS SOCCER CLUB					
EIGHTY-SIXERS		(no location name)	S		**FIRESTONE NON-SKIDS**		
Vancouver	S				Akron	Bk	
		FALCONS-WARSAW					
ELECTRICS		(no location name)	S		**FIRESTONES**		
Buffalo	B				Akron	Bk	
Schenectady County	T	**FALCOS**					
		Holyoke	S		**FLAMES**		
ELITE GIANTS		Newark	S		Atlanta*	H	
Baltimore*	B				Calgary*	H	
Columbus*	B	**FEDERALS**			Fort Wayne	IS	
Nashville*	B	Indianapolis	B				
Washington*	B	Washington	F		**FLAMINGOS**		
					Florida	T	
ELITES		**FEDS**					
Cleveland	B	Brooklyn	B		**FLASH**		
		Newark	B		Las Vegas	RH	
ELM CITYS					New York	RH	
New Haven	B	**FEVER**			Rochester	S	
		Indiana	Bk				
EMPERORS		Philadelphia	IS		**FLOORING**		
California	S				Indiana	S	
		FIELD CLUB					
ESKIMOS		New York	S				
Duluth	F	New York	S				

FLORIDIANS
   (no location name)* Bk
   Miami* Bk

FLYERS
   Baltimore S
   Muncie F
   Philadelphia H

FOG
   San Francisco IS

FOOTBALL CLUB
   Brooklyn S
   Fall River S
   Fall River S
   Philadelphia S
   Portland S
   Seattle S

FORCE
   Cleveland IS
   San Antonio AF
   Toronto RH

FOREST CITYS
   Cleveland B
   Rockford B

FOREST DRAGONS
   Portland AF

FORTY-NINERS
   San Francisco F

FOXES
   Colorado S

FOXFORCE
   Hartford T

FREEDOM
   Miami S

FREEDOMS
   Philadelphia T

FREEZZ
   Utah IS

FREIGHTERS
   New Jersey Bk

FRIARS
   San Diego T

FROGS
   St. Louis S

FURY
   (no location name) RH
   Detroit AF
   Philadelphia S

FUSILIERS
   Northern H

FUSION
   Miami S

FYRE
   Chicago T

GALAXY
   Los Angeles S

GALES
   Golden Gate S
   San Francisco S

GALLAGHER TROJANS
   Kankakee Bk

GAMBLERS
   Houston F

GAMECOCKS
   El Paso-Juarez S

GATOS
   Miami S

GEARS
   Chicago Bk

GEMS
   Detroit Bk

GENERAL ELECTRICS
   Fort Wayne Bk

GENERALS
   Georgia S
   Jacksonville IS
   New Jersey F
   New York S

GEORDIES
   Newcastle IS

GERMAN-AMERICANS
   Philadelphia S

GERMANS
   Baltimore S
   Buffalo Bk
   Newark S
   Philadelphia S

GIANTS
   Chicago B
   Cleveland B
   Harrisburg B
   Hilldale B
   New York* B
   New York B
   New York F
   New York F
   New York S
   New York S
   St. Louis B
   San Francisco* B

GLADIATORS
   Brooklyn B
   Pittsburgh AF

GLORY
   Atlanta Bk

GOLD
   Charlotte S
   Denver F
   Sacramento S

GOLD BUGS
   Providence S

GOLD MINERS
   Sacramento F

GOLDEN BLADES
New York   H

GOLDEN GATERS
(no location name)   T

GOLDEN SEALS
California   H

GOLDEN SPIKERS
Utah   S

GOODYEAR WINGFOOTS
Akron   Bk

GOODYEARS
Akron   Bk

GOTHAMS
Brooklyn*   Bk
New York   B
New York*   Bk

GRAYS
Brooklyn   B
Homestead*   B
Louisville   B
Milwaukee   B
Milwaukee   B
Providence   B
Washington Homestead*
                    B

GREEKS
New York   S

GREEN STOCKINGS
New York   B

GREY SOX
Montgomery   B

GRIZZLIES
Memphis   F
San Jose   IS
Vancouver   Bk

GUARDS
Fort Wayne   Bk
Middletown   Bk

GULLS
Herne Bay   RH

GUNNERS
St. Louis   F

GUNSLINGERS
San Antonio   Bk
San Antonio   F

HABS
Montreal   H

HAKOAH
Brooklyn*   S
New York*   S
New York   S

HAKOAH ALL-STARS
(no location name)   S

HAKOAH-AMERICANS
New York   S

HAKOAHS
New York   Bk

HAMMERHEADS
Florida   RH

HAMMERS
Hamilton   RH

HAMPTONS
New York   T

HARLEM YANKEES
New York*   Bk
Saratoga*   Bk

HARTFORDS
Brooklyn*   B
Hartford*   B

HAWAIIANS
(no location name)* F
Honolulu*   F

HAWKS
Atlanta*   Bk
Columbus   RH
Milwaukee*   Bk

St. Louis*   Bk
Waterloo   Bk

HAYMAKERS
Troy   B
Troy   Bk

HEAT
Charlotte   T
Harrisburg   IS
Los Angeles   S
Miami   Bk

HEBREWS
Philadelphia   Bk

HELLIONS
Hartford   IS

HEPS
Boston   B

HERALDS
Detroit   F

HEURICH BREWERS
Washington   Bk

HEURICHS
Washington   Bk

HIGHLANDERS
New York   B
Trenton   S

HILLTOPPERS
New York   B

HISPANO
Brooklyn   S

HOOFEDS
Indianapolis   B

HOOSIERFEDS
Indianapolis   B

HOOSIERS
Fort Wayne   Bk
Hammond   F
Indianapolis   B
Indianapolis   B

Indianapolis	B		
Indianapolis	B		
HOOTERS			
Miami	AF		
HOP-BITTERS			
Rochester	B		
HORIZONS			
Chicago	IS		
HORNETS			
Charlotte	Bk		
Charlotte	F		
Chicago	F		
Cleveland	B		
HORSE-LIONS			
Brooklyn	F		
HORSEMEN			
Brooklyn	F		
HOT RODS			
Los Angeles	AF		
HOTSHOTS			
Houston	IS		
HUNGARIA			
Bridgeport	S		
HUNGARIAN AMERICANS			
(no location name)	S		
HURRICANE			
Houston	S		
HURRICANES			
Carolina	H		
Hartford	Bk		
HUSKIES			
Toronto	Bk		
HUSTLERS			
Baltimore	Bk		

IMPACT
Hershey — IS
Montreal — S/IS

INDEPENDENTS
Rock Island — F

INDIANS
Akron — F
Brooklyn* — Bk
Brooklyn — Bk
Buffalo — F
Camden* — Bk
Cleveland — B
Cleveland — F
Cleveland — F
Cleveland — F
Hammond — F
Oorang — F
Shawsheen — S
Westchester — Bk

INFANTS
Cleveland — B

INFERNO
Colorado — RH
Phoenix — IS

INNOCENTS
Pittsburgh — B

INTER
New York — S

INVADERS
Canton* — IS
Chicago — B
Columbus* — IS
New York — B
Oakland — F

IRISH
Newark — S

IRISH-AMERICANS
(no location name) — S
Kearny — S

IRONMEN
Pittsburgh — Bk

ISLANDERS
New York — H

ITALIANS
Brooklyn* — S
Inter-Brooklyn* — S

JACKALS
Florida* — RH
Miami* — RH
Orlando* — RH

JACKAWAYS
New Britain — Bk

JAGUARS
Jacksonville — F

JAWS
San Diego — S

JAWZ
Long Island — RH

JAZZ
New Orleans* — Bk
Utah* — Bk

JEEPS
Toledo — Bk

JEFFERSONS
Rochester — F

JERSEYMEN
Newark — B

JETS
Indianapolis — Bk
Los Angeles — Bk
New York — F
Winnipeg — H

JEWELS
Brooklyn* — Bk
New Haven* — Bk
New York* — Bk

JIM WHITE CHEVROLETS
Toledo — Bk

JOE FAYS		
Newark	Bk	
JUNIORS		
Boca	S	
KANGAROOS		
Kalamazoo	IS	
KARDEX		
Tonawanda	F	
KATS		
Nashville	AF	
KAUTSKYS		
Indianapolis	Bk	
KEKIONGAS		
Fort Wayne	B	
KELLEYS		
Duluth	F	
KELLYS		
Cincinnati	B	
KEYSTONES		
Philadelphia	B	
Pittsburgh	B	
KICK		
Indiana	IS	
New York	IS	
KICKERS		
California*	S	
Hollywood*	S	
KICKS		
Minnesota	S/IS	
KIDS		
Cincinnati	IS	
KILLERS		
Cincinnati	B	
KING CLOTHIERS		
Richmond	Bk	

KINGS		
Hartford	S	
Kansas City*	Bk	
Kansas City-Omaha*	Bk	
Los Angeles	H	
Richmond	Bk	
Sacramento*	Bk	
KIXX		
Philadelphia	IS	
KNICKERBOCKERS		
New York	Bk	
KNIGHTHAWKS		
Rochester	L	
KNIGHTS		
Jersey	H	
New York	AF	
Sacramento	IS	
LA RAZA		
Monterrey	IS	
LAKERS		
Los Angeles*	Bk	
Minneapolis*	Bk	
LANCERS		
Rochester	S	
LARKS		
Denver	Bk	
LASERS		
London	RH	
San Jose	Bk	
Springfield	T	
LASSIES		
Kalamazoo*	B	
Muskegon*	B	
LAUNDRYMEN		
Washington	Bk	
LAZERS		
Los Angeles	IS	
Southern California	S	

LEGION		
Racine	F	
LEIS		
Hawaii	T	
LIBERTY		
New York	Bk	
LIGHTNIN'		
Carolina	S	
LIGHTNING		
Detroit	IS	
Manchester	IS	
Tampa Bay	H	
LINCOLN GIANTS		
New York	B	
LIONS		
British Columbia	F	
Brooklyn	F	
Detroit	F	
English	RH	
London	RH	
Orlando	S	
LOBSTERS		
Boston	T	
LOGGERS		
Ottawa	RH	
LORD BALTIMORES		
Baltimore	B	
LOVES		
Detroit	T	
Indiana	T	
Indiana	T	
LUMBERMEN		
Tonawanda	F	
LUSITANO		
Ludlow	S	
LYNX		
Minnesota	Bk	

MAD DOGS		**MAULERS**		**MINUTEMEN**	
Memphis	F	Pittsburgh	F	Boston	S
MAGIC		**MAUMEES**		**MIRACLE**	
Columbus	S	Toledo	B	Orlando	Bk
Manchester	IS				
Orlando	Bk	**MAVERICKS**		**MOLLY McGUIRES**	
		Dallas	Bk	Cleveland	B
MAJORS		Dallas	IS		
Chicago	Bk	Houston	Bk	**MONARCHS**	
				Kansas City	B
MANIC		**MERCURY**		Monroe	B
Montreal	S/IS	Phoenix	Bk	Sacramento	Bk
MANSFIELDS		**METROPOLITANS**		**MONUMENTALS**	
Middletown	B	Dayton	Bk	Baltimore	B
		New York	B		
MAPLE LEAFS		Seattle	H	**MOOSE**	
Toronto	H			Trenton	Bk
		METROS		Trenton	Bk
MARAUDERS		Boston	S		
Massachusetts	AF	Dayton	Bk	**MOTOR CITY MUSTANGS**	
		Toronto	S	Detroit	RH
MARCOS					
Dayton	B	**METROS-CROATIA**		**MOUNTAIN CITYS**	
		Toronto	S/IS	Altoona	B
MARINERS					
San Diego	H	**METROSTARS**		**MOUNTIES**	
Seattle	B	New York-New Jersey		Vancouver	Bk
			S		
MARINES				**MULES**	
Minneapolis	F	**METS**		New Britain*	Bk
		New York	B	Newark*	Bk
MARKSMEN		New York	B	St. Louis	S
Fall River	S				
		MIGHTY DUCKS		**MUSKIES**	
MARLINS		Anaheim	H	Minnesota	Bk
Florida	B				
		MILLERETTES		**MUSTANGS**	
MAROONS		Minneapolis	B	Chicago	S
Kenosha*	F			Detroit	S
Montreal	H	**MILLIONAIRES**		Milwaukee	AF
Pottsville	F	Renfrew	H		
St. Louis	B	Vancouver	H	**MUTINY**	
St. Louis	B			Tampa Bay	S
Toledo*	F	**MINERS**			
Vancouver	H	Pittsburgh	S	**MUTUALS**	
		St. Louis	B	New York	B
MARYLANDS		Scranton	Bk		
Baltimore	B			**MYSTICS**	
				Washington	Bk

NAPS		
Cleveland	B	

NATIONALS		
Boston	B	
New York	S	
New York	S	
Ottawa	H	
Philadelphia	B	
Philadelphia	S	
Syracuse	Bk	
Washington	B	
Washington	B	
Washington	B	
Washington	B	
Washington	B	

NEON		
Detroit	IS	

NETS		
Cleveland	T	
New Jersey*	Bk	
New York*	Bk	
Sun Belt	T	

NEW HAVENS		
New Haven	B	

NEWFEDS		
Newark	B	

NEWFIELD STEELERS		
Bridgeport	Bk	

NIGHT		
New Orleans	AF	

NOISE		
Nashville	Bk	

NOMADS		
San Diego	S	

NORDIQUES		
Quebec	H	

NORTH AMERICANS		
Michigan*	RH	
Port Huron*	RH	

NORTH STARS		
Minnesota	H	

NORTHMEN		
Toronto	F	

NUGGETS		
Denver	Bk	
Denver	Bk	

OAKS		
Oakland	Bk	
Oakland	Bk	

OCEANEERS		
New England*	S	
Rhode Island*	S	

OIL KINGS		
Edmonton	H	

OILERS		
Alberta[1]	H	
Edmonton[1]	H	
Houston[2]	F	
Tennessee[2]	F	

OLYMPIA		
(no location name)	S	

OLYMPIANS		
Indianapolis	Bk	

OLYMPICS		
Washington	B	

OLYMPIQUE		
Montreal	S	

ONTARIOS		
Toronto	H	

ORANGES		
Anaheim*	T	
California*	T	

ORIGINAL CELTICS		
New York	Bk	

ORIOLES		
Baltimore	B	
Baltimore	B	
Baltimore	B	
Baltimore	Bk	
Baltimore	Bk	

ORPHANS		
Chicago	B	

OTBZZ		
New York	T	

OTTOWAS		
Altoona	B	

OUTLAW REDS		
Cincinnati	B	

OUTLAWS		
Arizona*	F	
Oklahoma*	F	
Oshawa	RH	

PACERS		
Indiana	Bk	

PACKERS		
Anderson	Bk	
Chicago	Bk	
Green Bay	F	
Kansas City	B	
Schenectady	Bk	

PADRES		
San Diego	B	

PALACE FIVE		
Washington	Bk	

PALACES		
New Britain	Bk	

PALACIANS		
Washington	Bk	

PANHANDLES		
Columbus	F	

PANTHERS		
Carolina	F	
Cleveland	F	
Detroit	F	
East Liverpool	Bk	
Florida	H	

Michigan	F
Paterson	Bk
Portland	T

PASSON
Philadelphia	S

PATRIOTS
Boston*	F
New England*	F

PEACHES
Rockford	B

PEARLS
Philadelphia	B

PENGUINS
Minnesota	T
Pittsburgh	H

PENN OILERS
Warren	Bk

PENNS
Warren	Bk

PEPPERS
Newark	B

PEPS
Newark	B

PERFECTOS
St. Louis	B

PHANTOMS
Pittsburgh	RH
Pittsburgh	S

PHARAOHS
Memphis	AF

PHIL-PITT
(no location name)	F

PHILADELPHIAS
Philadelphia	B

PHILLIES
Passon	S
Philadelphia	B

Philadelphia	B
Philadelphia	Bk

PILGRIMS
Boston	B
Boston	B

PILOTS
Seattle	B

PIONEERS
Pittsburgh	Bk
Utah	S

PIPERS
Cleveland	Bk
Minnesota*	Bk
Pittsburgh*	Bk

PIRANHAS
Anaheim	AF

PIRATES
Chicago	B
Pittsburgh	B
Pittsburgh	Bk
Pittsburgh	F
Pittsburgh	H
Shreveport	F

PISTONS
Detroit*	Bk
Fort Wayne*	Bk

PITTSFEDS
Pittsburgh	B

PLANETS
Toronto	RH

PLYMOUTH ROCKS
Boston	B

POLISH FALCONS
Elizabeth	S

POMPEI
Baltimore	S

PORKERS
Cincinnati	B

PORTUGUESE
Newark	S

POSSE
Las Vegas	F
Pennsylvania	RH

POTOMACS
Washington	B

POWER
Chicago	IS
Portland	Bk
Washington	RH

PREDATORS
Nashville	H
Orlando	AF

PRIDE
Altoona	B
Phoenix	IS
Portland	IS
Toledo	IS

PROS
Akron	F
Hammond	F
Memphis	Bk
Utica	Bk
Washington	F

PULASKI POST FIVE
Detroit	Bk

PURITANS
Boston	B

PYTHONS
Portland	IS

QUAKERS
Philadelphia	B
Philadelphia	B
Philadelphia	Bk
Philadelphia	F
Philadelphia	H

QUEST
Columbus	Bk

QUICKSILVERS		Pawtucket	S	Cincinnati	B
Las Vegas	S	Texas	B	St. Louis	B
QUICKSTEPS		**RAPIDS**		**RED WINGS**	
Washington	B	Colorado	S	Detroit	H
Wilmington	B				
		RAPTORS		**REDJACKETS**	
RACERS		Toronto	Bk	Minneapolis	F
Detroit	RH				
Indianapolis	H	**RATTLERS**		**REDLEGS**	
		Arizona	AF	Cincinnati	B
RACQUETEERS					
Milwaukee	T	**RAVENS**		**REDS**	
		Baltimore	F	Boston	B
RACQUETS		St. Louis	B	Boston	B
Arizona	T			Boston	B
Denver*	T	**REAL**		Cincinnati	B
Phoenix*	T	Santa Barbara	S	Cincinnati	F
San Antonio	T			Jersey*	Bk
		REBELS		Passaic	Bk
RAD'Z		Cleveland	Bk	St. Louis	B
Calgary	RH	Pittsburgh	B	Union City*	Bk
RAGE		**RECRUITS**		**REDSKINS**	
Charlotte	AF	Chicago	B	Boston*	F
Philadelphia*	Bk			Washington*	F
Portland	RH	**RED CAPS**			
Richmond*	Bk	Boston	B	**REDWINGS**	
		Jacksonville	B	Peoria	B
RAIDERS					
Los Angeles*	F	**RED DEVILS**		**REIGN**	
New York	H	Passaic	Bk	Seattle	Bk
Oakland*	F				
Ontario	L	**RED DOGS**		**REMNANTS**	
Pittsburgh	Bk	New Jersey	AF	Chicago	B
RAINMAKERS		**RED MAN TOBACCOS**		**RENAISSANCES**	
Chicago	B	Toledo	Bk	Pittsburgh	Bk
RAMPAGE		**RED SKINS**		**RENEGADES**	
Grand Rapids	AF	Sheboygan	Bk	Orlando	F
RAMS		**RED SOX**		**RENS**	
Cleveland*	F	Boston	B	Dayton	Bk
Los Angeles*	F	Cleveland	B	Pittsburgh	Bk
St. Louis*	F	Memphis	B		
				RESOLUTES	
RANGERS		**RED STOCKINGS**		Elizabeth	B
Buffalo	F	Boston	B		
New York	H	Boston	B	**REVOLUTION**	
		Boston	B	New England	S

RHINOS
San Jose — RH

RHODE ISLANDERS
Providence — B

RIDGEWOODS
Brooklyn — B

RIOT
New York — RH

RIPTIDE
Victoria — S

RIVER RATS
Sacramento — RH

ROADRUNNERS
Montreal — RH
Phoenix — H

ROBINS
Brooklyn — B

ROCK
Toronto — L

ROCKERS
Cincinnati — AF
Cleveland — Bk
Detroit — IS

ROCKETS
Baltimore — S
Chicago — F
Denver — Bk
Houston* — Bk
New Jersey — IS
San Diego* — Bk
Toronto — S

ROCKIES
Colorado — B
Colorado — H
Utah — Bk

ROCKIN' ROLLERS
New Jersey* — RH
New York/New Jersey* — RH

ROESSLERS
Bridgeport — Bk

ROGUES
Memphis — IS
Memphis — S/IS

ROLLERBEES
Utah — RH

ROLLERGATORS
Orlando — RH

ROLLIN' THUNDER
Tampa Bay — RH

ROSEBUDS
Portland — H
Portland — H

ROSENBLUMS
Cleveland — Bk

ROSES
Lancaster — Bk

ROUGH RIDERS
Ottawa — F

ROUGHNECKS
Tulsa — S/IS

ROUGHRIDERS
Saskatchewan — F

ROVERS
Boston — S

ROWDIES
Tampa Bay — IS
Tampa Bay — S
Tampa Bay — S/IS

ROYAL BENGALS
Trenton — Bk

ROYAL CANADIANS
Vancouver — S

ROYAL GIANTS
Brooklyn — B

ROYALS
Cincinnati* — Bk
Kansas City — B
New Westminster — H
Rochester* — Bk
Toronto-Buffalo — T
Vancouver — S

RUBY LEGS
Worcester — B

RUSTLERS
Boston — B

SABERCATS
San Jose — AF

SABRES
Buffalo — H

SAFARI
Detroit — IS

SAILS
San Diego — Bk

ST. GERARDS
Baltimore — S

ST. PATRICKS
Toronto — H

SAINTS
New Jersey* — L
New Orleans — F
New York* — L
St. Paul — B
San Francisco — Bk

SALLIES
Springfield — B

SALSA
Los Angeles — S

SAND SNIPERS
Atlantic City — Bk

SANDSHARKS
Arizona — IS

SCHAEFER BREWERS
New Jersey   S

SCORPIONS
Syracuse   S

SCOTS
Kearny   S

SCOTS-AMERICANS
(no location name)   S

SCOUTS
Kansas City   H

SCREAMING EAGLES
Miami   H
Swindon   RH

SEA WOLVES
New England   AF

SEADOGS
Seattle   IS

SEAGULLS
Las Vegas   S

SEAHAWKS
Miami   F
Seattle   F

SEALS
California*   H
Oakland*   H

SENATORS
Columbus   B
Harrisburg   Bk
Ottawa   H
Ottawa   H
Sacramento   S
Victoria   H
Washington   B
Washington   B
Washington   B
Washington   B
Washington   F

SETS
New York   T

SEVENTY-SIXERS
Philadelphia   Bk

SHAMROCKS
Boston   F
Montreal   H
Toronto   H

SHARKS
Jacksonville   F
Los Angeles   H
Miami   S
New England   S
San Francisco   H
San Jose   H

SHEIKS
Saskatoon   H

SHIPYARDS
Todd   S

SHOCCERS
Chicago   IS

SHOCK
Detroit   Bk

SHOOTING STARS
Toronto   IS

SHOWBOATS
Memphis   F

SIDEKICKS
Dallas   IS

SILK SOX
Paterson   S

SILVER KINGS
Cobalt   H

SILVERBACKS
Cincinnati   IS

SITCH
Newark   S

SKATES
Oakland   RH

SKEETERS
Newark   S

SKYHAWKS
Los Angeles   S

SKYLINERS
New York   S

SLATERS
Pawtucket   Bk

SLED DOGS
Edmonton   RH

SLICKERS
Oklahoma City   S

SLIMS
St. Louis   T

SLOUFEDS
St. Louis   B

SMASH
Delaware   T
Phoenix   T
Syracuse   L

SNEAKERS
Idaho   T

SOCCER CLUB
Baltimore   S
Detroit   S
Fall River   S
Harrison   S
Hartford   S
Inter   S
Inter   S
Ludlow   S
New York   S
Roma   S

SOCKERS
San Diego   S/IS

SOL
Miami   Bk

SOLONS		
Columbus	B	
SOMERSETS		
Boston	B	
SOUNDERS		
Seattle	S	
Seattle	S/IS	
SOUNDS		
Memphis	Bk	
SOUTHMEN		
Memphis	F	
SOVIETS		
(no location name)	T	
SPARKS		
Los Angeles	Bk	
SPARTANS		
Philadelphia	S	
Philadelphia	S	
Portsmouth	F	
SPEEDBOYS		
Boston	B	
SPHAS		
Philadelphia	Bk	
SPIDERS		
Cleveland	B	
SPIN		
Washington	RH	
SPIRIT		
Baltimore	IS	
Charlotte	Bk	
Penn-Jersey	S	
Pittsburgh	IS	
St. Louis	IS	
SPIRITS		
Sacramento	S	
St. Louis	Bk	

SPLASH		
Anaheim	IS	
SPURS		
Chicago*	S	
Denver	H	
Kansas City*	S	
San Antonio	Bk	
SQUIRES		
Virginia	Bk	
STAGS		
Chicago	Bk	
Michigan	H	
STALEYS		
Chicago*	F	
Decatur*	F	
STALLIONS		
Baltimore	F	
Birmingham	F	
Buffalo	IS	
Dallas	RH	
STAMPEDE		
Buffalo	RH	
Oklahoma City	S	
St. Louis	AF	
STAMPEDERS		
Calgary	F	
STAPES		
Stapleton*	F	
Staten Island*	F	
STAPLETONS		
Staten Island	F	
STARS		
Baltimore[1]	F	
Baltimore	S	
Charlotte[2]	F	
Cleveland	S	
Cuban	B	
Dallas	H	
Dallas	T	
Detroit	B	
Harrisburg-St. Louis[3]	B	
Houston	S	

Los Angeles[4]	Bk	
New Jersey	T	
New Orleans-St. Louis[3]		
	B	
New York[2]	F	
Newark	B	
Philadelphia	B	
Philadelphia[1]	F	
St. Louis	B	
St. Louis[3]	B	
St. Louis	S	
Syracuse	B	
Syracuse	B	
Tacoma	IS	
Tacoma	IS	
Utah[4]	Bk	
Washington	S	
STARS (EAST)		
Cuban	B	
STARS (WEST)		
Cuban	B	
STARZZ		
Utah	Bk	
STATESMEN		
Washington	B	
Washington	B	
STEAGLES		
(no location name)	F	
STEAM ROLLER		
Providence	F	
STEAMER		
Shreveport	F	
STEAMERS		
St. Louis	IS	
St. Louis	IS	
STEAMROLLERS		
New England	AF	
Providence	Bk	
STEEL		
Bethlehem	S	

STEELERS		
Pittsburgh	F	
STEERS		
Kansas City	Bk	
STING		
Charlotte	Bk	
Chicago	S/IS	
Las Vegas	AF	
Philadelphia	RH	
Salt Lake	S	
STINGERS		
Cincinnati	H	
New England	RH	
Pittsburgh	IS	
STINGRAYS		
Long Beach	Bk	
STOGIES		
Pittsburgh	B	
STOKERS		
Cleveland	S	
STOMPERS		
Oakland	S	
STONERS		
Pennsylvania	S	
STORM		
Buffalo	S	
Manchester	RH	
Memphis	IS	
Portland	F	
St. Louis	IS	
Seattle	Bk	
Seattle	S	
Tampa Bay	AF	
STRIKERS		
Fort Lauderdale	S	
Fort Lauderdale*	S/IS	
Minnesota*	S/IS	
Sheffield	IS	

STRINGS		
Los Angeles	T	
STUDEBAKER FLYERS		
Chicago	Bk	
STUDEBAKERS		
Chicago	Bk	
SUMMIT SOCCER		
Houston	IS	
SUN		
Fort Lauderdale*	S	
South Florida*	S	
Southern California	F	
SUN DOGS		
Utah	RH	
SUN-NETS		
Fresno	T	
SUNS		
Florida	F	
Phoenix	Bk	
Syracuse	S	
SUNSETS		
Phoenix	T	
SUNSHINE		
California	S	
SUPERBAS		
Brooklyn	B	
SUPERSONICS		
Seattle	Bk	
SURF		
California	S/IS	
SURGE		
Orlando	RH	
TAMS		
Memphis	Bk	

TAPERS		
New York*	Bk	
Philadelphia*	Bk	
TATE STARS		
Cleveland	B	
TEA MEN		
Jacksonville*	S/IS	
New England*	S/IS	
TEAM		
America	S	
Hawaii	S	
TECUMSEHS		
Toronto	H	
TERRAPINS		
Baltimore	B	
TERRIERS		
St. Louis	B	
TERROR		
Tampa Bay	IS	
Texas	AF	
TEXANS		
Dallas	AF	
Dallas	F	
Dallas	F	
Houston	F	
Houston	F	
San Antonio	F	
THOUROTS		
North Hudson	Bk	
THRASHERS		
Atlanta	H	
THUNDER		
Arizona	IS	
Atlanta	T	
Baltimore	L	
Denver*	IS	
Illinois*	IS	
Louisville	IS	
Portland	F	
San Antonio	S	

THUNDERBEARS		
Houston	AF	
THUNDERBOLTS		
Cleveland*	AF	
Columbus*	AF	
THUNDERCATS		
Florida	IS	
Florida*	RH	
Philadelphia*	RH	
THUNDERHAWKS		
Toronto	IS	
TIDES		
Tacoma	S	
TIGER-CATS		
Hamilton	F	
TIGERS		
Boston	S	
Brighton	RH	
Brooklyn[1]	F	
Brooklyn	F	
Buffalo	F	
Calgary	H	
Chicago	F	
Cincinnati	B	
Cleveland	F	
Columbus	F	
Detroit	B	
Detroit	F	
Gary[2]	S	
Hamilton	H	
Hammond	F	
Indiana[2]	S	
Philadelphia	B	
Rochester[1]	F	
Toledo	B	
Trenton	Bk	
TIMBERS		
Portland	S	
Portland	S/IS	
TIMBERWOLVES		
Minnesota	Bk	

TIP-TOPS		
Brooklyn	B	
TITANS		
(no location name)	RH	
New York	F	
Tennessee	F	
TORNADO		
Dallas	S/IS	
TORNADOES		
Newark*	F	
Orange*	F	
Racine	F	
Tulsa	S	
TOROS		
Los Angeles*	S	
Mexico	IS	
Miami	S	
San Diego*	S	
Toronto	H	
TORPEDOES		
Toronto	RH	
TRAIL BLAZERS		
Portland	Bk	
TRIANGLES		
Dayton	F	
Pittsburgh	T	
TRIBE		
Manchester	RH	
TRITONS		
Tampa Bay	RH	
TROJANS		
Boston	Bk	
Troy	B	
TROLLEY DODGERS		
Brooklyn	B	
TRUCKERS		
Uhrik	S	

TURBOS		
(no location name)	RH	
Detroit	L	
TURFS		
Columbus	B	
TWINS		
Minnesota	B	
TWIST		
Florida	T	
TWISTERS		
Indiana*	IS	
Indianapolis*	IS	
TYPHOON		
(no location name)	RH	
UKRAINIAN NATIONALS		
Philadelphia	S	
UKRAINIAN SITCH		
Newark	S	
UNCLE SAMS		
Portland	H	
UNIONS		
Altoona	B	
Baltimore	B	
Boston	B	
Kansas City	B	
UNIQUES		
Chicago	B	
UNITED		
D.C.	S	
Fall River	S	
London	IS	
Los Angeles	IS	
New York	S	
Northeast	S	
VAGABOND KINGS		
Detroit	Bk	
VIKINGS		
Minnesota	F	

VIPERS
Carolina — IS
St. Louis — RH

VIRGINIANS
Richmond — B

VISITATIONS
Brooklyn* — Bk
Paterson* — Bk

VOODOO
Vancouver — RH

VULCANS
Birmingham — F

VULTURES
Chicago — IS
Virginia — RH

WANDERERS
Brooklyn — S
Brooklyn — S
Brooklyn — S
Montreal — H

WARRIORS
Golden State* — Bk
Philadelphia — Bk
Philadelphia* — Bk
San Francisco* — Bk

WARTHOGS
Washington — IS

WASHINGTONS
Washington — B

WAVE
(no location name) — RH
Milwaukee — IS
Toronto — RH
Washington — L

WESTCHESTERS
New York — Bk

WESTERNS
Keokuk — B

WHALERS
Hartford* — H
New Bedford — S
New Bedford — S
New England* — H

WHALES
Chicago — B

WHEELS
Detroit — F
Ottawa — RH

WHIPS
Washington — S

WHIRLWINDS
Boston — Bk
Paterson — Bk

WHITE HORSES
Cleveland — Bk

WHITE SOX
Chicago — B
Louisville — B

WHITE STOCKINGS
Chicago — B
Chicago — B
Philadelphia — B

WHITECAPS
St. Paul — B
Vancouver — S/IS

WHITES
Philadelphia — B

WILD
Minnesota — H

WILDCATS
Connecticut — S
Los Angeles — F

WINDS
Chicago — F

WINGS
Buffalo — RH
Buffalo — RH
Delaware — S
Los Angeles — AF
Philadelphia — L
San Antonio — F
Virginia — RH
Wichita — IS

WIZ
Kansas City — S

WIZARDS
Kansas City — S
Washington — Bk

WOLVERINES
Detroit — B
Detroit — F

WOLVES
Los Angeles — S

WONDER WORKERS
Boston — S

WONDERS
Brooklyn — B

WRANGLERS
Arizona — F
Arizona — F
Oklahoma — AF

XPLOSION
Colorado — Bk

YANKEES
Bronx[1] — Bk
Brooklyn-New York[2] — F
Connecticut — S
New York — B
New York[1] — Bk
New York — F
New York — F
New York[2] — F

New York	S	YARN		ZEPHYRS	
Schenectady	Bk	Fleisher	S	Chicago	Bk
YANKS		YELLOW JACKETS		ZOLLNER PISTONS	
Boston*	F	Frankford	F	Fort Wayne	Bk
New York*	F				

Part 4

Team Name Origins

This section contains information on the origins or the significance of the names of most of the teams featured in this book. The meaning of *every* name has not been documented, therefore not every team appears here. Research continues on those clubs.

Each name which *has* been identified appears only once, even if multiple teams have used the same name. In most cases, later teams simply copied the name of the original team to use the name. A parenthetical notation alerts the reader to names that have been used by more than one team, and the *first* team to use that name is then identified. The text presents the appropriate information if there is a story behind the naming of subsequent teams with the same name.

In some instances, major league teams copied the names of previous minor league teams. Some of these organizations may not have done so deliberately, but the information is considered of enough interest to be presented here.

Akron Firestone Non-Skids: Named for the fact that the team was formed by the Firestone Tire Company. A "Non-Skid" was a type of Firestone tire.

Akron Firestones: Shortened form of the name Akron Firestone Non-Skids (see).

Akron Goodyear Wingfoots: Named for the fact that the team was formed by the Goodyear Tire Company. The "wingfoot," or a foot bearing a wing, is part of the Goodyear logo, and a "Wingfoot" was a type of Goodyear tire.

Akron Goodyears: Shortened form of the name Akron Goodyear Wingfoots (see).

Akron Indians: Named for the American Indian population indigenous to the Akron area. The name was copied from at least two previous independent football teams.

Akron Pros: Short for "professional," as this team was officially the Akron Professional Football Club.

Albany Capitals: Named for the fact that Albany is the state capital of New York.

Albany Firebirds: This team's two owners were driving home from Boston one day and were suggesting names back and forth for their new franchise. One of the names mentioned during the drive was "Firebirds." They both liked it, thought about it, and eventually decided that this would be the team's name.

Alberta Oilers: Named in a fan contest which featured thousands of entries. The name reflects the fact that, in 1949, a large oil discovery 15 miles south of Edmonton resulted in huge growth in the province of Alberta. The city of Edmonton is located in the region which produces the most oil in all of Canada.[3] The location name "Alberta" was used originally because the team was supposed to have been shared between Edmonton and Calgary, Alberta. That idea fell through, however, and the team played exclusively in Edmonton.

Altoona Mountain Citys: Named for the fact that the city of Altoona is very near the Appalachian Mountains.

Altoona Ottowas: Likely named for a Native American tribe (the Ottawas), although the spelling is a bit curious.

Altoona Pride: Likely referred to a sense of civic pride for Altoona.[4]

Altoona Unions: Named for the Union Association in which the team played.

Anaheim Amigos: Reflects the Hispanic culture of the city of Anaheim. The word *amigo* is Spanish for "friend." The name was suggested by Anaheim resident Tom Voigt in a name-the-team contest.[5]

Anaheim Angels: Revised form of the team's previous name of California Angels (and see *Los Angeles Angels*). The name was changed when the Walt Disney Company bought the team.

Anaheim Bullfrogs: Named by the Silver family, the team's owners. The team played at Arrowhead Pond in Anaheim, and a bullfrog is an animal that is often found in a pond.

Anaheim Mighty Ducks: Named by the Walt Disney Company, which owned the team, for the Disney movie *The Mighty Ducks*, which was about a boys' hockey team by the same name.

Anaheim Oranges: Named for a popular fruit for which California is famous. In 1978, when this tennis team played the New York team, it was the Oranges versus the Apples.

Anaheim Piranhas: Named in a call-in name-the-team contest. This team played at Arrowhead Pond in Anaheim, and the team was marketed with the slogan "Piranhas Are in the Pond," as well as with the phrase "Football with a Bite." The name was announced on November 14, 1995.

Anderson Duffey Packers: Named for Duffey's, Inc., a meat-packing plant which sponsored the team.

Anderson Packers: Shortened form of the team's previous name of Anderson Duffey Packers (see).

Arizona Cardinals: Revision of team's former name of Phoenix Cardinals (and see *Racine Cardinals*). The location name "Arizona" is meant to appeal to a larger fan base.

Arizona Condors: Named for an endangered bird once common in Arizona. Condors, which are members of the vulture family, were once prevalent throughout the southern United States and ranged from Mexico to Canada. Their population was vastly reduced 10,000 years ago when the late Pleistocene extinction of large mammals occurred, decimating many of the condors' food sources (including mastodons, giant sloths, and saber-toothed cats). By the 1930s condors were found only in California, and by 1985 only nine wild birds remained. Those nine were brought into captivity and a breeding program begun to try to repopulate the species. By the time this soccer team was formed in 1989, the Arizona Game and Fish Department's Nongame Branch was surveying potential release sites to reintroduce the bird into Arizona. The team folded following the 1990 season, but six condors were successfully released into the Arizona skies in October of 1996.

Arizona Diamondbacks: Named for a snake indigenous to the Phoenix area. Founding owner Jerry Colangelo, in referring to the Tampa Bay team formed at the same time with its selection of the name of the friendly devil ray, stated, "You don't ride or pet a diamondback rattlesnake. We wanted to put a little BITE into our nickname!" The team had to purchase the rights to the name from the Chandler Diamondbacks, a minor winter league baseball team in Chandler, Arizona. The five finalists for the team name were Coyotes, Diamondbacks, Phoenix, Rattlers, and Scorpions.

Arizona Outlaws: Name carried over from Tulsa, Oklahoma (see *Oklahoma Outlaws*). This was a merged team, and the name is actually a combination of *Arizona* Wranglers and Oklahoma *Outlaws*.

Arizona Racquets: Named for the tennis racquet.

Arizona Rattlers: Named for the rattlesnakes indigenous to Arizona.

Arizona Thunder: Named in a contest from among 2000 entries.

Arizona Wranglers: (2 teams) The first team to be called the Arizona Wranglers was the one which played in the United States Football League in 1983. A "wrangler" is a cowboy, so the name reflects some of the Western history of the Phoenix area.

Atlanta Attack: This name was chosen because team owners wanted a name beginning with the letter *A* that would flow with "Atlanta." Ironically, the team kept the name when it moved to Kansas City, Missouri.

Atlanta Black Crackers: This Negro League team copied and slightly altered the name of Atlanta's minor league white baseball team at the time, the Atlanta Crackers. The Atlanta Crackers, in turn, were named for a former nickname of the state of Georgia, the "Cracker State." This nickname came from the days when horses and buggies were a common sight in Georgia, and a common sound was the crack made by the drivers' whips as they forced the horses to run faster.

Atlanta Braves: For this baseball team, see *Boston Braves.*

Atlanta Chiefs: (2 teams) The first team to be called the Atlanta Chiefs was the one which played in the outdoor National Professional Soccer League in 1967. Some of the team's backers were owners of the Atlanta Braves, so the name "Chiefs" was selected to create a connection with the baseball team.

Atlanta Falcons: Named in a contest held by team officials and radio station WSB. Among 40 contestants, the winner was Miss Julia Elliot, a high school teacher from Griffin, Georgia, who wrote the following in her contest essay: "The Falcon is proud and dignified, with great courage and fight. It never drops its prey. It's deadly and has a great sporting tradition."[6] Other names suggested in the contest included Bombers, Crackers, Fireballs,

Firebirds, Knights, Lancers, Rebels, Thrashers, and Thunderbirds.[7]

Atlanta Fire Ants: Named for an insect prevalent in Atlanta and in the state of Georgia. These particular ants, which are a different species than the native variety found in Texas, are themselves not native to the United States. They were accidentally imported prior to the 1920s, possibly because of nests in potted plants or in ballast on ships traveling from South America to Mobile, Alabama, and they spread from there. They are very aggressive and will sting a perceived enemy repeatedly.

Atlanta Flames: Named in a fan contest, chosen from among 10,000 entries, judged by the Atlanta media. The name recalls the capture and burning of Atlanta by General Sherman during the Civil War.[8]

Atlanta Glory: Named for certain stanzas in the song "Battle Hymn of the Republic," as well as for the glory of the Olympic Games, which Atlanta hosted the same year this team began play (1996). Reebok, the team's sponsor, also liked the name.

Atlanta Hawks: See *Milwaukee Hawks.*

Atlanta Thrashers: Named for the brown thrasher, the state bird of Georgia. This name was the choice of owner Ted Turner, who first discussed it with his wife, Jane Fonda, while the two were riding horses in Montana. The team faced a legal challenge from High Speed Publications, Inc., which produced a magazine called *Thrasher.* *Thrasher* was a national publication devoted to skateboarding. The magazine had been founded in 1981 and had made the name "Thrasher" popular among many young people in the country. The two organizations eventually settled out of court, and both now have rights to the name.

Atlantic City Bacharach Giants: Originally formed as an independent team in Jacksonville, Florida, called the Duvall Giants (for Duvall County, of which Jacksonville is a part), this team moved to Atlantic City and was named for Atlantic City mayor Henry Bacharach.[9] Like many Negro League teams, this club also copied and altered the name of a popular white major league baseball team (in this case, the New York Giants).

Atlantic City Sand Snipers: Named for a shorebird (usually called a sandpiper) indigenous to the Atlantic City area. In his book *Can You Name That Team?,* David Biesel explains that Sand Snipers "is a variant spelling of

Sandpiper and is rarely used. It might be that it was an intentional play on words—a sniper—or that it was an early typographical error that just never got corrected."[10]

Aztecs: Named by World Roller Hockey League founder David McLane. Aztecs were early Mexican Indians who were conquered by Cortez in 1520. The word *aztec* translates as "place of the heron."[11]

Baltimore Americans: (3 teams) The first team to be called the Baltimore Americans was the one which played in the second American Soccer League in 1939. All three teams were likely named for the United States of America as well as the second American Soccer League in which they played. In the midst of many other ethnic names, the title "Americans" became a very popular one in the American Soccer Leagues, especially just before and during World War II.

Baltimore Baltfeds: This team played in the Federal League, and the name is a combination of "Baltimore" and "Federal."

Baltimore Banners: This tennis team was likely named for "The Star Spangled Banner," which was written in Baltimore by Francis Scott Key during the War of 1812. Key was inspired to write the national anthem when he witnessed the British attack on Fort McHenry, located in the Baltimore harbor, from September 13–14, 1914. The team's logo featured the stars and stripes.

Baltimore Bays: (2 teams) The first team to be called the Baltimore Bays was the one which played in the outdoor National Professional Soccer League in 1967. Both teams were probably named for Chesapeake Bay, on which Baltimore is situated.

Baltimore Black Sox: Like many Negro League teams, this club took and altered the name of popular white major league baseball teams (in this case, the Boston Red Sox and Chicago White Sox).

Baltimore Blades: This hockey team was named for one of the most important pieces of hockey equipment: the blade on the bottom of the skate.

Baltimore Blast: Owner Ed Hale renamed this team when it moved from Houston, Texas, where it was Houston Summit Soccer. After selling the team to J. W. "Bill" Stealey, who renamed it the Spirit, Hale bought it back in 1998 and revived the Blast name.

Baltimore Bullets: (2 teams) The first team to be called the Baltimore Bullets was the one which played in the Basketball Association of America in 1947. The name may have been chosen in 1944 for a nearby foundry which produced ammunition for American soldiers in World War II. The *Baltimore Sun* also explained that the team had "explosive talent and speed in humbling the opposition."

Baltimore Canaries: Named for the yellow silk jerseys worn by the team.

Baltimore CFL Colts: Baltimore had previously had two football teams called the Baltimore Colts. This team, which played in the Canadian Football League, attempted by its name both to maintain the "Colts" tradition and to distinguish itself as a CFL team. The NFL's Indianapolis Colts (formerly the second Baltimore Colts) filed a lawsuit against this team, however, and the club changed its name to Baltimore CFLs (see) before the season began.

Baltimore CFLs: Formerly called the Baltimore CFL Colts, the team was forced to drop the name "Colts" because of a lawsuit filed by the NFL's Indianapolis Colts (formerly the second Baltimore Colts). "CFL" stood for the Canadian Football League in which the team played.

Baltimore Claws: Named in a contest for part of the crabs for which Baltimore and the state of Maryland are famous. This team folded before ever playing a game in Baltimore.

Baltimore Clippers: Named for the clipper ships which frequented Baltimore's harbors in the nineteenth century.

Baltimore Colts: (2 teams) The first team to be called the Baltimore Colts was the one which played in the All-America Football Conference and came to Baltimore from Miami, Florida, in 1947. That team was originally called the Miami Seahawks, and when the team moved to Baltimore, the name "Seahawks" did not seem to fit Baltimore's image. So a contest was held, and the name "Colts" won. It was suggested by Charles Evans, who said, "Colts are the youngest entry in the league, Maryland is famous for its race-horses, and it is short, easily pronounced, and fits well in newspaper headlines."[12]

Baltimore Elite Giants: See *Nashville Elite Giants.*

Baltimore Germans: Like many soccer teams, this club was named for the ethnic origins of the players and/or the population which supported it.

Baltimore Hustlers: Named for the style of play team management wished its players to practice, but before the season began, the league office of the American Basketball Association convinced management to change the name because of the negative connotations of the word "Hustler." The team's arena was located in a somewhat seedy part of town, and the name can be a slang term for prostitutes.

Baltimore Lord Baltimores: Named for George Calvert (1580?–1632), an English colonist in America who became the governor of the British colony of Maryland, and who was known as the first Baron Baltimore, or Lord Baltimore.

Baltimore Marylands: Named for the state of Maryland in which the team played.

Baltimore Monumentals: Named for the nickname of the city of Baltimore, the "Monument City," so named because of its many historical monuments. Battle Monument, for example, recalls the Battle of North Point, where the bombardment of Fort McHenry by the British in 1814 inspired Baltimore's Francis Scott Key to compose "The Star Spangled Banner." This team's primary name was the Baltimore Unions; an Eastern League team used the name Monumentals at the same time. The major league team played at Monumental Park in Baltimore. However, only one game was played there, on August 25, 1884, and as the field surface proved to be somewhat uneven and bumpy, the team moved back to Belair Lot, where it had played previously.

Baltimore Orioles: (5 teams) The first team to be called the Baltimore Orioles was the baseball team which played in the American Association in 1882. It was named for the state bird of Maryland. The fifth team to use the name is the one which plays in the American League and came to Baltimore from St. Louis, Missouri, in 1954. That team adopted the name in an attempt to change its losing ways from its days as the St. Louis Browns, reviving the old Baltimore tradition of the two previous Oriole baseball teams.

Baltimore Ravens: This team's name was inspired by Edgar Allan Poe's poem "The Raven." Poe himself was a resident of the city of Baltimore. When team owner Art Modell moved football's first Cleveland Browns to Baltimore and announced that he would change the name, NFL Properties presented him with a list of over 100 possible names from which to choose. Club executives trimmed that list to 17 names, and then a focus group of 200 people from the Baltimore area cut it down to 6. A telephone survey of 1000 fans reduced it to 3 names—Americans, Marauders, and Ravens. The *Baltimore Sun* then conducted a phone-in poll for fans, and out of 33,288 voters, a total of 21,108 chose the name Ravens.

Baltimore Soccer Club: The rather unimaginative name "Soccer Club," along with "Field Club" and "Football Club," was commonly used by soccer teams when nicknames were uncommon, especially in the early part of the twentieth century.

Baltimore Spirit: Baltimore Blast owner J. W. "Bill" Stealey and his wife Laura were trying to come up with a new name for the team when it switched from the defunct Major Soccer League to the indoor National Professional Soccer League. The name was created when Laura said, "We need to rekindle the spirit the indoor soccer team had in the early '80s."[13]

Baltimore Stallions: This was the Canadian Football League team formerly called the Baltimore CFL Colts, which was forced to drop the name "Colts" (see *Baltimore CFL Colts*). It probably chose the name "Stallions" because of its relationship to "Colts." The name "Stallions," incidentally, had been reserved by the NFL for a potential expansion team in St. Louis, Missouri. When the Los Angeles Rams moved to St. Louis from Los Angeles, however, the NFL gave the rights to the "Stallions" name to Baltimore's CFL franchise.

Baltimore Stars: (2 teams) The first team to be called the Baltimore Stars was the one which played in the second American Soccer League in 1972. For the second, a football team, see *Philadelphia Stars.*

Baltimore Terrapins: A terrapin is a North American turtle which is common to the Atlantic coast. The name has also long been used by the University of Maryland. In 1994, seventy-nine years after this team folded, the diamondback terrapin was named the state reptile of Maryland.

Baltimore Thunder: Named by the Eagle Pro Box Lacrosse League, which owned and named nearly all the teams in the league.

Baltimore Unions: Named for the Union Association in which the team played.

Battle Creek Belles: See *Racine Belles.*

Bethlehem: Used no team name, but only the name of the city which this soccer team represented.

Bethlehem Steel: Named for Bethlehem Steel, the company which sponsored the team.

Birmingham Americans: Named for the United States of America in which the team played.

Birmingham Black Barons: This Negro League team copied and altered the name of Birmingham's minor league white baseball team, the Birmingham Barons.

Birmingham Bulls: Derived from the team's previous name of Toronto Toros (*toro* being Spanish for "bull").

Birmingham Vulcans: In Roman mythology, Vulcan was the god of fire and craftsmanship. A 55-foot iron statue of the god, on a pedestal 124 feet high, overlooks Birmingham atop Red Mountain. The city itself is built on one of the mountain's slopes.

Blast: Named by World Roller Hockey League founder David McLane.

Boca Juniors: Copied the name of the famous Boca Juniors soccer team from Argentina, because this New York team was owned by a group of local Argentineans. Boca is a very poor neighborhood in Buenos Aires where the Argentinean team's stadium is located. The area is frequented by tourists because of its colorful houses and the *Caminito*, a street where paintings and other works of local art can be bought. The name "Juniors" was chosen by the original team in the early 1900s because the club wanted a rather non-serious name, and wanted an English name in order to pay tribute to England and its storied soccer history.

Boston: Used no team name, but only the name of the city which this soccer team represented.

Boston Americans: Named for the American League in which the team played.

Boston Bays: Recalls the nickname of Massachusetts, the "Bay State."

Boston Beacons: Probably named for Beacon Hill near Boston's Back Bay, where the descendants of the city's Puritan founders now live. The State House is also located there, as well as a lighthouse built by the Puritans.

Boston Beaneaters: (2 teams) The first team to be called the Boston Beaneaters was the one which was primarily known as the Boston Bostons in the National League in 1883. The name developed through common usage by newspapers. It was used because of Boston's nickname of "Beantown."

Boston Bees: Renamed from Boston Braves in 1936, "perhaps out of desperation to stimulate sagging attendance, or to shake off an image of endless futility."[14] The name was selected in a contest from among 10,000 entries and 1327 different names. The winner was Arthur J. Rockwood of East Weymouth, Massachusetts, who received two season tickets for his entry. Other suggested names were Beacons, Blues, Bulldogs, Bulls, Bunker Hills, Minute Men, Pilgrims, and Puritans.[15]

Boston Blazers: See *New England Blazers.*

Boston Bostons: Named for the city of Boston in which the team played.

Boston Braves: (2 teams) The first team to be called the Boston Braves was the baseball team which played in the National League in 1912. After names such as Heps and Rustlers did not seem to encourage much fan support, new club President John M. Ward selected the name Braves after the 1911 season for owner Jim Gaffney, a chieftain or political "brave" from Tammany Hall. (Tammany Hall itself honors a Native American chief named Tammany.) The football Boston Braves selected the same name because they played at the baseball Braves' field.

Boston Bruins: Named in a contest. Owner Charles Adams wanted a name which would match the team colors of brown and yellow (which, not coincidentally, also matched the colors of the stores he owned in Boston). He also wanted a name which would suggest strength and power. "Bruins" fit the bill, because a bruin (or bear) is usually dark brown, and is also fierce and deadly.[16]

Boston Bulldogs: (3 teams) The first team to be called the Boston Bulldogs was the one which played in the first American Football League in 1926. All three teams were named for the Boston terrier or "bull terrier," which is also known as a bulldog (and which, in 1979, would be named the state dog of Massachusetts). The name of the third team lasted for only 12 hours (and no actual games) before it was changed to "Bulls" by club president Howard Baldwin.[17]

Boston Bulls: Named by club president Howard Baldwin, who switched from the name "Bulldogs" after only 12 hours under the original name. The team moved to New York as the New York Stars before it actually played under either name.[18]

Boston Celtics: Adapted from a team called the Original Celtics in the 1920s, one of the first truly successful professional basketball teams. The Original Celtics themselves developed from the New York Celtics in 1914, who came from a settlement house on Manhattan's tough west side. In 1946, Boston Celtics' founder Walter Brown was searching for a name for his new franchise, and he exclaimed to his publicist, J. Howard McHugh, "Wait, I've got it—the Celtics. We'll call them the Boston Celtics! The name has a great basketball tradition. And Boston is full of Irishmen. Yes, that's it. We'll put them in green uniforms and call them the Boston Celtics."[19]

Boston Doves: Named for owner John Dovey.

Boston Heps: Named for new owner William Hepburn Russell. Also called the Boston Rustlers for the same reason.

Boston Lobsters: Named for the crustacean seafood for which Boston is famous. The word "lob" is also a tennis term for a ball hit in a slow, high arc.

Boston Minutemen: Named for the militiamen in and near Boston during the Revolutionary War who pledged to be ready to fight at a moment's notice, and were thus called Minutemen. The war began when British troops fired on Minutemen in Lexington, Massachusetts, near Boston on April 19, 1775.

Boston Nationals: Named for the National League in which the team played, in order to distinguish it from the Boston Americans of the American League.

Boston Patriots: Named in a contest. The name was selected in honor of the eighteenth century colonists who helped declare independence from Britain, and Patriot's Day is celebrated in honor of Paul Revere's ride through Boston.

Boston Pilgrims: (2 teams) The first team to be called the Boston Pilgrims was the one which played in the American League in 1901. The name was used by newspapers in honor of the settlers who first landed in Boston.

Boston Plymouth Rocks: Named for the famous landmark in Boston, which marks the place where the Pilgrims supposedly landed.

Boston Puritans: Used by newspapers. Named for the popularity of this Protestant sect in Boston in the sixteenth and seventeenth centuries. It was Puritans who founded Boston, and they were called Puritans because they wanted to "purify" the teachings of the Church of England.

Boston Red Caps: Named for the team's red hats. The name was derived from the team's original name of Boston Red Stockings, which was in turn inspired by the Cincinnati Red Stockings.

Boston Red Sox: Shortened form of the team's previous name of Boston Red Stockings. The name was probably shortened in an effort to economize on newspaper space. Additionally, owner John Taylor thought the team needed a zippier name (it was also called the Boston Americans at the time), and his son (some tales say daughter) liked the color of the stockings worn by the players.

Boston Red Stockings: (3 teams) The first team to be called the Boston Red Stockings was the one which debuted in the National Association in 1871. It was named by manager Harry Wright, who had also managed the Cincinnati Red Stockings of 1869 and 1870. When Cincinnati decided not to field a professional team in 1871, many members of the team, including Wright, went to Boston to join that city's new team. Wright brought the uniform design of the Cincinnati Red Stockings with him (featuring the unique red stockings that had made the appearance of the Cincinnati team so distinct), and thus were born the Boston Red Stockings.

Boston Reds: (3 teams) The first team to be called the Boston Reds was the one which debuted in the National Association in 1871. The name was an alternate, shorter version of the team's original name of Boston Red Stockings (see).

Boston Redskins: This football team was previously called the Boston Braves because it played at the same field as baseball's Boston Braves. When the team moved to Fenway Park, home of baseball's Boston Red Sox, owner George Marshall and first coach Will "Lone Star" Dietz, himself a Native American, changed its name to Redskins in an effort to connect it with the Red Sox, thus establishing good relations with the team's landlord while at the same time retaining the Native American idea. The players even wore feathers and war paint for their first team photo.

Boston Rovers: This name was carried over from Dublin, Ireland, where the team had played as the Shamrock Rovers.

Boston Rustlers: Named for new owner William Hepburn Russell. Also called the Boston Heps for the same reason.

Boston Shamrocks: Named for the Irish population in the city of Boston. The shamrock is considered the national emblem of Ireland.

Boston Somersets: Named for owner Charles Somers.

Boston Speedboys: Probably so named because the players on the team were said to be fast runners.

Boston Unions: Named for the Union Association in which the team played.

Boston Whirlwinds: Copied the name of a previous independent barnstorming basketball team called the New York Whirlwinds, which had been organized by Tex Rickard.[20]

Boston Wonder Workers: Named for the Wonder Works factory, the company which sponsored the team.

Boston Yanks: Short for "Yankees," which is slang for "Americans." Owner Ted Collins had always wanted a New York franchise which could play at Yankee Stadium. Failing that, he used the name Yanks in Boston as a second-best option.[21]

Bridgeport Bears: This basketball team copied the name of a minor league baseball team which had played in the Eastern League from 1924–32.

Bridgeport Hungaria: Like many soccer teams, this club was named for the ethnic origins of the players and/or the population which supported it.

Brighton Tigers: This roller hockey team took the name of a previous ice hockey team in Brighton. That team played into the early 1960s and even defeated the Russian national team, so the name of this club was meant to rekindle happy memories for Brighton fans.

British Columbia Lions: Named for two prominent mountain peaks on Vancouver's North Shore that tower over the city. These peaks are called the Lions. The team's logo reflects a North American mountain lion.

Bronx Americans: Originally formed as a minor league team called the Brooklyn Americans, this team was likely named for the United States of America in which it played.

Bronx Yankees: This basketball team copied the name of baseball's New York Yankees. To create an even closer connection with that team, it soon changed its name to New York Yankees halfway through its only season.

Brookhattan: See *New York Brookhattan.* This team in reality used no team name, but only "Brookhattan" as a combination of "Brooklyn" and "Manhattan," the two boroughs in New York which it represented.

Brookhattan-Galicia: Revised form of the team's previous name of Brookhattan (see). "Galicia" was possibly an ethnic name which referred to an area in Spain. Like many soccer teams, this club was in part named for the ethnic origins of the players and/or the population which supported it.

Brooklyn Americans: For this hockey team, see *New York Americans.*

Brooklyn Arcadians: Named for Arcadia, the hall in which the team played.[22]

Brooklyn Atlantics: (2 teams) The first team to be called the Brooklyn Atlantics was the one which formed as an amateur team in 1855 and joined the National Association in 1872. The team was originally called Atlantic of Brooklyn, because it played on Atlantic Avenue in Brooklyn.

Brooklyn Bridegrooms: Named for the fact that there were at least four newlyweds on the team.

Brooklyn Brookfeds: This team played in the Federal League, and the name is a combination of "Brooklyn" and "Federal."

Brooklyn Celtics: (4 teams) The first major league team to be called the Brooklyn Celtics was the one which played in the first American Basketball League in 1926. That team took the name of the original, independent New York Celtics of 1914, a team which was named for the predominantly Irish population of the west side of New York where it was organized.[23] Like many others, the two soccer clubs were named for the ethnic origins of the play-ers and/or the population which supported them. The name "Celtics" refers to the Irish.

Brooklyn Dodgers: (3 teams) The first team to be called the Brooklyn Dodgers was the baseball team which played in the National League in 1911. The name is a shortened form of the team's previous name of Brooklyn Trolley Dodgers (see).

Brooklyn Eckfords: This team was composed of ship-wrights and mechanics, and they named the club after Brooklyn shipbuilder Henry Eckford.[24]

Brooklyn Feds: This team played in the Federal League, and "Feds" is a shortened form of "Federal."

Brooklyn Football Club: This team used the worldwide term "football" for soccer. This name, along with "Soccer Club" and "Field Club," was commonly used by soccer teams when nicknames were uncommon, especially in the early part of the twentieth century.

Brooklyn Gothams: For this basketball team, see *New York Gothams.*

Brooklyn Grays: Probably named for the colors the team wore.

Brooklyn Hakoah: Copied the name of Hakoah, a famous all-Jewish soccer team from Vienna, Austria. "Hakoah" is derived from the Hebrew word *Koach* or *Hakoach,* meaning "power" or "strong ones."

Brooklyn Hartfords: See *Hartford Hartfords.*

Brooklyn Hispano: Like many soccer teams, this club was named for the ethnic origins of the players and/or the population which supported it.

Brooklyn Horse-Lions: This was a combined name of two teams which merged: the Brooklyn Horsemen and the Brooklyn Lions. In the words of football historian Stan Grosshandler in his article "The Brooklyn Dodgers," this team "disbanded after the season, saving the world from a potentially horrifying logo."[25]

Brooklyn Horsemen: This football team was named for two of the team's players, Harry Stuhldreher and Elmer Layden, who were formerly two of the Four Horsemen of Notre Dame. That name, in turn, was coined by Grantland Rice, a sports reporter for the *New York Herald Tribune.* These two players, along with Jim Crowley and Don

Miller, helped Notre Dame defeat Army at New York, 13-7, on October 18, 1924. Rice was inspired to write: "Outlined against a blue-grey sky the Four Horsemen rode again. In dramatic lore they are known as Famine, Pestilence, Destruction and Death. These are only aliases, their real names are: Stuhldreher, Crowley, Miller and Layden."[26]

Brooklyn Indians: (2 teams) The first team to be called the Brooklyn Indians was the one which played in the second American Basketball League in 1942. That team carried the name over from Camden, New Jersey. (See *Camden Indians*.)

Brooklyn Italians: Like many soccer teams, this club was named for the ethnic origins of the players and/or the population which supported it.

Brooklyn Ridgewoods: Named for Ridgewood Park where the team played. Ridgewood is a neighborhood on the border between Brooklyn and Queens in New York.

Brooklyn Robins: Named for manager Wilbert Robinson, who was known affectionately to many as "Uncle Robbie."

Brooklyn Royal Giants: Named for the Royal Cafe in Brooklyn, which sponsored the team.[27] Like many Negro League teams, this club also copied and altered the name of a popular white major league baseball team (in this case, the New York Giants).

Brooklyn Superbas: The manager of this team was Ned Hanlon, and because there was a popular vaudeville act at the time called "Hanlon's Superbas," the team copied the name.

Brooklyn Tip-Tops: Owner Robert B. Ward also owned 13 Tip-Top bakeries. He was at first hesitant to call this team the Tip-Tops because of the blatancy of the advertising, so he originally called it the Brookfeds (see *Brooklyn Brookfeds*). However, he relented shortly thereafter.

Brooklyn Trolley Dodgers: The ballpark in which this team played was located in Eastern Park, near Jamaica Bay. The team was named for the fact that fans had to "dodge" the electric trolleys on Washington Avenue on their way to the ballpark.

Brooklyn Visitations: Named for the Visitation Church which organized the team. This team would move to Paterson, New Jersey, and become the Paterson Visitations

for the first game of the 1936 season, and then would immediately return to Brooklyn.[28]

Brooklyn Wonders: Named for owner John Ward's Wonder Bread Company.[29]

Brooklyn-New York Yankees: This team was a merger of two teams, and the name was a combination of their previous names: Brooklyn Dodgers and New York Yankees.

Buffalo All-Americans: The term "All-American" was developed by Caspar W. Whitney in 1889 to describe the selection of the best college football players in the country.

Buffalo Bandits: Named by the Major Indoor Lacrosse League, which owned and named nearly all the teams in the league.

Buffalo Bills: (2 teams) The first team to be called the Buffalo Bills was the one which played in the All-America Football Conference in 1947. It was named in a contest by Jimmy Dyson, who suggested it in honor of the historical figure named Buffalo Bill Cody, a hero of the Old West and the American Frontier. It so happened that team owner Jim Breuil also owned Frontier Oil, and he felt that the team was indeed opening a new frontier in sports in western New York. For his suggestion, Dyson won a silver tea set.

Buffalo Bisons: (7 teams) The first team to be called the Buffalo Bisons was the baseball team which played in the National League in 1879. The name is a play on the city name of Buffalo, and it has been used by numerous minor league teams as well as the seven major league teams listed in this book. In fact, this full name has been used by more major league teams than any other. Today, the name is *still* used in minor league baseball. Technically, the buffalo and the bison are different animals, though closely related. There have never actually been any buffalo in the Buffalo area, and one story of how the city got its name claims it is a mispronunciation of the French *beau fleuve*, meaning "beautiful river." (The river in question would be the Niagara River.)

Buffalo Blizzard: Named in a contest.

Buffalo Blues: Probably named for the colors the team wore.

Buffalo Braves: Named for the American Indian population indigenous to the Buffalo area. The team was named in a contest from among 14,000 submissions. The winner was David Lajewski of Dunkirk, New York, who received two season tickets for his efforts.[30] (See also *Buffalo Indians*.)

Buffalo Buffeds: This team played in the Federal League, and the name is a combination of "Buffalo" and "Federal."

Buffalo Destroyers: Named in a contest from among 18,000 entries and 1200 responses to a survey conducted by Eric Mower and Associates. The name was chosen because residents of the Buffalo area had made it clear that they wanted a name that was aggressive, that represented the city, and that commanded respect. The name "Destroyers" accomplished all that, while at the same time incorporating Buffalo's rich naval history and creating a connection to the naval destroyer anchored at the Buffalo Naval and Servicemen's Park. That park is located near the Marine Midland Arena where the team plays. The name was actually not even one of the top ten submitted. Those ten names, in order, were Blitz, Stampede, Wings, Blast, Blaze, Storm, Blazers, Bombers, Bullets, and Bobcats.

Buffalo Germans: Named for the predominantly German population on the east side of the city of Buffalo. This team copied the name of an earlier independent team which was organized in 1895.

Buffalo Indians: Named for the American Indian population indigenous to the Buffalo area, especially the Iroquois.

Buffalo Sabres: Named in a fan contest and chosen from among 13,000 entries. Team owners wanted a name that was not currently in use, that would lend itself easily to newspaper articles and headlines, and that would not follow the traditional buffalo-type names (e.g., Buffalo Bisons). From among four final suggestions, the name "Sabres" was chosen via drawing. The winner of the contest was Robert Sonnelitter, who won a pair of season tickets to the Sabres' games for his efforts. In a press release, team Public Relations director Chuck Burr explained: "A sabre is renowned as a clean, sharp, decisive, and penetrating weapon on offense, as well as a strong parrying weapon on defense."[31] Other suggested names included Bees, Border Riders, Comets, Flying Zeppelins, Herd, Knoxen, and Mugwumps.[32]

Buffalo Stampede: A play on the city name of Buffalo, referring to the animal of the same name and its occasional tendency to stampede.

Buffalo Wings: (2 teams) The first team to be called the Buffalo Wings was the men's team which first played in Roller Hockey International in 1997. The second, a women's team, was owned by the first and even used the same logo. The name is a play on the chicken appetizers of the same name.

Calgary Boomers: Named in recognition of the fact that Calgary became a "boom" town in the 1970s and early 1980s because of the rise of the oil industry in the area.[33]

Calgary Broncos: This hockey team copied and slightly altered the name of three previous minor league baseball teams, all of which were called the Calgary Bronchos and the first of which played in the Western Canada League in 1907. The name reflects the Western history and culture of the city of Calgary. This team moved to Cleveland before ever playing a game.

Calgary Cowboys: Reflects the history and culture of Calgary as a huge Canadian cattle-raising center.

Calgary Flames: See *Atlanta Flames*.

Calgary Stampeders: Named for the Calgary Stampede, an annual 10-day rodeo-type festival which has been held in Calgary since 1912. The festival features such events as calf roping, barrel racing, bull riding, chuck wagon racing, the Stampede Stock Show, and a state fair.

Calgary Tigers: This hockey team copied the name of a rugby team which played as the Calgary Tigers from 1908 to 1923, and which had originally been the Calgary City Rugby Foot-ball Club.

California Angels: Originally the Los Angeles Angels (see), the location name was changed from "Los Angeles" to "California" in an attempt to appeal to a more generic population base, and because of the team's impending move from Los Angeles to Anaheim.

California Clippers: Revised form of the team's original name of Oakland Clippers (see) in an effort to gain wider regional appeal.

California Golden Seals: Revised form of the team's previous name of Oakland Seals and original name of California Seals (see) combined with the nickname of the state of California (the "Golden State"). The name was changed by new owner Charles O. Finley.

California Kickers: See *Hollywood Kickers*.

California Oranges: See *Anaheim Oranges.*

California Seals: Named for a sea animal indigenous to the Oakland area. Though this was a hockey team, the name also followed a minor league baseball tradition in the area, as three separate teams called the San Francisco Seals had previously played in the San Francisco Bay area, the first in the Pacific Coast League in 1903. A minor league hockey team called the San Francisco Seals had also played in hockey's minor Western League. The NHL team chose the location name "California" in an attempt to represent San Francisco as well as Oakland. The team changed its location name to "Oakland" after a couple of months, however, because it realized that it was not attracting followers in San Francisco. Later, the team would become the California Golden Seals.

California Sunshine: Named for the almost constant sunny days for which southern California is famous.

California Surf: Named for the waves, or surf, common on the California coast.

Camden Brewers: Named for the fact that the team was sponsored by a local brewer in Camden.

Camden Indians: Named for the Native American population indigenous to the Camden area.

Canton Bulldogs: Copied the name of a previous independent football team which had played in Canton from 1905–06.

Canton Invaders: This indoor soccer team was named by owner Steve Paxos. Paxos was a fan of the NFL's Oakland Raiders, and he wanted a name similar to "Raiders" without copying it exactly, so he came up with "Invaders."

Capital Bullets: Formerly the second Baltimore Bullets (see), the location name "Capital" was used when the team reached Washington, D.C., not only because the team represented the capital of the United States, but also because it played at Capital Centre in Landover, Maryland.

Card-Pitt: This team was a merger of the Chicago Cardinals and the Pittsburgh half of Phil-Pitt (formerly the Pittsburgh Steelers). The name is a combination of "Cardinals" and "Pittsburgh." This club was sometimes jokingly referred to as the Carpets, because it was said that the rest of the league "walked all over" this team.

Carolina Cobras: According to principal owner Roddy Jones, the team "wanted a name that was different and one that sounds intimidating." He added, "I know cobras aren't indigenous to North Carolina, obviously. But they do invoke a measure of respect and fear when you hear the word. And it sounds good with 'Carolina.'"[34]

Carolina Copperheads: Named for a snake indigenous to the Charlotte area.

Carolina Cougars: Name chosen by General Manager Don DeJardin.

Carolina Hurricanes: Named by team officials on May 5, 1997, for the fierce storms which blow in to the North Carolina coast from the Atlantic Ocean.

Carolina Panthers: Named for the black panther, which is actually the rarest of all spotted leopards. An excellent athlete (hence the inspiration for naming a football team after it), it can jump 25 feet in distance and 12 feet in height. Black panthers are generally larger then other spotted leopards, because their dark coats make them more difficult to see. They are therefore able to stalk prey more easily, and as a result have better diets. The spotted leopard is an endangered species in the United States. In North Carolina, the mountain lion is sometimes referred to as a panther (or Carolina panther), but this animal is practically extinct there today.

Carolina Vipers: Named for the snakes common to the Charlotte area.

Charlotte Cobras: Named by the Major Indoor Lacrosse League, which owned and named nearly all the teams in the league.

Charlotte Gold: Named for the fact that Charlotte was the location of the country's first gold rush in the late 1700s and early 1800s. In fact, the government began operating a mint in Charlotte in 1837. The gold mines closed once gold was discovered in California in 1849, although they reopened briefly in the 1930s.

Charlotte Hornets: (2 teams) The first team to be called the Charlotte Hornets was the football team which played in the World Football League in 1974. Several minor league teams have also used the name, including at least four minor league baseball teams, the first of which used it in the Virginia-North Carolina League in 1901. The name comes from an event which occurred during the Revolutionary War, when British General Charles Cornwallis, who was engaged in heavy fighting in the Carolinas, sent a battle report to the King of England and stated something like, "This place is like fighting in a hornet's nest," or possibly, "There's a rebel behind every bush. It's a veritable nest of hornets."[35] When Charlotte received its basketball franchise in 1988, team officials formed a committee to which they delegated the responsibility of finding a team name. The committee chose the name Charlotte Spirit, but the public did not respond well to this choice. Team ownership then decided to hold a contest in conjunction with the *Charlotte Observer*, and from the entries in that contest the owners selected six names from which fans would vote. Ownership today cannot recall two of the names, but the other four were Gold (because of a discovery of gold in Charlotte even before the California Gold Rush; see *Charlotte Gold*), Hornets, Knights (because Charlotte's nickname is the "Queen City"), and Spirit. The name "Hornets" won by a landslide among Charlotte fans.[36]

Charlotte Spirit: When Charlotte received its basketball franchise in 1988, team officials formed a committee to which they delegated the responsibility of finding a team name. The committee chose the name Charlotte Spirit, but the public did not respond well to this choice. Team ownership then decided to hold a contest in conjunction with the *Charlotte Observer*, and from that contest the team would be named the Charlotte Hornets before ever playing a game as the Spirit. (See *Charlotte Hornets*.)

Charlotte Stars: See *New York Stars*.

Charlotte Sting: Like many WNBA teams, this club was named to create a connection with the NBA team which shared the same city (in this case, basketball's Charlotte Hornets).

Chicago Aces: (2 teams) The first team to be called the Chicago Aces was the one which played in World Team-Tennis in 1974. Both were tennis teams which were named for a tennis term. An "ace" is a serve which is not returned by one's opponent.

Chicago American Gears: This team represented the American Gear Company.

Chicago American Giants: Like many Negro League teams, this club copied and altered the name of a popular white major league baseball team (in this case, the New York Giants). It may have used "American" as part of its name to distinguish it from the Chicago Giants, another team in the same league.

Chicago Americans: Likely named for the United States of America as well as the second American Soccer League in which the team played. In the midst of many other ethnic names, the title "Americans" became a very popular one in the American Soccer Leagues.

Chicago Babes: Named for the fact that raids from new American League teams forced this team to use young, unproven players.

Chicago Bears: Named in an attempt to create a connection in the public mind with the Chicago Cubs, a team that was already enjoying much success. Owner George Halas also figured that his football players were more ruggedly built than baseball's Cubs, so "Bears" was selected as the more "grown-up" version.

Chicago Black Hawks: In 1926, the first owner of this team was Major Frederic McLaughlin, a World War I veteran who had served in an artillery unit called the Black Hawk division. The name also honors Chief Black Hawk of the Sauk Indians who roamed the Midwest in the 1800s and led the Sauks in a two-year battle against the Illinois State Militia over land disagreements in the Black Hawk War of 1831.

Chicago Blackhawks: Revised form of the team's original name of Chicago Black Hawks (see). The names were joined into a single word when owners discovered in 1985 that it was one word in the team charter.

Chicago Blitz: (2 teams) The first team to be called the Chicago Blitz was the one which played in the United States Football League in 1983. It was named in a contest from among 20,000 entries and 3351 different names. The winner was Mike Wehrli of Oak Park, Illinois, who received four season tickets for his entry. Coach and part owner George Allen announced the name on July 23, 1983. He said, "Blitz is my kind of name. I wanted a short, aggressive, attacking, physical name. The definition of 'blitz' refers to ground attack and air attack. My definition is to hit the enemy with everything you have. A team effort—offense, defense, special teams, coaches, staff, and fans."[37] (A "blitz" is a football play in which the linebackers and safeties rush the offensive line in an effort to tackle the quarterback on a passing play.)

Chicago Bluesmen: Named in reference to the claim that Chicago is the blues music capital of the world.

Chicago Browns: Probably named for the colors the team wore.

Chicago Bruins: (2 teams) The first team to be called the Chicago Bruins was the one which played in the first American Basketball League in 1925. A "bruin" is a bear. Both teams were probably named in order to create a connection with both the Chicago Cubs and the Chicago Bears. The second team to bear this name (no pun intended), formerly the Chicago Stags, folded before ever playing a game as the Bruins.

Chicago Bulls: (2 teams) The first team to be called the Chicago Bulls was the one which played in the first American Football League in 1926. That team was likely named for the city's longtime association with stockyards.[38] The National Basketball Association team was named by its first owner, Richard Klein. Klein felt that the name fit his team because, as is known from centuries of bullfighting, the bull has a relentless fighting attitude and an instinct to never quit.[39]

Chicago Cardinals: See *Racine Cardinals.*

Chicago Chifeds: This team played in the Federal League, and the name is a combination of "Chicago" and "Federal."

Chicago Colleens: This women's baseball team, like most in the All-American Girls Professional Baseball League, was assigned a feminine name so that the league could emphasize the femininity of the women who played. The league believed that to be the only way to build a following for itself.

Chicago Colts: Named for the fact that player/manager Cap Anson once appeared in a play called *Runaway Colt.*

Chicago Condors: This basketball team was named in a contest from among 4000 entries. Rejecting several names because of possible trademark infringement, the team actually preferred the name Chicago Cobras, but learned that there was a semipro soccer team by that name, so they opted for "Condors" instead. The name was submitted by 15-year-old Jeff Feyerer of Tinley Park, who won a pair of season tickets and a trip for four to Walt Disney World. Other finalists in the contest were Wind, Breeze, and Skyscrapers. In explaining his entry, Feyerer said, "It was kind of original. No one else had it." Ironically, within a matter of days, the head coach of a rugby team called the Chicago Westside Condors spoke up and pointed out that his team was about to begin its 20th season and had been using the name continuously since its inception. The two franchises traded barbs, but a legal fight never developed and the basketball team has since folded.

Chicago Cubs: Named by writers George Rice and Fred Hayner. It was first used in the 1890s as an alternate name for the Chicago Colts, but appeared to stay on March 27, 1902, when these writers used it in an attempt to find a short name for the club. It also fit because American League raiders were forcing the team to use many young, unproven players.

Chicago Fire: (3 teams) The first team to be called the Chicago Fire was the one which played in the World Football League in 1974. All three teams were named for the Great Fire of 1871, which burned most of the city and left one-third of Chicago's citizens homeless. That fire also left the first Chicago White Stockings without uniforms, equipment, business records, or a ballpark.

Chicago Fyre: Alternate form of the name "Chicago Fire" (see). This was a tennis team which eventually changed its name to Chicago Fire.

Chicago Gears: Shortened form of the team's primary name of Chicago American Gears (see).

Chicago Giants: Like many Negro League teams, this club copied the name of a popular white major league baseball team (in this case, the New York Giants).

Chicago Horizons: Named for Rosemont Horizon, the arena in which the team played.

Chicago Hornets: Name changed from Chicago Rockets in an effort to shake the team's losing image.

Chicago Invaders: Named for the fact that this team and the rest of the American League "invaded" Chicago (National League territory) in 1900.

Chicago Mustangs: Name selected to represent a "spirited" team.[40]

Chicago Orphans: Named in 1898, when manager "Pop" Anson, considered a father figure to many of the team's young players, was fired after 19 years at the helm.

Chicago Packers: Name announced by team President David Trager on May 15, 1961. The name was possibly selected because of the fact that the team played at the Amphitheater in the stockyards, where many meat-packing companies were located.[41]

Chicago Power: So named to signify the team's strength.

Chicago Rainmakers: Named for the long fly balls hit by the team. (Such a fly was sometimes called a "rainmaker.")

Chicago Remnants: This team, which was originally known as the first Chicago White Stockings, lost its uniforms, equipment, business records, and ballpark in the Great Chicago Fire of 1871. As a result the club had to go on hiatus for two years, and when it returned in 1874, it was sometimes referred to as the Remnants because of those losses.

Chicago Rockets: Name selected to represent something "new and deadly," as World War II had recently ended and the V-2 rockets used by Germany were a new innovation.[42]

Chicago Shoccers: A play on the words "shock" and "soccer."

Chicago Stags: Name announced on October 17, 1946, by club President Judge John Sbarbaro.[43]

Chicago Staleys: Name carried over from Decatur, Illinois. The Decatur Staleys were named for owner A. E. Staley and his Staley Starchworks company. When Staley sold the team to George Halas (who moved it to Chicago) for $5000, he paid Halas to retain the "Staleys" name for one year.

Chicago Sting: Possibly named for the movie *The Sting*, which was set in Chicago.

Chicago Studebaker Flyers: The first Chicago Bruins adopted this name when they were purchased by the United Auto Workers, many of whom worked in Chicago's Studebaker plant.

Chicago Studebakers: Shortened form of the team's primary name of Chicago Studebaker Flyers (see).

Chicago Whales: Renamed from Chicago Chifeds in a contest. The winner was D. J. Eichoff of Chicago, who pointed out that the best commercial whales were found in the North, and this team played on the north side of Chicago. In addition, "to *whale* meant to lash, thrash, or drub, and a whale is anything extraordinary, particularly in size."[44]

Chicago White Sox: Shortened form of the team's previous name of Chicago White Stockings. It was first employed by sportswriters Sy Sanborn and Earl Green, who used it in order to break any connection with the first Chicago White Stockings (the National League team which had become the Chicago Cubs).

Chicago White Stockings: (2 teams) The first team to be called the Chicago White Stockings was the one which played in the National Association in 1871, and which was formed in the amateur NA in 1870. This team was a contemporary of the Cincinnati Red Stockings, and, inspired by that first professional team, named itself after a part of its uniform.

Chicago Winds: Named for the nickname of Chicago, the "Windy City." Incidentally, Chicago is not so named because of the gusts which often blow in from Lake Michigan, but rather for its reputation of having rather boisterous and verbose politicians.

Chicago Zephyrs: Named in a contest from among 2000 entries and 236 different names. The winner was Richard L. Jakubauskas of Chicago, who received a $500 savings bond as his prize.[45] The name was probably meant to be a derivation of the name "Winds," recalling Chicago's nickname of the "Windy City." (A "zephyr" is a windstorm.)

Cincinnati Bengals: (2 teams) The first team to be called the Cincinnati Bengals was the one which played in the second American Football League in 1937. The team took its name from the movie *The Lives of a Bengal Lancer*. The second team's coach, Paul Brown, in meeting with owners Dave Gamble and John Sawyer, met at Cincinnati's Queen City Club to choose a name for their new expansion franchise. Names other than Bengals which were considered included Buckeyes (which was already being used by Ohio State University and which Brown considered too regional anyway),[46] Celts, Cincis (for Cincinnati), Krauts (for Cincinnati's German heritage), Rhinos (also for Cincinnati's German heritage, referring to the Rhineland), Romans (because Cincinnati, with its seven hills, is considered a sister city to Rome), and Tigers (since Gamble and Sawyer both attended Princeton University, which uses the name Tigers, besides the fact that Brown once coached the Massillon High School Tigers). All these names were rejected. (Brown's daughter even pointed out that rhinos are slow and dumb.) Brown decided to go with tradition, and "Bengals" was chosen because of the previous team which had borne this name.[47]

Cincinnati Buckeyes: Named for the nickname of the state of Ohio, the "Buckeye State." (The word "buckeye" is literally "eye of a buck" or "eye of a deer," which is what the nut resembles.) An amateur team had used this name as early as the 1860s, and baseball's Cincinnati Reds used it briefly as an independent team in 1881.

Cincinnati Celts: Named for the Irish population which immigrated to Cincinnati in the 1840s.

Cincinnati Clowns: Originally formed as an independent team called the Miami Clowns and later the Ethiopian Clowns, this team toured often as a comedic, clowning squad to help boost attendance. The name reflected the team's antics.

Cincinnati Cubans: Revised form of the team's original name of Cuban Stars. This Negro League team was possibly named in an effort to overcome racial prejudice, as the players may have tried to pass themselves off as Cubans.[48] After one season, this team would return to the name Cuban Stars.

Cincinnati Kellys: Named for the team's manager, Mike "King" Kelly.

Cincinnati Kids: Named for the movie *The Cincinnati Kid*.

Cincinnati Killers: This team was also called the Cincinnati Kellys (see), and the name derives from the fact that it was sometimes called "Kelly's Killers."

Cincinnati Outlaw Reds: Name derived from the Cincinnati Reds of the National League. This team played in the Union Association, considered an "outlaw" league since it was a rival of the NL.

Cincinnati Porkers: Named for the pork industry in Cincinnati and the city's nickname of "Porkopolis."

Cincinnati Red Stockings: Named for the unique red stockings which were a part of the team's uniform.

Cincinnati Redlegs: Derivation of the team's original name of Cincinnati Red Stockings (see) and previous name of Cincinnati Reds (see). Since the name "Reds" is also a moniker for the Communist party, the name was changed from Reds to Redlegs twice—once during World War II and once following that war during the Cold War—in order to avoid implications of any connection with the Communist party.

Cincinnati Reds: (2 teams) The first team to be called the Cincinnati Reds was the baseball team which played in the National League under this name beginning in 1878. The name is a shortened form of the team's original name of Cincinnati Red Stockings (see).

Cincinnati Rockers: This arena football team recalled the fact that arena football is promoted as "rock 'n' roll football."

Cincinnati Royals: See *Rochester Royals*.

Cincinnati Silverbacks: A silverback is a type of gorilla which has a stripe of silver fur on its back.

Cincinnati Stingers: Named in a fan contest.

Cincinnati Tigers: Like many Negro League teams, this club copied the name of a popular white major league baseball team (in this case, the Detroit Tigers).

Cleveland Allmen Transfers: Named for the Allmen Transfer Company owned by Stan Allmen, a moving and storage company which sponsored the team.[49]

Cleveland Barons: Copied from several minor league hockey teams which had previously borne this name. The original, minor league Cleveland Barons were first called the Cleveland Falcons, and in 1937 the team built a new arena and held a fan contest in the newspapers to rename the team. The name "Barons" signified the team's—and hockey's—aristocracy, especially during the Depression years.

Cleveland Bluebirds: Named for the color of the team's uniforms.

Cleveland Blues: (3 teams) The first team to be called the Cleveland Blues was the one which played in the National League in 1879. The team was named for the color of its uniforms. The third Cleveland Blues, who played in the American League in 1901, used it as a shortened form of their original name of Cleveland Bluebirds (see).

Cleveland Brass: Shortened form of the team's original and primary name of Cleveland Chase Brassmen (see).

Cleveland Bronchos: This team was previously called the Cleveland Bluebirds. Its players considered that name too effeminate, and chose "Bronchos" as an aggressive alternative.

Cleveland Browns: (3 teams) The first team to be called the Cleveland Browns was the baseball team which played in the first Negro National League in 1924. Like many

Negro League teams, that club may have copied the name of a popular white major league baseball team (in this case, the St. Louis Browns). The second was a football team which was formed in the All-America Football Conference in 1946. A contest was held in 1945 to name this team, and the winning name was Cleveland Panthers, submitted by John J. Harnett. The reasoning for this choice was that it could be easily animated for promotional use, and a logo could as easily be created for the team. Harnett received a $1000 war bond for his entry. However, Paul Brown (the team's first coach) soon discovered that a semipro team in the area was already using the name, and was not having much success on the field. Not wanting to be associated with a loser of any kind, Brown held a new contest, and as some stories go, many entries suggested the name Cleveland Brown Bombers in honor of boxer Joe Louis, the "Brown Bomber." The winner from among those who submitted this name was William E. Thompson, who also received a $1000 war bond as a prize. Brown then shortened the name to "Browns." At the same time, the owner is said to have denied that he named the team after himself.[50] However, Brown's son, Mike Brown, as owner of the second Cincinnati Bengals, claimed,

> They had a campaign up there to say the Browns were named for Joe Louis or something. But that's simply not true. The way that happened was my dad ran a contest. "Name the new team," and the name that came back was Panthers. My dad thought that that was, shall we say, not appropriate. So he just named the team the Browns. That's how it happened. . . . In hindsight, it was rather daring. But no one thought much about it at the time.[51]

When the first Cleveland Browns moved to Baltimore, Maryland, in 1996, the city of Cleveland fought to retain the rights to the name "Browns," and owner Art Modell agreed and renamed his team "Ravens." Thus, the "Browns" name would be applied to the second Cleveland football team in 1999.

Cleveland Buckeyes: See *Cincinnati Buckeyes.*

Cleveland Bulldogs: The owner of football's second Cleveland Indians, Sam Deutsch, bought the Canton Bulldogs for $1500, transferred all the team's best players to his Indians, then renamed the Indians the Cleveland Bulldogs. At the same time he put the Canton Bulldogs on hiatus. The next season, Deutsch sold the Canton Bulldogs back to Canton for $3000.

Cleveland Cavaliers: Named in a fan contest, voted for by over 2000 fans. The winner was Jerry Tomko, who stated that the name "represents a group of daring, fearless men, whose life's pact was never surrender, no matter what the odds."[52]

Cleveland Chase Brassmen: Named for the Chase Brass Company which sponsored the team.

Cleveland Crunch: Owner George S. Hoffman and General Manager Al Miller sat down one day and started brainstorming for a name that would sound good with "Cleveland." They came up with "Crunch."

Cleveland Crusaders: Named in a newspaper contest from among 8000 entries.

Cleveland Cubs: Like many Negro League teams, this club may have copied the name of a popular white major league baseball team (in this case, the Chicago Cubs). Originally the Nashville Elite Giants, this team may have changed its name upon moving to Cleveland in order to avoid confusion with a former team called the Cleveland Elites.

Cleveland Force: This team was created when the movie *Star Wars* was extremely popular, and was likely named for the mystical energy field called the Force in that film.

Cleveland Forest Citys: Named for the nickname of Cleveland, called the "Forest City" because of its thousands of trees.

Cleveland Giants: Like many Negro League teams, this club copied the name of a popular white major league baseball team (in this case, the New York Giants).

Cleveland Indians: (4 teams) The first team to be called the Cleveland Indians was the baseball team which currently plays in the American League, first so named in 1915. It was named in a newspaper contest in honor of former player Lou Sockalexis, a popular American Indian who played for the Cleveland Spiders from 1897 to 1899, and who had died in 1913.

Cleveland Molly McGuires: Named for manager Jim McGuire. The name was derived from the Molly Maguires, a secret organization of Pennsylvania coal miners in 1876 who protested against the deplorable working conditions in the mines. Reports from the period indicate that this group, which consisted of several thousand members and covered an area 50 miles long and 40 miles wide, operated under the guise of the Ancient Order of Hibernians but in reality was little more than a powerful band of assassins and terrorists. These workers supposedly copied the name from a similar group which had previously gained fame (or infamy) in Ireland.

Cleveland Naps: Named in a contest for star player/manager Napoleon ("Nap") Lajoie.

Cleveland Nets: Named for the tennis net that is such an integral part of the game.

Cleveland Rams: Named by owner Homer Marshman and General Manager Buzz Wetzel, because Wetzel liked the name of college football's Fordham Rams. Marshman added, "Wild rams butt harder than any other animal."[53]

Cleveland Red Sox: Like many Negro League teams, this club copied the name of a popular white major league baseball team (in this case, the Boston Red Sox).

Cleveland Rockers: Named for the fact that the Rock 'n' Roll Hall of Fame and Museum is located in Cleveland.

Cleveland Rosenblums: Named for Max Rosenblum, who owned a department store in Cleveland and sponsored the team.

Cleveland Spiders: Named for the fact that many of the team's players were tall, thin, and wiry, and management decided it would be advantageous to emphasize their physical characteristics.

Cleveland Stokers: This team originated in Stoke-on-Trent, Stafford, England, and was originally known as Stoke City when it played in Europe as an independent team.

Cleveland Tate Stars: Named for George Tate, an officer of the team and the vice president of the first Negro National League in which the club played.

Cobalt Silver Kings: Named for the fact that most of the team's players also worked in a silver mine, and sometimes were even paid in silver nuggets.

Cole's American Giants: Revised form of the team's original name of Chicago American Giants (see). The rechristened squad was named for owner Robert J. Cole.[54] When Cole sold the team to H. G. Hall, it went back to the name Chicago American Giants.

Colorado Avalanche: Named by the team's ownership group as a reminder of the Rocky Mountains which surround the Denver area. Shortly before the season began, ownership had narrowed the name possibilities to two: the Colorado Avalanche and the Rocky Mountain Avalanche. Other suggested or rumored names had been the Bighorns, the Black Bears, the Cougars, the Rocky Mountain Extreme, and the Storm. The name "Avalanche" was also used by a previous indoor soccer team called the Denver Avalanche (see).

Colorado Foxes: Named for the presence of the many foxes throughout Colorado and North America in general.

Colorado Inferno: This team's owners also owned a real estate office, and the receptionist at that office and her daughter created the name. The name was selected at least in part because it matched Major League Roller Hockey's slogan "Too Hot for Ice."

Colorado Rapids: Reflective of the Colorado River and the impressive geography of the Denver area. The name also suggests speed and dynamism. The location name "Colorado" was selected as a way of representing the entire region.

Colorado Rockies: (2 teams) The first team to be called the Colorado Rockies was the hockey team which played in the National Hockey League in 1976. It was named for the Rocky Mountains for which the Denver area is famous. The second team with this name—the baseball team—was named by the club's ownership group, and that group wanted to employ the location name "Colorado" in order to give the team a wider regional appeal.

Colorado Xplosion: Some of the other names which the American Basketball League preferred for this team had already been taken, so "Xplosion" was chosen to represent an explosion of power.

Columbus Athletic Supply: Named for the Columbus Athletic Supply Company which sponsored the team.

Columbus Blue Jackets: Named in a contest held by the *Columbus Dispatch* and Wendy's Restaurants from among 14,000 entries as a tribute to the large number of Ohioans who served in the Union Army during the Civil War. (Union Army uniforms featured blue coats, or jackets.) Contrary to rumors which became popular at the time, the team was not named for Blue Jacket, a Shawnee leader in the Columbus area in the nineteenth century. Other names suggested in the contest were Aces, Armada, Blades, Blizzard, Chaos, Clash, Cobras, Comets, Convicts (because the team's arena was next to the site of the old Ohio Penitentiary), Cruisers, Crusaders, Crush, Discovery, Explorers, Freeze, Herd, Ice Cats, Idiot Drivers, Justice, Mad Cows, Millennium (since the team began play in the year 2000), Orange Barrels (due to a great deal of ongoing road construction in the area), Outlaws, Puckeyes, Traffic, Wardens, and Wolves. Team officials submitted ten names to the National Hockey League for approval, and the NHL sent back two: Blue Jackets and Justice. Of the two, team management said they did not really understand the name "Justice," so they chose "Blue Jackets" instead. The team mascot is a yellow jacket who, incidentally, is green, and wearing a blue jacket.

Columbus Buckeyes: (3 teams) The first major league team to be called the Columbus Buckeyes was the one which played in the American Association in 1883. However, the name had been used by a minor league baseball team as early as 1877. The name comes from the nickname of the state of Ohio, the "Buckeye State." (The word "buckeye" is literally "eye of a buck" or "eye of a deer," which is what the nut resembles.)

Columbus Capitals: Named for the fact that Columbus is the state capital of Ohio.

Columbus Crew: Reflects the hard-working attitude of the Columbus community. The name implies teamwork and a show-me-don't-tell-me attitude.

Columbus Elite Giants: See *Nashville Elite Giants.*

Columbus Hawks: Named by team president Fred Drew. Drew had developed a fascination for the red-tailed hawk, a bird of prey which exists throughout North America but which is especially prevalent in the Columbus area. Drew did some research on this bird, and after discovering that Native Americans had once called it the white hawk, he planned to name his team the Columbus White Hawks. He later changed his mind and decided on Ohio Hawks, but eventually altered that to Columbus Hawks. Drew developed a relationship with the Columbus Zoo and arranged for a red-tailed hawk by the name of Jama to be present at all the team's home games. In return, a portion of all the team's merchandising sales was donated to the Songbird Aviary at the Columbus Zoo.

Columbus Invaders: See *Canton Invaders.*

Columbus Panhandles: Named for the fact that most of the team's players were employed by the Panhandle Division of the Pennsylvania Railroad.

Columbus Quest: Named in a contest, chosen by the team's coach and others in Columbus.

Columbus Senators: Named for the Ohio State Senate, since the team played in the state capital of Ohio.

Columbus Tigers: This team was originally called the Columbus Panhandles because most of its players also worked for the Panhandle Division of the Pennsylvania Railroad. When the majority of the players were no longer railroad employees, the team changed its name to "Tigers."

Connecticut Bicentennials: See *Hartford Bicentennials.*

Connecticut Coyotes: A coyote is a prairie wolf, and the name "coyote" was possibly derived from the Native American Coyotero Apaches.

Connecticut Yankees: The term "Yankee" is slang for "American." This team likely made reference to William Shakespeare's play *A Connecticut Yankee in King Arthur's Court*, as well as to the state song of Connecticut, "Yankee Doodle."

Corpus Christi Advantage: The word "advantage" is a tennis term. A player must usually win by two points, and when a tennis match goes into overtime, the player who gets the next point to break the tie is said to have the "advantage."

Cosmos: Revised form of the team's original name of New York Cosmos (see). The team would eventually change its name back to New York Cosmos.

Cuban Stars: This Negro League team was possibly named in an effort to overcome racial prejudice, as the players may have tried to pass themselves off as Cubans.[55]

Cuban Stars (East): This Negro League team was possibly named in an effort to overcome racial prejudice, as the players may have tried to pass themselves off as Cubans.[56] The "(East)" was to differentiate this New York team from another squad called the Cuban Stars (West) which played in Cincinnati, Ohio.

Cuban Stars (West): Revised form of the team's original name of Cuban Stars (see). The "(West)" was to differentiate this Cincinnati team from another squad called the Cuban Stars (East) which played in New York.

D.C. United: Name focuses on international appeal. It represents the community of the District of Columbia while also taking on a global appearance. The name "United" is a very popular and deeply traditional one among soccer teams, especially in South America and Europe. It denotes the fact that the team plays together as a unit.

Dallas Americans: Named for the United States of America in which the team played.

Dallas Burn: Using the logo of a fire-breathing mustang, this name represents the raw horsepower of the team and the game of soccer.

Dallas Chaparrals: Named by one of the team's investors during a meeting at the Dallas Sheraton in the Chaparral Room. The investor suggested the name when he looked at a napkin with a chaparral on it. "Chaparrals" are famous thickets and trees prominent in Texas and nearby Mexico. A "chaparral cock" is a roadrunner. After a one-year term as the Texas Chaparrals, this team would return to the location name "Dallas."

Dallas Cowboys: After team officials had decided to name this team the Dallas Rangers, General Manager Tex Schramm discovered that a minor league baseball team had used that name a mere two years previously, and was currently playing as the Dallas-Fort Worth Rangers. Consequently, he called a meeting of the team's owners in order to rename the team and thus avoid interference and confusion. The name "Cowboys" is reflective of the history and culture of the Dallas area.[57]

Dallas Express: Named by owner John Y. Brown. Brown owned the Buffalo Braves and had planned to move the team to Dallas and name them the Express. The move fell through, however, and the club never actually played in Dallas. Brown instead took the team to San Diego and renamed it the Clippers.[58]

Dallas Mavericks: (2 teams) The first team to be called the Dallas Mavericks was the basketball team which began play in the National Basketball Association in 1980. The team was named on May 1, 1980, through a contest held by WBAP radio. It was chosen from among 4600 entries submitted to owner Donald Carter. The name was seen as tying in well with the world-famous cowboy image of Dallas.[59] The term originally came from Samuel Maverick,

a Texas freedom fighter who did not brand his calves (and thus did not conform).[60]

Dallas Sidekicks: Named for the side kick in soccer. The name also conjures up images of Western heroes and their sidekicks.

Dallas Stallions: Recalls the Western history and culture of the city of Dallas.

Dallas Stars: (2 teams) The first team to be called the Dallas Stars was the tennis team which played in Team-Tennis from 1982–83. The later hockey team shortened its previous name of Minnesota North Stars, which it used when it was located in Bloomington, Minnesota. (See *Minnesota North Stars.*) When this team first moved to Dallas, it was rumored that it would be named the Dallas Lone Stars after the nickname of Texas, the "Lone Star State," but "Stars" was chosen instead. The star itself is a very recognizable symbol of the state of Texas.

Dallas Texans: (3 teams) The first team to be called the Dallas Texans was the football team which played in the National Football League in 1951. While all three teams were obviously named for the fact that they played in the state of Texas, the second football team was named specifically by founder Lamar Hunt, a hometown native of Dallas.

Dallas Tornado: Named for the windstorms common in the western United States.

Darby Daisies: See *Hilldale Daisies.*

Dayton Aeros: Likely named for the fact that Dayton is famous for airplanes and flight. Before ever playing a game, this team would move to Houston, Texas, where its name would fit perfectly with the presence of the aerospace industry.

Dayton Rens: Name carried over from New York, New York, where the team played as an independent all-black team. The name of the New York Rens was short for "New York Renaissance Five." It was so named because it played at the Renaissance Casino Ballroom in Harlem.

Dayton Triangles: Named for a "triangle" of plants in downtown Dayton which sponsored the team: the Dayton Engineering Laboratories Company (DELCO), Dayton Metal Products (DMP), and the Domestic Engineering Company (DECO, which later became DELCO Light).[61]

Decatur Staleys: Named for owner A. E. Staley and his Staley Starchworks, the company which the team represented.

Delaware Smash: Named for a tennis term. A "smash" is a very hard hit ball.

Denver Avalanche: Named for the Rocky Mountains which surround the Denver area.

Denver Broncos: Named in a contest. The name was seen to symbolize the toughness and determination of the West. The name was previously used by a minor league baseball team in the 1920s.

Denver Dynamos: Took the name of the Soviet sports club called Dynamo, and especially soccer's famous Moscow Dynamo.[62]

Denver Gold: Named for the gold that was discovered in Denver in 1858 and the resulting gold rush in 1859.

Denver Larks: Named for the lark bunting, the state bird of Colorado. This team changed its name to "Rockets" before ever playing a game.

Denver Nuggets: (2 teams) The first team to be called the Denver Nuggets was the one which played in the National Basketball League in 1948. This team was named for the gold which was discovered in Denver in 1858 and the resulting gold rush in 1859, at a period when both gold and silver mining were booming. The second team, formerly the Denver Rockets (see), was renamed in a name-the-team contest.

Denver Racquets: Named for the tennis racquet.

Denver Rockets: Named for the fact that the team's owner also ran Rocket Truck Lines. The team changed its name to Denver Nuggets when its league, the American Basketball Association, folded, and it joined the National Basketball Association, which already featured the Houston Rockets.

Denver Spurs: Reflects the Western history and culture of the Denver area.

Detroit Cougars: (2 teams) The first team to be called the Detroit Cougars was the hockey team which played in the National Hockey League in 1926. This team was named for the fact that team owners bought the entire franchise of the Western Hockey League's Victoria Cougars to help stock their new team when the WHL folded. The soccer team, which played from 1967–68, was sponsored by the Ford Motor Company and was named for the Mercury Cougar which Ford produced.

Detroit Drive: This name recalls the fact that Detroit is the automobile capital of the world. "Drive" is also a football term, referring to a team's steady progress down the field while it has possession of the ball.

Detroit Falcons: (2 teams) The first team to be called the Detroit Falcons was the hockey team which played in the National Hockey League in 1929. The team, formerly known as the Detroit Cougars, was renamed because it had had bad luck as the Cougars and was attempting to change its fortunes. The name change didn't help much, however.

Detroit Fury: This Arena Football League team was named in a contest from among 10,000 entries. Nineteen people had suggested the name, and the winner by random drawing was Jim Lyons of Novi, Michigan, who won four season tickets and a chance to accompany the team during a road trip. The other 18 people who had entered the name received four tickets each to the team's home opener. Tom Wilson, President of Palace Sports and Entertainment, the team's owner, explained the choice of the name by saying, "The word embodies the vision we've set for this team, the way the product will be represented on the field, and what our fans can expect to experience when they attend our games. Ultimately, football is a game of fury." The other nine finalists for the name were Cougars, Demolition, Diesel, Knights, Mustangs, Overdrive, Panthers, Pride, and Thunderbirds.

Detroit Gems: Named for the fact that the team was owned by jeweler Maurice Winston.

Detroit Lions: Team officials, particularly owner G. A. Richards, originally wanted to call this team the Detroit Tigers after the successful American League baseball team, but feared causing confusion among fans. Because of the Tigers' success, however, and the presence of a previous football team called the Detroit Panthers, the officials decided to choose another jungle cat. Said Vice President and General Manager Cy Houston, "The Lion is monarch of the jungle, and we hope to be monarch of the league. It is our ambition to make the Lion as famous as the Detroit ball club has made the Tiger."[63]

Detroit Loves: Named for a tennis score. "Love" is when a player has no points. (For example, "Fifteen-Love" is a score of 15–0.) The tennis term "love," incidentally, comes from the French word for "egg." Because of the numeral's oval shape, a score of "0" in any sport has long been associated with an egg, and even today, when shut out, players or teams are said to have scored an "egg," or, more commonly, a "goose egg." The French word for "egg" is *oeuff* (pronounced "oov"). The definite article is *le*, but before another vowel is shortened to *l'*. The word for "egg," therefore, is *l'oeuff* (pronounced "loov"), which eventually became "love."

Detroit Motor City Mustangs: Detroit's nickname is the "Motor City" because of its famous automobile manufacturing.

Detroit Neon: This team formed a marketing partnership with Chrysler Corporation, and was named after Chrysler's automobile the Neon.

Detroit Pistons: See *Fort Wayne Pistons*. When this team moved from Fort Wayne to Detroit, the name fit right in with Detroit's image as the auto-making capital of the world.

Detroit Pulaski Post Five: Named for Pulaski Post No. 270, which sponsored the team.[64] The "Five" signifies the number of players allowed on the basketball court per team at one time.

Detroit Racers: Likely named in recognition of the fact that Detroit is considered the auto-making capital of the world. This team folded before ever playing a game.

Detroit Red Wings: In 1932, new Detroit Falcons' owner James Norris renamed his team in honor of a Canadian hockey team for which he himself had once played: the Winged Wheelers of the Montreal Athletic Association.[65] The Wheelers' logo was a wheel with red wings, so Norris was inspired to create the name "Red Wings" for his club and to adopt the logo.

Detroit Rockers: Named in a name-the-team contest.

Detroit Safari: Name changed from Detroit Neon (see) when the team switched from a marketing partnership with Chrysler to a sponsorship deal with Pontiac/GMC.

Detroit Shock: Named for shock absorbers. Like many WNBA teams, this club was named to create a connection with the NBA team which shared the same city (in this case, the Detroit Pistons). Shock absorbers and pistons are both car parts.

Detroit Soccer Club: The rather unimaginative name "Soccer Club," along with "Field Club" and "Football Club," was commonly used by soccer teams when nicknames were uncommon, especially in the early part of the twentieth century. This team played in 1972 and was a throwback. After only a brief time under this name, however, it switched to the name "Detroit Mustangs."

Detroit Tigers: (2 teams) The first team to be called the Detroit Tigers was the baseball team which has played in the American League since 1901. Some stories say that the name of this team was inspired by its yellow and black stocking stripes in 1901. Some give credit to George Stallings, who managed a minor league baseball team in the Western League by the same name in 1896, others to an unidentified writer with the *Detroit Free Press* as early as 1895. But the earliest recorded team by this name was apparently a minor league team in the Western Association in 1892.

Detroit Turbos: Named by the Major Indoor Lacrosse League, which owned and named nearly all the teams in the league.

Detroit Vagabond Kings: Named for owner King Boring and the fact that the team had no home arena (thus "Vagabond").[66]

Detroit Wheels: Likely named in recognition of the fact that Detroit is considered the automobile capital of the world.

Detroit Wolverines: (2 teams) The first team to be called the Detroit Wolverines was the baseball team which played in the National League in 1881. It was named for the nickname of the state of Michigan, the "Wolverine State."

Duluth Eskimos: Renamed from previous name of Duluth Kelleys when the team acquired Ernie Nevers. They were promoted as "Ernie Nevers' Duluth Eskimos."

Duluth Kelleys: Named for a hardware store which sponsored the team.

Edmonton Drillers: (2 teams) The first team to be called the Edmonton Drillers was the one which played in the outdoor North American Soccer League in 1979. Both teams were named for the oil industry for which Edmonton is famous.

Edmonton Eskimos: (2 teams) The first major league team to be called the Edmonton Eskimos was the one which played in the Western Canada Hockey League in 1921. The football team, which played in the Canadian Football Council in 1956, actually used the name first, however, as an independent rugby team in 1910. A minor league baseball team had used it even earlier, however, in 1909 in the Western Canada League. All these teams were named for the Eskimo Indians indigenous to Alaska and Northern Canada. The name "Eskimo," incidentally, is Indian for "eater of raw fish." Eskimos were originally aborigines of the northern coast of North America, Greenland, and Labrador.[67]

Edmonton Oil Kings: Named for the oil industry in the city of Edmonton. This name was never actually used, however, and was changed to "Alberta Oilers" (see) before the season began. Owner Bill Hunter also owned a junior hockey team called the Edmonton Oil Kings.

Edmonton Oilers: See *Alberta Oilers.*

Edmonton Sled Dogs: Named for the animals which pull sleds in the cold, snowy regions of Edmonton and Canada in general. The name was derived from an Inuit (Eskimo) mode of transportation.

El Paso-Juarez Gamecocks: A "gamecock" is a rooster which has been trained for cockfighting.

Elizabeth Polish Falcons: Originally the Elizabeth Falcons, this team was renamed for the ethnic origins of the players and/or the population which supported it. After two years the club would return to the name Elizabeth Falcons.

Elmira Colonels: This basketball team copied the name of two previous minor league baseball teams, the first of which played in the New York State League from 1908–17.

English Lions: Likely named for the fact that the lion is the symbol of England. A lion was featured on the Great Seal of Richard I in the late twelfth century, and the Royal Arms of the United Kingdom have borne three lions since very shortly thereafter.

Express: Named by World Roller Hockey League founder David McLane.

Falcons Soccer Club: Formerly the Elizabeth Falcons, this team took the rather unimaginative name "Soccer Club," which, along with "Field Club" and "Football Club," was commonly used by soccer teams when nicknames were uncommon, especially in the early part of the twentieth century.

Falcons-Warsaw: Formerly the Falcons Soccer Club and earlier the Elizabeth Falcons and the Elizabeth Polish Falcons (see), this team kept the "Falcons" name and combined it with the name of the capital city of Poland (Warsaw). Like many soccer teams, this club was named for the ethnic origins of the players and/or the population which supported it.

Fall River Football Club: (2 teams) The first team to be called the Fall River Football Club was the one which played in the first American Soccer League in 1931. Both teams used the worldwide term "football" for soccer. This name, along with "Soccer Club" and "Field Club," was commonly used by soccer teams when nicknames were uncommon, especially in the early part of the twentieth century.

Fall River Marksmen: Previously known as the Fall River United, this team was renamed for new owner Sam Mark, a local businessman, when Mark bought the club.

Fall River Soccer Club: The rather unimaginative name "Soccer Club," along with "Field Club" and "Football Club," was commonly used by soccer teams when nicknames were uncommon, especially in the early part of the twentieth century.

Fall River United: Employed a very popular and deeply traditional name among soccer teams, especially in Europe and South America. It denotes the fact that the team plays together as a unit.

Fleisher Yarn: Named for Fleisher Yarn, the company which sponsored the team.

Flint Chemicals: See *Midland Chemicals.*

Flint Dow A.C.'s: See *Midland Dow A.C.'s.*

Florida Blazers: Named for the "blazing sun" for which Florida is famous.

Florida Bobcats: Named for an animal common in Florida and North America in general. The bobcat is believed to have spread into North America from Asia, and is smaller than original bobcats because of competition with early puma species. In Florida, bobcats are found mainly in swamp areas.

Florida Breakers: Named for the cresting waves common and popular on the Florida coast. This team moved to Minnesota before ever playing a game in Florida.

Florida Flamingos: Named for a bird indigenous to Miami and other tropical areas. A minor league baseball team called the Greater Miami Flamingos (formerly the Miami Beach Flamingos) also played in the Florida International League in 1954.

Florida Hammerheads: Named for a shark indigenous to the Miami area. A hammerhead shark has a flattened head which looks like a double-headed hammer, with an eye at the end of each extension.

Florida Jackals: See *Orlando Jackals.*

Florida Marlins: Three previous minor league baseball teams were called the Miami Marlins: one in the International League in 1956, and two in the Florida State League—the first in 1962 and the second in 1982. The name of the National League team was chosen by owner Wayne Huizenga, who called the marlin a "fierce fighter and an adversary that tests your mettle."[68]

Florida Panthers: Named for the Florida Panther, a rare animal indigenous to the Miami area. The animal is presently threatened with extinction.

Florida Suns: Named for the sunshine for which Florida is famous, and for the state nickname of Florida, the "Sunshine State." This team changed its name to "Blazers" before ever playing as the Suns.

Floridians: See *Miami Floridians.* The team dropped "Miami" from its name when it began to play games all over the state of Florida. While it still played most of its games in Miami, it also played some in Jacksonville, some in St. Petersburg, and some in Tampa.

Football Club Portland: This soccer team used the worldwide term "football" for soccer, and recalled many years of tradition established by teams which had used the simple name "Football Club" or its abbreviation "FC."

Football Club Seattle: This soccer team used the worldwide term "football" for soccer, and recalled many years of tradition established by teams which had used the simple name "Football Club" or its abbreviation "FC."

Fort Lauderdale Strikers: (2 teams) The first team to be called the Fort Lauderdale Strikers was the one which played in the outdoor North American Soccer League in 1977. A "striker" is an offensive player in soccer.

Fort Lauderdale Sun: Named for the brightness and warmth of the sun for which southern Florida is famous, and for the state nickname of Florida, the "Sunshine State."

Fort Wayne Caseys: Named for the local Knights of Columbus (K.C.s) who sponsored the team.[69]

Fort Wayne Daisies: This women's baseball team, like most in the All-American Girls Professional Baseball League, was assigned a feminine name so that the league could emphasize the femininity of the women who played. The league believed that to be the only way to build a following for itself.

Fort Wayne General Electrics: Named for the fact that the team was formed by the General Electric plant in Fort Wayne.

Fort Wayne Hoosiers: This basketball team copied the name of two previous minor league baseball teams, the first of which played in the Northwestern League from 1883–84. All these teams were named for the nickname of the state of Indiana, the "Hoosier State." The following legendary stories illustrate the possible origin of the word "Hoosier": 1) Travelers knocking on doors across the state would hear a peculiarly accented form of "Who's there?" from the people beyond those doors, causing the question to sound more like "Hoosier?" 2) At a time when brawling was very common, Indiana rivermen gained notoriety by consistently defeating or "hushing" their opponents. They therefore became known as "hushers," which developed into "Hoosiers." 3) A contractor named Hoosier hired Indiana laborers to work on the Louisville and Portland Canal. 4) Indiana boatmen used to take corn to New Orleans, and "Hoosier" developed from an Indian word for corn known as *hoosa.* This theory was put forth by Governor Joseph Wright, but no such Indian word is known to exist. 5) A traveler who witnessed a barfight in which a man's ear was partially bitten off heard a bystander who picked up the ear asking, "Whose ear?" and making it sound more like "Hoosier?" 6) The most likely explanation is that the term comes from an English word in the Cumberland dialect known as *hoozer.* Developed from the Anglo-Saxon term *hoo,* meaning "hill" or "high," it was attached to hill dwellers from Cumberland whose descendants eventually settled in the hills of southern Indiana.

Fort Wayne Kekiongas: Kekionga was the name of the original Miami Indian village located at the site which is now Fort Wayne. The word *kekionga* is Indian for "clipped hair."[70]

Fort Wayne Pistons: Shortened form of the team's original name of Fort Wayne Zollner Pistons (see).

Fort Wayne Zollner Pistons: Named for owner Fred Zollner's piston plant in Fort Wayne.

Fort Worth Cavalry: Named for the troops which fought on horseback in the Old West in and around Fort Worth.

Fresno Sun-Nets: A combination of the word "sun," as California is famous for its sunshine, and "nets," referring to the tennis net.

Fury: Named by World Roller Hockey League founder David McLane.

Galicia: Shortened form of the team's previous name of Brookhattan-Galicia (see).

Galicia-Honduras: This team was a merger of Galicia and an independent team called Honduras. Like many soccer teams, this club was named for the ethnic origins of the players and/or the population which supported it. (See *Brookhattan-Galicia*.)

Glens Falls-Saratoga: Used no team name, but only the names of the two New York cities (Glens Falls and Saratoga Springs) which this basketball team represented.

Golden Bay Earthquakes: See *San Jose Earthquakes.* The location name "Golden Bay" refers to nearby San Francisco Bay while also making use of California's nickname of the "Golden State."

Golden Gate Gales: Named for the fierce winds which are sometimes common in the San Francisco Bay area. The Golden Gate is a strait which is two miles wide and five miles long and which connects San Francisco Bay to the Pacific Ocean. The Golden Gate Bridge is a famous landmark which spans the strait from San Francisco to the Marin Peninsula. Nearby, Golden Gate Park is also situated in San Francisco.

Golden Gaters: Named for the Golden Gate, a strait which is two miles wide and five miles long and which connects San Francisco Bay to the Pacific Ocean. The Golden Gate Bridge is a famous landmark which spans the strait from San Francisco to the Marin Peninsula. Nearby, Golden Gate Park is also situated in San Francisco.

Golden State Warriors: See *Philadelphia Warriors.* After playing as the San Francisco Warriors, in Oakland the team used the location name "Golden State" after the nickname of the state of California in the hopes of attracting a wider fan base throughout the state. (Incidentally, California's nickname the "Golden State" comes from the fact that the golden poppy is the official state flower, as well as from the fact that gold was discovered there in 1848.)

Grand Rapids Chicks: See *Milwaukee Chicks.*

Green Bay Blues: Name changed from Green Bay Packers by coach Earl "Curly" Lambeau for cosmetic reasons. The name did not catch on, however, and it quickly reverted to "Packers."

Green Bay Packers: This team was founded in 1919 by Earl "Curly" Lambeau and George Calhoun and was called the Acme Packers because it represented the Acme Packing Company, which was later bought out by the Indian Packing Company, in Green Bay. Lambeau, who worked for the packing company, successfully lobbied Frank Peck of the corporation to provide $500 for team uniforms and equipment, and also gained the use of the company's practice field. The team name was changed to the Green Bay Packers when the buyout was made. The company folded before the first season had been completed, but the team lives on.

Haileybury Comets: Possibly a play on the name "Haileybury" with reference to Halley's Comet. (This supposition is undocumented.)

Hakoah All-Stars: This team was a merger of Brooklyn Hakoah and the minor league New York Hakoahs. Both teams had copied the name of Hakoah, a famous all-Jewish soccer team from Vienna, Austria, and then called themselves All-Stars when they joined together. "Hakoah" is derived from the Hebrew word *Koach* or *Hakoach,* meaning "power" or "strong ones."

Hamilton Tiger-Cats: This team was the result of a merger between two football teams, and the name reflects the names of both former teams: the Hamilton Tigers and the Hamilton Wildcats.

Hamilton Tigers: Name copied from the rugby team, formed in 1869, which eventually became the Hamilton Tiger-Cats (see).

Hammond Calumet Buccaneers: Buccaneers were pirates who terrorized the West Indies in the seventeenth century. More specifically, they were French, English, or Dutch pirates who originally settled in Haiti and, from the native Indians there, learned a special technique of sun-drying meat called "buccaning," from which they got their name. The word "Calumet" refers to the Grand Calumet River which flows through Hammond, and so the name could have referred to old river pirates on this waterway.

Hammond Ciesar All-Americans: See *Whiting Ciesar All-Americans.*

Hammond Hoosiers: Named for the nickname of the state of Indiana, the "Hoosier State." This was an alternate name for the Hammond Pros, and was used primarily by newspapers in Canton, Ohio. For a description of the derivation of the word "Hoosier," see *Fort Wayne Hoosiers.*

Hammond Indians: Named for the Native American population indigenous to Hammond and the state of Indiana (and from which Indiana got its name). This was an alternate name for the Hammond Pros and was used only by a few newspapers.

Hammond Pros: Short for "professional."

Hammond Tigers: This was an alternate name for the Hammond Pros and was used only by a few newspapers.

Harrisburg Giants: Like many Negro League teams, this club copied the name of a popular white major league baseball team (in this case, the New York Giants).

Harrisburg Heat: Named in a contest held by the *Harrisburg Herald News,* chosen from over 1000 entries. Other suggested names included Capitals and Hurricanes.

Harrisburg Senators: This basketball team copied the name of four previous minor league baseball teams, the first of which played in the Pennsylvania State League in 1895. All these teams were named for the Pennsylvania State Senate, as Harrisburg is the state capital of Pennsylvania.

Harrison Soccer Club: The rather unimaginative name "Soccer Club," along with "Field Club" and "Football Club," was commonly used by soccer teams when nick-

names were uncommon, especially in the early part of the twentieth century.

Hartford Americans: Likely named for the United States of America as well as the first American Soccer League in which the team played. In the midst of many other ethnic names, the title "Americans" became a very popular one in the American Soccer Leagues.

Hartford Bicentennials: Named for the American Bicentennial, celebrated in 1976, which was imminent when this team was formed in 1975. The state of Connecticut was one of the 13 original American colonies which declared independence in 1776.

Hartford Blues: Originally formed as the independent Waterbury Blues before 1924, this team was likely named for the color of its jerseys.

Hartford Dark Blues: Most likely named for the colors the team wore.

Hartford FoxForce: Named by owners Brian Foley and Lisa Wilson Foley after their Blue Fox Run Golf Club in Avon, Connecticut, and their Blue Fox Rock-n-Bowl in Simsbury, Connecticut.

Hartford Hartfords: Named for the city of Hartford in which the team played.

Hartford Soccer Club: The rather unimaginative name "Soccer Club," along with "Field Club" and "Football Club," was commonly used by soccer teams when nicknames were uncommon, especially in the early part of the twentieth century.

Hartford Whalers: See *New England Whalers.*

Hawaii Chiefs: Named in honor of the chiefs of the multitude of tribes that have lived on the Hawaiian islands.[71]

Hawaii Leis: Named for the garlands of flowers, or leis (pronounced "lays"), worn around the neck for which Hawaii is famous.

Hawaiians: See *Honolulu Hawaiians.*

Herne Bay Gulls: Named for a bird indigenous to Herne Bay and the coastal areas of Great Britain.

Hilldale: Used no team name. "Hilldale" may at one time have been the name of a street in Darby, Pennsylvania, near Philadelphia, where this team played.

Hilldale Daisies: "Daisy" was a slang expression in the 1920s meaning "an excellent or first-rate person or thing."[72] (See also *Hilldale*.)

Hilldale Giants: Like many Negro League teams, this club copied the name of a popular white major league baseball team (in this case, the New York Giants). Primarily called simply Hilldale (see), the team's players would respond with the name "Giants" when asked the name of their club.

Hollywood Kickers: Named for the most popular action in soccer: kicking.

Homestead Grays: Previously an independent team called the Murdock Grays, this team was likely named for the "grayness" of the city of Homestead in which it played. Homestead was near the steel mills of the Carnegie Steel Corporation (now the U.S. Steel Corporation), and soot and smoke from those mills permeated the town.[73]

Honolulu Hawaiians: This football team was named for the state of Hawaii in which it played. This was also the name of a minor league baseball team in 1948.

Houston Aeros: See *Dayton Aeros*.

Houston Astros: This team changed its name from Houston Colt .45s when it moved from Colt Stadium into the Astrodome. The name was also a reminder of the new space center and astronautic program in Houston.

Houston Colt .45s: Named for the famous six-shooter that "won the West." When ground was broken at the Astrodomain, where the Astrodome would soon be built, owner Judge Hofheinz celebrated by firing a Colt .45 into the ground.

Houston Comets: Like many WNBA teams, this club was named to create a connection with the NBA team which shared the same city (in this case, the Houston Rockets).

Houston E-Z Riders: Reflects the Western history and culture of the city of Houston.

Houston Gamblers: Reflects the history and culture of the Houston area, part of the Old West. Gambling was a large part of that Old Western heritage. The team was named by part owner Jerry Argovitz, who said that "the name symbolized the bold, imaginative, gambling style" of the team.[74]

Houston Hotshots: Likely named for the "shots," or fierce kicks, taken by indoor soccer players, and because the name sounded good with "Houston."

Houston Hurricane: Named in a contest from among 9000 entries. The winner received an all-expense paid trip with the team to one of its road games. Other suggested names included Kickers and Stars.[75]

Houston Mavericks: This basketball team was named for an animal which reflects the history and culture of the Houston area. The name originally came from Samuel Maverick, a Texas freedom fighter who did not brand his calves (and thus did not conform).[76] A previous team in the failed Professional Basketball League of America had also used the name in 1947.

Houston Oilers: Named for founder K. S. "Bud" Adams' ADA Oil Company (established in 1947), the forerunner of his Adams Resources and Energy, Inc., the profits from which allowed Adams to buy the team. He named the team "Oilers" on October 31, 1959, "for sentimental and social reasons."[77]

Houston Rockets: See *San Diego Rockets*. When the team moved to Houston, the name fit perfectly with the presence of NASA and the space program in Houston.

Houston Stars: Possibly named to fit the presence of the aerospace industry in Houston. It may also reflect the state nickname of Texas, the "Lone Star State."

Houston Summit Soccer: This team was named for the arena in which it played: The Summit.

Houston Texans: (2 teams) The first team to be called the Houston Texans was the one which played in the World Football League in 1974. Both teams were named for the state of Texas in which they played. The second, an NFL team, was so named to project a sense of the heritage of the people of Texas and the modern and progressive image of Houston. The name was announced by owners Bob and Janice McNair on September 6, 2000. Mr. McNair stated, "I feel that we have developed a name and logo that fans throughout the area and around the country will embrace for years to come. . . . The name and logo embody the pride, strength, independence and achievement that make the people of Houston and our area special."

Hungarian Americans: Like many soccer teams, this club was named for the ethnic origins of the players and/or the population which supported it. Several soccer teams combined their ethnic names with that of "Americans."

Idaho Sneakers: Named in the hopes that Diamond Sports, Inc., the team's owner, would secure a major shoe sponsor for the team. The attempt failed, but the team kept the name.

Indiana Fever: Named by the team's management and the WNBA. According to Chief Operating Officer Kelly Krauskopf, "It goes without saying that Indiana has the most passionate and loyal basketball fans. We worked with the League office to develop a name that captures that passion and appeals to all ages of our fan base." In developing both the team's name and its logo, the WNBA's Creative Services Department and the team's owner, Pacer Sports and Entertainment, had three main objectives: to create a concept that appealed to both children and adults, to preserve a link with the NBA's Indiana Pacers, and to capture the spirit and passion of Indiana's basketball fans. Said Donnie Walsh, President of Pacer Sports and Entertainment, "We want everyone in Indiana to catch the Fever and we will do everything we can to expose them to it."

Indiana Flooring: This team played in New York and was named for Indiana Flooring, the company which sponsored the club.

Indiana Kick: Named for the most common activity in indoor soccer: the kick.

Indiana Loves: (2 teams) The first team to be called the Indiana Loves was the one which played in World Team-Tennis in 1975. The team was named for a tennis score. "Love" is when a player has no points. (For example, "Fifteen-Love" is a score of 15–0.) The tennis term "love," incidentally, comes from the French word for "egg." Because of the numeral's oval shape, a score of "0" in any sport has long been associated with an egg, and even today, when shut out, players or teams are said to have scored an "egg," or, more commonly, a "goose egg." The French word for "egg" is *oeuff* (pronounced "oov"). The definite article is *le*, but before another vowel is shortened to *l'*. The word for "egg," therefore, is *l'oeuff* (pronounced "loov"), which eventually became "love."

Indiana Pacers: So named because the team was intended to "set the pace" in the new American Basketball Association and in professional basketball in general. General Manager Mike Storen is also said to have created a con-

nection with the famous Indianapolis 500, with its renowned pace cars.

Indiana Twisters: See *Indianapolis Twisters.*

Indianapolis ABC's: Named for the American Brewing Company which sponsored the team.[78]

Indianapolis All-Americans: The term "All-American" was developed by Caspar W. Whitney in 1889 to describe the selection of the best college football players in the country. It was later adapted for other sports, and some professional teams, like this basketball squad, used it.

Indianapolis Athletics: Like many Negro League teams, this club may have copied the name of a popular white major league baseball team (in this case, the Philadelphia Athletics).

Indianapolis Blues: Probably named for the colors worn by the team.

Indianapolis Browns: Probably named for the colors worn by the team.

Indianapolis Clowns: See *Cincinnati Clowns.*

Indianapolis Colts: See *Baltimore Colts.*

Indianapolis Crawfords: See *Pittsburgh Crawfords.*

Indianapolis Federals: Named for the Federal League in which the team played.

Indianapolis Hoofeds: Shortened form of the team's alternate name of Indianapolis Hoosierfeds (see).

Indianapolis Hoosierfeds: Combination of the team's alternate names of Indianapolis Federals (see) and Indianapolis Hoosiers (see).

Indianapolis Hoosiers: (4 teams) The first team to be called the Indianapolis Hoosiers was the one which played in the National League in 1878. The team was named for the nickname of the state of Indiana, the "Hoosier State." For a description of the derivation of the word "Hoosier," see *Fort Wayne Hoosiers.*

Indianapolis Jets: Name changed from Indianapolis Kautskys when the team switched from the National Basketball League to the Basketball Association of America.

The BAA did not want teams to have commercial sponsors, like the Kautskys.[79]

Indianapolis Kautskys: Named for head coach Frank Kautsky.

Indianapolis Olympians: Named for the fact that much of the team was recruited from the graduating class of 1949 from the University of Kentucky—a team which had not only been NCAA champions, but had won the 1948 Olympic gold medal as well.

Indianapolis Racers: Named for the sport of auto racing for which Indianapolis is world famous, especially because of the Indianapolis 500.

Indianapolis Twisters: Named in a contest from among 250 suggestions. Marc Morrison and Dusty Pope were the winners, although they had actually suggested the name "Tornadoes." Each won two season tickets for their entry. Additional names entered included Dentists and Speed.

Indianapolis-Cincinnati Clowns: See *Cincinnati Clowns.*

Inter Soccer Club: (2 teams) The first team to be called the Inter Soccer Club was the one which played in the second American Soccer League in 1960. "Inter" was short for "international." While many teams in the American Soccer Leagues were using ethnic names, this one was comprised of players of a number of different nationalities. The rather unimaginative name "Soccer Club," along with "Field Club" and "Football Club," was commonly used by soccer teams in the ASLs.

Inter-Brooklyn Italians: This was a merged team, and combined the names of the first Inter Soccer Club and the Brooklyn Italians (see).

Iowa Barnstormers: The term "barnstormers" was first applied to people who traveled across the country presenting plays, speeches, or similar events. The name also applies to pilots and planes who travel to fairs or carnivals and give exhibitions of stunt-flying. In sports, it has been used to describe teams who have traveled the country playing exhibition games. This arena football team uses a set of wings in its logo, emphasizing the stunt-flying reference of the name.

Irish-Americans: Like many soccer teams, this club was named for the ethnic origins of the players and/or the population which supported it. Several soccer teams combined their ethnic names with that of "Americans."

J & P Coats: Named for J & P Coats, a textile manufacturing company which sponsored the team.

Jacksonville Bulls: Named in a contest.

Jacksonville Generals: Probably named for the fact that the city of Jacksonville is itself named for General Andrew Jackson. Jackson once fought to defend settlers in neighboring Alabama and Georgia against attacks from Seminole Indians from Florida. In 1821, he was appointed by President James Monroe as the first governor of Florida.

Jacksonville Jaguars: This name was announced before a franchise was even awarded to Jacksonville. The team was named by Touchdown Jacksonville! Ltd., a nine-member partnership which became the team's owners, and the name was announced on December 6, 1991.

Jacksonville Red Caps: So named because most of the team's players also had jobs as redcaps, or porters, at the local train station.[80]

Jacksonville Sharks: Named for a sea animal indigenous to the Jacksonville area.

Jacksonville Tea Men: See *New England Tea Men.*

Jersey City: Used no team name, but only the name of the city which this soccer team represented.

Jersey City Celtics: Like many soccer teams, this club was named for the ethnic origins of the players and/or the population which supported it. The name "Celtics" refers to the Irish.

Jersey Knights: Named by the World Hockey Association when the team moved from New York, New York (where it was the New York Golden Blades) to Cherry Hill, New Jersey.

Jersey Reds: See *Union City Reds.*

Kalamazoo Lassies: See *Muskegon Lassies.*

Kankakee Gallagher Trojans: Named for the fact that most of the team's players were from the Gallagher Business School in Kankakee, which in turn had as its nickname "Trojans."[81]

Kansas City Athletics: See *Philadelphia Athletics.*

Kansas City Attack: See *Atlanta Attack.*

Kansas City Blues: (2 teams) The first team to be called the Kansas City Blues was the baseball team which played in the American Association in 1888. The team was probably named for the colors the players wore.

Kansas City Chiefs: Named by owner H. L. Hunt in honor of Kansas City mayor H. Roe "The Chief" Bartle.[82]

Kansas City Cowboys: (4 teams) The first team to be called the Kansas City Cowboys was the baseball team which played in the Union Association in 1884. The name reflects Kansas City's history and culture as a Western town.

Kansas City Explorers: This tennis team was sponsored by local Ford dealerships, and at the request of those dealerships was named for the Ford Explorer, a sports utility vehicle which is very popular among tennis players.

Kansas City Kings: See *Kansas City-Omaha Kings*.

Kansas City Monarchs: Copied the name of a previous minor league baseball team which played in Kansas City in the early 1900s.

Kansas City Packers: Reflects the fact that Kansas City is famous for its stockyards and meat-packing industry.[83]

Kansas City Royals: Named in a fan contest from among 17,000 entries. The winner was Sanford Porte of Overland Park, Kansas, who explained: "Kansas City's new baseball team should be called the Royals because of Missouri's billion dollar livestock income, Kansas City's position as the nation's leading stocker and feeder market and the nationally known American Royal parade and pageant."[84] For his entry, Porte won an all-expense paid trip to the 1969 All-Star game at the Astrodome in Houston, Texas. Other names suggested in the contest were: Bluebirds, Blues, Cowpokes, Mules, Steers, and Studs.[85] There was also an independent barnstorming baseball team in the 1940s called the Kansas City Royals.

Kansas City Scouts: Named for the scouts who accompanied wagon trains westward, and for those who worked for the U.S. Army. There could be a Native American connection as well, since there is an Indian memorial at Penn Valley Park in Kansas City called "The Scout."

Kansas City Steers: Named for Kansas City's famous stockyards and meat-packing industry.[86]

Kansas City Unions: Named for the Union Association in which the team played.

Kansas City Wiz: Named in a month-long contest by the *Kansas City Star,* selected from over 3200 entries. The winning submission was actually "Wizards," sent in by six people, and the Grand Prize winner was 9-year-old Sarah Starr of Lee's Summit, who received two season tickets to the team's inaugural campaign. A minor league team in the United Systems of Independent Soccer Leagues called the Delaware Wizards held the trademark rights to the name, however, so it was shortened to "Wiz." The team did want a unique name, and felt that this shortened version fit the league's marketing image well. (See also *Kansas City Wizards*.)

Kansas City Wizards: Revised form of the team's original name of Kansas City Wiz (see). The team originally wanted the name "Wizards," but was prevented from using it by minor league soccer's Delaware Wizards, who held the trademark rights. When an eastern electronics firm by the name of Nobody Beats the Wiz Inc. questioned whether the team was infringing upon *its* trademark rights, the Delaware Wizards, in showing support for Major League Soccer, released their claim to the "Wizards" name to the Kansas City franchise.

Kansas City-Omaha Kings: Named by public vote. When the Cincinnati Royals moved to Kansas City and Omaha from Cincinnati, Ohio, team ownership decided to change the team's name in order to avoid confusion with major league baseball's Kansas City Royals and with minor league baseball's Omaha Royals. The name "Kings" is different, yet retains the idea of the original. Other names suggested for the change were: Barons, Crowns, Plainsmen, Regals, River Kings, Scouts, Stars, Steers, and Tornadoes.[87]

Kearny Americans: Likely named for the United States of America as well as the second American Soccer League in which the team played. In the midst of many other ethnic names, the title "Americans" became a very popular one in the American Soccer Leagues, especially just before and during World War II.

Kearny Celtic: Alternate name for the Irish-Americans (see). Like many soccer teams, this club was named for the ethnic origins of the players and/or the population which supported it. The name "Celtic" refers to the Irish.

Kearny Celtics: See *Newark Celtics*.

Kearny Irish-Americans: Like many soccer teams, this club was named for the ethnic origins of the players and/or the population which supported it. Several soccer teams combined their ethnic names with that of "Americans."

Kearny Scots: Like many soccer teams, this club was named for the ethnic origins of the players and/or the population which supported it.

Kenosha Maroons: See *Toledo Maroons.*

Kentucky Colonels: Named for those who have received the famous honorary title of Kentucky Colonel from the state of Kentucky.

Keokuk Westerns: Originally called the Western Base Ball Association of Keokuk.

Kingston Colonials: This basketball team was named for the Colonial Cities Services gas station which sponsored the team. There had also been previous basketball teams in Kingston by the same name,[88] as well as two previous minor league baseball teams, the first of which played in the Hudson River League from 1903–05.

Lancaster Roses: Named for the nickname of Lancaster, the "Red Rose City." There are many references to red roses in Lancaster, including the bus system, which is called the Red Rose Transit Authority. Lancaster was named after Lancashire, England, which was in turn named for the House of Lancaster. This House began as an earldom for Edmund, the son of King Henry III, and took as its badge a red rose. Competition with the House of York for the throne led to a series of civil wars, and as the House of York used a white rose as its symbol, these conflicts were referred to as the War of the Roses. Today, Lancaster, Pennsylvania, named for Lancashire, is known as the "Red Rose City," and nearby York, Pennsylvania, named for York, England, is called the "White Rose City."

Las Vegas Americans: See *Memphis Americans.*

Las Vegas Coyotes: Named for an animal indigenous to the western United States. A coyote is a prairie wolf, and the name "coyote" was possibly derived from the Native American Coyotero Apaches.

Las Vegas DustDevils: Las Vegas and the state of Nevada are renowned for their deserts. A "dust devil" is a transient desert whirlwind.

Las Vegas Flash: Likely named for the flash (or flashiness) of the city of Las Vegas, which is famous for its casinos, neon signs, and spectacular shows.

Las Vegas Posse: Named in a fan contest from among 2000 suggestions sent in by over 1200 people. The name "Posse" was suggested by six people, but the winner was Janet Negrete of Las Vegas, because she also suggested the team colors of black, white, and desert sand. These colors, she said, were the same a person would see looking at the terrain surrounding the city of Las Vegas. Negrete said that she chose the name "Posse" because, when she arrived in Las Vegas from Toronto, Ontario, 32 years previously, the Nevada city was "just a cowboy town."[89]

Las Vegas Quicksilvers: The city of Las Vegas is located in the state of Nevada, nicknamed the "Silver State" because of its many silver deposits. "Quicksilver" is actually mercury, and Nevada ranks high among the states in the production of this metal.

London Lions: Likely named for the fact that the lion is the symbol of England. A lion was featured on the Great Seal of Richard I in the late twelfth century, and the Royal Arms of the United Kingdom have borne three lions since very shortly thereafter.

London United: Employed a very popular and deeply traditional name among soccer and indoor soccer teams, especially in Europe and South America. It denotes the fact that the team plays together as a unit. This team folded before ever playing a game.

Long Beach Breakers: Named for the cresting waves common and popular on the California coast.

Long Beach Chiefs: See *Hawaii Chiefs.*

Long Beach StingRays: Named in a contest for an animal indigenous to the Long Beach area. The American Basketball League office liked the name, and embraced it to some degree because many other names had already been taken.

Los Angeles Angels: This baseball team copied the name of two previous minor league teams, the first of which played in the California League in 1894, and the second in the Pacific Coast League in 1903. The name reflects the fact that the team played in Los Angeles, which translates from Spanish as the "City of Angels."

Los Angeles Avengers: Named by team owner and president Casey Wasserman, who explained,

> I'm a huge sports fan, and I wanted a name for my team that would captivate the Los Angeles community and capture the spirit and imagination of Los Angeles. The name "Avengers" to me implies power and energy. The name is representative of how I feel this team is going to perform and entertain the fans of Los Angeles.

Los Angeles Aztecs: Named for the early Mexican Indians who were conquered by Cortez in 1520. The word *aztec* translates as "place of the heron."[90]

Los Angeles Blades: Likely named for the roller blades which constitute a fundamental part of the roller hockey uniform.

Los Angeles Buccaneers: Buccaneers were French, English, or Dutch pirates who originally settled in Haiti and, from the native Indians there, learned a special technique of sun-drying meat called "buccaning," from which they got their name.

Los Angeles Chargers: Named in a fan contest. The winner was Gerald Courtney of Hollywood, California, who won an all-expense paid trip to Mexico City and Acapulco for his efforts. The name was selected by owner Barron Hilton, who chose it to represent an electrical charge, because the San Diego club stationery had the symbol of a horse charging, and because his Hilton Hotel chain had recently unveiled the Carte Blanche charge card.[91] Some sources indicate he selected the name because of the cries of "Charge!" he would hear at University of Southern California football games. He also thought that the name sounded dynamic.[92]

Los Angeles Clippers: See *San Diego Clippers.*

Los Angeles Dodgers: For this baseball team, see *Brooklyn Dodgers.*

Los Angeles Dons: Reflects the Hispanic culture of the city of Los Angeles. "Don" was a title used by Christian Spaniards of high rank, and the term has also been used simply to refer to a Spanish gentleman. The name also referred to the team's owner, actor Don Ameche.

Los Angeles Galaxy: So named because of a galaxy's relationship to the sun, because Los Angeles is famous for its sunshine. (Our sun is one of billions of stars in our galaxy, which is called the Milky Way. Our galaxy, in turn, is one of billions in the universe.)

Los Angeles Hot Rods: Named for the souped-up cars that sometimes cruise southern California roadways. This team folded before ever playing a game.

Los Angeles Kings: Selected in a contest by owner Jack Kent Cooke.

Los Angeles Lakers: See *Minneapolis Lakers.*

Los Angeles Raiders: See *Oakland Raiders.*

Los Angeles Rams: See *Cleveland Rams.*

Los Angeles Salsa: Likely reflects the Hispanic influence on the Los Angeles area. The term "salsa" is the name of a Hispanic dance, as well as of a type of Mexican food.

Los Angeles Sharks: Named for a sea animal indigenous to the Los Angeles area. This team was previously called the Los Angeles Aces, but when the San Francisco Sharks moved to Quebec before ever playing a game, the Aces adopted the name "Sharks," also before ever playing a game.

Los Angeles Sparks: Named by the father of a team employee. Brandi Bratcher was the Assistant to the President, and her father was a welder. Her father suggested the name because of the sparks that would always fly when he was welding.

Los Angeles Stars: Probably named for the movie stars in Los Angeles. Two minor league baseball teams, the first of which played in 1926, previously played in nearby Hollywood and were both called the Hollywood Stars.

Los Angeles Strings: Likely named for the strings on a tennis racquet.

Los Angeles Toros: Reflects the Hispanic culture and influence in Los Angeles. (The word *toro* is Spanish for "bull.")

Los Angeles United: Employed a very popular and deeply traditional name among soccer and indoor soccer teams, especially in South America and Europe. It denotes the fact that the team plays together as a unit.

Los Angeles Wildcats: Named for Wildcat Wilson, a popular player in independent football in Los Angeles.

Los Angeles Wolves: Named for the city of Wolverhampton, Stafford, England, in which this team originally played as the independent Wolverhampton Wanderers.

Louisiana Buccaneers: Named for the pirates who terrorized the West Indies and the Gulf of Mexico off New Orleans beginning in the seventeenth century. Buccaneers were French, English, or Dutch pirates who originally settled in Haiti and, from the native Indians there, learned a special technique of sun-drying meat called "buccaning," from which they got their name. This team changed its name to the New Orleans Buccaneers before ever playing a game.

Louisville Brecks: Possibly a shortened form of the name Breckenridge, which would indicate that the Breckenridge family may have sponsored the team.[93]

Louisville Buckeyes: See *Cincinnati Buckeyes*. The team kept the name even when it moved to Kentucky.

Louisville Colonels: (2 teams) The first team to be called the Louisville Colonels was the baseball team which played in the National League in 1876. The team was named for those who have received the famous honorary title of Kentucky Colonel from the state of Kentucky.

Louisville Eclipse: Named for American Eclipse, a famous racehorse which had been retired to stud in Kentucky.[94]

Louisville Grays: Probably named for the colors worn by the team.

Louisville White Sox: Like many Negro League teams, this club copied the name of a popular white major league baseball team (in this case, the Chicago White Sox).

Ludlow Lusitano: Like many soccer teams, this club was named for the ethnic origins of the players and/or the population which supported it. The name "Lusitano" refers to Lusitania, which is the ancient name for Portugal.

Ludlow Soccer Club: The rather unimaginative name "Soccer Club," along with "Field Club" and "Football Club," was commonly used by soccer teams when nicknames were uncommon, especially in the early part of the twentieth century.

Maryland Bays: Likely named for Chesapeake Bay, near which this team played.

Memphis Americans: Named for the United States of America in which the team played.

Memphis Grizzlies: Named for an animal indigenous to the Memphis area. This team changed its name from Southmen after the World Football League folded in the hopes that it would be accepted into the National Football League. It was thought that the name "Grizzlies" would fit better with the names of other NFL teams. The team was not accepted into the NFL, however, and never actually played as the Grizzlies.

Memphis Pharaohs: Recalls the fact that Memphis took its name from the ancient Egyptian city of Memphis. The original city of Memphis was the capital of ancient Egypt, located on the Nile River approximately 12 miles south of Cairo. The Tennessee city copied the name because it is similarly situated on the Mississippi River. A "pharaoh" was an ancient Egyptian king.

Memphis Pros: Renamed from New Orleans Buccaneers when the team moved from New Orleans to Memphis. Shortly before the move, the team had spent $1000 for new jerseys which had the name "BUCS" across the front. Coach Babe McCarthy wanted to rename the team but did not want to waste the $1000, so he cut the *B*, *U*, and *C* off a jersey and replaced these letters with *P*, *R*, and *O*. He planned to rename the team again the following year, but "Pros" stuck for two years, when the franchise was purchased by Charles O. Finley, who then renamed it the "Tams."[95]

Memphis Red Sox: Like many Negro League teams, this club copied the name of a popular white major league baseball team (in this case, the Boston Red Sox).

Memphis Showboats: Named for the showboats famous for cruising the Mississippi River in Memphis. Such boats would carry troupes of actors and performers and would stage shows while cruising the river.

Memphis Sounds: Named for the fact that the city of Memphis is famous for its music, which began with blues and melancholy ballads once sung by slaves, and was eventually heightened by the emergence of Elvis Presley.

Memphis Southmen: This team moved to Memphis from Toronto, Ontario, where it was called the Toronto Northmen because it was the northernmost team in the World Football League. The name "Southmen," adopted when the team moved to a southern town, is in juxtaposition to the former name.

Memphis Tams: A "tam" is a type of hat, and the team's logo included such a hat. The team was named in a contest from among 20,000 entries, and the name was selected by owner Charles O. Finley. The winner was Bill Barrett of West Point, Mississippi, who received a $2500 prize. Barrett wished the letters *T, A,* and *M* to represent Tennessee, Arkansas, and Mississippi, the three states from which Finley hoped to create a fan base.

Mexico Toros: The word *toro* is Spanish for "bull."

Miami Americans: For this soccer team, see *New Jersey Americans.*

Miami Beach Breakers: (2 teams) The first team to be called the Miami Beach Breakers was the one which played in TeamTennis in 1985. Both teams were named for the cresting waves common and popular on the Florida coast.

Miami Breakers: (2 teams) See *Miami Beach Breakers* for both teams.

Miami Dolphins: Named in a 1965 contest from among 20,000 entries. The winning name was submitted by Mrs. Robert Swanson of West Miami, Florida, who was awarded two lifetime passes to the team's games for her entry. Owner Joe Robbie explained his choice by saying, "The dolphin is one of the fastest and smartest creatures of the sea. Dolphins can attack and kill a shark or a whale. Sailors say bad luck will come to anyone who harms one of them."[96] Other names suggested in the contest included Marauders, Marines, Missiles, Moons, Mustangs, Sharks, and Suns.[97]

Miami Floridians: Named for the state of Florida in which the team played.

Miami Fusion: According to Major League Soccer commissioner Douglas G. Logan, "The name Fusion symbolizes the relationship between the world's most exciting sport and Miami's multicultural makeup." Investor-Operator Kenneth A. Horowitz added, "Soccer and Miami each embody the diversity of ethnic and multinational groups. The name Fusion represents the unification of soccer fans of all nationalities with the force, power and passion of soccer."[98]

Miami Gatos: Reflects the Hispanic culture and influence on the Miami area. The word *gato* is Spanish for "cat" or "tomcat."

Miami Heat: Named in a contest from among 20,000 entries. The winner was Stephanie Freed, who received two season tickets as well as two tickets to see part owner Julio Iglesias in concert. The top three choices for the name were Flamingos, Heat, and Wave, and a panel of sportswriters selected Heat. Team general partner Zev Bufman explained the choice of the name by saying, "We're Miami. When you think of Miami, that's what you think of."[99] He added that it "graphically can be turned into something very exciting, with colors like reds, yellows, and oranges."[100] Other names suggested in the contest included Barracudas, Beaches, Dolphins, Floridians, Palm Trees, Shade, Sharks, Suntan, and Tornadoes.[101]

Miami Hooters: Owner-President Dave Lageschulte also owned Hooters of Southern Florida, and named the team after his restaurants.

Miami Jackals: See *Orlando Jackals.*

Miami Seahawks: Named for a bird indigenous to the Miami area.

Miami Sharks: Named for a sea animal indigenous to the Miami area.

Miami Sol: Named for the sun for which Florida is famous and for the state nickname of Florida, the "Sunshine State." It also creates a connection with the Hispanic community in the Miami area, since *sol* is the Spanish word for "sun." Like the names of many WNBA teams, this one was also created to forge a bond with the NBA team which shared the same city (in this case, the Miami Heat). Michael A. McCullough, Executive Vice President, Team Sports for both the Heat and the Sol, explained,

> The sun conveys our beautiful weather, while the Spanish word *sol* embraces the wonderful diversity that makes South Florida so special. Both the colors and name establish a link to the Heat. All of this makes our team the heart and "Sol" of South Florida.

Miami Toros: Reflects the Hispanic culture and influence on the Miami area. The word *toro* is Spanish for "bull."

Michigan Blast: Named in a contest. Since this team was located in the city of Flint, many of the entries were related to the auto industry or to fire and sparks (connecting to the meaning of "Flint"). Ultimately, the name "Blast" was selected because it was seen as being marketable and fun. This team folded before ever playing a game as the Blast.

Michigan North Americans: Named for the continent of North America on which the team played, likely in an attempt to draw fans from both the United States and Canada. The city of Port Huron in which the team was formed is located in Michigan near the Canadian border, and the team's logo even combined an American flag with a Canadian maple leaf. This team changed its name to Port Huron North Americans before ever playing a game.

Michigan Panthers: So named to create a resemblance to Detroit's other football team, the Lions.

Middletown Mansfields: Named for General Joseph Mansfield, a Union general in the Civil War who was killed at the Battle of Antietam at Sharpsburg, Maryland.[102]

Midland Chemicals: Named for the Dow Chemical Company which sponsored the team. (See also *Midland Dow A.C.'s.*)

Midland Dow A.C.'s: Named for the Dow Chemical Company, which sponsored the team and which helped transform the city of Midland, Michigan, from a lumbering town into a culturally active city. "A.C." was a popular abbreviation for "Athletic Club."

Milwaukee Badgers: Named for the nickname of the state of Wisconsin, the "Badger State." Incidentally, the state nickname does not come from actual animals, but from lead miners in southwestern Wisconsin. These miners were nicknamed "badgers" because they lived in caves which reminded people of badgers' burrows.

Milwaukee Braves: For this baseball team, see *Boston Braves.*

Milwaukee Brewers: (5 teams) The first team to be called the Milwaukee Brewers was the one which played in the National League in 1878. The name is a salute to the beer-making capital of the nation.

Milwaukee Bucks: Named in a contest on May 22, 1968, from among 14,000 entries. Among 45 entries for "Bucks," the winner was R. D. Trebilcox of Whitefish Bay, Wisconsin, who won a new car for his efforts. The name was seen as fitting the wildlife atmosphere of Wisconsin, as being unique, and as being easily adaptable to promotional use. Trebilcox explained, "Bucks are spirited, good jumpers, fast and agile. These are exceptional qualities for basketball players."[103] General Manager John Erickson also pointed out that bucks are indigenous and very common to the Milwaukee area. Other names suggested in the contest included Badgers, Beavers, Braves, Hornets, Packers, Ponies, Skunks, Stags, and Stallions. Many people also sent in the names of Indian tribes.[104]

Milwaukee Chicks: This women's baseball team, like most in the All-American Girls Professional Baseball League, was assigned a feminine name so that the league could emphasize the femininity of the women who played. The league believed that to be the only way to build a following for itself.

Milwaukee Chiefs: Named for the American Indians indigenous to the Milwaukee area.

Milwaukee Cream Citys: (2 teams) The first team to be called the Milwaukee Cream Citys was the one which played in the National League in 1878. The name reflects the nickname of Milwaukee—the "Cream City"—so named because of Milwaukee's status as the brewing capital of the nation, recalling cream ales, cream stouts, etc. Another story, however, states that the nickname comes from Milwaukee's building bricks which are made from a local clay.

Milwaukee Deuce: Named for a tennis term. A "deuce" is a score in which each player or team has 40 points or 5 or more games, and either player or team must therefore win two consecutive points or games to win the match or set. This team changed its name to "Racqueteers" before ever playing as the Deuce.

Milwaukee Grays: (2 teams) The first team to be called the Milwaukee Grays was the one which played in the National League in 1878. The team was probably named for the colors the players wore.

Milwaukee Hawks: Shortened version of the team's previous name of Tri-Cities Blackhawks (see), used in Davenport, Iowa; Moline, Illinois; and Rock Island, Illinois.

Milwaukee Mustangs: Named by owner Andrew Vallozzi, who simply compiled a list of possibilities and decided that this one sounded best.

Milwaukee Racqueteers: A play on words. A "racketeer" is someone engaging in illegal business or, more appropriately, someone engaged in causing a racket (or uproar). The name "Racqueteers" combines that idea with that of the tennis racquet.

Milwaukee Wave: Named by one of the team's original owners because of Milwaukee's proximity to Lake Michigan.

Minneapolis Lakers: Named for the thousands of lakes in the state of Minnesota. The state motto, in fact, is "The Land of 10,000 Lakes."

Minneapolis Marines: Possibly reflective of the meaning of the name of the city of Minneapolis. "Minneapolis" is a combination of Indian and Greek words meaning "water city."

Minneapolis Millerettes: This women's baseball team copied and feminized the name of a men's minor league baseball team which was playing in the American Association at the same time, the Minneapolis Millers. A previous minor league team had also used that name in the late nineteenth century.

Minneapolis Redjackets: Possibly named for an American Indian chief by the name of Red Jacket, who got his name when he was given a red jacket by a British officer.[105]

Minnesota Arctic Blast: Named for the frequently icy weather in the state of Minnesota.

Minnesota Blue Ox: (2 teams) The first team to be called the Minnesota Blue Ox was the one which played in Roller Hockey International in 1995. Both teams were likely named for the legendary tale of Paul Bunyan, a giant lumberjack who was said to have walked from Maine, where he was supposedly born, westward, and whose footprints were said to have filled with water to form the Great Lakes. Paul's companion was a huge blue ox named Babe, whose horns measured 42 axe handles and a plug of Star Chewing Tobacco from tip to tip.

Minnesota Buckskins: Named for the deer and deer-hunting prevalent in Minnesota.

Minnesota Fighting Pike: Refers to Minnesota's many fishermen and lakes. The pike, a popular game fish, has a long snout and sometimes reaches four feet in length.

Minnesota Fighting Saints: (2 teams) The first team to be called the Minnesota Fighting Saints was the one which played in the World Hockey Association in 1972. The name was likely a play on the city name of St. Paul in which the team played.

Minnesota Kicks: Named in a contest for the most common activity in indoor soccer: the kick.

Minnesota Lynx: Like many WNBA teams, this club was named to create a connection with the NBA team which shared the same city (in this case, the Minnesota Timberwolves). The name was announced on December 5, 1998, and Chief Operating Officer Roger Griffith explained, "The Lynx resembles the Timberwolf in many ways. Both animals are indigenous to this area and have been in danger of extinction at different times in their history." He went on to point out, "The Timberwolves and the Lynx share a bond as they are both historical predators inhabiting the northern regions of Minnesota and Canada."

Minnesota Muskies: Named for a fish prevalent in Minnesota's thousands of lakes.

Minnesota North Stars: Named in a contest. The name was submitted by several fans, and was chosen because of Minnesota's state nickname of *Etoile du Nord,* or "Star of the North."[106]

Minnesota Pipers: See *Pittsburgh Pipers.*

Minnesota Strikers: See *Fort Lauderdale Strikers.*

Minnesota Timberwolves: Named in a contest from among 6000 entries. When the choices from those 6000 had been narrowed to 2—Timberwolves and Polars—public forums were held throughout the state of Minnesota to vote, and the name "Timberwolves" won by a 2–1 margin. The name was selected because the timberwolf is indigenous to Minnesota (and Minnesota is the only state besides Alaska to contain a significant number of this breed of wolf), it is a unique name (no other professional team has used it), and it is extremely marketable, even lending itself well to logo designs. "Minnesota" was used as the location name rather than "Minneapolis" because the team was meant to represent a great portion of the Midwest. (The closest NBA teams to Minneapolis were located in Milwaukee, Chicago, and Denver.)[107]

Minnesota Twins: Named for the Twin Cities of Minneapolis and St. Paul in an effort to avoid ill feeling because of the spirited and ongoing rivalry between those two cities. The team was originally to be called the Twin Cities Twins, but owner Calvin Griffith decided to go with the location name "Minnesota" to honor the entire state, since the team was already straying from the tradition of naming a team after a single city.

Minnesota Vikings: Named by General Manager Bert Rose because of Minnesota's rich Nordic background. Rose said, "A nickname should serve a dual purpose. It should represent an aggressive person or an animal imbued with the will to win. Secondly, if possible, it is desirable to have it connote the region that the team represents."[108] A large part of this region contains many people of Scandinavian descent, whose ancestors, the Vikings, were "a fierce band of tireless warriors."[109]

Minnesota Wild: As team CEO Jac K. Sperling explained,

> The selection of our team name is obviously an important step in developing our team's identity. We think it best represents what Minnesota hockey fans hold most dear—our rugged natural wilderness, the premier brand hockey that's native to Minnesota and the great enthusiasm of all of our hockey fans.

The other five finalists for the team name were Blue Ox, Freeze, Northern Lights, Voyageurs, and White Bears.

Monterrey La Raza: *La raza* is an idiomatic Spanish expression meaning "friends." It is used in Monterrey as well as in other regions of northern Mexico.

Montgomery Grey Sox: Likely named for the color of the team's uniform stockings.

Montreal Alouettes: (3 teams) The first team to be called the Montreal Alouettes was the one which played in the Canadian Football Council in 1956. *Alouettes* is a French word meaning "Larks."

Montreal Canadiens: This team was founded in 1909 by J. Ambrose O'Brien, who called it the Club de Hockey Canadien. That year, only French-Canadians were allowed on the team. In 1910, O'Brien sold the team to George Kennedy, who named it the Club Athletique Canadien. In 1916, it was renamed the Club De Hockey Canadien.[110] The name "Canadien," which employs the French spelling for "Canadian," has been consistent throughout.

Montreal Expos: Named for the World Exposition of 1967, which was held in Montreal.

Montreal Habs: "Habs" is a shortened form of "Habitants." The French name was *Les Habitants,* applied to the team in 1909, meaning "inhabitants of the country." Habitants were actually the first settlers along the St. Lawrence River.

Montreal Impact: Named by an American company which offered suggestions for the team name.

Montreal Manic: Named for the Manicouagan River in northern Quebec.[111]

Montreal Maroons: Named for the color of the team's jerseys.

Montreal Olympique: Possibly named in honor of the impending 1976 Olympic Games. (This team first played in 1971.)

Montreal Shamrocks: Named for the Irish population in the city of Montreal. The shamrock is considered the national emblem of Ireland.

Muskegon Belles: See *Racine Belles.*

Muskegon Lassies: This women's baseball team, like most in the All-American Girls Professional Baseball League, was assigned a feminine name so that the league could emphasize the femininity of the women who played. The league believed that to be the only way to build a following for itself.

Nashville Elite Giants: Like many Negro League teams, this club copied and altered the name of a popular white major league baseball team (in this case, the New York Giants).

Nashville Kats: This name has something to do with country music star Travis Tritt, who, according to the Arena Football League office, "looks like a Kat," and, in fact, a bit like the team mascot.

Nashville Noise: Named as a result of cooperation between the Nashville community, newspapers, and ad agencies. The name was alliterative and also reflected the musical importance of Nashville. It was also one of the few team investigated which had not been taken.

Nashville Predators: So named because the remains of a saber-toothed tiger and its possible lair were discovered in downtown Nashville in 1971. They were located beneath the First American Center and were preserved under concrete. The name therefore represents the city of Nashville and creates a tie to the Ice Age (with an obvious connection to ice hockey). The final four choices for the team's name were Fury, Ice Tigers, Predators, and Tigers. The name Predators was chosen through balloting, focus groups, and a telephone poll.

New Bedford Whalers: (2 teams) The first major league team to be called the New Bedford Whalers was the one which played in the first American Soccer League in 1924. Both of these soccer teams copied the name of two previous minor league baseball teams, the first of which played in the New England League from 1895–98. The name reflects the whaling history of New Bedford and the entire New England area. The city of New Bedford itself, in fact, was once a whaling port. (The first New Bedford Whalers moved to Fall River and were absorbed by the first Fall River Football Club, who later moved to New Bedford and became the second New Bedford Whalers.)

New England Blazers: Named by the Major Indoor Lacrosse League, which owned and named nearly all the teams in the league. This particular team was named for the Chevy Blazer, because Chevrolet was a sponsor of the team.

New England Blizzard: Named by team management in conjunction with focus groups to reflect the harshness of New England winters. It was also thought that the name would appeal to children.

New England Oceaneers: See *Rhode Island Oceaneers.*

New England Patriots: See *Boston Patriots.*

New England Revolution: Named in a name-the-team contest held by the *Boston Globe* and Reebok International Limited (the team's official outfitter). The name was submitted by Joseph Bracken, a 17-year-old high school student from Quincy, Massachusetts, who said it seemed especially fitting because of New England's rich history and proud patriotic heritage. (The American Revolution began in Massachusetts on April 19, 1775.)

New England Sea Wolves: Named for the Seawolf submarine. President and General Manager Neil Smith explained that the name "is derived from the Seawolf submarine, which is based in nearby Groton. The Seawolf submarine is among the elite in attack submarines, and we expect to make this organization the benchmark for arena football excellence."[112]

New England Steamrollers: Took the name of the Providence Steam Roller (see).

New England Stingers: This team played in Portland, Maine, and the name may have something to do with the fact that the honeybee is the state insect of Maine.

New England Tea Men: Named for the Lipton Tea Company, which owned the team.

New England Whalers: Reflects the whaling history of the New England area. The first three letters of the name "Whalers" also lent themselves to promotion of the World Hockey Association, or WHA, the league in which the team first played.

New Haven Elm Citys: Named for the nickname of New Haven, the "Elm City," so-called because of its multitude of elm trees. These trees are especially prevalent on the New Haven Green, which is one of nine "squares" in the city's village plan.

New Haven New Havens: Named for the city of New Haven in which the team played.

New Jersey Americans: (2 teams) The first team to be called the New Jersey Americans was the basketball team which played in the American Basketball Association in 1967. That team was likely named for the ABA in which it played, while the American Soccer League team was likely named for *its* league. In the midst of many other ethnic names, the title "Americans" became a very popular one in the American Soccer Leagues.

New Jersey Brewers: Shortened form of the team's original name of New Jersey Schaefer Brewers (see).

New Jersey Devils: Named in a fan contest consisting of 2400 contestants and 10,000 entries. The field was narrowed to a top 10, and then fans voted. The team's name is based on the legend of the New Jersey Devil, a half man/half beast that for 250 years was said to stalk the Pine Barrens of South Jersey. A second legend says that the creature was the thirteenth child of Mother Leeds, who was said to have been jinxed by gypsies she discovered on her land in Estelville in Atlantic County, New Jersey.[113] Other names suggested in the contest were Americans, Blades, Coastals, Colonials, Generals, Gulls, Jaguars, Lightnings, Meadowlanders, Meadowlarks, and Patriots.[114] There was also a previous minor league hockey team by this name.

New Jersey Freighters: This basketball team was named by owner Arthur J. Brown for his ABC Freight Forwarding Company.[115] The team never actually played under this name, however, changing its name to "New Jersey Americans" before the season began.

New Jersey Generals: Refers to the regional nature of the team, which represented New Jersey and the New York metropolitan area.[116]

New Jersey Nets: See *New York Nets.*

New Jersey Red Dogs: Named in a name-the-team contest. The name was one of the first entered, and it quickly became a favorite of club officials. It remained so even after hundreds of entries poured in.

New Jersey Rockets: Named by owner Ed Tepper, who announced the name on August 29, 1981.[117]

New Jersey Rockin' Rollers: A play on the term "rock 'n' roll," referring to music, and roller hockey.

New Jersey Saints: This team played at the Meadowlands Arena, which it shared with the New Jersey Devils. The name "Saints" was created to be in contrast to the name "Devils."

New Jersey Schaefer Brewers: Named for the Schaefer Brewing Company which sponsored the team.

New Orleans Buccaneers: See *Louisiana Buccaneers.*

New Orleans Jazz: Named in a contest from among 6500 entries for the style of music for which New Orleans is most famous. The winner of the contest was Steve Brown, who received a season pass and a ticket to the NBA All-Star Game. Brown explained, "The name should be something indigenous to the city. Everyone identifies Jazz with the city."[118] Other suggested names included Cajuns, Crescents, Deltas, Dukes, Knights, and Pilots. The two most popular were Dukes and Jazz. The city is reputed to be the birthplace of jazz, and its nickname is the "jazz capital of the world."

New Orleans Saints: Named on January 9, 1967, for the fact that the franchise was awarded to the city on All Saints Day (November 1), 1966. The name also refers to the song "When the Saints Come Marching In," reflecting New Orleans' great love for jazz music.[119]

New Westminster Royals: Possibly named for the fact that, although Canada has an independent government, the sovereign of the country is the British monarch.

New York Americans: (5 teams) The first team to be called the New York Americans was the hockey team which played in the National Hockey League in 1925.

After faltering in the Canadian cities of Quebec and Hamilton, this team moved to New York and was probably so named not only because it played in the United States of America, but also because it was one of the very first American teams in major league hockey. Ironically, the NHL split into a Canadian Division and an American Division, and the Americans were the only American team playing in the Canadian Division. The football team was named for the third American Football League in which it played. When football's second New York Yankees were sold by Douglas Hertz to William D. Cox, Hertz retained the rights to the "Yankees" name, so Cox was forced to rename the club. The first basketball team was named for the second American Basketball League in which it played. For the second basketball team, see *New Jersey Americans.*

New York Apollo: Name changed from New York Greeks when the second American Soccer League instituted a prohibition on ethnic nicknames. The name "Apollo" retained the Greek identity, since Apollo was the Greek god of the sun, prophecy, music, medicine, and poetry.

New York Apples: Named for the nickname of the city of New York: the "Big Apple." This term was first used by jazz musicians in the 1930s, who referred to all cities as "apples." Playing in New York was considered hitting the big time, and New York was therefore the "Big Apple." In 1978, when this tennis team played the Anaheim team, it was the Apples versus the Oranges.

New York Black Yankees: Like many Negro League teams, this club copied and altered the name of a popular white major league baseball team (in this case, the New York Yankees). This team actually wore the old uniforms of the white New York Yankees, however. The team was originally formed in 1931 as an independent squad, and despite the owners' desire to call the team the Black Yankees from the start, they settled on the name Harlem Stars because the team played its games at both Yankee Stadium and the Polo Grounds. Since the Polo Grounds were the home of the Yankees' rivals, the New York Giants, the owners did not deem the name "Black Yankees" appropriate that first year.[120]

New York Brickley's Giants: The name "New York Giants" was copied from the original baseball team (see), coupled with the name of head coach George Brickley.

New York Brookhattan: Named for Brooklyn and Manhattan, the two boroughs in New York which this team represented.

New York Bulldogs: This team moved to New York from Boston, Massachusetts, where it was called the Boston Yanks. Playing in the National Football League, the team did not carry the name "Yanks" from Boston because it wished to avoid confusion with baseball's New York Yankees of the American League and with football's New York Yankees of the All-America Football Conference, so it chose "Bulldogs" instead. (This choice may have had something to do with the fact that there had been two previous football teams in Boston called the Boston Bulldogs.) The following year, however (after the AAFC football team had folded), the team did change its name to "New York Yanks."

New York Celtics: For this basketball team, see *Brooklyn Celtics.*

New York CityHawks: This arena football team was so named for two reasons: 1) There was once a New York street hockey team in the late 1950s which wore Montreal Canadiens' jerseys. The jerseys read "CHK" across the front, so the team created the name "Cityhawks" so that it could claim the jerseys as its own. 2) In 1996, some nearly extinct hawks started appearing in Central Park; no one knows how or why. The name recalls that event as well.

New York Cosmos: Named in a contest to refer to a well-organized, smooth-running team.

New York Cubans: This Negro League team was possibly named in an effort to overcome racial prejudice, as the players may have tried to pass themselves off as Cubans.[121]

New York Field Club: (2 teams) The first team to be called the New York Field Club was the one which played in the first American Soccer League in 1921. "Field Club" was a commonly used name for soccer teams, especially in the early twentieth century.

New York Generals: Named for RKO-General, at first a partial sponsor of the team.[122]

New York Giants: (6 teams) The first team to be called the New York Giants was the baseball team which played in the National League in 1885. The team was inadvertently named by manager Jim Mutrie, who, after a particularly exciting victory, was heard exclaiming to his players, "My big fellows! My Giants! We are the people!"

He was also said to have called his players "not only giants in stature but in baseball ability."[123] Football's second New York Giants were so named in 1925 because they played at the Polo Grounds, the same park used by baseball's first New York Giants.

New York Golden Blades: Named for the blade on a hockey skate.

New York Gothams: (2 teams) The first team to be called the New York Gothams was the baseball team which played in the National League in 1883. Both teams were named for the nickname of the city of New York, "Gotham City."

New York Greeks: Like many soccer teams, this club was named for the ethnic origins of the players and/or the population which supported it.

New York Green Stockings: Named for the color of the team's uniform stockings.

New York Hakoah: (2 teams) The first team to be called New York Hakoah was the one which played in the first American Soccer League in 1931. This team was originally known as Brooklyn Hakoah, and then as the Hakoah All-Stars. Both teams copied the name of Hakoah, a famous all-Jewish soccer team from Vienna, Austria. "Hakoah" is derived from the Hebrew word *Koach* or *Hakoach,* meaning "power" or "strong ones."

New York Hakoah-Americans: Revised form of the team's previous name of New York Hakoah (see). Several soccer teams combined their ethnic names with that of "Americans." Additionally, this team had earlier absorbed soccer's New York Americans.

New York Hakoahs: This basketball team likely copied the name of Hakoah, a famous all-Jewish soccer team from Vienna, Austria. (See also *New York Hakoah.*) "Hakoah" is derived from the Hebrew word *Koach* or *Hakoach,* meaning "power" or "strong ones."

New York Hamptons: Named for the Hamptons, the region of New York in which this team plays.

New York Harlem Yankees: This team copied the name of baseball's New York Yankees (see) and combined it with the New York neighborhood of Harlem.

New York Highlanders: Named for the fact that the team's ballpark was built on high ground. Also, the team's first president was Joseph Gordon, and there was at the time a famous regiment in the British army called Gordon's Highlanders.

New York Hilltoppers: Named for the fact that the team played at Hilltop Park.

New York Inter: Revised from the team's previous name of Inter Soccer Club, the second to use the name. "Inter" was short for "international." While many teams in the American Soccer Leagues were using ethnic names, this one was comprised of players of a number of different nationalities.

New York Islanders: Named by owner Ray Boe for the fact that the team was located in Nassau County on Long Island, New York. This name had also been a runner-up in a contest to name the second New York Mets 11 years earlier.

New York Jets: This team nearly went bankrupt while it was called the New York Titans, and new owner Sonny Werblin said, "We need a new image. So we'll begin with a successful established coach and a new name—one not so grandiose."[124] The name was chosen to reflect the fact that the country was entering the "Jet Age" or the "Space Age," and also because Shea Stadium was to be built between LaGuardia and Idlewild (now John F. Kennedy) Airports. Also, it was a short name which could be used easily by headline writers.[125] Finally, it rhymed with "New York Mets."

New York Kick: Named for the most common activity in indoor soccer: the kick.

New York Knickerbockers: Knickerbockers, or knickers, are long trousers banded at the knee which were worn by the descendants of Dutch settlers in New York. The word, when capitalized, has come to refer to New Yorkers themselves. The very first team to use this name was actually the very first known baseball team in all of history, Alexander Cartwright's New York Knickerbockers of 1845. That team was named after a volunteer fire department to which Cartwright and several other players belonged.

New York Liberty: Named for the Statue of Liberty for which New York is famous.

New York Lincoln Giants: This New York team copied the complete name of the Lincoln Giants, a previous team which had played in Lincoln, Nebraska, in 1890.

New York Metropolitans: Named for the metropolis of New York City.

New York Mets: (2 teams) The first team to be called the New York Mets was the one which played in the American Association in 1883. For this team, the alternate name of "Mets" was simply a shortened form of the team's original name of "Metropolitans" (see). The corporate name of the second franchise with this name was actually the Metropolitan Baseball Club, Inc. Owner Mrs. Joan Payson chose the name "Mets" in a public poll conducted from among the names Avengers, Burros, Continentals, Islanders, Jets, Mets, Meadowlarks, NYBs, Rebels, and Skyliners.[126] The name Skyliners, which would later become the name of a major league soccer team, finished second. (See *New York Skyliners*.)

New York Mutuals: Originally called Mutual of New York. In its amateur days the team was named by club owner Bill Cammeyer for the firemen of Mutual Hook and Ladder Company Number 1 who formed it.

New York Nationals: (2 teams) The first team to be called the New York Nationals was the one which played in the first American Soccer League in 1927. Owner Charles Stoneham also owned baseball's first New York Giants, and would have preferred to have called his soccer team by the same name. Another soccer team in the same league had already taken the name, however, so Stoneham settled on the name "Nationals" for his soccer squad.

New York Nets: Named for the basketball net. The name was also chosen because it rhymed with "New York Mets" and "New York Jets."

New York Original Celtics: Copied the name of the original, independent New York Celtics of 1914, a team which was named for the predominantly Irish population of the west side of New York where it was organized, and the Original Celtics of 1918.[127]

New York OTBzz: This tennis team was named for Off-Track Betting (formally Capital District Regional Off-Track Betting Corporation), the company which owned the team. Based in Schenectady, the company has branches in many states as well as in Canada. Off-Track Betting, or OTB, provides legalized wagering on horse racing and lotteries and distributes the profits to local governments and to the racing industry. This method is called "off-track" because it provides betting away from the racetrack; the company has even set up clubhouses with theater screens and televisions for people to watch the races. Betting can take place by phone or over the Internet. This tennis team used a bee as its mascot and in its logo, thus the two *z*'s at the end of the name.

New York Rangers: Named for owner Tex Rickard, for whom the team was affectionately called "Tex's Rangers."

New York Saints: See *New Jersey Saints.*

New York Sets: Named for a tennis term. A "set" is a group of games which makes up a match. Additionally, the name rhymes with "New York Mets," "New York Jets," and "New York Nets."

New York Skyliners: Named for the world-famous New York skyline.

New York Soccer Club: The rather unimaginative name "Soccer Club," along with "Field Club" and "Football Club," was commonly used by soccer teams when nicknames were uncommon, especially in the early part of the twentieth century.

New York Stars: Credit for this name is given to coach Babe Parilli. On a flight from Boston to New York, Parilli said to his assistant, Dusty Rhodes, "I finally feel like a star." She replied, "Yeah, a New York Star," and Parilli exclaimed, "That's it!"[128]

New York Tapers: Named for the Technical Tape Corporation which owned the team.[129]

New York Titans: Probably named in an attempt to create a connection (or competition) with football's second New York Giants. In Greek mythology, the Titans were huge, powerful primordial gods who were the children of Uranus and Gaea, and who were eventually overthrown by the more popularly known Olympian gods.

New York United: Employed a very popular and deeply traditional name among soccer teams, especially in South America and Europe. It denotes the fact that the team plays together as a unit.

New York Westchesters: Named for Westchester County just north of the city of New York, where the team played.

New York Yankees: (6 teams) The first team to be called the New York Yankees was the baseball team which has played in the American League under this name since 1913. The name was supposedly first used in 1909, when the team was called the New York Highlanders, by sportswriter Jim Price, during an era of spirited nationalism. The name was shorter and thus easier to use in headlines than "Highlanders." The term "Yankee" is slang for "American."

New York Yanks: After one season of being called the New York Bulldogs in order to avoid confusion with other teams called the New York Yankees (see *New York Bulldogs*), this team fetched its original name of "Yanks" from Boston, Massachusetts. Boston owner Ted Collins had always wanted a New York franchise that could play at Yankee Stadium. Failing that, he originally used the name "Yanks" in Boston as a second-best option. "Yanks" is short for "Yankees," which is slang for "Americans."

New York-New Jersey MetroStars: Named for the energy of the city of New York and the surrounding area.

New York/New Jersey Rockin' Rollers: See *New Jersey Rockin' Rollers.* This team had planned to move from East Rutherford, New Jersey, to Morristown, New Jersey and New York, New York, but folded before the season began.

Newark: Used no team name, but only the name of the New Jersey city which this soccer team represented.

Newark Americans: Likely named for the United States of America as well as the first American Soccer League in which the team played. In the midst of many other ethnic names, the title "Americans" became a very popular one in the American Soccer Leagues.

Newark Bears: (2 teams) The first team to be called the Newark Bears was the football team which played in the first American Football League in 1926. It was named by George Halas, who copied the name from the other football team he owned, the Chicago Bears. Three previous minor league baseball teams had also used the name, the first of which played in the International League from 1917 until 1919.

Newark Celtics: Formerly the Newark Irish, this team changed its name but kept the meaning. Like many soccer teams, it was named for the ethnic origins of the players and/or the population which supported it. The name "Celtics" refers to the Irish.

Newark Dodgers: Like many Negro League teams, this club copied the name of a popular white major league baseball team (in this case, the Brooklyn Dodgers).

Newark Feds: Short for "Federal," named for the Federal League in which the team played.

Newark Germans: Like many soccer teams, this club was named for the ethnic origins of the players and/or the population which supported it.

Newark Irish: This team came over from Kearny, New Jersey, where it had played as the Kearny Irish-Americans. Like many soccer teams, this club was named for the ethnic origins of the players and/or the population which supported it.

Newark Jerseymen: Named for the fact that the team played in the state of New Jersey.

Newark Newfeds: Combination of the names "Newark" (the city in which the team played) and "Federal" (for the Federal League in which the team played).

Newark Peppers: Named in a contest. The word "pepper" has been used in baseball to denote liveliness (for instance, if a pitch has a lot of movement on the ball, it is said to "have some pepper on it"), and the game of Pepper is an informal one in which a baseball is thrown among several players who attempt to demonstrate their skill and speed.

Newark Peps: Shortened form of the name "Peppers" (see *Newark Peppers*).

Newark Portuguese: Like many soccer teams, this club was named for the ethnic origins of the players and/or the population which supported it.

Newark Sitch: Shortened form of the team's previous name of Newark Ukrainian Sitch (see).

Newark Ukrainian Sitch: Like many soccer teams, this club was named for the ethnic origins of the players and/or the population which supported it. In Ukraine in the seventeenth and eighteenth centuries, serf labor peasants who no longer wished to work for their landlords were running away to the outlying districts of the country. Settlements of fugitive peasants therefore began to spring up in these areas. These peasants would later form a military unification known as the *Kozachestvo,* and the soldiers were called *kozaki.* Under Russian Queen Ekaterina the Great, when Ukraine was a part of Russia, these *kozaki,* or kozaks, were used by the tsarist government to guard the borders. Kozaks then began to form their own settlements, and these settlements were called sitches. The main kozak

settlement was in Zaporozhye, and this region therefore began to be known as Zaporozhskaya Sitch.

Newcastle Geordies: The term "Geordie" generally refers to citizens of the city of Newcastle-Upon-Tyne, Tyne and Wear, England, although there is some dissension concerning exactly who is a Geordie and where the term originated. One account relates that it has to do with the fact that, in the seventeenth and eighteenth centuries, the town came under attack and was occupied on several occasions by Scottish armies, who referred to England's King George I by various disparaging nicknames, among them "Wee Geordie of Hanover" and "The Wee German Geordie." A second account goes back to the thirteenth century, when a fisherman named George, who was also known as Geordie, built himself a house on the banks of the Tyne River. He eventually had 11 children, and when asked the children would tell people, "We're Geordie's kids," eventually creating an identifying nickname for the area's settlers. This team folded before ever playing a game.

North Hudson Thourots: Possibly named for a family which sponsored the team. Hudson is a county in New Jersey where the team played.[130]

Northeast United: Employed a very popular and deeply traditional name among soccer teams, especially in South America and Europe. It denotes the fact that the team plays together as a unit.

Northern Fusiliers: This team was part of the 228th Battalion of the Northern Fusiliers of Canada. It was the only military team to become a major league team in any of the ten sports featured in this volume. It was often listed in the standings as the "228th Battalion." It left the league during World War I when the entire unit was ordered overseas to France. Incidentally, a "fusilier" was a soldier who used a fusil, which was a type of flintlock musket.

Oakland Aces: Named for a tennis term. An "ace" is a serve which is not returned by one's opponent.

Oakland Americans: Likely named for the American Basketball Association in which the team was formed. This squad became the second Oakland Oaks before ever playing a game as the Americans.

Oakland Athletics: See *Philadelphia Athletics.*

Oakland Breakers: Named for the cresting waves common and popular on the California coast.

Oakland Buccaneers: Buccaneers were French, English, or Dutch pirates who originally settled in Haiti and, from the native Indians there, learned a special technique of sun-drying meat called "buccaning," from which they got their name.

Oakland Clippers: Named for the clipper ships which used to sail through the harbors of San Francisco Bay many years ago.

Oakland Invaders: This USFL team copied the name of a minor league baseball team which played in the Central California Baseball League in 1910. The name was also similar to that of the NFL's Oakland Raiders.

Oakland Oaks: (2 teams) The first team to be called the Oakland Oaks was the one which played in the third American Basketball League in 1962. This basketball team copied the name of a minor league baseball team which played in the Pacific Coast League beginning in 1903. The name itself is likely a play on the city name of Oakland.

Oakland Raiders: This team was originally called the Metropolitan Oakland Area Football Club, but deeming that title too long for public use, team officials sanctioned a fan contest conducted by the Oakland Chamber of Commerce. When the name Oakland Señors was chosen as the winner, the team officials rejected it and chose their own name.[131] They chose "Raiders" because their team originally featured players from seven other teams.

Oakland Seals: See *California Seals.*

Oakland Skates: A play on words. This roller hockey team combined the idea of a roller skate with that of a sea animal indigenous to the Oakland area.

Oakland Stompers: Possibly named for grape-stomping, reflecting California's grape or wine industry.[132]

Oklahoma City Stampede: Recalls the Western culture and history of Oklahoma City.

Oklahoma Coyotes: Named for an animal indigenous to the Oklahoma City plains area. A coyote is a prairie wolf, and the name "coyote" was possibly derived from the Native American Coyotero Apaches.

Oklahoma Outlaws: Named by owners William Tatham, Sr. and William Tatham, Jr. Gil Swalls, the team's head of media relations, explained that they wanted an aggressive name similar to those which other teams in the United States Football League were using (such as Bandits, Gamblers, Invaders, and Wranglers). He said that some fans objected, claiming it put the state's history in a negative light. "But we explain, with tongue in cheek," he said, "that the team is starting as a renegade."[133]

Oklahoma Wranglers: This Arena Football League team was named in a contest from among 1041 entries submitted in a 72-hour period. Eleven people suggested the winning name. Team owner Ed Gatlin explained, "We wanted a name that would be something indigenous to the area, and Wranglers certainly does that. The AFL's pioneering spirit is a reflection of Oklahoma's heritage."

Oorang Indians: Named for the fact that the team was comprised entirely of American Indians, including the great Jim Thorpe. The team was organized by Walter Lingo, the owner of Oorang Dog Kennels in LaRue, Ohio. Lingo created the team for the sole purpose of advertising his dog kennels and the Airedale breed of dog which he promoted. The Indians played only one home game, which they had to play in nearby Marion since LaRue did not have a field. Lingo liked his team to play road games so that he could advertise in different localities. Pregame and halftime entertainment frequently consisted of performances by the Airedale dogs or by the players themselves. One player, whose name was Long Time Sleep, sometimes wrestled a bear as part of that entertainment.

Orlando Jackals: Named by the club's front office staff. Everyone on the staff submitted names, and a vote was taken. The name "Jackals" was the highest vote-getter.

Orlando Magic: Named in a contest sponsored by the *Orlando Sentinel.* Entries were narrowed down to two names: Magic and Juice. These two were sent to a panel of local community leaders, who selected the name Magic. Team General Manager Pat Williams explained, "Magic is synonymous with this area. We are the tourist capital of the world. We have the Magic Kingdom and Disney World. The tourism slogan is 'Come to the Magic.'"[134]

Orlando Miracle: Named by RDV Sports and the WNBA for three reasons: 1) It appeals to both children and adults. 2) It preserves a link with the NBA's Orlando Magic. 3) It captures the spirit of the WNBA in the Orlando community and across the country. RDV Sports Senior Executive Vice President Pat Williams pointed out, "It truly is a miracle we will be playing women's professional basketball before what we believe will be capacity crowds in a few short months." The team was granted the right to use the name "Miracle" by the Ft. Myers Miracle, a member of baseball's minor Florida State League.

Orlando Predators: Named for the alligators and crocodiles indigenous to Florida's swamps.

Orlando Renegades: Named in a contest sponsored by the *Orlando Sentinel* from among 10,000 entries. A seven-member selection committee was set up to choose the name, and this committee was not required to use any of the submitted names. The 10 finalists for the team name, in order of preference, were: Renegades, Lazers, Lightning, Lynx, Condors, Avengers, Thunders, Wildcats, Juggernauts, and Tribe. Four names were then submitted to the USFL league office for approval. In order of the team's preference, those names were: Renegades, Lazers, Condors, and Lynx. The league immediately eliminated the name "Lazers" because of a conflict with the MISL's Los Angeles Lazers. The name "Renegades" was approved and registered with the league in October of 1984. It had been submitted in the contest by 26 people, and the winner by random drawing was Blake Harper, a plumber from Christmas, Florida, who won an all-expense paid trip to the 1985 USFL Championship Game in Pontiac, Michigan (a game which ultimately was never played because the league folded during the 1985 season). Harper explained, "I thought Renegades would be a good name since it would be along the same line as the [Tampa Bay] Bandits, the [Oklahoma] Outlaws and other teams in the league. I thought of it when I was on the job." Managing general partner Don Dizney stated, "We're very happy with it. Any time you comb your hair differently you have to have a little renegade blood in you. And we hope to be a little different."

Orlando RollerGators: Named for the sport of roller hockey as well as for the alligators prevalent in Florida.

Ottawa Civics: Named for the Ottawa Civic Center in which the team played.

Ottawa Loggers: Reflects Ottawa's origins as a logging outpost in the nineteenth century.

Ottawa Nationals: This hockey team copied the name of a minor league baseball team which played in the Border League in 1947. The name may also be indicative of the fact that Ottawa is the national capital of Canada.

Ottawa Rough Riders: Name copied from a previous rugby team which was formed in 1876. The name proba-

bly referred to lumberjacks, called Rough Riders, who rode logs down the Ottawa River.

Ottawa Senators: (2 teams) The first team to be called the Ottawa Senators was the one which played in the National Hockey Association in 1909, and before that in the amateur Canadian Hockey Association in 1885. The name refers to the Canadian Senate, as Ottawa is the capital of Canada.

Ottawa Wheels: Likely named for the wheels on a roller hockey skate.

Passaic Bengal Tigers: Followed a common tradition in the Passaic and northern New Jersey area of using a name relating to tigers or bengals.[135]

Passon Phillies: "Philly" is the nickname of Philadelphia, the city in which this team played. "Passon" referred to owner Harry Passon.

Paterson Caledonians: Like many soccer teams, this club was named for the ethnic origins of the players and/or the population which supported it. The name "Caledonians" refers to the Scottish.

Paterson Crescents: (2 teams) The first team to be called the Paterson Crescents was the one which played in the first American Basketball League in 1929. That team was likely named for the nickname of Paterson, the "Crescent City." Crescents may have also been some kind of social organizations.[136]

Paterson Silk Sox: Named for the silk industry in Paterson, which for a number of years was the primary source of income for the city. Paterson was founded as a textile town in 1792 by Alexander Hamilton and his Society for Establishing Useful Manufactures.

Paterson Visitations: See *Brooklyn Visitations*.

Paterson Whirlwinds: Copied the name of a previous independent barnstorming basketball team called the New York Whirlwinds, which had been organized by Tex Rickard.[137]

Pawtucket Rangers: This team, formerly called J & P Coats for the Pawtucket manufacturing company which sponsored it, was renamed by its new management when J & P Coats ran into financial problems and sold the club.

Pawtucket Slaters: This basketball team copied the name of a minor league baseball team which had played in the New England League from 1946–49. Both teams were named for Samuel Slater, the Father of the American Industrial Revolution. Slater was a British immigrant who came to the United States in 1789 and built the first successful water-powered textile mill in Pawtucket in 1793.

Pennsylvania Posse: Named by Charlie Yoder of Harrisburg, the team's Director of Hockey Operations.

Peoria Redwings: While the origin of this women's baseball team's name is uncertain, it may have been influenced by two previous men's minor league teams called the Peoria Reds, the first of which played in the Northwestern League from 1883–84.

Phil-Pitt: This team was a merger of the Philadelphia Eagles and the Pittsburgh Steelers. The name is a combination of "Philadelphia" and "Pittsburgh."

Philadelphia: Used no team name, but only the name of the city which this soccer team represented.

Philadelphia Americans: Shortened form of the team's previous, alternate name of Philadelphia German-Americans (see). The team was likely named for the United States of America as well as the second American Soccer League in which it played. In the midst of many other ethnic names, the title "Americans" became a very popular one in the American Soccer Leagues.

Philadelphia Athletics: (4 teams) The first team to be called the Philadelphia Athletics was the one which played in the National Association in 1871, and which had been formed as an independent team in 1860. The team was probably named for the athleticism of the team, as many teams used similar names promoting their skills. This team was, of course, an athletic club, and was originally called Athletic of Philadelphia. The second Philadelphia Athletics, who played in the American Association from 1882 to 1890, were replaced in that league in 1891 by a former Players League club called the Philadelphia Quakers, and the Quakers were "awarded" the name Athletics upon entering the AA.

Philadelphia Atoms: Named in a contest from among 3000 entries. The winner was Sarah Fletcher of Lakewood, New Jersey, who received a trip for two to London, England, for the English soccer Cup Final for her suggestion. The name was announced by team owner Tom McCloskey.[138]

Philadelphia Bell: Named for the Liberty Bell, a famous national landmark in Philadelphia.

Philadelphia Blue Jays: In 1943, new Philadelphia Phillies' owner R. R. M. Carpenter, Jr. was perhaps "weary with the perennial losers image of two decades,"[139] so he held a contest to rename the team. From among 5064 entries and 635 different names, the winner was "Blue Jays," suggested by Mrs. John L. Crooks of Philadelphia. Mrs. Crooks received a $100 savings bond (or "war" bond) and a season pass for her entry. She explained that the name Blue Jays "reflects a new team spirit. The Blue Jay is colorful in personality and plumage. His plumage is a brilliant blue, a color the Phillies could use decoratively and psychologically."[140] The name "Blue Jays" didn't last long, however, reverting back to "Phillies" after only two seasons. Even when the team was called the Blue Jays, the uniforms still bore the name "Phillies."

Philadelphia Bulldogs: This roller hockey team copied the name of a previous minor league football team, which played in the Continental Football League in 1965.

Philadelphia Celtic: Like many soccer teams, this club was named for the ethnic origins of the players and/or the population which supported it. The name "Celtic" refers to the Irish.

Philadelphia Centennials: This team played at Centennial Park in 1875. It was almost time for the centennial celebration of the 1776 signing of the Declaration of Independence which took place in Philadelphia, and the team name looked forward to that anniversary.

Philadelphia Eagles: Named by co-owner Bert Bell for President Franklin D. Roosevelt's National Recovery Administration (NRA), which had the American Eagle as its symbol. Designed in 1933 to help the nation recover from the stock market crash of 1929, the NRA had enormous power over business and industry. It was headed by Hugh S. Johnson, a former general who said the agency needed a visible, unique symbol. He chose the Blue Eagle, which was inspired by a Navajo thunderbird ideogram.

Philadelphia Field Club: (2 teams) The first team to be called the Philadelphia Field Club was the one which played in the first American Soccer League in 1921. "Field Club" was a commonly used name for soccer teams, especially in the early twentieth century.

Philadelphia Fillies: A play on the nickname of the city of Philadelphia ("Phillie"). A "filly" is a young female horse. The team would soon change the spelling and would thus be the second to adopt the name "Phillies."

Philadelphia Flyers: Named in a contest from among 25,000 entries. The winner was chosen by General Manager Bud Poile and the team's Board of Directors. The name was selected simply because it sounded proper after "Philadelphia."[141]

Philadelphia Football Club: This team used the worldwide term "football" for soccer. This name, along with "Soccer Club" and "Field Club," was commonly used by soccer teams when nicknames were uncommon, especially in the early part of the twentieth century.

Philadelphia Freedoms: The city of Philadelphia is intimately connected with the idea of liberty, resulting mainly from the fact that the Declaration of Independence was signed there on July 4, 1776. The Liberty Bell is a reminder of this ideal. The term "Philadelphia freedom" is a similar development.

Philadelphia German-Americans: Alternate form of the team's original, primary name of Philadelphia Germans (see). Several soccer teams combined their ethnic names with that of "Americans."

Philadelphia Germans: Like many soccer teams, this club was named for the ethnic origins of the players and/or the population which supported it. This club was formed as an independent team called the Philadelphia German Rifle Club, which later became the First German Soccer Club.

Philadelphia Hebrews: Named for the fact that the team was sponsored by the South Philadelphia Hebrew Association.

Philadelphia Keystones: Named for the nickname of the state of Pennsylvania, the "Keystone State." A keystone is the central stone in an arch that locks the others together, and Pennsylvania got its nickname because, as one of the 13 original states, it was located at the center of the infant nation. Six states were situated to the north and east of it, and six to the south. The team also played at Keystone Park. This team played in 1884, but a previous amateur team had used the name as early as 1865.

Philadelphia Kixx: Named for the most common activity in indoor soccer: the kick.

Philadelphia Nationals: (2 teams) The first team to be called the Philadelphia Nationals was the baseball team which played in the National League in 1883. That team was probably named for the National League in which it played.

Philadelphia Passon: Named for owner Harry Passon.

Philadelphia Philadelphias: Named for the city of Philadelphia in which the team played.

Philadelphia Phillies: (3 teams) The first team to be called the Philadelphia Phillies was the baseball team which played in the National Association in 1875. It was named for the nickname of the city of Philadelphia ("Phillie") in which it played. The owner of the second baseball team, Horace Fogel, began an unsuccessful campaign in 1910 to rename the team, stating, "The name Phillies is too trite and Quakers [a former name of the team] stands for peaceful people who will dodge a fight. Why don't you fellas [meaning sportswriters] call the club the 'Live Wires'?"[142] The basketball team changed its name to Philadelphia Warriors (see) in order to avoid confusion with the baseball team.

Philadelphia Quakers: (5 teams) The first team to be called the Philadelphia Quakers was the baseball team which played in the National League in 1883. The name refers to the Society of Friends, a popular religious denomination in Philadelphia, the members of which are called Quakers by outsiders.

Philadelphia Rage: See *Richmond Rage.*

Philadelphia Seventy-Sixers: Named in a contest in honor of the signing of the Declaration of Independence on July 4, 1776, by the Continental Congress at Independence Hall in Philadelphia. The name evoked a spirit of liberty.

Philadelphia Sphas: Named for the South Philadelphia Hebrew Association (S.P.H.A.) which sponsored the team. The name may have been suggested by Bill Scheffer, a sportswriter for the *Philadelphia Inquirer.*

Philadelphia Stars: (2 teams) The first team to be called the Philadelphia Stars was the baseball team which played in the second Negro National League in 1934. Whether intentional or otherwise, both this team and the later United States Football League team copied the name of an independent football team which had first used it as early as 1901.

Philadelphia Tapers: See *New York Tapers.*

Philadelphia Tigers: Like many Negro League teams, this club copied the name of a popular white major league baseball team (in this case, the Detroit Tigers).

Philadelphia Ukrainian Nationals: Like many soccer teams, this club was named for the ethnic origins of the players and/or the population which supported it.

Philadelphia Warriors: (2 teams) The first team to be called the Philadelphia Warriors was the one which played in the first American Basketball League in 1927. That team was originally called the Philadelphia Phillies (after the major league baseball team), when owner Jules Aronson changed it in order to distinguish it from baseball's Phillies. Gordon Mackay of the *Philadelphia Inquirer* reported Aronson as saying, "I saw a picture of Hannibal last night, and the name popped right into my head. Warriors, that's the name for our bunch. And that's the name we will take."[143]

Philadelphia White Stockings: Named for the color of the team's stockings.

Philadelphia Whites: Shortened form of the team's alternate name of Philadelphia White Stockings (see).

Philadelphia Wings: This lacrosse team copied the name of a previous professional lacrosse team in Philadelphia.

Phoenix Cardinals: See *Racine Cardinals.*

Phoenix Coyotes: Named for an animal indigenous to the Phoenix area. The name was chosen by team management in a name-the-team contest, and was announced on April 8, 1996. A coyote is a prairie wolf, and the name "coyote" was possibly derived from the Native American Coyotero Apaches.

Phoenix Fire: The city of Phoenix is named for the mythical bird called the phoenix which rose up from its own ashes. This team's name may have referred to the flames which caused the phoenix to burn. This team folded before ever playing a game and, unlike the phoenix, did *not* rise again.

Phoenix Mercury: Like many WNBA teams, this club was named to create a connection with the NBA team which shared the same city (in this case, the Phoenix Suns). The sun is at the center of our solar system, and Mercury is the first planet.

Phoenix Pride: So named because the team was claimed to be the pride of Phoenix.[144]

Phoenix Racquets: See *Denver Racquets.*

Phoenix Roadrunners: Named for a swift-running bird indigenous to the Phoenix area. The name also belonged to a previous minor league hockey team in Phoenix which played in the Western Hockey League in 1973.

Phoenix Smash: Named for a tennis term. A "smash" is a very hard hit ball.

Phoenix Suns: Named in a contest in which everyone entering was to receive a free ticket to a future game. The winner received $1000, two season tickets, and a one-year membership to the Stadium Club. From among 28,000 entries, 465 different names were suggested, and the name "Suns," the most frequent entry, was chosen because of Arizona's constant sunshine and tropical climate. Other suggested names were Dudes, Dust Devils, Gems, Rattlers, Scorpions, Sunspots, Suntanos, and Wrens.[145]

Phoenix Sunsets: Likely a play on words, combining "sun," since Phoenix has almost constant sunshine (see *Phoenix Suns*) and "set," a tennis term for a group of games which make up a match.

Pittsburgh Alleghenies: Named for the Allegheny River. In its first year (1882) this team played at the original Exposition Park Lower Field, which was located on the Allegheny River. This is the current site of Three Rivers Stadium. The name was first used by a minor league baseball team which played in the International Association in 1877.

Pittsburgh Americans: Named for the second American Football League in which the team played.

Pittsburgh Bulls: Named by the Major Indoor Lacrosse League, which owned and named nearly all the teams in the league.

Pittsburgh Burghers: A "burgher" was a member of the mercantile class of a medieval city. However, the word could also simply refer to a solid citizen. The name was likely a play on the city name "Pittsburgh."

Pittsburgh Condors: Chosen as an alternate when legal problems created complications over the team's selection of the name "Pittsburgh Pioneers" (see).

Pittsburgh Crawfords: Originally an independent team called the Crawford Colored Giants, this team was so named because it was organized by Jim Dorsey, director of the Crawford Recreation Center.[146]

Pittsburgh CrosseFire: Named in a contest. The name is a play on words, combining the idea of a dangerous crossfire with that of the sport of lacrosse. The other four finalists for the team name were Beavers, Jackals, Panic, and Piranhas.

Pittsburgh Innocents: This name was used facetiously when the team "traitorously" abandoned the American Association for the National League. Another story is that the team was stealing players from other teams, and the name was used facetiously in this instance as well.

Pittsburgh Ironmen: As Pittsburgh is the "Steel Capital of the World," named for the fact that iron is one of the elements in steel.

Pittsburgh Keystones: Named for the nickname of the state of Pennsylvania, the "Keystone State." A keystone is the central stone in an arch that locks the others together, and Pennsylvania got its nickname because, as one of the 13 original states, it was located at the center of the infant nation. Six states were situated to the north and east of it, and six to the south.

Pittsburgh Maulers: Named as a tribute to Pittsburgh's steelworkers.

Pittsburgh Miners: Reflects the mining industry popular in Pittsburgh and in many parts of Pennsylvania.

Pittsburgh Penguins: Named in a contest. Team Public Relations assistant Cindy Heine explained, "There is no direct reasoning behind the name. It was just chosen as a nickname."[147]

Pittsburgh Pioneers: When Haven Industries, Inc. bought the Pittsburgh Pipers, the new owners desired a name change to try to promote a new image and a new attitude for the team, so they held a fan contest. The contest rules stipulated that each entrant was to enter a name and also an essay stating the *reason* for the suggested name in 25 words or less. The winning entry was "Pittsburgh Pioneers," but a woman sued the team because the winning essay was more than 25 words in length. Nearby college Point Park, a member of the National Association of Intercollegiate Athletics (NAIA) also threatened to sue, because its team already used the name Pioneers. To avoid all the potential legal problems, team ownership chose the name "Condors" instead.

Pittsburgh Pipers: Named by owner Gene Rubin, who liked the alliteration of the name and who also felt that it made a connection with bagpipes and thus with the Scottish-Irish people who settled the area.

Pittsburgh Pirates: (4 teams) The first team to be called the Pittsburgh Pirates was the baseball team which first played in the National League in 1891 under the name. In 1889, second baseman Louis Bierbauer played for the second Philadelphia Athletics in the American Association. In 1890, the Players League was formed, and Bierbauer abandoned the Athletics for the Brooklyn Wonders in the PL. The Athletics were ejected from the AA anyway after the 1890 season. The PL also folded at that time, and rules were created stating that the rights to all players in the PL returned to their original 1889 teams. The second Athletics were replaced in the AA by the second Philadelphia Quakers of the PL, who then changed their name to Athletics. Bierbauer's rights reverted to this replacement team, but through a clerical error, the Pittsburgh Innocents of the National League signed him. The team was then said to have "pirated" Bierbauer from Philadelphia. The name "Pittsburgh Pirates" is also the only primary name to have been used by major league teams in baseball, football, basketball, and hockey. (The name "Philadelphia Quakers" has also been used in those four sports, but in basketball was an alternate to the primary names "Philadelphia Phillies" and "Philadelphia Warriors.")

Pittsburgh Pittsfeds: This team played in the Federal League, and the name is a combination of "Pittsburgh" and "Federal."

Pittsburgh Raiders: Possibly so named to create a connection with baseball's Pittsburgh Pirates.

Pittsburgh Rebels: Formerly the Pittsburgh Pittsfeds, this team was renamed for manager "Rebel" Oakes when Oakes replaced Doc Gessler after the season's first month.[148]

Pittsburgh Renaissances: Possibly named for the famous New York Renaissance Five, a team which had played independently in the 1920s and which had eventually become the Dayton Rens. That team was named for the Renaissance Casino Ballroom in Harlem where it played.

Pittsburgh Rens: Shortened form of the team's original, primary name of Pittsburgh Renaissances (see). The name "Rens" was the one more commonly used.

Pittsburgh Steelers: Formerly called the Pittsburgh Pirates, this team's name was changed by owner Art Rooney in order to better represent Pittsburgh as the "Steel Capital of the World."[149] Rooney supposedly got the idea from the wife of the team's ticket manager.[150]

Pittsburgh Triangles: Likely named for the fact that Pittsburgh's downtown area is called the Golden Triangle, so named because the Allegheny and Monongahela Rivers meet there to form the Ohio River.

Port Huron North Americans: See *Michigan North Americans.*

Portland Capitals: Name carried over from Regina, Saskatchewan. The Regina Capitals were so named because Regina is the capital of the province of Saskatchewan. They kept the name in Portland despite the fact that Portland is not the capital of Oregon. (That distinction belongs to the city of Salem.)

Portland Fire: Like many WNBA teams, this club was named to create a connection with the NBA team which shared the same city (in this case, the Portland Trail Blazers). It was named by NBA Creative Services in coordination with the team to reflect the energy, intensity, and emotion the franchise planned to bring to the city. Head Coach and General Manager Linda Hargrove said, "Fire is what I look for in a player and it's what all fans will see in this team. I can't think of a better word to describe the intensity I expect this team to bring to the floor every night." Harry Hutt, Senior Vice President of Marketing Operations for the Portland Trail Blazers, added, "Fire describes not just the intensity of the team, but also the fervor of our fans, who have been extremely supportive of our local sports teams for many, many years."

Portland Forest Dragons: Named by team consultant Jon Spoelstra. Spoelstra was a former vice president of the New Jersey Nets, and he wanted to rename that team the Swamp Dragons. The National Basketball Association approved the name, but the team's Executive Committee did not, and opted to keep the name "Nets." Spoelstra later went into private business, became a consultant for Portland's arena football team and, inspired by his near-miss with "Swamp Dragons," changed the name a bit and created the name "Forest Dragons" because of Portland's many forests and the importance of the lumber industry there.

Portland Power: Named largely by default, as many of the other names the American Basketball League wanted for this team had already been taken.

Portland Pride: Named in a name-the-team contest.

Portland Pythons: Named in a contest. This team was originally called the Portland Pride when it played in the Continental Indoor Soccer League. When the CISL folded, the league still held the rights to the team's name and logo, so the club was forced to abandon that identity and adopt a new one. The five finalists in the contest were Bigfoot, Panthers, Pythons, Steelhead, and Storm. Sample logos were designed for four of those names (Bigfoot, Pythons, Steelhead, and Storm), and team officials then decided on the "Pythons" name.

Portland Rosebuds: (2 teams) The first team to be called the Portland Rosebuds was the one which played in the Pacific Coast Hockey Association in 1914. The name reflects Portland's renown for its many beautiful roses and rose gardens, including those in the annual Rose Festival which has been held every June since 1907. Portland is even nicknamed the "Rose City."

Portland Timbers: (2 teams) The first team to be called the Portland Timbers was the one which played in the outdoor North American Soccer League in 1975. The name recalls the many forests in Portland, and the importance of the lumber industry both to the city and to the state of Oregon as a whole.

Portland Trail Blazers: Named in a contest from among 10,000 entries. The name "Trail Blazers" was entered by 172 people. Founder Harry Glickman explained the choice by saying it "reflects both the ruggedness of the Pacific Northwest and the start of a major league era in our state."[151] The name reflects the role that explorers played in settling the Pacific Northwest.

Portland Uncle Sams: Named for Uncle Sam, a character which personifies the United States. The prevailing theory concerning the origin of Uncle Sam is that the character comes from Samuel Wilson, a meat-packer in Troy, New York, during the War of 1812. Supposedly Wilson shipped meat to the U.S. Army and stamped the barrels "U.S." Someone suggested that the "U.S." stood for "Uncle Sam" Wilson, and a legend was born.

Pottsville Maroons: Named for the color of the team's jerseys. In 1924, team manager Dr. J. G. Striegel placed an order with Joseph Zacko, the owner of a local sporting goods store, for 25 matching jerseys. Striegel told Zacko, "The color isn't important." Zacko then delivered 25 maroon jerseys, and the team was called the "Maroons."[152]

Prague: Not much is known about this team. It was likely composed of Czechoslovakian players and named itself after the famous Czech city.

Providence Clamdiggers: This soccer team copied the name of a minor league baseball team which played in the Eastern League in 1905. Both teams were at least in part named for the fact that clams and other shellfish account for approximately half of Rhode Island's total fish catch.

Providence Grays: Probably named for the colors the team wore.

Providence Rhode Islanders: Named for the state of Rhode Island in which the team played.

Providence Steam Roller: According to founder Pierce Johnson, this team was named by sports editor Charles Coppen of the *Providence Journal* in 1916. During the team's first game, when it was simply an independent squad called Providence, the team had built up a 52–0 lead when Coppen overheard a spectator remark, "Gee, they're steamrolling them." Coppen then started calling the team the Providence Steam Roller. He preferred the singular form because he reasoned that it was a single team and therefore deserved a singular name.[153]

Providence Steamrollers: Took the name of the Providence Steam Roller (see).

Quebec Nordiques: Named in a contest for the fact that this was the northernmost team in major league hockey. The name (meaning "Northerners") makes reference to where the team is located, and it even does so in Quebec's dominant language: French.

Queens Bohemians: Like many soccer teams, this club was named for the ethnic origins of the players and/or the population which supported it. The name "Bohemians" refers to Czechoslovakians.

Racine Belles: This women's baseball team, like most in the All-American Girls Professional Baseball League, was assigned a feminine name so that the league could emphasize the femininity of the women who played. The league

believed that to be the only way to build a following for itself. A previous men's minor league team had also used the name, however, in the Wisconsin-Illinois League from 1909–14.

Racine Cardinals: The name "Cardinals" was actually used informally for this team as early as 1898, when it was officially known as the Morgan Athletic Club. "Cardinal" described the color of the team's jerseys, which were maroon and which had been obtained from the University of Chicago by owner Chris O'Brien. Upon his purchase, O'Brien stated, "That's not maroon, it's Cardinal Red." The name "Racine" refers to Racine Avenue in Chicago, the street on which the team's field was located. It dropped the name "Racine" and adopted "Chicago" in order to avoid confusion when the Racine Legion entered the league from Racine, Wisconsin.

Racine Legion: Named for an American Legion post which sponsored the team.[154]

Real Santa Barbara: A Spanish name reflecting the strong Hispanic influence and history in the city of Santa Barbara. The name *Real* (pronounced "reh-AL") is a popular and very traditional one for soccer teams in Spanish-speaking countries, and translates as "Royal."

Regina Capitals: Named for the fact that Regina is the capital of the province of Saskatchewan.

Renfrew Creamery Kings: Likely named for the fact that the city of Renfrew was called the Creamery Capital of the Ottawa Valley.

Renfrew Millionaires: In the early 1800s, a lumber boom attracted many settlers to the city of Renfrew. So much money was made from the surrounding forests that the team was given this name in 1909.

Rhode Island Oceaneers: Named for the state nickname of Rhode Island, the "Ocean State."

Richmond King Clothiers: Named for King Clothiers, the company which sponsored the team.

Richmond Kings: Shortened form of the team's original, primary name of Richmond King Clothiers (see).

Richmond Rage: Chosen by the American Basketball League office because it was a powerful, aggressive name which sounded good with "Richmond." When this team moved to Philadelphia, it kept the name "Rage" because it had become well-liked and familiar to fans.

Richmond Virginians: Named for the state of Virginia in which the team played. The team's formal name was Virginia of Richmond.

Rochester Braves: See *Syracuse Braves.*

Rochester Centrals: Named for Central Avenue in Rochester, where the team was first organized as an independent squad.[155]

Rochester Hop-Bitters: Named for two previous minor league baseball teams which bore the same name and played in 1879 and 1880. The original team played in 1879 in the minor National Association, a league of nine teams located in New York and New England. This team was backed financially by Asa T. Soule, who had made a fortune selling an alcohol-based medicine called Hop Bitters, which he promoted as "the Invalid's Friend." On Soule's team, each player received a tablespoon of the elixir before each game to help spur the team on to victory. (This method was largely unsuccessful.)[156]

Rochester Knighthawks: Named by the Major Indoor Lacrosse League, which owned and named nearly all the teams in the league.

Rochester Royals: Named in a contest. The winner was 15-year-old Richard Paeth, who stated that Webster defines a royal as "pertaining to a king or crown, befitting or like a King, majestic."[157]

Rockford Forest Citys: Named for the nickname of the city of Rockford in which the team played, the "Forest City," so named by its citizens because it averages approximately 100 trees per block. The formal name of the team was Forest City of Rockford, Illinois.

Rockford Peaches: This women's baseball team, like most in the All-American Girls Professional Baseball League, was assigned a feminine name so that the league could emphasize the femininity of the women who played. The league believed that to be the only way to build a following for itself.

Roma Soccer Club: This team played in Paterson, New Jersey, but was likely made up of Italian players and used the location name "Roma" to refer to Rome, Italy (although this is not documented). The rather unimaginative name "Soccer Club," along with "Field Club" and "Foot-

ball Club," was commonly used by soccer teams when nicknames were uncommon, especially in the early part of the twentieth century.

Sacramento Capitals: Named for the fact that Sacramento is the state capital of California.

Sacramento Gold: Named for the California Gold Rush in the nineteenth century, of which Sacramento was a part.

Sacramento Gold Miners: Named on January 15, 1993, in honor of the hard-working people in search of prosperity during the California Gold Rush.

Sacramento Kings: See *Kansas City-Omaha Kings.*

Sacramento Knights: Named in a name-the-team contest held by the *Sacramento Bee* and radio stations KFBK and KRCX. The name is consistent with the "royal" tradition of the National Basketball Association's Sacramento Kings.

Sacramento Monarchs: Like many WNBA teams, this club was named to create a connection with the NBA team which shared the same city (in this case, the Sacramento Kings).

Sacramento Senators: This soccer team was named for the California state Senate, since Sacramento is the capital of California. This name was also used by a minor league baseball team which played in the California League from 1889–91.

St. Louis Aces: This tennis team was named for two reasons. First, "ace" is a tennis term which refers to a serve which is not returned by one's opponent. Second, since a tennis team is comprised of four players, the name refers to the four aces in a deck of cards.

St. Louis All-Stars: Optimistically named by owner Ollie Kraehe (before he had even signed any players for his team).

St. Louis Ambush: See *Tulsa Ambush.*

St. Louis Blues: Named for the song "St. Louis Blues" by W. C. Handy. Owner Sid Salomon said of his team, "It's part of the city where W. C. Handy composed his famed song while thinking of his girl one morning. . . . No matter where you go in this town there's singing. It's the spirit of St. Louis."[158] Other names suggested for the team were Apollo and Mercury.[159]

St. Louis Bombers: Probably reflects the fact that an important part of St. Louis' industry is the manufacturing of military aircraft.

St. Louis Brown Stockings: (2 teams) The first team to be called the St. Louis Brown Stockings was the one which played in the National Association in 1875. The team was named for the color of its uniform stockings, and the name was likely inspired by the Cincinnati Red Stockings of 1869–70.

St. Louis Brownies: This team played in the Federal League. It was probably named for the team colors and for the name of a previous team called the St. Louis Browns and a concurrent team in the rival American League also called the St. Louis Browns (see).

St. Louis Browns: (2 teams) The first team to be called the St. Louis Browns was the one which played in the American Association in 1883. The name was a shortened form of its original name of St. Louis Brown Stockings (see). The second team, which began play in the American League in 1902, copied the name of this team and was also named for the color of the trim on the players' uniforms.

St. Louis Cardinals: (2 teams) Ironically, the two teams to bear this name acquired it independently of one another. The first team to be called the St. Louis Cardinals was the baseball team which has played in the National League under this name since 1900. It was first used by William McHale, a sportswriter for the *St. Louis Republic,* who had overheard a woman remark, upon catching sight of the red on the team's jerseys, "What a lovely shade of Cardinal."[160] The football team carried its name over from Chicago, Illinois, where it was known as the Chicago Cardinals, but originally as the Racine Cardinals because it played on Racine Avenue in Chicago. The name was acquired in somewhat similar fashion: Owner Chris O'Brien bought the team's supposedly maroon jerseys from the University of Chicago, and was heard to remark, "That's not maroon, it's Cardinal Red."

St. Louis Giants: Like many Negro League teams, this club copied the name of a popular white major league baseball team (in this case, the New York Giants).

St. Louis Gunners: As an independent team this club was at first sponsored by the National Guard's 126th Field Artillery and was called the Battery A Gunners. When the National Guard withdrew its sponsorship, the name was changed to St. Louis Gunners.[161]

St. Louis Hawks: See *Milwaukee Hawks.*

St. Louis Maroons: (2 teams) The first team to be called the St. Louis Maroons was the one which played in the American Association in 1883, and which was better known as the St. Louis Browns. Both teams were likely named for their uniform colors.

St. Louis Mules: Likely named for an animal popular throughout Missouri's history. Mules were first introduced to the state in the 1820s and immediately became popular with farmers and settlers because of their ruggedness. They pulled pioneer wagons to the West in the nineteenth century, and helped move supplies and troops in World Wars I and II. For many years, Missouri was the premier producer of mules in the United States. This soccer team played in 1972, but in 1995, the Missouri mule was named the official state animal.

St. Louis Rams: See *Cleveland Rams.*

St. Louis Ravens: This name was used for only one season as an alternate to the team's more established name of St. Louis Browns. The "Ravens" name was used by a St. Louis newspaper in 1906 when the team temporarily abandoned the brown piping on its uniforms and replaced it with black.

St. Louis Red Stockings: Named for the color of the team's uniform stockings. The name was likely inspired by the Cincinnati Red Stockings of 1869–70.

St. Louis Reds: Shortened form of the team's original name of St. Louis Red Stockings (see).

St. Louis Sloufeds: This team played in the Federal League, and the name is a combination of "St. Louis" and "Federal."

St. Louis Spirit: Likely a variation of "Spirit of St. Louis." (See also *Spirits of St. Louis.*)

St. Louis Stampede: Reflects the Western culture and heritage of the St. Louis area.

St. Louis Steamers: (2 teams) The first team to be called the St. Louis Steamers was the one which played in the Major Indoor Soccer League in 1979. Both teams were named for the steamships which used to travel the Mississippi River to and from St. Louis in the early to mid-1800s.

St. Louis Storm: Named in a contest from among 1000 submissions. Owner Milan Mandaric liked the name because it was scary, and he hoped the team would scare the opposition. The four finalists for the team name were Dynamos, Lightning, Spirit, and Storm.[162]

St. Mary's Celtics: (2 teams) The first team to be called the St. Mary's Celtics was the one which played in the second American Soccer League in 1935. This team's name was a revised form of the team's original name of Brooklyn Celtics (see). "St. Mary's" likely referred to a parish in Brooklyn with which the teams were affiliated.

St. Paul Saints: Likely a play on the name of the city of St. Paul in which the team played.

St. Paul Whitecaps: Likely named for the tops of the waves, or "whitecaps," on the thousands of lakes around St. Paul and throughout the state of Minnesota.

Salt Lake Sting: Likely named for the sting of a bee, since the nickname of the state of Utah is the "Beehive State." The nickname comes from the fact that Utah was once called Deseret, a name from the Book of Mormon which translates as "honeybee."

San Antonio Gunslingers: (2 teams) The first team to be called the San Antonio Gunslingers was the one which was to have played in the American Basketball Association in 1973, but which then became the San Antonio Spurs before the season began. The football team was named in a contest, chosen by majority stockholder Clinton Manges. General Manager Roger Gill explained, "We wanted to get away from typical animal names and be unique. Gunslingers seemed appropriate to our territory."[163]

San Antonio Racquets: Named for the tennis racquet.

San Antonio Spurs: When the Dallas Chaparrals moved to San Antonio from Dallas, the name "Chaparrals" was not considered appropriate for San Antonio's image. Management originally planned to call the team the Gunslingers, but they held a contest, and the name "Spurs" was chosen because it represents the Western heritage of Texas, it easily adapted itself to a logo, and it is short enough for broad use by the media.[164]

San Antonio Texans: Named for the state of Texas in which the team played.

San Antonio Thunder: Named in a contest.

San Antonio Wings: Likely named for the four air bases near San Antonio.

San Diego Barracudas: Named for a fish indigenous to the San Diego area.

San Diego Chargers: See *Los Angeles Chargers.*

San Diego Clippers: Named for the clipper ships which used to pass through the harbors of San Diego many years ago.

San Diego Conquistadors: Named in a contest from among 10,000 entries for the Spanish conquerors in Mexico (and Peru) in the sixteenth century. Hispanic influence in San Diego, which is just north of the Mexican border, is strong.

San Diego Friars: Likely named for the Franciscan friars who helped pioneer and settle the San Diego area over 400 years ago. (See also *San Diego Padres.*)

San Diego Jaws: Named for the most dangerous part of the sharks that are indigenous to the San Diego area.

San Diego Mariners: Named for the shipping and boating industry which has had a major impact on the formation and growth of San Diego through the last several centuries.

San Diego Padres: Named in a contest for the Franciscan padres who helped pioneer and settle the San Diego area over 400 years ago. The name was also copied from a previous minor league baseball team which played in the Pacific Coast League in 1936.

San Diego Rockets: Named in a fan contest. The name was said to reflect San Diego's theme of a "City in Motion," based on the growth of "space age" industries in the city. When the team moved to Houston, Texas, the name fit perfectly with the presence of NASA and the space program in Houston.[165]

San Diego Sails: Named for the pastime of sailing which is so popular in San Diego.

San Diego Sockers: A play on words, combining the idea of a powerful "sock" with that of the game of soccer.

San Diego Toros: See *Los Angeles Toros.*

San Francisco Fog: Named for the rolling fog which is so prevalent in San Francisco Bay.

San Francisco Forty-Niners: Named for those who participated in the California Gold Rush in 1849. The name was suggested by part owner Alan Sorrell, who suggested it to principal owner Tony Morabito and pointed out that the team, as one of the few west of the Mississippi River when it was formed, was taking a big risk, as did those prospectors during the Gold Rush.

San Francisco Gales: Named for the fierce winds which are sometimes common in the San Francisco Bay area.

San Francisco Giants: For this baseball team, see *New York Giants.*

San Francisco Saints: Likely named for the fact that Franciscan friars, who revered the saints, pioneered and settled much of the West Coast. Many cities and towns along the California coastline, in fact, are named for saints, and San Francisco itself is named for St. Francis of Assisi.

San Francisco Sharks: Named for a sea animal indigenous to the San Francisco area. When this team moved to Quebec before it ever played a game, the name "Sharks" was taken by the Los Angeles Aces before *they* ever played a game.

San Francisco Warriors: See *Philadelphia Warriors.*

San Jose Clash: Named for the fact that the team promised strong and decisive action in every match.

San Jose Earthquakes: (2 teams) The first team to be called the San Jose Earthquakes was the one which played in the outdoor North American Soccer League in 1974. Both teams were named for the large number of earthquakes which occur on the West Coast of the United States.

San Jose Grizzlies: Named for the grizzly bear, the state animal of California.

San Jose Lasers: The women's American Basketball League wanted to name this team the San Jose Missions, but the team itself preferred the name "Lasers" because of the high-tech Silicon Valley in which San Jose is located.

San Jose Rhinos: Named in a fan ballot of San Jose Sharks' hockey fans. Questionnaires were distributed at one of the National Hockey League Sharks' home games in 1993, asking fans what name they would prefer for the soon-to-be Roller Hockey International roller hockey team in San Jose. The number one choice was actually the name "Dragons." Soon after the ballots were counted, however, team officials learned that one of the largest Asian gangs in North America and nearby San Francisco was called the Dragons, so they went with the number two choice instead. That name was "Rhinos."

San Jose SaberCats: Named for the saber-toothed tiger or saber-toothed cat. This formidable prehistoric animal, which became extinct during the Ice Age, widely inhabited both Europe and the United States, but it is believed that the largest concentration was in what is now California. The largest number of saber-toothed cat fossils in the world have been found in Southern California's La Brea Tar Pits, and due to the enormous number that have been discovered there, the saber-toothed cat has been named California's official state fossil.

San Jose Sharks: Named in a contest which consisted of 2300 submissions from a total of 5700 entrants. The top 15 were Blades, Breakers, Breeze, Condors, Fog, Gold, Golden Gaters, Golden Skaters, Grizzlies, Icebreakers, Knights, Redwoods, Sea Lions, Sharks, and Waves. The name "Sharks" was actually the second choice of team officials. The first choice was the name "Blades," which was later rejected because it was thought that it sounded too much like a Knife and Gun Club on a Saturday night.[166] The name "Sharks" was then chosen, and the grand prize was a trip for two to the 1991 NHL all-star game weekend in Chicago, Illinois. The name was selected because it appealed to both children and adults, and because it would lend itself well to a logo. The Pacific Ocean is home to seven varieties of sharks (the great white, leopard, mako, seven-gill, blue, soupfin, and spiny dog). A part of the Bay Area near San Jose, in fact, is called the "red triangle" because of its large shark population. There is a great deal of shark research performed in the San Jose area. Matt Levine, the team's Executive Vice President of Marketing and Broadcast, explained, "Sharks are relentless, determined, swift, agile, bright and fearless. We plan to build an organization that has all those qualities."

Santa Barbara Condors: Named for the California condor, an endangered bird once common in California. Condors, which are members of the vulture family, were once prevalent throughout the southern United States and ranged from Mexico to Canada. Their population was vastly reduced 10,000 years ago when the late Pleistocene extinction of large mammals occurred, decimating many of the condors' food sources (including mastodons, giant sloths, and saber-toothed cats). By the 1930s condors were found only in California, and by 1977, when this soccer team was formed, fewer than 30 birds remained. A captive breeding program began in 1980, and today there are over 90 condors in several states.

Saratoga Harlem Yankees: See *New York Harlem Yankees.*

Saskatchewan Roughriders: Named for horseback riders in Regina and throughout the province of Saskatchewan.

Saskatoon Crescents: Named in a contest in late December of 1919 for the Crescent Arena in which the team played. The winner received a set of season tickets to the team's inaugural campaign. The arena itself was likely named for the multitude of streets in Saskatoon which are called "crescents" because of their shape.

Saskatoon Sheiks: Named for the hit song of the day, "The Sheik of Araby," and for the fact that many men were referred to as sheiks because they had adopted Rudolph Valentino haircuts (extra long and well plastered with Vaseline).

Schenectady County Electrics: At least in part named for the fact that the city of Schenectady has been known as the "first electrical city" of the United States since Thomas Edison opened a shop there in 1886. The General Electric Company set up headquarters there in 1892, and electrical equipment has long been a staple of the city's economy.

Schenectady Yankees: "Yankee" is a slang term for "American."

Scotland Eagles: This roller hockey team played in the city of Ayr near Glasgow in 1997, and may have derived its name from the Ayr Scottish Eagles, an ice hockey team which had begun play in the Ice Hockey Superleague a year earlier.

Scots-Americans: Revised form of the team's original name of Kearny Scots (see). Several soccer teams combined their ethnic names with that of "Americans."

Scranton Miners: This basketball team copied the name of five previous minor league baseball teams, the first of which had played in the International League in 1887. The name reflects the mining industry popular in Scranton and in many parts of Pennsylvania.

Sea-Port Cascades: Named for the Cascade Mountains near Seattle and Portland. (The location name "Sea-Port" is short for "Seattle-Portland.")

Seattle Cascades: See *Sea-Port Cascades.*

Seattle Mariners: Named in a contest for the fishing and boating industry in Seattle. The name was selected on August 24, 1976, from among 600 entries. Winner Roger Symodis explained, "I've selected Mariners because of the natural association between the sea and Seattle and her people, who have been challenged and rewarded by it."[167]

Seattle Metropolitans: Likely named for the fact that Seattle has long been considered *the* major metropolis of the state of Washington.

Seattle Pilots: Named in a contest for the fact that Seattle has long been a leader in both maritime and air activities. Seattle is home to many shipping operations and to the Boeing plant.

Seattle Reign: A play on words. This team was named for the rain which is prevalent in Seattle, but the spelling and logo denoted a female athlete as having a majestic bearing.

Seattle SeaDogs: Chosen through an informal poll of elementary school students. Announced on November 15, 1994, the name recalls the importance of water life to Seattle. A "sea dog" is a seal or a similar marine mammal, and the term can also refer to an experienced sailor.

Seattle Seahawks: A 1974 contest produced 20,365 entries. The name "Seahawks," which had been entered by 151 people, was chosen on June 17, 1975, and General Manager John Thompson explained, "Our new name shows aggressiveness, reflects our soaring northwest heritage, and belongs to no other major league team."[168] Other suggested names included Lumberjacks, Mariners (*before* the baseball team was created), Pioneers, Seagulls, Skippers, Sockeyes, Spacers, and Spinmakers.[169]

Seattle Sounders: (2 teams) The first team to be called the Seattle Sounders was the one which played in the outdoor North American Soccer League in 1974. This team was named in a contest, and both were named for Puget Sound, on which the city of Seattle is situated.

Seattle Storm: (2 teams) The first team to be called the Seattle Storm was the soccer team which played in the Western Soccer League in 1986. Both teams were named for Seattle's frequently stormy weather. When the second team, a WNBA franchise, announced its name on January 6, 2000, just prior to its inaugural season, Senior Director of WNBA Operations Karen Bryant stated, "We're so happy to have a name that reflects Seattle and the intensity this team will bring to the floor. From now until opening night this summer, Seattle is on a Storm watch." She went on to say, "In the process of searching for a name, the Storm kept coming up with fans we met, in letters we received and on radio call in shows. It's such a perfect fit, it really was the obvious choice."

Seattle SuperSonics: Named in a contest from among 25,000 entries. The name was suggested by 163 people. The winner was Howard E. Schmidt of Seattle, who, for his efforts, won a trip to Palm Springs, California, and season tickets for the team's 1967–68 season. The name was suggested because of the presence of the Boeing plant in Seattle and the proposed Supersonic Transport which was never actually created. General Manager Don Richman said that the name "best expresses Seattle's people, its present, and future."[170] The name "Sonics" was also entered by 200 people.[171]

Shawsheen Indians: Named for the Native American population indigenous to Massachusetts. Shawsheen is the name of the county in Massachusetts in which the team played.

Sheboygan Red Skins: Named for the American Indian population indigenous to the Sheboygan area who gave the city its name. Sheboygan contains many Indian burial mounds in the shape of panthers and deer. One unlikely legend of how Sheboygan got its name involves a settlement of wigwams along the Wisconsin side of Lake Michigan. The settlement did not yet have a name. A middle-aged Native American came into the trading post one winter and was warming himself by the pot-bellied stove. The Native American did not speak English well, and he told the storekeeper, "Gottim another papoose in our wigwam." The storekeeper knew that the man already had six boys, so he asked, "Is it a girl this time?" The Native American replied, "No, she boy 'gin."[172] In reality, *sheboygan* is an Indian term meaning "place of ore" or "rumbling underground," likely a reference to the sound of the falls three miles up the Sheboygan River.

Sheffield Strikers: Named for a soccer term. A "striker" is an offensive player in soccer or indoor soccer. This team folded before ever playing a game.

Shreveport Pirates: This Canadian Football League team was so named in January of 1994 because, according to President Lonie Glieberman, "we're a pirate team in a pirate league."[173] The name was also copied from two past minor league baseball teams: The first played in the Southern Association in 1904, and the other in the Texas League in 1908.

Shreveport Steamer: Named for the steamboats which once navigated the Red River in Shreveport.

South Bend Blue Sox: Named for the color of the team's uniform stockings.

South Carolina Fire Ants: Named for an insect prevalent in the state of South Carolina. These particular ants, which are a different species than the native variety found in Texas, are themselves not native to the United States. They were accidentally imported prior to the 1920s, possibly because of nests in potted plants or in ballast on ships traveling from South America to Mobile, Alabama, and they spread from there. They are very aggressive and will sting a perceived enemy repeatedly.

South Florida Breakers: See *Miami Beach Breakers.*

South Florida Sun: See *Fort Lauderdale Sun.*

Southern California Sun: Named in a contest for the ever-popular sunny weather in Anaheim and the rest of Southern California.

Soviets: This team was actually an all-star tennis team which represented the entire Soviet Union in World TeamTennis. Incidentally, a *soviet* is "one of the popularly elected legislative assemblies existing at local, regional, and national levels, organized on the basis of the workers', soldiers', and peasants' councils of the revolutionary period."[174]

Spirits of St. Louis: Likely named for the famous airplane flown by Charles Lindbergh. The *Spirit of St. Louis* was a small monoplane, and on May 20–21, 1927, Lindbergh flew it nonstop from New York to Paris, becoming the first man to fly across the Atlantic Ocean. The plane is now in the Smithsonian Institution in Washington, D.C.

Springfield Lasers: Named at a city promotional function for the team when the club was formed. City employees were asked to make suggestions for the name, and the Springfield Greene County Park Board then chose the one it liked best.

Springfield Sallies: This women's baseball team, like most in the All-American Girls Professional Baseball League, was assigned a feminine name so that the league could emphasize the femininity of the women who played. The league believed that to be the only way to build a following for itself.

Stapleton Stapes: Shortened form of the team's primary name of Staten Island Stapes (see). The location name "Stapleton" refers to the neighborhood of Stapleton on Staten Island, where the team played.

Staten Island Stapes: Shortened form of the team's original name of Staten Island Stapletons (see).

Staten Island Stapletons: Named for the neighborhood of Stapleton on Staten Island, where the team played.

Steagles: This team was a merger of the Pittsburgh Steelers and the Philadelphia Eagles. The name is a combination of "Steelers" and "Eagles." (See also *Phil-Pitt*.)

Sun Belt Nets: Named for the tennis net. The Sun Belt is a large region of the southern United States which includes New Orleans, where this team played.

Syracuse All-Americans: The term "All-American" was developed by Caspar W. Whitney in 1889 to describe the selection of the best college football players in the country. It was later adapted for other sports, and some professional teams, like this basketball squad, used it.

Syracuse Braves: Recalls the Native American population indigenous to the Syracuse area.

Syracuse Nationals: Possibly named for the National Basketball League in which the team first played.

Syracuse Smash: This lacrosse team was named by the team's owner, who also owned a minor league hockey team called the Syracuse Crunch and was creating a common theme.

Syracuse Stars: (2 teams) The first team to be called the Syracuse Stars was the one which played in the National League in 1879, and before that in the minor International League in 1878. This team played at the first Star Park in Syracuse, and the second team at the second Star Park. The team name was copied from a previous minor league team which played in the Keystone Association in 1877, and independently as early as 1876.

Tacoma Tides: Named for the tides rolling in to the shores of Tacoma from Puget Sound.

Tampa Bay Bandits: This team was partially owned by Burt Reynolds, and it was named after the nickname of his character in the movie *Smokey and the Bandit*.

Tampa Bay Buccaneers: Named in a contest held by radio station WFLA. The winner was Dr. Richard Molloy of Tampa, who won a television set and a set of season tickets for 1976 for his entry. Team committee chairman James M. McEwen explained, "Water people first settled in the area. Boating is a way of life and our history is rich in pirate stories. We believe it embraces the area."[175] Owner Hugh F. Culverhouse expounded,

> It catches the spirit. I think of the coast-line community and the rich history of so-called freebooters whom they tell me took charge in their days of pirating and buccaneering. Well, we want our football team to be as aggressive, high-spirited, and colorful as were the old buccaneers.[176]

Incidentally, buccaneers were French, English, or Dutch pirates who originally settled in Haiti and, from the native Indians there, learned a special technique of sun-drying meat called "buccaning," from which they got their name. Other names suggested for this team included Crackers, Rough Riders, Sailors, and 76ers.[177]

Tampa Bay Devil Rays: Named for a fish indigenous to the Tampa Bay area. A fan contest resulted in approximately 7000 submissions, the largest percentage containing some form of the name "rays." Team owners ruled out the name "Stingrays" because they didn't want the team named for a harmful fish. The devil ray is a smaller cousin of the manta ray. Founding owner Vince Naimoli said that the devil ray's "only wish, it seems, is to float peacefully in its water, taking in mouthfuls of its favorite foods, which are called plankton. It looks like a huge floating blanket. It jumps out of the water and sails 20 feet in the air. [Rays] are so gentle they will let humans pet them and ride them." Many people officially registered many potential team names, as allowed by Florida law, hoping for a big payoff from the new ownership group when Tampa/St. Petersburg finally got a team. Naimoli refused to buy the rights to any name. When the name "Devil Rays" was first announced, it created a public outcry, in large part because of the word "devil" in the name. Naimoli then had fans vote between "Devil Rays" and "Manta Rays," and of the two, "Devil Rays" was the winner.

Tampa Bay Lightning: Named by general partner Phil Esposito. Esposito was inspired while he was eating in a restaurant in Tampa in 1991, when he looked outside and saw a bolt of lightning.

Tampa Bay Mutiny: While the name recalls the seafaring history of the Tampa Bay area, it and the team's futuristic logo (comprised of green-winged cyber-mutants) were meant to portray a high-tech, ominous force on the soccer field.

Tampa Bay Rollin' Thunder: A play on the name of the sport of roller hockey while also recalling the sometimes tropical stormy weather in the Tampa Bay area.

Tampa Bay Rowdies: (3 teams) The first team to be called the Tampa Bay Rowdies was the one which played in the outdoor North American Soccer League in 1975. This team was named in a contest, and all three were named for the unruly behavior sometimes exhibited by soccer players and fans.

Tampa Bay Terror: Named in a contest from among 1000 entries. The name refers to the potential terror caused by the presence of sharks in the Tampa Bay area.

Tampa Bay Tritons: Triton was a minor god of the sea in ancient Greek mythology. He was the son of Poseidon (the god of the sea) and Amphitrite, and had the head and trunk of a man and the tail of a fish. The term also referred to a mythological race of lesser sea deities. The team's name reflects the importance of the sea to the Tampa Bay area.

Team America: This team literally represented the entire United States of America, as it was soccer's U.S. National Team which, for one season, joined the outdoor North American Soccer League. After that season, it continued to play as the U.S. National Team, and still does so today.

Team Hawaii: This team was . . . well . . . a team.

Tennessee Oilers: See *Houston Oilers.*

Tennessee Titans: Renamed from Tennessee Oilers because the name "Oilers," which had been carried over from Houston, Texas, was not considered relevant to Tennessee. The new name was chosen by owner K. S. "Bud" Adams, who explained, "We wanted a new nickname to reflect strength, leadership and other heroic qualities." He continued, "Titans come from early Greek mythology and the fact that Nashville is known as the 'Athens of the South' makes the Titans name very appropriate."[178] (Spe-

cifically, Titans were huge, powerful primordial gods who were the children of Uranus and Gaea, and who were eventually overthrown by the more popularly known Olympian gods.) The New York Jets, who had previously been the New York Titans, stated that they had no problem with the Nashville team taking the name. On July 28, 1998, the Nashville franchise and the National Football League had applied to the U.S. Patent and Trademark Office for the following 39 potential new names: Ambush, Bandits, Blitz, Bobcats, Commanders, Conquerors, Copperheads, Cougars, Cruisers, Daredevils, Dynamos, Firestorm, Fury, Generals, Legends, Marauders, Nighthawks, Pioneers, Power, Presidents, Rampage, Rapids, Rattlers, Renegades, River Bandits, Siege, Smokies, Sound, Stallions, Stampede, Stingers, Talon, Tempest, Thunder, Titans, Tornadoes, Tradition, Troopers, and Vipers. The three finalists chosen by Adams were Titans, Pioneers, and Tornadoes. NFL Commissioner Paul Tagliabue agreed to retire the name "Oilers," so that no future league franchise may use it.

Texas Chaparrals: This team was formerly called the Dallas Chaparrals (see), and the shift to the location name of "Texas" was made in an effort to get the entire state interested in the team. After one year, however, the attempt was given up, and the team returned to its former name.

Texas Rangers: Named in a fan contest. The name honors the legendary state police force of Texas. The location name "Texas" is also used because the team represents *two* Texan cities—Dallas and Fort Worth. Also, in the past there have been two minor league baseball teams called the Dallas Rangers, another called the Fort Worth Rangers, and one called the Dallas-Fort Worth Rangers.

Texas Terror: Named in a "Name Your Team" contest from among 500 entries. The winner was Mike Pendley of Conroe, Texas, who won the right to take part in the Opening Night coin toss, as well as two tickets to the team's opening game, a Terror jersey, and a Terror helmet.

Titans: Named by World Roller Hockey League founder David McLane. In Greek mythology, the Titans were huge, powerful primordial gods who were the children of Uranus and Gaea, and who were eventually overthrown by the more popularly known Olympian gods.

Todd Shipyards: Named for the company which sponsored the team.

Toledo Blue Stockings: Named for the color of the team's uniform stockings.

Toledo Chevies: Shortened form of the team's original, primary name of Toledo Jim White Chevrolets (see).

Toledo Crawfords: See *Pittsburgh Crawfords.*

Toledo Jeeps: Named for the Jeep manufacturing plant, a longtime mainstay in Toledo. There are several versions of how the Jeep got its name: 1) The Jeep was a vehicle which was originally built for the Army. The military called it a General Purpose vehicle, or GP, which was eventually slurred into "Jeep." 2) According to Colonel A. W. Herrington, the name was used in Oklahoma as early as 1934 to refer to trucks which were equipped to dig oil wells. 3) The name came from "Eugene the Jeep," a character in a 1936 Popeye comic strip by E. C. Edgar. The character was a small, imp-like being which could travel between dimensions. 4) Test driver Irving "Red" Haussman picked up the name from soldiers at Camp Holsbird. Haussman later gave a demonstration ride in the new vehicle to dignitaries, including *Washington Daily News* reporter Katherine Hillyer, who used it in a 1941 headline which read, "Jeep Creeps Up Capitol Steps." This marked the first use of the name by the media.

Toledo Jim White Chevrolets: Named for the Jim White Chevrolet dealership which sponsored the team.[179]

Toledo Maroons: Named for the color of the team's jerseys. The name had also been used by a previous independent team which played from 1911–20.

Toledo Maumees: Copied the name from an earlier, minor league team which played in the Tri-State League in 1888. The name refers to the Maumee River, which runs through Toledo.

Toledo Red Man Tobaccos: Named for Red Man Tobacco, a product of the Pinkerton Tobacco Company which sponsored the team. This team was sometimes referred to as the Toledo Redmen or Toledo Red Men, much to the consternation of team management, who insisted that "Red Man Tobaccos" was the correct name. The Red Men were a National Fraternal Order with whom the team had no connection.[180]

Toledo Tigers: Like many Negro League teams, this club copied the name of a popular white major league baseball team (in this case, the Detroit Tigers).

Tonawanda Kardex: Named for the Rand Kardex Bureau, Inc., the company which sponsored the team. "Kardex" refers to the card-index system which the company produced.[181]

Tonawanda Lumbermen: Named for the lumber industry for which Tonawanda is famous. The industry, which focuses on white pine, began in the region in the year 1867, and by 1900 Tonawanda and North Tonawanda were jointly known as "The Lumber City." They briefly formed the largest lumber supply center in the world, and for many years afterward were second only to Chicago.

Toronto Arenas: Named for their home court, Mutual Street Arena.

Toronto Argonauts: In Greek mythology, an Argonaut was a person who sailed with Jason aboard the ship the *Argo* in search of the Golden Fleece. The name makes sense in light of the fact that this football club originated as a rowing team called the Argonaut Rowing Club.

Toronto Blizzard: (2 teams) The first team to be called the Toronto Blizzard was the one which played in the outdoor North American Soccer League in 1971. This team had previously been called the Toronto Metros-Croatia, and desired a non-ethnic name which could still be identified with Canada. Team President Paul Morton stated, "We wanted a name which could meet the perception of Canada held by most North Americans and Europeans."[182]

Toronto Blue Jays: Named in a contest from among 30,000 entries. The name "Blues" was the most frequently submitted, but the University of Toronto was already using that name. The name "Blue Jays," one of the other 10 finalists, was chosen on August 12, 1976. It was submitted by 154 people, and was inspired by the multitude of blue jays living in the provincial area surrounding Toronto. The winner by drawing was Dr. William Mills of Etobicoke, Ontario, who received for his efforts an all-expense paid trip for himself and his family to the team's training camp in Dunedin, Florida, as well as a set of season tickets for 1977.[183] The company which owned the team also owned "Blue" label beer, and the hope was that the name would be shortened in common usage to "Blues." It wasn't.

Toronto Blueshirts: Named for the color of the team's jerseys.

Toronto City: Copied the name of two previous minor league soccer teams, the first of which played in the first International Soccer League in 1926, and the second in the

Eastern Canadian Professional Soccer League from 1961–62 and 1964–65.

Toronto Force: Named for Force Sports, the company which owned the team. Force Sports manufactured pants, girdles, sticks, and replacement blades for roller hockey, and purchased Major League Roller Hockey's Toronto Torpedoes during the 1998 season. It renamed the club "Force" in preparation for the 1999 campaign, but the league suspended operations and the team folded before ever playing under its new name.

Toronto Huskies: Named for a type of dog popular to the Toronto area in honor of the inventor of basketball, James Naismith. Naismith was born in Almonte, Ontario, where huskies were common, and he grew up working on his family's farm and in Canadian logging camps.

Toronto Maple Leafs: Named for the Maple Leaf Regiment, a famous Canadian World War I fighting unit. Additionally, approximately half of the province of Ontario is covered by vast forests which contain a great many maple trees.[184] When owner Conn Smythe took over the Toronto St. Patricks, he wanted a more secular name for the team, so he chose this one. The maple leaf itself has become a proud symbol of the nation of Canada, and is displayed prominently on the national flag. The name was also copied from a minor league baseball team which first used it in the Eastern League in 1902.

Toronto Metros: Likely named for the metropolitan area of Toronto, which is a rather huge city.

Toronto Metros-Croatia: This was a merged team, consisting of the major league Toronto Metros (see) and a semipro team called Croatia. Ethnic names were used for a long time in soccer, and most of the time reflected the nationality or ethnicity of their teams' members. When the Metros merged with Croatia, they adopted the combined name of "Metros-Croatia" despite the fact that the North American Soccer League had banned ethnic names. The team was attempting to draw the support of the Croatian community in Toronto. Because of the ban on ethnic nicknames, during a televised game in 1976, commentator Jon Miller was prohibited by league officials from saying "Metros-Croatia" on the air.

Toronto Northmen: This team was named for the fact that it was the northernmost of the charter members of the World Football League in 1974. It moved to Memphis, Tennessee, before the season began in order to avoid conflict with the Toronto Argonauts of the Canadian Football League. In Memphis, the team emphasized its newfound southern culture by changing its name from Northmen to Southmen.

Toronto Ontarios: Named for the province of Ontario in which the team played. The word *ontario* is Indian for "beautiful hills, rocks, rivers."

Toronto Raptors: Named in a contest held by Professional Basketball Franchise Inc. which consisted of more than 2000 entries. The 10 finalists were Beavers, Bobcats, Dragons, Grizzlies, Hogs (after Toronto's nickname of Hogtown), Raptors, Scorpions, T-Rex, Tarantulas, and Terriers. The name "Raptors" was chosen because of the success of the movie *Jurassic Park* and the resulting increased popularity of dinosaurs with youngsters.

Toronto Rock: President and Managing Director Bill Watters explained, "Toronto 'Rock' signifies everything that is exciting, fast-paced, and high-energy in the sport [of lacrosse]. I know that fans will appreciate the athleticism of these talented players and the game they play."[185]

Toronto St. Patricks: After several losing seasons as the Toronto Arenas, this team hoped to get the luck of the Irish by using this name. The name emphasizes the strong Irish heritage in Toronto. (St. Patrick is the patron saint of Ireland.)

Toronto Shamrocks: Named in honor of the strong Irish heritage in Toronto. The shamrock is considered the national emblem of Ireland.

Toronto Shooting Stars: Named in honor of Tecumseh (see also *Toronto Tecumsehs*). *Tecumseh* is an Indian name which means "shooting star." The team's logo, in fact, contained a shooting star which resolved into the face of an Indian.

Toronto Tecumsehs: Named for Tecumseh, a Shawnee Indian chief who attempted to unite Indians against encroachments by whites in Illinois and Indiana during the late 1700s and early 1800s. During the War of 1812, he joined the British in Canada as a brigadier general, and he was killed during the Battle of the Thames on October 5, 1813. Tecumseh is buried on Walpole Island, Ontario.[186]

Toronto ThunderHawks: Name announced by team management, including owner Neil Jamieson, in June of 2000 along with the slogan "Come Feel the Thunder."

Toronto Toros: Named by owner John Bassett. "Toros" includes the first four letters of the name "Toronto," and *toro* is also Spanish for "bull."

Toronto-Buffalo Royals: While the origin of this tennis team's name is uncertain, there was once a minor league baseball team called the Toronto Royals which played in the Eastern League in 1901.

Trenton Americans: Likely named for the United States of America as well as the second American Soccer League in which the team played. In the midst of many other ethnic names, the title "Americans" became a very popular one in the American Soccer Leagues.

Trenton Athletics: Named for the fact that this was an athletic club. The second American Soccer League in which this team played was attempting to attract a wider audience in the late 1940s by toning down the ubiquitous ethnic team nicknames, and this new club complied immediately.

Trenton Bengals: (2 teams) The first team to be called the Trenton Bengals was the one which played in the first American Basketball League in 1928. For that team, the name was a shortened form of the team's original, primary name of Trenton Royal Bengals (see). Both teams followed a common tradition in the Trenton and northern New Jersey area of using a name relating to tigers or bengals.[187]

Trenton Highlanders: Like many soccer teams, this club was likely named for the ethnic origins of the players and/or the population which supported it. The name "Highlanders" refers to the Scottish, making reference to the Highlands in Scotland.

Trenton Moose: (2 teams) The first team to be called the Trenton Moose was the one which played in the second American Basketball League in 1933. Both teams were named for the fact that they were sponsored by a local lodge of the Loyal Order of Moose.[188]

Trenton Royal Bengals: Followed a common tradition in the Trenton and northern New Jersey area of using a name relating to tigers or bengals.[189]

Trenton Tigers: Named carried over in part from Passaic, New Jersey, where the team had played as the Passaic Bengal Tigers. The team had originally followed a common tradition in the Passaic and northern New Jersey area

of using a name relating to tigers or bengals. It continued that tradition when it moved to Trenton.[190]

Tri-Cities Blackhawks: Named for Chief Black Hawk of the Sauk Indian tribe, whose tribe was located in Rock Island, Illinois, and who was an integral part of the Black Hawk War of 1831–33 against the Illinois State Militia over land disagreements. The location name "Tri-Cities" referred to the region which includes Davenport, Iowa; Moline, Illinois; and Rock Island, Illinois. The same region today also includes Bettendorf, Iowa, and is known as Quad Cities.

Troy Celtics: (2 teams) The first team to be called the Troy Celtics was the one which played in the second American Basketball League in 1939. That team was named for the Irish population predominant in the Troy area.

Troy Haymakers: (2 teams) The first team to be called the Troy Haymakers was the baseball team which played in the National Association in 1871, and in the amateur NA as early as 1869. A "haymaker" was a powerful punch, and this team had a reputation for its roughhouse style of play. In addition, it played at the Haymakers' Grounds in Troy.

Troy Trojans: Named for the fact that the team played in the city of Troy.

Tulsa Ambush: Named for the Western culture and heritage of the Tulsa area.

Tulsa Tornadoes: Named for the windstorms common in the western United States.

Turbos: Named by World Roller Hockey League founder David McLane.

Typhoon: Named by World Roller Hockey League founder David McLane.

Uhrik Truckers: Formerly the Philadelphia Americans (see), this team was named for new owner Tony Uhrik and his trucking company when Uhrik bought the club in 1953.

Union City Reds: As an independent team this squad had been called the Union City Redlegs, and was likely named for the color of its uniform stockings.

Utah Freezz: Followed a growing tradition in Utah of creating sports names which contain two *z*'s. (The state has also hosted major and minor league teams called the Utah Jazz, Utah Grizzlies, Salt Lake Buzz, Utah Starzz, and Utah Pioneerzz, among others.)

Utah Golden Spikers: Named for railroad spikes, because the completion of the transcontinental railroad occurred in Utah on May 10, 1869. This event is commemorated at Golden Spike National Historic Site in Promontory, Utah.

Utah Jazz: See *New Orleans Jazz.*

Utah Pioneers: Named for the pioneers who settled Utah. Specifically, Utah was settled by the Mormons, who first arrived on July 21, 1847. Brigham Young arrived on July 24, 1847, and the date of his arrival is now celebrated throughout the state as Pioneer Day.

Utah Rockies: Named for the Rocky Mountains in Utah. This team never had a chance to use the name (or to be relocated to Salt Lake City from St. Louis, where it had played as the Spirits of St. Louis) because the American Basketball Association folded following the 1975–76 season.

Utah Rollerbees: Combination of "roller" hockey and "bees," since the nickname of the state of Utah is the "Beehive State." The nickname comes from the fact that Utah was once called Deseret, a name from the Book of Mormon which translates as "honeybee."

Utah Stars: See *Los Angeles Stars.*

Utah Starzz: Like many WNBA teams, this club was named to create a connection with the NBA team which shared the same city (in this case, the Utah Jazz). Salt Lake City has a growing tradition of teams whose names end with two *z*'s. (The state has also hosted major and minor league teams called the Utah Jazz, Utah Grizzlies, Salt Lake Buzz, Utah Freezz, and Utah Pioneerzz, among others.) The team also recalled a bit of history, copying and altering the name of a previous team in the American Basketball Association called the Utah Stars.

Utica Pros: Short for "professional."

Vail Eagles: Named for a bird indigenous to the Vail area.

Vancouver Canucks: Named for the legend of Johnny Canuck, a great logger, skater, and hockey player.[191] The name was also used previously by a team in the minor Western Hockey League. The word "Canuck" is a slang term for a Canadian.

Vancouver Eighty-Sixers: Name suggested by former Canadian National Team soccer coach Tony Waiters. Waiters pointed out that similar numerical team names have been used throughout history (for example, the Philadelphia 76ers, San Francisco 49ers, FC Schalke 04, and Hannover 96). The name commemorates the founding of the team, which occurred in 1986, as well as the founding of the city of Vancouver, which happened in 1886.

Vancouver Grizzlies: This basketball team was named for an animal indigenous to the Vancouver area. The name was also copied from a Canadian football team which played in the Western Interprovincial Football Union in 1941.

Vancouver Maroons: Named for the colors of the team's uniforms.

Vancouver Millionaires: So named because of the team's huge (for the time) payroll.

Vancouver Mounties: This basketball team attempted to copy the name of two previous minor league baseball teams, the first of which had played in the Pacific Coast League from 1956–62. All these teams were named for the Royal Canadian Mounted Police. This police force was established in parts of Canada in 1873 as the North-West Mounted Police, became the Royal Canadian Mounted Police in 1920, and assumed provincial policing duties in British Columbia in 1950. The major league team changed its name to Vancouver Grizzlies before ever playing a game, however, when it met with resistance from the Royal Canadian Mounted Police.

Vancouver Royal Canadians: The term "Royal Canadian" refers to the fact that, although Canada has an independent government, the sovereign of the country is the British monarch.

Vancouver Royals: Shortened form of the team's original name of Vancouver Royal Canadians (see).

Vancouver Whitecaps: Named for both the white-capped mountains and the white-capped ocean waves which surround Vancouver.

Victoria Riptide: A riptide, or rip tide, is a current of water which is disturbed by an opposing current. These tides are not uncommon around Victoria, which is located on Vancouver Island on Juan de Fuca Strait.

Victoria Senators: Named for the British Columbia Senate, since Victoria is the capital of the province of British Columbia.

Virginia Ambassadors: See *Washington Ambassadors.*

Virginia Squires: The term "squire" refers to a landowner in colonial days, and therefore reflects the colonial heritage of the state of Virginia.[192]

Warren Penn Oilers: Named for the Hyvis Oil Company which sponsored the team in Pennsylvania.[193]

Warren Penns: Shortened form of the team's original and primary name of Warren Penn Oilers (see). "Penns" is short for Pennsylvania.

Washington Ambassadors: Named in recognition of the fact that Washington, the capital of the United States, plays host to many ambassadors from a multitude of nations. The team was named in a contest from among 16,000 entries and 1500 different names. The winners were Mr. and Mrs. Richard S. Berardino of Laurel, Maryland, who won $1000 for their suggestion.[194] Owner Joseph Wheeler originally wanted to name this World Football League team the Washington Americans, but the Birmingham Americans of the WFL beat him to the name.

Washington Black Senators: Like many Negro League teams, this club copied and altered the name of a popular white major league baseball team (in this case, the Washington Senators).

Washington Brewers: Shortened form of the team's previous name of Washington Heurich Brewers, originally called the Washington Heurichs (see).

Washington Bullets: See *Baltimore Bullets.*

Washington Capitals: Named in a contest, chosen by owner Abe Pollin. The name "Comets" was the most frequently submitted, but Pollin chose "Capitals" to go with his basketball team (the Capital Bullets), because Washington is the capital of the United States, and because the team played at Capital Centre.

Washington Capitol's: Named for the Capitol Building in Washington. The use of the apostrophe in the name is an unexplained curiosity.[195]

Washington Capitols: (4 teams) The first team to be called the Washington Capitols was the one which played in the Basketball Association of America in 1946. It was named for the Capitol Building in Washington.

Washington Diplomats: (3 teams) The first team to be called the Washington Diplomats was the one which played in the outdoor North American Soccer League in 1974. It was named by Sandi Finci, the wife of team president Mike Finci. All three teams were named for the thousands of diplomats who have worked and resided in Washington, which is the capital of the United States.

Washington Elite Giants: See *Nashville Elite Giants.*

Washington Federals: Named in recognition of the fact that Washington, the capital of the United States, is the seat of the country's federal government.

Washington Heurich Brewers: Expanded form of the team's original name of Washington Heurichs (see).

Washington Heurichs: Pronounced "HI-ricks," this team was named for the Christian Heurich Brewing Company, the company which sponsored it. This brewing company was formed in Washington on August 2, 1873, by German immigrant Christian Heurich. The founder's son, Christian Heurich, Jr., was the force behind the sponsorship of this basketball team, as well as several other sports teams in the Washington area. The brewery today is known as the Olde Heurich Brewing Company.

Washington Homestead Grays: See *Homestead Grays.* Under this combined name, the team actually played solely in Washington.

Washington Laundrymen: Named for owner George Preston Marshall's Palace Laundry in Washington.[196]

Washington Mystics: Like many WNBA teams, this club was named to create a connection with the NBA team which shared the same city (in this case, the Washington Wizards).

Washington Nationals: (5 teams) The first major league team to be called the Washington Nationals was the one which played in the National Association in 1871. This team also played at Nationals Grounds. The second major league team by this name, which played in the NA in 1872, was actually named first, as an amateur team in 1859. The name likely reflects the fact that Washington is the national capital of the United States. The fifth Washington Nationals, formerly baseball's third Washington Senators, adopted the name in a contest in an attempt to dissociate themselves from the two defunct Senators teams of the 1800s. The winner was F. L. McKenna, who wrote:

> My reasons for the name "Nationals" is that it has greater significance and will be more appreciated than "Senators" and incite the players to greater efforts. I believe the people of Washington will support a winning club. When Washington had a club called the "Nationals" it was a winner and the people were proud of it and supported it.[197]

The name never caught on, however, and "Senators" was eventually brought back.

Washington Olympics: This team played at Olympic Grounds in Washington.

Washington Palace Five: Named for owner George Preston Marshall's Palace Laundry in Washington.[198] The "Five" signifies the number of players allowed on the basketball court per team at one time.

Washington Palacians: Alternate form of the team's original name of Washington Palace Five (see).

Washington Potomacs: Named for the Potomac River which flows through Washington.

Washington Pros: Short for "professional."

Washington Quicksteps: "Quickstep" is a musical term for the march accompanying military quick time. The word was also used as a name by some early fire companies, and there could possibly be such a connection here.[199]

Washington Redskins: See *Boston Redskins.*

Washington Senators: (5 teams) The first team to be called the Washington Senators was the first baseball team by this name, which played in the National League in 1886 and which was also known as the first Washington Statesmen. It was named in honor of those who have served as members of the United States Senate, since the team played in the capital of the United States. The football team's primary name was actually Washington Pros (see), and the name "Senators" was only used for the team by newspapers in Canton, Ohio.

Washington Statesmen: (2 teams) The first team to be called the Washington Statesmen was the one which

played in the National League in 1886 and which was also known as baseball's first Washington Senators. It was named in recognition of the fact that the team played in the capital of the United States, the home of many statesmen.

Washington Washingtons: Named for the city of Washington in which the team played. The name "Washington," of course, comes from George Washington, the first President of the United States.

Washington Wave: Named by the Eagle Pro Box Lacrosse League, which owned and named nearly all the teams in the league.

Washington Whips: Named in a contest, possibly for the political whips present in Washington. A "whip" is a member of a legislative body who is charged with enforcing discipline and ensuring the attendance of party members.

Washington Wizards: Name changed from Washington Bullets when team management decided that, at a time when more and more children were falling victim to gunfire, the name "Bullets" was no longer appropriate.

Waterloo Hawks: The name of this basketball team was probably short for Black Hawks, in honor of Chief Black Hawk of the Sauk Indian tribe, whose tribe was located in Rock Island, Illinois, and who was an integral part of the Black Hawk War of 1831–33 against the Illinois State Militia over land disagreements. Waterloo, in fact, is located in Black Hawk County, and the state nickname of Iowa is the "Hawkeye State." The team name was actually used by two previous minor league baseball teams, the first of which played in the Mississippi Valley League in 1922, and the second in the Western League in 1936.

Wave: Named by World Roller Hockey League founder David McLane.

Wellington Aces: Named for a tennis term. An "ace" is a serve which is not returned by one's opponent.

Westchester Indians: Primarily known as the New York Westchesters (see), this team was named for the Native American population indigenous to the Westchester County area where it played.

Whiting Ciesar All-Americans: Named for owner Eddie Ciesar and the fact that the team featured numerous All-Americans.[200] The term "All-American" was developed by Caspar W. Whitney in 1889 to describe the selection of the best college football players in the country. It was later adapted for other sports, and some professional teams, like this basketball squad, used it.

Wichita Advantage: The word "advantage" is a tennis term. A player must usually win by two points, and when a tennis match goes into overtime, the player who gets the next point to break the tie is said to have the "advantage."

Wichita Wings: Named for the fact that the city of Wichita is considered the "Air Capital of the United States." The city is the home of Boeing, Cessna, Lear Jet, and Beech Aircrafts.

Wilkes-Barre Barons: (2 teams) The first major league team to be called the Wilkes-Barre Barons was the one which played in the second American Basketball League in 1938. That team copied the name of three previous minor league baseball teams, the first of which had played in the Atlantic Association in 1889. All these teams were named for the coal barons common in the Wilkes-Barre area at one time. Several minor league basketball teams[201] and later minor league baseball teams have also used the name.

Wilmington Quicksteps: "Quickstep" is a musical term for a march accompanying military quick time. The word was also used as a name by some early fire companies, and there could possibly be such a connection here.[202]

Winnipeg Blue Bombers: Named in 1936 during a game against the University of North Dakota, when a reporter took a line from sportswriter Grantland Rice and said of the Winnipeg team, "These are the Blue Bombers of Western Football." (Rice had once described boxer Joe Louis as the "Brown Bomber.")

Winnipeg Jets: The name refers to the fact that, before the formation of the National Hockey League, hockey was played in recreational leagues in Winnipeg called the Junior and Senior Hockey Leagues. Ben Hatskin renamed these leagues the "Jets" Leagues. Also, the name ties in with Bobby Hull of the Chicago Blackhawks, whose nickname was the "Golden Jet." Finally, it connects with the popularity of Elton John's song "Benny and the Jets" in Winnipeg.[203]

Worcester Brown Stockings: Named for the color of the team's uniform stockings.

Worcester Ruby Legs: Likely named for the color of the team's uniform stockings.

Notes

1. Marc Okkonen, "Team Nicknames 1900–1910," in *The Baseball Research Journal* 27, ed. Mark Alvarez (Cleveland, OH: Society for American Baseball Research, 1998), 37.

2. Ibid., 39.

3. Mike Lessiter, *Names of the Games* (Chicago, IL: Contemporary Books, 1988), 107.

4. David B. Biesel, *Can You Name That Team?* (Metuchen, NJ: Scarecrow Press, 1991), 2.

5. Ibid.

6. Lessiter, 56.

7. Ibid.

8. Ibid., 104.

9. Biesel, 3.

10. Ibid., 4.

11. E. Wendell Lamb, Josephine Lamb, and Lawrence W. Schultz, *More Indian Lore* (Carmel, IN: Schultz-Davis, 1968, 1994), 135.

12. Louis Phillips and Burnham Holmes, *Yogi, Babe, and Magic: The Complete Book of Sports Nicknames* (New York: Prentice Hall, 1994), 194.

13. *Cincinnati Silverbacks 1995–96 Game Program* (Cincinnati, OH: Cincinnati Silverbacks, 1995), 38.

14. Marc Okkonen, *Baseball Uniforms of the 20th Century* (New York: Sterling, 1991), 11.

15. Biesel, 6.

16. Lessiter, 115–16.

17. Biesel, 50.

18. Ibid.

19. Lessiter, 73.

20. Biesel, 8.

21. Ibid.

22. Ibid.

23. Ibid., 9.

24. Ibid., 10.

25. Stan Grosshandler, "The Brooklyn Dodgers," in *The Coffin Corner* 12, Professional Football Researchers Association web site, <http://www.geocities.com/Colosseum/Sideline/5960/brooklyn.htm> (6 May 1999).

26. Miles Aiken and Peter Rowe, *Guinness American Football: The Records* (Enfield, Middlesex, England: Guinness Books, 1986), 78.

27. Biesel, 11.

28. Ibid.

29. Ibid.

30. Ibid., 12–13.

31. Lessiter, 117.

32. Ibid.

33. Biesel, 13.

34. ArenaFan Online web site, <http://www.news-observer.com/daily/1999/11/12/sports10.html> (22 Nov. 1999).

35. Phillips, 187.

36. Lessiter, 99.

37. Biesel, 15–16.

38. Phillips, 186.

39. Lessiter, 74.

40. Biesel, 17.

41. Ibid.

42. Ibid.

43. Ibid.

44. Ibid., 18.

45. Ibid.

46. Lessiter, 40.

47. Andy Furman, "Bengals Derived Name from Hollywood," *Cincinnati Post,* 20 Dec. 1996, 2B.

48. Biesel, 23.

49. Ibid., 20.

50. Lessiter, 41.

51. John Donovan, "Team Name Received Brown's Own Touch," *Cincinnati Post,* 12 Dec. 1995.

52. Phillips, 186.

53. Ibid., 195.

54. Biesel, 19.

55. Ibid., 23.

56. Ibid.

57. Lessiter, 58.

58. Biesel, 13.

59. Lessiter, 86.

60. Biesel, 32.

61. Ibid., 25.

62. Ibid.

63. Lessiter, 59.

64. Biesel, 27.

65. Lessiter, 106.

66. Biesel, 28.

67. Lamb, *More Indian Lore,* 15.

68. Bruce Schumacher, ed., *Indianapolis Indians 1995 Souvenir Program* (Indianapolis, IN: Indians, Inc., 1995), 24.

69. Biesel, 29.

70. E. Wendell Lamb and Lawrence W. Schultz, *Indian Lore* (Carmel, IN: Schultz-Davis, 1964, 1993), 178.

71. Biesel, 31.

72. Ibid.

73. Ibid., 32.

74. Ibid.
75. Ibid.
76. Ibid.
77. Lessiter, 44.
78. Biesel, 33.
79. Ibid.
80. Ibid., 34.
81. Ibid.
82. Phillips, 193–94.
83. Biesel, 35.
84. Lessiter, 14.
85. Ibid.
86. Biesel, 35.
87. Lessiter, 94.
88. Biesel, 36.
89. *Canadian Football League: 1994 Facts, Figures and Records* (Chicago, IL: Triumph, 1994).
90. Lamb, *More Indian Lore,* 135.
91. Biesel, 37.
92. Phillips, 193.
93. Biesel, 38.
94. Ibid.
95. Ibid., 39.
96. Lessiter, 47.
97. Ibid.
98. Major League Soccer News, <http://www.mlsnet.com/pressbox/pr/expand.html> (30 July 1997).
99. Lessiter, 100.
100. Phillips, 187.
101. Lessiter, 100.
102. Biesel, 41.
103. Lessiter, 78.
104. Ibid.
105. Biesel, 42.
106. Lessiter, 109.
107. Ibid., 101.
108. Ibid., 62.
109. Phillips, 196.
110. Lessiter, 119.
111. Biesel, 44.
112. Arena Football League web site, "New England Sea Wolves Set to Kick Off 1999 Season," <http://www.arenafootball.com/tempf.html> (18 Jan. 1999).
113. Lessiter, 120.
114. Ibid.
115. Biesel, 46.
116. Ibid.
117. Ibid.
118. Ibid., 46.
119. Lessiter, 63.
120. Biesel, 47.
121. Ibid., 23.
122. Ibid., 48.
123. Phillips, 191.
124. Lessiter, 49.
125. Ibid.
126. Biesel, 49.
127. Ibid., 9.
128. Ibid., 50.
129. Ibid.
130. Ibid., 51.
131. Lessiter, 46.
132. Biesel, 52.
133. Ibid.
134. Lessiter, 102.
135. Biesel, 53.
136. Ibid.
137. Ibid., 8, 54.
138. Ibid., 54.
139. Okkonen, *Baseball Uniforms of the 20th Century,* 63.
140. Biesel, 55.
141. Lessiter, 123.
142. Ibid., 32.
143. Biesel, 55.
144. Ibid., 57.
145. Lessiter, 92.
146. Biesel, 58.
147. Lessiter, 124.
148. Biesel, 58–59.
149. Lessiter, 50.
150. Phillips, 196.
151. Lessiter, 93.
152. Joe Horrigan, Bob Braunwart, and Bob Carroll, "1925 Pottsville Maroons," Professional Football Researchers Association web site, <http://www.geocities.com/Colosseum/Sideline/5960/potts-25.htm> (7 May 1999), 2.
153. Biesel, 59.
154. Ibid., 60.
155. Ibid.
156. Tim Wolter, "The Rochester Hop Bitters," in *The National Pastime* 17, ed. Mark Alvarez (Cleveland, OH: Society for American Baseball Research, 1997), 38.
157. Biesel, 60.
158. Lessiter, 110.
159. Ibid.
160. Ibid., 35.
161. Biesel, 61–62.
162. Ibid., 62.
163. Ibid.

164. Lessiter, 95.

165. Ibid., 89.

166. Phillips, 185.

167. Lessiter, 19.

168. Ibid., 52.

169. Ibid.

170. Ibid., 96.

171. Ibid.

172. Lamb, *More Indian Lore,* 218.

173. *Canadian Football League: 1994 Facts, Figures and Records.*

174. William Morris, ed., *The American Heritage Dictionary* (Boston, MA: Houghton-Mifflin, 1980), 1236.

175. Lessiter, 68.

176. Ibid.

177. Ibid.

178. Associated Press, "Oilers Changing to Titans in 1999," *Cincinnati Enquirer,* 15 Nov. 1998.

179. Biesel, 66.

180. Ibid., 66–67.

181. Ibid., 67.

182. Ibid.

183. Lessiter, 21.

184. Ibid., 111.

185. National Lacrosse League web site, "'Toronto Rock' to Play at Gardens in 1999," <http://www.be-lax.com/text/120398.html> (7 Dec. 1998).

186. *Compton's Interactive Encyclopedia,* Compton's NewMedia, Inc. (1993, 1994).

187. Biesel, 53.

188. Ibid., 68.

189. Ibid., 53.

190. Ibid.

191. Lessiter, 112.

192. Biesel, 69.

193. Ibid.

194. Ibid.

195. Ibid., 70.

196. Ibid., 71.

197. Ibid., 70.

198. Ibid., 71.

199. Ibid., 72.

200. Ibid., 71.

201. Ibid., 71–72.

202. Ibid., 72.

203. Lessiter, 113.

Bibliography

Aiken, Miles, and Peter Rowe. *Guinness American Football: The Records.* Enfield, Middlesex, England: Guinness Books, 1986.

American Automobile Association. *AAA Florida Tourbook.* Heathrow, FL: American Automobile Association, 1993.

———. *AAA Illinois/Indiana/Ohio Tourbook.* Heathrow, FL: American Automobile Association, 1993.

———. *AAA Kentucky/Tennessee Tourbook.* Heathrow, FL: American Automobile Association, 1993.

———. *AAA Michigan/Wisconsin Tourbook.* Heathrow, FL: American Automobile Association, 1993.

———. *AAA New York Tourbook.* Heathrow, FL: American Automobile Association, 1995.

———. *AAA North Central Tourbook.* Heathrow, FL: American Automobile Association, 1993.

———. *AAA Today.* Heathrow, FL: American Automobile Association, 1995.

———. *AAA Tourbook: Arkansas/Kansas/Missouri/Oklahoma.* Heathrow, FL: American Automobile Association, 1996.

Arena Football League web site. "New England Sea Wolves Set to Kick Off 1999 Season." <http://www.arenafootball.com/tempf.html> (18 Jan. 1999).

ArenaFan Online web site. <http://www.news-observer.com/daily/1999/11/12/sports10.html> (22 Nov. 1999).

Arizona Cardinals web site. "Franchise History." <http://www.azcardinals.com/history/history.html> (17 Mar. 1999).

Associated Press. "Devils Appear Tennessee Bound," *Cincinnati Post*, 28 June 1995.

———. "Oilers Changing to Titans in 1999," *Cincinnati Enquirer*, 15 Nov. 1998.

Bae, Eun S., ed. *The Official 1996 Major League Soccer Yearbook.* New York: International Sports Publishing, 1996.

Biesel, David B. *Can You Name That Team?* Metuchen, NJ: Scarecrow Press, 1991.

Bradley, Robert. "NBA Team Roots." Association for Professional Basketball Research web site. <http://members.aol.com/bradleyrd/apbr.html> (1 June 1999).

Braunwart, Bob. "All Those A.F.L.'s: N.F.L. Competitors, 1935–41." Professional Football Researchers Association web site. <http://www.geocities.com/Colosseum/Sideline/5960/afl35-41.htm> (30 June 1998).

Braunwart, Bob, and Bob Carroll. "The Ohio League." *The Coffin Corner* 3, 1981. Professional Football Researchers Association web site. <http://www.geocities.com/Colosseum/Sideline/5960/ohiolgue.htm> (1 July 1998).

———. "The Rock Island Independents." *The Coffin Corner* 5, 1983. Professional Football Researchers Association web site. <http://www.geocities.com/Colosseum/Sideline/5960/rockisla.htm> (6 May 1999).

Canadian Football League: 1994 Facts, Figures and Records. Chicago, IL: Triumph, 1994.

Canadian Football League web site. "A Brief History of the CFL: 1861–1900." <http://www.cfl.ca/CFLArchives/1861_1900.html> (29 June 1998).

———. "A Brief History of the CFL: 1901–1950." <http://www.cfl.ca/CFLArchives/1901_1950.html> (29 June 1998).

———. "A Brief History of the CFL: 1951–1997." <http://www.cfl.ca/CFLArchives/1951_1997.html> (29 June 1998).

Carolina Panthers web site. "The Black Panther." <http://panther.alltel.net/fun%5Fgames/blkpanther.html> (21 Oct. 1999).

Carroll, Bob. "Ollie's All-Stars." *The Coffin Corner* 5, 1983. Professional Football Researchers Association web site. <http://www.geocities.com/Colosseum/ Sideline/5960/ollieas.htm> (6 May 1999).

———. "Steamrollered: 1928." Professional Football Researchers Association web site. <http://www.geocities. com/Colosseum/Sideline/5960/00-1928.htm> (10 May 1999).

———. "The Grange War: 1926." Professional Football Researchers Association web site. <http://www. geocities.com/Colosseum/Sideline/5960/00-1926.htm> (10 May 1999).

———. "The Packers Crash Through: 1929." Professional Football Researchers Association web site. <http:// www.geocities.com/Colosseum/Sideline/5960/00-1929.htm> (10 May 1999).

———. "The Town That Hated Pro Football." *The Coffin Corner* 3, 1981. Professional Football Researchers Association web site. <http://www.geocities.com/Colosseum/Sideline/5960/rochster.htm> (6 May 1999).

Cincinnati Enquirer, 1988–2000.

Cincinnati Post, 1988–2000.

Cincinnati Silverbacks 1995–96 Game Program. Cincinnati, OH: Cincinnati Silverbacks, 1995.

Collins, Bud, and Zander Hollander, eds. *Bud Collins' Modern Encyclopedia of Tennis.* Detroit, MI: Visible Ink, 1994.

Compton's Interactive Encyclopedia. Compton's NewMedia, Inc., 1993, 1994.

Couch, Kim, ed. *World TeamTennis: Super Tiebreaker.* Cleveland, OH: IMG Promotions, 1995, 1996.

Daly, Dan, and Bob O'Donnell. *The Pro Football Chronicle.* New York: Collier/Macmillan, 1990.

Delury, George E., ed. *The World Almanac and Book of Facts,* 1977 and 1978 editions. New York: Newspaper Enterprise Association, 1977, 1978.

Donnelly, Tracey, ed. *World TeamTennis 1996 Media Guide.* Cleveland, OH: IMG Promotions, 1996.

Donovan, John. "Team Name Received Brown's Own Touch," *Cincinnati Post,* 12 Dec. 1995.

Filichia, Peter. *Professional Baseball Franchises.* New York: Facts on File, 1993.

Frommer, Harvey. *Sports Roots.* New York: Atheneum, 1979.

Furman, Andy. "Bengals Derived Name from Hollywood," *Cincinnati Post,* 20 Dec. 1996.

Gallner, Sheldon M., with contributions by Michael Dennis. *Pro Sports: The Contract Game.* New York: Charles Scribner's Sons, 1974.

Gill, Bob. "PCPFL: 1940–45." *The Coffin Corner* 4, 1982. Professional Football Researchers Association web site. <http://www.geocities.com/Colosseum/Sideline/5960/pcpfl-40.htm> (1 July 1998).

Grosshandler, Stan. "All-America Football Conference." Professional Football Researchers Association web site. <http://www.geocities.com/Colosseum/Sideline/5960/aafc.htm> (30 June 1998).

———. "The Brooklyn Dodgers." *The Coffin Corner* 12. Professional Football Researchers Association web site. <http://www.geocities.com/Colosseum/Sideline/5960/brooklyn.htm> (6 May 1999).

Hammond's World Atlas: Classics Edition. Philadelphia, PA: The Publishers Agency, 1955.

Hickok, Ralph. *The Encyclopedia of North American Sports History.* New York: Facts on File, 1992.

Hill, Bob, and Randall Baron. *The Amazing Basketball Book: The First 100 Years.* Louisville, KY: Dyrven, 1988.

Hillman, Bob, executive ed. *Arenaball: The Official Game Magazine of the Arena Football League: Cincinnati Rockers vs. Detroit Drive.* Custer, SD: Hagen Marketing & Communications, 30 May 1992.

Hogrogian, John. "The Hartford Blues Part 1." *The Coffin Corner* 4, 1982. Professional Football Researchers Association web site. <http://www.geocities.com/Colosseum/Sideline/5960/hartfrd1.htm> (7 May 1999).

———. "The Staten Island Stapletons." *The Coffin Corner* 6, 1984. Professional Football Researchers Association web site. <http://www.geocities.com/Colosseum/Sideline/5960/stapes.htm> (7 May 1999).

———. "The Steam Roller." *The Coffin Corner* 2, 1980. Professional Football Researchers Association web site. <http://www.geocities.com/Colosseum/Sideline/5960/provdnce.htm> (7 May 1999).

Hollander, Zander. *The Complete Encyclopedia of Hockey.* Detroit, MI: Visible Ink, 1993.

Hollander, Zander, and Alex Sachare, eds. *The Official NBA Basketball Encyclopedia.* New York: Villard, 1989.

Holroyd, Steve. "The Year in American Soccer." U.S. Soccer History Archives web site. <http://www.sover.net/~spectrum/> (3 Feb. 1999).

Honig, Donald. *The American League: An Illustrated History.* New York: Crown, 1987.

Hoppel, Joe, ed. *Football: Facts, Feats, and Firsts.* New York: Galahad, 1985.

Horrigan, Joe. "National Football League Franchise Transactions." *The Coffin Corner* 18, 1996. Professional Football Researchers Association web site. <http://www.geocities.com/Colosseum/Sideline/5960/franchise.htm> (6 July 1999).

———. "The Tonawanda Kardex: The Forgotten Franchise." *The Coffin Corner* 6, 1984. Professional Football Researchers Association web site. <http://www.geocities.com/Colosseum/Sideline/5960/tonawanda.htm> (11 May 1999).

Horrigan, Joe, Bob Braunwart, and Bob Carroll. "1925 Pottsville Maroons." Professional Football Researchers Association web site. <http://www.geocities.com/Colosseum/Sideline/5960/potts-25.htm> (7 May 1999).

Ivor-Campbell, Frederick, Robert L. Tiemann, and Mark Ruckers, eds. *Baseball's First Stars.* Cleveland, OH: Society for American Baseball Research, 1996.

Jankowicz, Devi. "The Geordie FAQ." <http://www.cus.umist.ac.uk/%7Emosh/newcfaz.html> (8 Mar. 1999).

Johnson, Pearce, and PFRA Research. "When Did They Start?" Professional Football Researchers Association web site. <http://www.geocities.com/Colosseum/Sideline/5960/whenstart.htm> (11 May 1999).

Kane, Basil G. *Soccer for American Spectators.* Cranbury, NJ: A. S. Barnes, 1970.

Kelley, Joe, ed. *Cincinnati Reds 1994 Official Yearbook.* Cincinnati, OH: Cincinnati Reds, 1994.

Kiczek, Gene. *High Sticks and Hat Tricks: A History of Hockey in Cleveland.* Euclid, OH: Blue Line, 1996.

Koppett, Leonard. *The Man in the Dugout.* New York: Crown, 1993.

LaBlanc, Michael L. *Professional Sports Team Histories: Basketball.* Detroit, MI: Gale Research, 1994.

———. *Professional Sports Team Histories: Football.* Detroit, MI: Gale Research, 1994.

———. *Professional Sports Team Histories: Hockey.* Detroit, MI: Gale Research, 1994.

LaBlanc, Michael L., and Richard Henshaw. *The World Encyclopedia of Soccer.* Detroit, MI: Visible Ink, 1994.

Lamb, E. Wendell, and Lawrence W. Schultz. *Indian Lore.* Carmel, IN: Schultz-Davis, 1964, 1993.

Lamb, E. Wendell, Josephine Lamb, and Lawrence W. Schultz. *More Indian Lore.* Carmel, IN: Schultz-Davis, 1968, 1994.

Lattimore, Reuben, consulting ed. *Street & Smith's Guide to Pro Football 1994.* New York: Ballantine, 1994.

Lessiter, Mike. *Names of the Games.* Chicago, IL: Contemporary Books, 1988.

Litterer, David A. "A History of Soccer in New England." U.S. Soccer History Archives web site. <http://www.soccerspot.com/soccerhistory/NewEngland.html> (4 May 1999).

———. "American Professional Soccer League, 1990–Present." U.S. Soccer History Archives web site. <http://www.cs.cmu.edu/afs/cs/usr/mdwheel/www/soccer/history/apsl-history.html> (2 Feb. 1996).

———. "American Soccer League I (1921–1933)." U.S. Soccer History Archives web site. <http://www.sover.net/~spectrum/asl.html> (29 Mar. 1999).

———. "American Soccer League II." U.S. Soccer History Archives web site. <http://www.sover.net/~spectrum/asl2.html> (29 Mar. 1999).

———. "American Soccer League III." U.S. Soccer History Archives web site. <http://www.sover.net/~spectrum/asl3.html> (7 Feb. 1996).

———. "Canadian Soccer League." U.S. Soccer History Archives web site. <http://www.cs.cmu.edu/~mdwheel/us-soccer/history/csl.html> (8 Aug. 1997).

———. "Continental Indoor Soccer League, 1993–Present." U.S. Soccer History Archives web site. <http://www.cs.cmu.edu/afs/cs/usr/mdwheel/www/soccer/history/cisl-history.html> (2 Feb. 1996).

———. "Major Indoor Soccer League." U.S. Soccer History Archives web site. <http://www.cs.cmu.edu/afs/cs/usr/mdwheel/www/soccer/history/misl.html> (2 Feb. 1996).

———. "National Professional Soccer League, 1984–Present." U.S. Soccer History Archives web site. <http://www.cs.cmu.edu/afs/cs/usr/mdwheel/www/soccer/history/npsl-history.html> (2 Feb. 1996).

———. "United Soccer League." U.S. Soccer History Archives web site. <http://www.cs.cmu.edu/~mdwheel/us-soccer/history/usl.html> (30 Jan. 1996).

———. "Western Soccer Alliance." U.S. Soccer History Archives web site. <http://www.sover.net/~spectrum/wsa.html> (7 Feb. 1996).

Lowry, Philip J. *Green Cathedrals*. Reading, MA: Addison-Wesley, 1992.

Maher, Ted. "In the Beginning." *The Coffin Corner* 15, 1993. Professional Football Researchers Association web site. <http://www.geocities.com/Colosseum/Sideline/5960/nflfirsts.htm> (27 Sept. 1999).

Major League Soccer News. Major League Soccer web site. <http://www.mlsnet.com/pressbox/pr/expand.html> (1996–99).

McKinley, Michael. *Hockey Hall of Fame Legends*. Toronto, ON: Viking, 1993.

Meserole, Mike, ed. *The 1994 Information Please Sports Almanac*. Boston, MA: Houghton-Mifflin, 1994.

Miller, Ray. "Pre-1900 NL Franchise Movement." Pp. 57–61 in *The National Pastime* 17, ed. Mark Alvarez. Cleveland, OH: Society for American Baseball Research, 1997.

Moffett, Cleveland. "The Overthrow of the Molly Maguires," in *McClure's Magazine* (1894). Reprinted at <http://www.history.ohio-state.edu/projects/coal/MollyMaguire/mollymaguires.htm> (29 Mar. 1999).

Morford, Paul. "Oakland Seals." <http://www.eskimo.com/~pem/oakseal.html> (22 Jan. 1999).

Morris, William, ed. *The American Heritage Dictionary*. Boston, MA: Houghton-Mifflin, 1980.

National Lacrosse League web site. "'Toronto Rock' to Play at Gardens in 1999." <http://www.be-lax.com/text/120398.html> (7 Dec. 1998).

Neft, David S., Richard M. Cohen, and Rick Korch. *The Football Encyclopedia*. New York: St. Martin's, 1994.

———. *The Sports Encyclopedia: Pro Football*, 12th edition. New York: St. Martin's, 1994.

Nemec, David. *The Great American Baseball Team Book*. New York: Plume, 1992.

———. *Great Baseball Feats, Facts and Firsts*. New York: Signet, 1989.

Okkonen, Marc. *Baseball Uniforms of the 20th Century*. New York: Sterling, 1991.

———. "Team Nicknames 1900–1910." Pp. 37–39 in *The Baseball Research Journal* 27, ed. Mark Alvarez. Cleveland, OH: Society for American Baseball Research, 1998.

Okrent, Daniel, and Harris Lewine, eds. *The Ultimate Baseball Book*. Boston, MA: Hilltown, 1991.

Olde Heurich Brewing Company web site. <http://www.oldeheurich.com/history.htm> (7 Apr. 1999).

Pagano, Richard, and C. C. Staph. "The Frankford Yellow Jackets Part 1: Pre-NFL." *The Coffin Corner* 9, 1987. Professional Football Researchers Association web site. <http://www.geocities.com/Colosseum/Sideline/5960/frank-1.htm> (6 May 1999).

PFRA Research. "1922: Birth and Rebirth." Professional Football Researchers Association web site. <http://www.geocities.com/Colosseum/Sideline/5960/1922a.htm> (10 May 1999).

———. "1924: Goodbye, Bulldogs, Hello." Professional Football Researchers Association web site. <http://www.geocities.com/Colosseum/Sideline/5960/1924a.htm> (6 May 1999).

Phillips, Louis, and Burnham Holmes. *Yogi, Babe, and Magic: The Complete Book of Sports Nicknames.* New York: Prentice Hall, 1994.

Pluto, Terry. *Loose Balls.* New York: Simon and Schuster, 1990.

"Professional Basketball League Teams Since 1935." <http://members.aol.com/apbrhoops/leagues.html> (30 June 1998).

Rhodes, Greg, and John Erardi. *The First Boys of Summer.* Cincinnati, OH: Road West, 1994.

Rizakis, Kris. "The Grand List." U.S. Soccer History Archives web site. <http://www.sover.net/~spectrum/soccerclub.html> (3 Feb. 1999).

Ronan, Margaret. *The Arrow Book of States.* New York: Scholastic, 1970.

Rote, Kyle, Jr., with Basil Kane. *Kyle Rote, Jr.'s Complete Book of Soccer.* New York: Simon and Schuster, 1978.

Royal Canadian Mounted Police web site. <http://www.north-van.rcmp-grc.gc.ca/history.html> (21 May 1999).

Ruck, Don V., ed. *Missile: Official Magazine of the Major Indoor Soccer League.* New York: Don V. Ruck Associates, 1978.

Scarr, Michael, ed. *Roller Hockey: The World's Leading Magazine of Street and Inline Roller Hockey* 4, no. 5 (June 1996). Los Angeles: Straight Line Communications.

Schmitz, Brian. "Christmas Resident Names USFL Team," *Orlando Sentinel,* 19 Oct. 1984, B-1, B-4.

Schumacher, Bruce, ed. *Indianapolis Indians 1995 Souvenir Program.* Indianapolis, IN: Indians, Inc., 1995.

Shatzkin, Mike, ed. *The Ballplayers.* New York: Arbor House, 1990.

Speck, Mark. "The 1974 Florida Blazers: A Study in 'Focus.'" Professional Football Researchers Association web site. <http://www.geocities.com/Colosseum/Sideline/5960/blazers.htm> (1 July 1998).

Steiner, Roger J. *The Bantam New College French & English Dictionary.* New York: Bantam, 1988.

Suehsdorf, A. D. "Monumental Failure." Pp. 67–68 in *The National Pastime* 19, ed. Mark Alvarez. Cleveland, OH: Society for American Baseball Research, 1999.

Sullivan, George. *This Is Pro Soccer.* New York: Dodd, Mead and Company, 1979.

Thorn, John, and Pete Palmer, eds. *Total Baseball,* 2nd edition. New York: Warner, 1991.

Tingay, Lance. *The Guinness Book of Tennis Facts and Feats.* Enfield, Middlesex, England: Guinness Superlatives Limited, 1983.

Wawrzyniak, Bruce R. *1998 NLL Guide & Record Book.* Buffalo, NY: National Lacrosse League, 1998.

Wendel, Tim. "United League Unveils Eight Teams for '96," *USA Today Baseball Weekly,* 23–29 Aug. 1995.

White, Paul, ed. *USA Today Baseball Weekly,* 1990–99.

Whitehead, Eric. *The Patricks: Hockey's Royal Family.* Garden City, NY: Doubleday and Company, 1980.

Whitney, David. "North American Soccer League 1967–1984." U.S. Soccer History Archives web site. <http://www.cs.cmu.edu/afs/cs/usr/mdwheel/www/soccer/history/nasl/naslhist.html> (7 Feb. 1996).

Williams, Edwin B. *The Bantam New College Spanish & English Dictionary.* New York: Bantam, 1968.

Wilson, Lyle K. "Harlem Globetrotters Baseball Team." Pp. 77–80 in *The National Pastime* 17, ed. Mark Alvarez. Cleveland, OH: Society for American Baseball Research, 1997.

Wolff, Rick, editorial director. *The Baseball Encyclopedia,* 8th and 9th editions. New York: Macmillan, 1990, 1993.

Wolter, Tim. "The Rochester Hop Bitters." Pp. 38–40 in *The National Pastime* 17, ed. Mark Alvarez. Cleveland, OH: Society for American Baseball Research, 1997.

Woods, Mark. "It's Official: 'Devil Rays' Will Stay," *USA Today Baseball Weekly,* 5–11 Apr. 1995.

About the Author

Thomas W. Brucato is a technical writer and a lifelong, fiercely loyal Cincinnati Reds' fan. He is a member of the Society for American Baseball Research, and has a Master of Divinity from Mount St. Mary's Seminary of the West. In his free time he enjoys writing, playing softball, traveling, writing music, collecting autographed baseballs, and driving his classic 1968 Pontiac LeMans, the *Gray Ghost*. He has been involved in both Korean and Japanese martial arts for over 25 years, currently holding a 5th degree black belt and serving as President of the Shukokai Kempo Karate Academy. He and his wife, Julie, live in Cincinnati with their two Yorkshire terriers, Disney and Magic.